WRITING
Creative
Nonfiction

**Instruction and insights
from the teachers of the
Associated Writing Programs**

Carolyn Forché and Philip Gerard

STORY PRESS
CINCINNATI, OHIO
http://www.writersdigest.com

Visit our Web site at http://www.writersdigest.com for information on more resources for writers.

To receive a free weekly e-mail newsletter delivering tips and updates about writing and about Writer's Digest products, send an e-mail with "Subscribe Newsletter" in the body of the message to http://newsletters.fwpublications.com or register directly at our Web site at www.writersdigest.com.

05   04   03   02   01   5   4   3   2   1

Library of Congress Cataloging-in-Publication Data

Writing creative nonfiction: instruction and insights from teachers of the Associated Writing Programs / edited by Carolyn Forché and Philip Gerard.
    p.   cm.
Includes index.
ISBN 1-88491-050-5 (alk. paper)
    1. English language—Rhetoric—Study and teaching. 2. Prose literature—Authorship—Study and teaching. 3. Creative writing (Higher education). 4. Prose literature—Authorship. 5. Creative writing. I. Forché, Carolyn. II. Gerard, Philip. III. Associated Writing Programs.

PE1404.W697   2001
808'.042'0711—dc21
                                    2001018408
                                          CIP

Edited by Jack Heffron and Meg Leder
Cover photo by Patrick McDonogh © Photonica
Production coordinated by John Peavler
Editors' photo by Harry Mattison

PERMISSIONS

ACKNOWLEDGMENTS

The editors are grateful for support from the Creative Writing Department of the University of North Carolina at Wilmington; in particular, we express our heartfelt thanks to Carlyn Coviello, Jerrica Gardner, Lorrie Smith, and Chad Thorson, editorial assistants.

In addition, the following people provided invaluable assistance with this project: Julie Checkoway and Laura Wexler helped lay the groundwork; David Fenza at the Associated Writing Programs shepherded it into being; and at Story Press, Jack Heffron, through his creative vision and hard work, and Meg Leder, through her smart and conscientious attention to the manuscript-in-progress, made this book a reality.

Finally, to all the writers who have graciously contributed to these pages without remuneration as an act of dedication to their craft and solidarity with the community of writers, thanks for giving something back of such value.

ABOUT THE EDITORS

Carolyn Forché is well-known as a poet—winner of the Yale Younger Poets Prize, the Lamont Prize, and the L.A. Times Book Award, among other honors. Her books *The Country Between Us* and *The Angel of History* are widely regarded as classics of contemporary poetry. Forché has also made an international reputation as an essayist, tackling difficult political and social subjects, including the U.S. intervention in El Salvador and human rights abuses around the world. Her editorial credits include *Against Forgetting: Twentieth Century Poetry of Witness*, among other extensive projects. She teaches in the MFA program at George Mason University.

Philip Gerard is the author of three novels and three books of nonfiction, including *Creative Nonfiction—Researching and Crafting Stories of Real Life* and *Writing a Book That Makes a Difference*. He's also written documentary scripts for public television and essays for National Public Radio. A graduate of the MFA program at the University of Arizona, he teaches in the Creative Writing Department at UNC-Wilmington and in the MFA summer residency program at Goucher College.

TABLE OF CONTENTS

Creative Nonfiction: An Adventure in Lyric, Fact, and Story

It seems fitting that this book about writing creative nonfiction should be brought to you by a poet and a novelist: The genre has become a fertile meeting ground for writers of all kinds, from investigative reporters to literary short story writers and lyric poets. Somehow all their diverse interests converge in a genre that seems expansive enough to connect the self to the larger world of experience, shaping its form to tell the truth of a particular moment.

Creative nonfiction has emerged in the last few years as the province of factual prose that is also *literary*—infused with the stylistic devices, tropes, and rhetorical flourishes of the best fiction and the most lyrical of narrative poetry. It is fact-based writing that remains compelling, undiminished by the passage of time, that has at heart an interest in enduring human values: foremost a fidelity to accuracy, to *truthfulness*.

Its very *literariness* distinguishes this writing from deadline reportage, daily journalism, academic criticism, and critical biography. It is storytelling of a very high order—through the revelation of character and the suspense of plot, the subtle braiding of themes, rhythms and resonance, memory and imaginative research, precise and original language, and a narrative stance that is intelligent, humble, questioning, distinctive, individual and implicitly alert to the world.

Creative nonfiction is, in one sense, a very new genre—the term has come into fashion only in the past few years. There's ongoing discussion about whether "creative nonfiction" is the most useful appellation—some have suggested "literary journalism," though that would exclude most memoir, or "narrative nonfiction," though the lyric essay, for instance, does not really unfold as conventional narrative. Creative nonfiction remains the most inclusive term for such diverse literary expression: memoir, lyric and personal essay, plotted narrative, biography, meditation, nature writing. Recognizing that this fact-based genre now has taken on a distinctive artistic character, university M.F.A. programs in Creative Writing have begun to include it as a third genre in their curricula.

Publishers' lists are bursting with new works of creative nonfiction, and trade magazines and literary journals are responding to readers' burgeoning interest in creative nonfiction, the authority of fact and true-life experience undergirding all manner of stories.

But though it feels young and vibrant, creative nonfiction has a long history and an honorable provenance. Its roots lie in the literary essays of Montaigne, Rousseau, and Thoreau; the humorous "true" adventures of Mark Twain; the documentary "immersion" journalism of Daniel Defoe, Charles Dickens, Jack London, and George Orwell; the timeless war correspondence of Stephen Crane and Martha Gellhorn; the artful memoirs of Ernest Hemingway, Beryl Markham, and Mary McCarthy; the cultural critiques of James Baldwin, Ralph Ellison, and Marvel Cooke; the New Journalism of Tom Wolfe and Ken Kesey; the "Gonzo" journalism of Hunter S. Thompson; the nature writing of Annie Dillard, Barry Lopez, Terry Tempest Williams, and a host of others. Seen in this light, *Life on the Mississippi*, *The People of the Abyss*, *Hiroshima*, and *In Cold Blood* are all towering works of creative nonfiction.

In the pages that follow, a gathering of working creative nonfiction writers who also teach their passion talk about what they do and how they do it. From Terry Tempest Williams's inspiring manifesto, "Why I Write," to Bob Reiss's "Surviving Overseas," these writers probe the many facets of creative nonfiction craft. Many of the instructive pieces are linked to companion essays or book excerpts that exemplify the principles of craft as the particular author espouses and practices them. These are by the same authors and appear in the last section of the book, the "Creative Nonfiction Reader."

In "But Tell It Slant: From Poetry to Prose and Back Again," Judith Ortiz Cofer explores the uses of poetry in discovering the story. Brenda Miller, in "A Braided Heart: Shaping the Lyric Essay," demonstrates implicitly the braiding of thematic strands into a lyrical essay.

"Saying Goodbye to 'Once Upon a Time,' or Implementing Postmodernism in Creative Nonfiction" by Laura Wexler takes on the practical problems of research, along with the profound issue of *which* truth the writer can tell—there may always be a hole in the center of the story, the great unknowable fact—and the writer must make choices informed not only by aesthetics but by ethics in order to present the story in its integrity.

Alan Cheuse in "Finding a Story, or Using the Whole Pig" gives practical as well as aesthetic advice for making the most out of the raw material of the world.

Creative nonfiction is far too complex and inclusive a genre to be limited only to memoir—though the personal voice and the author's memory and imagination certainly contribute in all sorts of ways. In "Writing Personal Essays: On the Necessity of Turning Oneself Into a Character" Phillip Lopate addresses the necessity for creating the narrative "I" as a living character on the page—and how that basic act defines the concerns of the essay.

Michael Pearson takes on the quest for one's own autobiography in "Researching Your Own Life." "Taking Yourself Out of the Story: Narrative Stance and the Upright Pronoun" challenges the writer to know just why he or she must become a character in the story. Robin Hemley ("The Loneliness of the Long-Distance Writer") explores another kind of challenge: how to shape a long memoir.

In "As Time Goes By; Creating Biography" and "Twelve Years and Counting: Writing Biography," two accomplished biographers, Philip Furia and Honor Moore, write about how to move beyond the clichés of biography. They address the issues of interviewing and doing imaginative research, what to do with that research, and how to make it serve the story in an integral way.

Beverly Lowry in "Not the Killing But Why" shows us a journalist hot on the trail of a living story.

Christopher Merrill and Bob Reiss explore the dangers—physical, emotional, psychological—that the writer encounters in writing about real people in real conflict. "The 'New' Literature" reminds us that one of the indispensable ingredients of the best creative nonfiction is courage—the courage of one's convictions, the courage to tell the truth, and sometimes even the courage to go into harm's way and discover the truth.

Dinty Moore ("The Comfortable Chair: Using Humor in Creative Nonfiction") shows us how humor can also lead to truth.

Stanley Colbert, one of the most distinguished editors, publishers, and literary agents of his generation, offers a primer on the practical business of drafting a book proposal, the common way to "place" a nonfiction manuscript. And two nationally renowned First Amendment attorneys, Nicholas Hentoff and Harvey Silverglate, team up to penetrate the mysteries of legal issues, such as defamation of character and invasion of privacy, that affect the writer of creative nonfiction.

We've included a section about what happens after publication: "Aftershocks—Responses to the Genre." The three responses by E. Ethelbert Miller, Lauren Slater, and Lee Gutkind all address critiques, misunderstandings, disagreements, conventional expectations, ongoing issues of aesthetics and ethics, and real consequences of publishing in the genre.

As a final gift to the reader, we've included the "Creative Nonfiction Reader" offering the companion pieces and other exemplary essays to inspire, delight, teach, and simply to enjoy.

It's a fascinating enterprise, this business of trying to tell the truth about the world through writing that is at once factual and literary. It calls for a reporter's investigative determination, a photographer's eye for detail, a historian's sense of documentation, a poet's passion for language, a storyteller's feel for narrative arc, a detective's nose for truth, a travel agent's ability to organize an itinerary, some wise forethought, a little courage to put yourself on the line, a pencil and paper, and a bit of luck.

So good reading. And good writing.

—*Carolyn Forché and Philip Gerard*

I
The Art, the Craft,
the Business

Why I Write

TERRY TEMPEST WILLIAMS

It is just after 4:00 A.M. I was dreaming about Moab, Brooke and I walking around the block just before dawn. I threw a red silk scarf around my shoulders and then I began reciting in my sleep why I write:

I write to make peace with the things I cannot control. I write to create fabric in a world that often appears black and white. I write to discover. I write to uncover. I write to meet my ghosts. I write to begin a dialogue. I write to imagine things differently and in imagining things differently perhaps the world will change. I write to honor beauty. I write to correspond with my friends. I write as a daily act of improvisation. I write because it creates my composure. I write against power and for democracy. I write myself out of my nightmares and into my dreams. I write in a solitude born out of community. I write to the questions that shatter my sleep. I write to the answers that keep me complacent. I write to remember. I write to forget. I write to the music that opens my heart. I write to quell the pain. I write to migrating birds with the hubris of language. I write as a form of translation. I write with the patience of melancholy in winter. I write because it allows me to confront that which I do not know. I write as an act of faith. I write as an act of slowness. I write to record what I love in the face of loss. I write because it makes me less fearful of death. I write as an exercise in pure joy. I write as one who walks on the surface of a frozen river beginning to melt. I write out of my anger and into my passion. I write from the stillness of night anticipating—always anticipating. I write to listen. I write out of silence. I write to soothe the voices shouting inside me, outside me, all around. I write because of the humor of our condition as humans. I write because I believe in words. I write because I do not believe in words. I write because it is a dance with paradox. I write because you can play on the page like a child left alone in sand. I write because it belongs to the force of the moon: high tide, low tide. I write because it is the way I take long walks. I write as a bow to wilderness. I write because I believe it can create a path in darkness. I write because as a child I spoke a different language. I write with a knife carving each word through the generosity of trees. I write as ritual. I write because I am not employable. I write out of my inconsistencies. I write because then I do not have to speak. I write with the colors of memory. I write as a witness to what I have seen. I write as a witness to what I imagine. I write by grace and grit. I write out of indigestion. I write when I am starving. I write when I am full. I write to the dead. I write out of the body. I write to put food on the table. I write on the other side of procrastination. I write for the children we never had. I write for the love of ideas. I write for the surprise of a sentence. I write with the belief of alchemists. I write knowing I will always fail. I write knowing words always fall short. I write knowing I can be killed by my own words, stabbed by syntax, crucified by both understanding and misunderstanding. I write out of ignorance. I write by accident. I write past the embarrassment of exposure. I keep writing and suddenly, I am overcome by the sheer indulgence, (the madness,) the meaninglessness, the ridiculousness of this list. I trust nothing especially myself and slide head first into the familiar abyss of doubt and humiliation and threaten to push the delete button on my way down, or madly erase each line, pick up the paper and rip it into shreds—and then I realize, it doesn't matter, words are always a gamble, words are splinters from cut glass. I write because it is dangerous, a bloody risk, like love, to form the words, to say the words, to touch the source, to be touched, to reveal how vulnerable we are, how transient.

I write as though I am whispering in the ear of the one I love.

EXERCISE

1. Why do you write?

But Tell It Slant: From Poetry to Prose and Back Again

JUDITH ORTIZ COFER

From poetry . . .

The Lesson of the Sugarcane
My mother opened her eyes wide
at the edge of the field
ready for cutting
"Take a deep breath,"
> *she whispered,*
"There is nothing as sweet:
Nada más dulce."
> *Overhearing,*
Father left the flat he was changing
in the road-warping sun,
and grabbing my arm, broke my sprint
toward a stalk:
"Cane can choke a little girl: snakes hide
where it grows over your head."
And he led us back to the crippled car
where we sweated out our penitence,
for having craved more sweetness
than we were allowed,
more sweetness than we could handle.
> *(from* The Latin Deli: Prose and Poetry,
> *W.W. Norton, 1993)*

To story . . .

We often had tire blowouts and car trouble. Everyone did then, and
so we knew the routine when we heard the familiar pop and Papi began
to maneuver the car off the paved road. Since it was sweltering hot,
Mami got out, looked around wherever we were to make sure it was
safe, then she'd let me and Mili come out for fresh air. She would take

these occasions to point out things about our país to us as if were turistas.

One day we had a flat by the side of a field of sugarcane that extended toward the horizon like a green sea. It was ready for harvesting. La zafra, the cutting season, is also the time of fiestas on the Island, and we were heading for Mami's pueblo to the festival of the town's patron saint, San Lázaro. We would stay with her mamá a few days and Papi would return to San Juan by himself since he had to go back to work.

Mami's happiness about going to her mamás' was evident in her movements, which were like a dancer's. In fact she had put on a mambo record to do her mopping the day before, and Mili and I had pranced around the house as she polished the floors while dancing with the mop to the sounds of Tito Puente and his orchestra.

Now her starched red cotton skirt and off-the-shoulder peasant blouse made her look like a movie star on vacation as she scanned the cane field, shading her eyes with one hand and holding both Mili's and my hands with the other. Papi's rule: if there is even the possibility of a moving vehicle in our path we must be securely attached to an adult by the hand. I was beginning to resent this at the age of ten, but Mami only obeyed Papi's excessively protective commandments when he was around, so we had a silent agreement, she and I. We humored him in exchange for other privileges we exacted from each other. Mili had not yet caught on to these tactics, however; she seemed impervious to the family negotiations that went on constantly as we circled one another trying to figure out how to gain the most territory without starting a war.

"What are you looking for, Mami?" Mili asked, now six, pretty, and vivacious as a Puerto Rican Shirley Temple with her mass of black curls, peach skin and pearly white teeth. Mami could not help but hug and kiss her at least once an hour, by my rough calculations. I liked her too but I knew she had a bad side. In fact I had saved her from herself quite a few times. Mili was impulsive, even reckless. And I was always to blame for her mishaps, as her older sister and custodian by default. I was beginning to suspect even then that her "charming" personality would be her downfall.

"I'm trying to see if the cane is ready to eat," Mami whispered, bending down to look us in the eyes, "there is nothing sweeter than la caña of this part of our Isla, hijas. Es pura azúcar." Then she crossed her lips for silence. I knew why she was speaking low. Papi did not allow us to eat anything that had not been "processed." That meant either it bore a seal from some U.S. government inspector, or he had examined the product for worms, decay, pits, bones, or fibers that would choke his little girls; of course that meant depriving us of much

of the island's bounty on which Mami had grown into the healthy woman he had married. "Country people learn early to deal with dangers you have not faced or will need to face," he had explained to me when I had been forbidden to suck on a quenepa, a slippery gooey fruit with a pit about the size of my gullet. One of my aunts had brought Mami a bunch from a tree in my abuela's yard. Papi's "No" had been firm enough to send me crying to my room. But when he left for work, Mami had brought in a few in a paper bag, then with deliberation she had shown me how to curl my tongue around the pepita so that it would not slide down my throat, and how to suck on the flesh of the fruit and savor it while rolling the pit back and forth in my mouth. It was a complicated but satisfying way to enjoy a forbidden fruit—absolutely worth the trouble and the price. Her indulgences meant that I had to accept the difficult role of keeping her little secrets, like about María Sereno's manicures and a few other things Papi could not know about.

Mili suddenly broke loose from Mami's grasp and ran into the field. We both called out her name and my father dropped the tire he was about to mount on the wheel and ran after Mili. We watched him grab her by the arm a little too roughly and hurry her back to Mami.

Caught by surprise, Mili was not sure what she had done wrong as she ran to Mami. Papi looked sternly into Mami's face as he said to us, "There might be snakes in those stalks. Your mother should be a little more careful about what she promises you."

He then opened the car doors and waited for us to get settled in seats so hot that our sweat-damp dresses stuck to the vinyl covers. It took him longer than usual to change the tire. No one said anything until he eased the car back onto the carretera militar that circled the island in its tortuous route.

"There are no poisonous serpientes *on our isla,"* my mother said *in a tone that told us,* this is a fact, nothing more need be said about the subject. *And nothing was.*

The poem is closer to my emotional memory of this incident; the prose is an extrapolation that began with the facts of the event. In both the poem and the prose, I wanted to get "off the subject" in order to throw a different slant on the truth of the subject.

In his extraordinary little book on the writing life, *The Triggering Town*, the poet Richard Hugo talks about writing "off the subject." The "town" that may trigger the poem will not be the final town in the poem, if there is a town at all left in it. In my own work I have often taken this process in a different direction and used my poems as triggers for my essays and fiction. For me, it's a mental shortcut, a bypassing of a few steps necessary for the creative impulse to kick in. It involves attaining a sort of out-of-body state for me. First I have to distance myself from the persona of the poem enough to be able to see myself as a character outside of me, the writer.

In the case of the sugarcane scene I vividly recall the family road trips around the Island, the macho driving, and the blowouts in the white hot tropical heat. As an adult I can now imagine the tensions those little contretemps must have generated between my parents, and for my purposes, I have assigned rays of meaning to these ordinary events. In the poem I focused on the triad of mother-father-daughter and the sexual politics between the adults that will also affect the girl at the subconscious level. It is the mother lode, the hoard of the writer, these buried insights that surface during the making of the poem or story.

Sometimes, after I finish a poem, the poem continues to haunt me. "You are not finished with me," it whines. "Give me a chance to explain myself." This was the case with "The Woman Who Was Left at the Altar," which eventually formed the nucleus of the essay "The Woman Who Slept With One Eye Open." If I succumb to its siren call (for me it's impossible to ignore an unfinished subject; like the unburied dead, it drifts in and out of your dreams and keeps you from going on to other things during your working hours), having exhausted its possibilities in one form, I then try to explore the character or event in another genre. "Tell all the Truth but tell it slant—" said Emily Dickinson, and what choice did she, does any writer, have? So I begin again. There were sugarcane fields, and trips in my father's Studebaker, and I was not allowed to suck the sweet juice of . . . Oh, please, I don't want to say it. OK, it was the sweet juice of life. And there are no poisonous snakes on the island, and my mother wanted me to know that I did not have to fear the knowledge of good and evil. And to this day I experience the thrill of the forbidden when I eat the forbidden fruit, when I find a new slant for an old story.

I still don't know the full meaning or the real lesson of the sugarcane, but it has stopped haunting me. I no longer care. I have given it as decent a last rite as I can manage with a eulogy in both poetry and prose. The process is both elegantly simple as well as mysteriously elusive. In writing the poem I make the connection, find the neural pathways to a deeply felt memory-generated emotion. That is how I know it is the Truth (not to be mistaken by the Fact). Once I have located the Truth, I have the Subject. Not the triggering subject, but the Thing that I must use as the basis of my essay or story. It is not

11

that the poem and the prose are the same Thing, only that they came from the same source.

I use this technique in order to answer the all-important questions I must ask before I commit my time, my energies, and my heart to a writing project: Is it worth part of my life? Who cares if I make this poem or story? If I am passionate enough about something to write a poem, then it *is* worth my time and no one else needs to care about it. It is necessary to me.

My writing students are often initially irritated at me for requiring that everyone in my workshops write poems. We move from poetry writing to prose and then back to the poem. My hope is that they will begin to understand that the process of creation begins with the identification of the Subject. The Subject is that which is worth writing about. Once the writer attempts to put her thoughts in the demanding form of the poem, she will soon discover that if there is no diamond embedded in the carbon, she will not be able to fake it. In my classes we read many poems before I ask them to write one of their own. If they are die-hard prose writers and claim to have no impulse for poetry, I ask them to write a version of a poem by a poet they admire, one that speaks to them out of a shared experience. Oh there is resistance, and the results are usually spectacularly uneven (as Oscar Wilde said: "All bad poetry springs from genuine feeling"). But the point of the exercise is that if it's not a true subject, it will not be made into art. It makes them more conscious of the writing process as one of self-discovery, not merely of self-expression.

The poems, good, bad, and mediocre, are revised and workshopped. The students are directed to find the Truth in their poems, to paraphrase them, and to begin transforming them into prose: prose made from the distilled, purified, and polished material the poems have produced. I find that the stories and essays that pass through this process begin at a much higher level of thought and technical proficiency than the prose work I get written "from scratch." The fact is that the poetry-to-prose technique I use and teach is probably very similar to the intensive revision process that most experienced writers practice. I see it simply as a way to arrive dramatically at the point that begins serious writing for me: a respect for language that poetry writing demands. Not that prose doesn't require great discipline; it does. I believe, though, that it usually takes longer for the inexperienced prose writer to come to terms with the cutting and compression required for good writing; the poet must face that painful decision almost immediately.

The poet must be asked to perform a particularly perverse experiment, like being asked "to paint a landscape on a grain of rice" (from the introduction to *Microfiction*). Precisely, I thought, like being asked to write a poem. I know how long and how hard I struggled with my assignment for the book. It was not until I saw it as a poem that the closing lines for my tiny story, "Kennedy in the Barrio," achieved its true closure: "I slipped in between them [my parents]. I smelled her scent of castile soap, café con leche, and cinnamon; I inhaled his mixture of sweat and Old Spice cologne—a man-smell that I was afraid to like too much."

It was finally a matter of condensing, of miniaturizing. These similarities allow me to allow the students to move toward the same results and still choose their genre: fiction or poetry. I admit to taking liberties with the Truth when I assure them that they have a choice. I am simply telling the truth, but with a slant. The moral is good writing is good writing is good writing. And that it begins with the pause of the artist before a blank canvas, the discipline of restraint that was best expressed by Richard Hugo when he advised the writer, "Think small, if you have a large mind it will show itself."

In teaching a multigenre workshop I try to keep an ongoing discussion on good writing as the basis for both prose and poetry. An advanced exercise I assign requires that each student in the entire class write a poem from a story and a story from a poem—with variations. These caveats include writing the essay from the poem or writing the poem from the story. The point is to continue the emphasis on control of language and craft from poem to prose. The poem as minutely planned as the creative nonfiction, which is nothing more and nothing less than a composite of the narrative poem and the finely crafted plotted story: a story as polished and economically constructed as a poem. The second half of the workshop is conducted along more traditional lines with the usual requirements of a full-length short story and poetry in various forms so that we can see the genres in the new light shed by the transformation. So rather than isolating each genre, I teach them as they exist in my life as a reader and writer, that is, as angles of light from the same source, transforming whatever they fall upon into something new.

EXERCISES

1. Write a short poem about a real-life event, personal or public, that interests you deeply.

2. In the above poem, identify the Subject that was triggered by the writing.

3. From the poem, write a piece of creative nonfiction about the same Subject.

A Braided Heart:
Shaping the Lyric Essay

BRENDA MILLER

I. THE LYRIC ESSAY

On the first day of my class "Writing the Lyric Essay", I bring in a loaf of *challah,* the braided bread traditionally eaten for the Jewish Sabbath dinner. I take it out of my bag and set it in on a white cloth at the center of the table. Before I say anything at all about it, I watch my students' reactions: some eye it warily, their eyes narrowed in suspicion. They know there must be *some* predetermined reaction I'm looking for, and so they sit back and refuse to give any at all; they cross their arms over their chests or begin to rustle through their backpacks for pencils or pens. Some of them, the ones who recognize the *challah*, are worried that this is going to be one of those "spiritual" writing classes; they look at the bread and glance away, then lean over to whisper something to their neighbors. Some gaze at the bread only with suppressed delight, hunger evident in their eyes. *Snack time*, they think, and with it the promise of an "easy" class, one that coddles and nurtures.

Any of them could be right. I pass out the syllabus and watch the stapled packets make a circuit around the room, the *challah* still sitting placidly in the center of the table, innocuous yet full of mysterious power. I don't talk about the bread, but I begin some forays into the "lyric essay" in general. What is it? That is the main question we all have; I might even write it on the board. *What is the lyric essay?* Not only *what is it* but *how do I make it?* What's the definition? What's the answer?

And I might tell them: *I don't know.* I might tell them, though they won't want to hear it, that we've entered a realm of unknowing, a place where definitions are constantly in flux, a place where answers are not as important as the questions to which they give rise.

II. THE *CHALLAH*

I loved *challah* when I was a child. It had to be bought from a special kosher bakery, the Delicious Bakery in the Hughes Shopping Center, and we had to get there at just the right time on Friday afternoons: before the loaves were sold out, and after they had just come from the oven, still warm, the egg wash and the sesame seed gleaming like gold. They seemed, in fact, the golden loaves of some fairy tale, minted from a factory deep inside a hidden cave, emerging on a conveyer belt and counted out for all the Jews of Northridge. There were a good many conservative congregations in the San Fernando valley, the "California Jews" whom the east coast Jews frowned upon, or dismissed. There's a joke: California Jews are not really Jews; they're Jew-*ish*.

And I suppose my family fit that description. We went to synagogue when necessary, and my brothers and I went to Hebrew school, and I thought the men looked both distinguished and ridiculous with their *yarmulkes* on: it was the contrast between the elegant black silk and the womanish bobby pins used to hold them in place. My brothers took them off as soon as they could, but sometimes my father absent-mindedly left his *yarmulke* on throughout the rest of that sanctified day, preoccupied with a piece of wood in his vise-grip on the bench in the garage, or sitting with his feet up on the La-Z-Boy recliner, watching a Lakers game, waiting for dinner to be served.

Though we were secular Jews, we were still Jewish enough to appreciate the quality of the Sabbath bread, that beautiful, glowing *challah*. I recently asked a rabbi on the Internet why the *challah* is braided, what is symbolic about it, and his e-mail reply said (in a voice so much like the rabbis of my youth! Slightly contemptuous, a little annoyed . . .) that the Sabbath bread must only look *different* from everyday bread, that it need not be braided; it could be circular or oblong or in the shape of a rhomboid, for that matter. The braid had become custom for eastern European Jews; some bakers used three strands, some four; this rabbi, he said with a hint of pride, used six!

As a child, I knew only that the braided bread simply tasted *better* than ordinary bread, the way texture will often affect flavor, the way presentation and form can sometimes offer sustenance in itself. I loved watching my mother cut through that jeweled crust, the heft of the buttered slice in my hands, the convoluted, lacquered outer surface giving way to the dense bread beneath. The inside was moist and delicious, tasted like an entire meal in itself. I often closed my eyes when I bit into it. Here was a bread that spoke of what it meant to have a sacred day: to bring the divine into one's small and common body.

III. BRAIDING THE *CHALLAH*

"Divide dough into four equal portions; roll each between hands to form a strand about 20 inches long. Place the 4 strips lengthwise on

a greased baking sheet, pinch tops together and braid as follows: pick up strand on right, bring it over next one, under the third, and over the fourth. Repeat always starting with the strand on the right, until braid is complete. Pinch ends together. Cover and let rise in a warm place until almost doubled. Using a soft brush or your fingers, spread egg yolk mixture evenly over braids; sprinkle with seed. Bake in a 350° oven for 30–35 minutes or until loaf is golden brown and sounds hollow when tapped."

IV. THE LYRIC ESSAY

"Lyric. Essay. How do you think the two fit together?" My students mull over the question, avoiding my eyes, their gaze landing on the glowing *challah* at the center of the table. "What would be the recipe for a lyric essay?" I ask, "What are the ingredients?"

"Imagery?" one student tentatively offers. I nod my head eagerly and lean forward in my chair. "Poetic language?" another asks. I get up and start writing on the board, as my students begin to call out words and phrases: *fragments, personal experience, metaphor, sentences, gaps, structure, white space, thesis, sensuality, voice, meditation, repetition, rhythm. . . .* When we're finished I have a blackboard full of possibilities, really a panoply of all the ways of writing itself. It's a little daunting. I sit down and ask them again: So what makes the lyric essay a lyric? What makes it an essay? Why not just write a poem, instead, if you want to be lyrical? Why not just write an essay, if you want to be prosaic?

Silence falls, so I tell my students that the lyric essay is quite an ancient form; it's nothing new. Writers like Seneca, Bacon, Sei Shōnagon in the tenth century, Montaigne, hundreds of others: all could be said to write essays whose forms were inherently lyric; that is, they did not necessarily follow a linear, narrative line. Many excellent writers and thinkers have tried to pin down the lyric essay, defining it as a collage, a montage, a mosaic. It's been called disjunctive, paratactic, segmented, sectioned. All of these are correct. All of these recognize in the lyric essay a tendency toward fragmentation that invites the reader into those gaps, that emphasizes what is unknown rather than the already articulated known. By infusing prose with tools normally relegated to the poetic sensibility, the lyric essayist creates anew, each time, a form that is interactive, alive, full of new spaces in which meaning can germinate. The *Seneca Review,* in its thirtieth anniversary issue devoted to lyric essays, characterized them as having "this built-in mechanism for provoking meditation. They require us to complete their meaning."

So, I underline *fragmentation* on the board. I underline the word *gaps*. I write the words *explode the narrative line!!* over the whole thing. My students nod; they write this down.

Then I go over and, with chalky hands, pick up the bread.

V. THE BRAIDED ESSAY

Writing has always—and always will, I'm sure—scared the hell out of me. I'll do just about anything to get out of it, and have been known to spend whole afternoons circling my desk like a dog, wary, unwilling to commit to writing a single word. What is so frightening about it? I still don't know. Perhaps it's the horrible knowledge that no matter how well you write, the resultant product will never correlate exactly to the truth, will never arrive with quite the melodious voice you hear in the acoustic cavity of your mind.

When I first started writing personal essays, I didn't know that's what I was doing. I had written poetry for many years, but at some point felt restricted by the poetic line. So I started wandering past the line break and ended up writing autobiographical prose that had a lilting, hesitant quality to it, as if it still didn't trust itself in this un-fenced yard.

But what I found was that this yard had just as many fences, just as many restrictions. I was struggling to write an essay that seemed very important to me, an essay about being a massage therapist for several years at a small hot springs resort in northern California. This work had defined me and created a center of self based on serving others. By the time I was writing the essay, in 1989, this center had dissolved: I no longer practiced massage and had yet to find another guiding principle to replace it. The urge to write was the urge to explain the sense of loss I felt, to bring coherence to an identity that now seemed fragmented, in flux, chaotic.

While I wrote, I kept looking at a photograph of myself from that time: I'm naked, in the hot tub of Orr Springs. The photographer (my boyfriend) chose to frame this scene through a windowpane misty with steam; we get a fragment of Jasmine bush, the blur of the water, my hands lifted to shield my face. The diffuse light centers on my abdomen (the site, it turns out, where much of my autobiographical material resides). I looked at this picture often, much the way I might gaze in a mirror: looking for a way into this body, a way for this image of the body to give up its secrets and make itself manifest in language. But as I tried to order this material of memory and image into a logical, linear narrative, the essay became flat, intractable, stubbornly refusing to yield any measure of truth.

By chance, I happened to be studying the personal essay form for an independent study class at the University of Montana. One of my classmates brought in an essay by the poet Albert Goldbarth. It was called "After Yitzl," and I had never before read anything like it. Written in numbered sections that at first seemed to have little to do with one another, the essay worked through a steady accretion of imagery and key repetitions; it spoke in a voice that grew loud, then whispered, that cut itself off, then rambled. I found myself tripping over the gaps, then laughing delightedly as I found myself sprawled on the ground. Something cracked open inside me. I saw how cavalierly Goldbarth had exploded his prose in order to put it together again in a new pattern that was inordinately pleasurable.

So I turned to my own essay and tried the same thing. I deserted a narrative line in favor of images that intuitively rose up in the work. I allowed for silence, the caesuras between words, and the essay began to take on voices that hardly belonged to me. This fragmentation allowed for those moments of "not knowing," which, to me, became the most honest moments in the essay. I abandoned my authority, and with that surrender came great freedom: I no longer had to know the answers. I didn't have to come to a static conclusion. Instead, the essay began to make an intuitive kind of sense.

When I arrived at the final draft, I had fragmented three different narratives—my work as a massage therapist, the story of a life-threatening miscarriage, and the birth of my godson. All of this material was highly emotional to me; the fragmentation, however, allowed me—almost forced me—not to approach this material head-on but to search for a more circuitous way into the essay. I had to expand my peripheral vision, to focus on images that at first seemed oblique to the stories. Sometimes your peripheral vision catches the most important details, those you might not have expected to carry significance. You give yourself over to chance sightings, arresting the image on the verge of skittering away. In the resultant essay, "A Thousand Buddhas," it was the image of my hands, those hands fluttering up in the photograph, that became a contextualizing force, yoking together the juxtaposed meditations on birth and death that surrounded it.

VI. TAKING RISKS

"For many bakers, kneading the soft dough is a lovely sensation, a sort of relaxing therapy. For others, the glorious moment comes with the first buttered bite of the fresh warm loaf. For everyone, the yeasty

aroma wafting from the oven as the bread bakes crowns the day with a sense of delicious achievement. . . .

Yeast bread baking has the reputation of being chancy and difficult. . . . It's true that you do need to be careful at first. You have to protect the baby dough to get it started. But after that the bread almost makes itself."

VII. CORNELL BOXES

"Somewhere in the city of New York there are four or five still-unknown objects that belong together. Once together they'll make a work of art."

In his lovely and diminutive book about the art of Joseph Cornell, *Dime-Store Alchemy,* Charles Simic elucidates the intuitive stance necessary not only for an artist like Cornell, who brings disparate objects together in order to create a sculpture, but for us writers too, the ones who look for the disparate strands of experience to come together and form a lyric essay. Simic portrays Cornell as a kind of wandering mystic, a man with a vision that looked beyond the surface of things to the inherent spirituality that lay beneath. "What Cornell sought in his walks in the city," Simic writes, "the fortune-tellers already practiced in their parlors . . . divination by contemplation of surfaces which stimulate inner visions and poetic faculties."

VIII. MAKING *CHALLAH*

There was a time in my life when I made all my own bread. I loved every part of it: reading the recipes, gathering the ingredients, kneading the dough, allowing it to rise. And all the praise I reaped from the task didn't hurt either. I remember, when I was in college, laying out perfectly browned loaves of whole wheat French bread on the kitchen counter in a house I shared with four men in Blue Lake; such love in their eyes, such devotion! I remember baking bread every day for children in a summer camp: big, oversized loaves of white bread that we cut and spread with churned butter. And the *challah,* of course. Sometimes I got ambitious and tried the kind of loaves you saw in synagogue: a four-strand base, with a smaller, three-strand braid on top, so that the whole thing became a monstrous labyrinth. Mine always emerged a little lopsided, but that only added to its charm.

All good bread makers develop a finely honed sense of intuition that comes into play at every step of the process: knowing exactly the temperature of the water in which to proof your yeast, testing it not with a thermometer but against the most sensitive skin at the underside of your wrist, with the same thoughtful stance as a mother testing a baby's formula. You add the warm milk, the butter, the salt, a bit of sugar. After a while you stop measuring the flour as you stir, knowing the correct texture through the way it resists your arm. You take the sticky dough in your hands and knead, folding the dough toward you, then pushing away with the heel of your hand, turning and repeating, working and working with your entire body—your legs, your abdomen, your strong heart. You work the dough until it takes on the texture of satin. You poke it with your index finger and it sighs against your touch.

You cover it and let it rise. You keep it in your mind as it combusts in the warm dark. You return to it, this living thing you've created with your hands. You shape it to please the eye and the mouth. You pull it apart and roll the dough into yeasty ropes and begin to braid it back into a different form. You hope it will come out all right, that the strands aren't too thick or too thin, that they aren't too long or too short, that they won't fall apart in the middle, or break. Sometimes you have to unravel what you've done, start again. You keep braiding with your heart in your throat, hoping for the best. You have the egg wash at the ready, to add the finishing touches, the small bowl of sesame seeds. In your mind you have a vision of the perfect *challah*, gleaming on its special platter.

You do what you can. At some point the bread "almost makes itself."

IX. FRENCH BRAIDS

When I first met Hannah and Sarah, the way into their hearts was to plait their hair into French braids. They had faith in all women over a certain age to be able to braid hair, and so when they came to me with combs and ribbons in hand, I didn't have the heart to disillusion them. It was like a test of my merit as an adult female companion, and their eyes were so eager, so trusting: How could I refuse?

But braiding hair is not as easy as braiding bread. Especially French braids, which require a certain dexterity of the fingers, an intuitive feel for the slippery hair of young girls. The hair slides from the fingers, breaks off, becomes unruly. I had to start over, again and again, and when I was finished they looked terrible, not really like braids at all but like some old sailor's rope, knotted and twisted and frayed.

But the girls were satisfied enough. They ran to the mirror and tilted their heads; luckily they couldn't see all the way around to the back. They patted their hair as if it were a nice, strange new animal and thanked me for my trouble. I knew why they wanted it so badly: Braided hair has an allure so much more exciting than "normal" hair;

it has texture and substance and mystery. Where does one strand originate and the next one begin? The eye travels, dizzy with delight, over the highlights, and the hair seems to shimmer more fully, takes on a coy illumination that beckons the hand to touch, to feel, to love.

X. A FINE CHAOS

The world is chaotic, certainly, and always clichéd. Face it: our lives are full of stories already told. Our parents die; our lovers leave us and, *surprise!*, begin to love others. The dog grows old and we watch our own aging faces in the mirror. What is new is not *what* we tell, but *how* we tell it. The lyric essay is one way to do this: it demands (or perhaps gently asks, with a knowing smile) that we stay awake to the chance associations and intuitive connections that make life bearable. Or really, to be more precise, it asks us to create those very connections through the act of writing, to follow a chain of those connections as far as they will go and pinch them together in the end.

XI. CORNELL

And this: *"Beauty is about the improbable coming true suddenly."*

And this: *"To submit to chance is to reveal the self and its obsession."*

XII. THE BRAIDED ESSAY

After that first essay, "A Thousand Buddhas," I began to adopt the structure of fragmented, numbered sections for much of my prose. And I began to see more clearly that this form wasn't just about fragmentation and juxtaposition; it wasn't really mosaic I was after. There was more of a sense of weaving about it, of interruption and continuation, like the braiding of bread, or of hair. I had to keep my eye on the single strands that came in and out of focus, filaments that glinted differently depending on where they had been. At the same time, I had to keep my eye focused on the single image that held them all together. As William Stafford wrote a few weeks before he died, "There's a thread you follow. It goes among/things that change. But it doesn't change."

As I began to adopt the braided essay more and more in my work, a strange, wonderful, and mysterious thing began to happen. While I was still writing "personal" essays, essays that mainly relied for their material on the experiences of my life, I found that they started to expand more outward, taking on myriad facts and stories of the outer world as well as the inner. New strands began to develop, but ones that still intersected with memories most important to me. I liked this.

It was as if I were creating the more complex, double-braided bread of the synagogue.

For instance, while at my first writing colony on an island in the Puget Sound, I happened to pick up an encyclopedia of Jewish religion from the library in the farmhouse. "Happened to" is the key phrase here; the essays of my own that I like the best arise out of happenstance, out of the material finding its way into my hands rather than vice versa. We must train ourselves into this state of "meditative expectancy," as Carolyn Forché calls the writer's stance; the world, after all, flies by us at millions of miles an hour, spewing out any number of offerings—it is the writer at her desk, the artist out perambulating, who will recognize a gift when she sees one. As I turned the pages of this marvelous book, I was struck by how little I, a Jewish woman who had gone to Hebrew school for most of her formative years, knew about my religion. In fact, I realized, I didn't have the foggiest idea how to pray.

I started writing down the quotes that interested me the most, facts about the kaballah, and the ritual baths, and *dybbuks,* and the Tree of Life. At the time, I was also writing about a recent trip I had taken to Portugal, and the news I had gotten there of my mother's emergency hysterectomy. I was also writing about my own yoga practice, and the volunteer work I did at a children's hospital in Seattle. As I kept all these windows open in my computer, the voice of the encyclopedia emerged as the binding thread, a way for me to create a spiritual self-portrait in the form of a complex braid.

This is what I love about all braided things: bread, hair, essays, rivers, our own circulatory systems pumping blood to our brains and our hearts. I love the fact of their separate parts intersecting, creating the illusion of wholeness, but with the oh-so-pleasurable texture of separation. It is not the same as a purely disjunctive form, the bits and pieces scattered like cookies on the baking sheet. Rather, the strands are separate, but together, creating a pattern that is lovely to the touch, makes the bread taste even better when we lift a slice of it to our tongues.

Poets, of course, have known this all along. They blow the world apart and put it back together again. Cornell wanders the city and is *"lunged into a world of complete happiness in which every triviality becomes imbued with significance. . . ."* Charles Simic comments, "The commonplace is miraculous if rightly seen, if recognized."

XIII. A BRAIDED HEART

Bread has always been a miracle. As has poetry. And language itself, this tremendous urge to communicate. To live our lives in our shattered ways and still be happy: this is miraculous. The Sabbath bread helps us see that an extraordinary pattern binds our days together. The braided loaf, set on a table, makes of that table an altar. Our hearts may give the illusion of one muscular organ, but think how the florid chambers converge, and of the many veins and arteries that wind their way by design to reach this fleshy core. They come together; they intersect; they beat an urgent rhythm beneath our skin.

XIV. MUSIC

I once wrote for a month at an artists' colony in upstate New York, and one of my fellow residents was a composer of operas. I am tone deaf, have no pitch whatsoever, and music for me has always been the most esoteric of languages. He played for us, on the piano, one of his arias. When he was finished, we applauded, and I asked him: "How do you know when a piece is finished?" I know now it was a naive question, even a little foolish.

But he answered me without pause. "When what I hear up here," he said, clasping a palm to his forehead, "corresponds to what's written down here." He pointed to the score. I followed the line of his fingers, saw a page full of inky hieroglyphics that wound in and out of the lined bars.

A writer must spend a great deal of time ushering her piece into the world. There is the creation of bulk, then the cutting down to the essential, resonant notes. When Cornell walks around New York City, he must pick up and discard any number of objects before finding the ones that *"belong together."* This process takes a terrible amount of patience, more than an inkling of faith. I wanted to spy on that composer through his window and see if he does what *I* do when I'm writing: sit with a blank stare, my pen poised over the empty page, my mouth hanging slightly ajar, waiting.

When I read the lyric essayists that I consider great—Albert Goldbarth, Anne Carson, Annie Dillard, Charles Simic, to name just a few—they all have the quality of a piece of music arrived whole from some distant place and played anew. I can go back and read these essays again and again because they seem neither static nor fixed. It's always a live performance: the white space expands and contracts, and I feel guest in a charmed province, the same one occupied by prayer.

XV. THE *CHALLAH*

We pass the bread around the seminar table. I ask my students each to tear off a chunk and hold it in their hands a moment, waiting until everyone has a piece. I want them to notice the heft of it, the yolky texture, the subtle yet amazing fact that within the loaf itself, once you cut it open, you see nary a sign of the braiding. You have a chunk of bread: whole, fine-grained, delicious.

The bread, of course, is good. All *challah* is good. And there are many ways to eat it. Some take it apart with their fingers, separating the strands, unwinding them and putting them one by one in their mouths. Some take big bites into the center of the bread, saving the golden crust for last. Some nibble at it, then leave it on their desks. After we're finished brushing off the crumbs, taking quick sips of water, we look at each other again. Some of the students seem a little more relaxed now, a little more willing; they look at me expectantly, their eyes bright, wondering what will happen next. Some of the students seem even more annoyed, already putting their pens away; I doubt I'll see them on the roster at the next class meeting.

What I'm hoping, for the students that remain, is that the idea of *braiding* has entered us, become a viable, perhaps natural, way of shaping our material, and even our lives, for the brief ten weeks we'll be together. What I'm hoping is that by the eating of this bread together we begin to respond to a hunger unsatisfied by everyday food, unvoiced in everyday language. We'll begin to formulate a few separate strands; we'll mull them over, roll them in our hands, and bring them together in a pattern that acts as mouthpiece to the sacred.

Recipe and quotes from *Sunset Cookbook of Breads* (Lane Publishing, 1978) and *Dime-Store Alchemy* (The Ecco Press, 1992).

EXERCISES

1. Take three disparate objects, at random, from your purse, your backpack, your shelves. Set them in front of you and begin writing, allowing fifteen minutes for each object. See if there is a common image or theme you can use to bind these together.

2. Go back to an essay that's been giving you problems. Look for the one image that seems to encapsulate the abstract ideas or concepts you're trying to develop. Explode the essay into at least three different strands, each focused on different aspects of that image, and begin weaving, transforming that image from beginning to end.

3. Cut apart an essay (or two, or three) with scissors, and lay the pieces out on the floor or a long table. Start moving them around like pieces of a puzzle and see what kind of patterns you can make through different juxtapositions of the texts.

Saying Good-Bye to "Once Upon a Time," or Implementing Postmodernism in Creative Nonfiction

LAURA WEXLER

Once upon a time is the most seductive line in literature.

Hearing it, we're immediately tantalized and calmed. Tantalized, because we know the story that follows will involve heroes and villains engaged in a fierce struggle. Calmed, because we know the heroes will prevail and live "happily ever after." The particulars may be different, but such a cocktail of excitement and ease can be found in nearly every fairy tale . . . and, for that matter, in every Hollywood blockbuster.

And yet, the fantasy of fairy tales has less to do with made-up characters and plot than with an illusion created about storytelling itself: the illusion that there always exists a single, true, and knowable version of What Happened.

Let's say that you, an aspiring creative nonfiction writer, decide to write about one of the most controversial events of the final decade of the twentieth century, the beating of Rodney King. Would it be possible for you to tell the story with the same calm omniscience as those who tell fairy tales? Would you be able to write the single, true version of What Happened, with a clear and certain idea of who did what to whom, and when and why?

Would your story paint the baton-wielding police officers as the villains and Rodney King the hero/victim—or would you cite the flawed use-of-force policies in the Los Angeles Police Department as a mitigating factor? And would you mention that Rodney King had been driving drunk and led the police on a chase? Would you tell the beating of Reginald Denney, a white man, by black men in the aftermath of the King trial, as a story about uncontrolled black anger—despite the fact those who rescued Denney were also black?

And how would you account for the fact that, in the rioting that followed the original not-guilty verdict of the officers, a conflict painted as a black-white thing, Korean businesspeople suffered the brunt of the property destruction? And what about the fact that one of the officers who beat Rodney King made a comment about *Gorillas in the Mist* several hours before the beating—does that mean he beat Rodney King because King was black, or because he (incorrectly) thought King was on the drug PCP? And what of the motives of the judge, the jury, the media, the citizens?

These questions make it clear that the Rodney King beating cannot be told as a fairy tale. There is no single, true version of What Happened. Because everything about it is up for grabs, everything is unstable: motives, actions, and interpretations. It seems we cannot, despite Rodney King's famous plea, "all get along"—because we tell different stories about the same events.

We always do.

An event like the Rodney King beating is simply a "hot spot" that brings our various and conflicting stories into high relief. It, like so many stories that reflect and perpetrate our national obsession with race, is a palimpsest. It is a particular story, certainly, but one that is freighted with all the conflicting stories about lynching, police brutality, and racism in the criminal justice system that have been told before. It is an event that occurred at a fixed point in time; nonetheless, it seems to exist more as an arrow, reaching into the past.

So as nonfiction writers, should we shy away from stories like this, stories that thwart our methods of researching and writing, our every effort to learn and record Truth? Absolutely not. Rather, we should recognize that the genre of creative nonfiction—with its emphasis on stories—is perfectly suited to deal with contested terrain, both in the past and present. We'll get tangled up, that's certain. But it can't be any other way.

A BRIEF AND REDUCTIVE DEFINITION OF POSTMODERNISM

The bedrock principle of postmodernism is *subjectivity*, the idea that the world looks different depending where you stand, both literally and figuratively. The fancy name for this is *positionality*; a variety of things—race, class, gender, sexual orientation, cultural background, educational level, experiences—combine to produce your positionality.

Your positionality affects your perceptions of the world and, at the same time, your perceptions of the world affect your positionality. Certainly there's a lot more to postmodernism, but for our purposes, it's important to acknowledge that different people almost always have different interpretations of the same event, and these different interpretations are illustrative of a whole range of interesting phenomena. The other thing that's crucial to realize is that seeing the world in a postmodern way makes it impossible—irresponsible at worst, uninteresting at best—to write any story like a fairy tale. Postmodernism shows us the impossibility of the existence of one true version of anything that matters.

Think about these ideas in terms of our nation's history. The Boston Tea Party—was it the act of patriots or insurgents? Depends whether you talk to the people who chucked the tea or the man who wore the British crown. The Civil War (or the War of Northern Aggression)— was it fought largely over slavery or states' rights? Depends whether you talk to a self-righteous Yankee or a devotee of the Lost Cause.

Then think about more recent events: The O.J. Simpson trial—was it long-denied justice finally served, or a travesty? The Elian Gonzalez brouhaha—was it a conflict over core politics or child rearing?

Or consider more run-of-the-mill events. A friend recently told me that several of her colleagues, who were Chinese men newly arrived to the United States, were asked to relocate to a different bureau to fill in a gap in their company's operations. The men perceived the relocation as a message that they were not performing well. Despite every attempt to convince them that the relocation was for logistical reasons, the men felt that they had dishonored the company, and themselves, and they resigned. Same action, different interpretations.

In an even more troubling—and thus illuminating—incident, a friend's wife, who is white, was waiting in line at the airport in Atlanta. It was crowded, and she stepped back to let a person pass through. That person—who was a black man—interpreted her stepping back as a sign of fear or distaste, and he told her so. She felt it was a gesture of consideration and politeness. Again, same action, different interpretations.

All of these cases deal with points of conflict. That's what makes them challenging to write about; that's also what makes them compelling. And certainly any journalist writing about events like these would seek out different people with different opinions in an effort to be objective. That's standard operating procedure. But implementing the principles of postmodernism in creative nonfiction means taking standard journalistic operating procedure further. It means creating literary structures and techniques that are the formal embodiment of these principles, such that readers have not only a cerebral, but also a visceral, experience.

STOPPING TO CONSIDER

As writers, it's easy to go about our business without much consideration to the theoretical implications of what we do. But think about it. What is really the main goal of the creative nonfiction writer?

To use research methods and literary techniques to re-create actual events and people on the page, you might say. And that's a good answer. Certainly there are many instances in which re-creating what happened—a ship going down in a storm, a climbing team perishing on Everest, a synagogue exploding in Atlanta—is an amazing reportorial and artistic enterprise, one that requires prodigious talent and skill. To borrow from Shakespeare, sometimes the play really *is* the thing.

But sometimes it isn't the *only* thing. Some stories are so contested that creative nonfiction writers must be as concerned with representing interpretations of those events as they are with re-creating the events themselves. In general, these are events that concern national hot spots, or secrets, or taboos; in the United States, the national taboo is, of course, race.

Consider one of the most fascinating history-made-current-affair stories to surface in the last few years: the question of whether Thomas Jefferson's sexual relationship with his slave Sally Heming led to a set of descendants that has never been recognized. "Jefferson's Blood," a documentary that aired on PBS's *Frontline*, dealt with this question by alternating scenes about life in Monticello during Jefferson's era with scenes from the current day, as people step forward claiming to be the secret descendants of Jefferson, and other people, in turn, deny those claims.

Again, the story is a palimpsest, a story whose modern chapters cannot be understood without understanding the history of race in America, as well as Thomas Jefferson's previously uncriticized place in that history. The documentary, at its end, does not solve the mystery. Rather, it provides insight into both our past and present by allowing us to see and hear clashing answers to the same question.

When I began writing my own book about the lynching of two black men and two black women in Walton County, Georgia, in 1946, my initial goal was to uncover who had fired the shots that killed the four victims—it was a lynching by bullet rather than by rope—and then re-create the story of the lynching on the page. I set out to do this in the same way I'd chased all the stories I'd ever written: I talked to people.

I talked to relatives of the victims, as well as white and black people who were living in Walton County at the time. I talked to people who were interviewed during the six-month FBI investigation in 1946 and others who had testified at the grand jury held in Athens, Georgia. After twenty or so interviews, I scanned my notebooks, looking to see what facts I'd collected, what I knew. I realized I had a lot of what people *thought* had happened, but very little I could confirm, very little that looked like truth.

Looking hard at my notebooks, I began to see that my hopes of re-creating a truthful and whole account of the lynching—much less solving it—would never be fulfilled. There was nobody living who could tell the story straight; there was, like with the Jefferson-Heming story, simply too much at stake for people. It was then I began to see that re-creating the lynching would be only part of my job. The other part was to investigate and represent the legacy of the lynching, which was the gossip, rumors, and beliefs I'd begun scribbling in my notebook. As soon as the last shot rang out that afternoon at the Moore's Ford Bridge in Walton County, the set of facts that was the lynching disappeared, and the lynching could, from that moment, live on only in stories.

People told, and tell, stories to deal with the surprise of the lynching. They tell stories to help themselves imagine the lynching even after it has occurred, a phenomenon Philip Gourevitch discusses in terms of the Rwandan genocide in his book *We Wish to Inform You That Tomorrow We Will Be Killed With Our Families*. They tell stories to serve their political, and their psychic, needs. Most of the stories aren't whole, and many can't be considered reliable. But their fragmentation, their unreliability, is the basis of their truth. People's stories about the lynching reveal as much about life in Georgia in 1946—and now—as the lynching itself. And the same holds true for any story that touches on a national taboo, secret, mystery, any event that's gone unstudied, undiscussed, unacknowledged.

And so, embracing the principles of postmodernism allows us to do several things as writers of creative nonfiction. It allows us, on both a theoretical and a practical level, to see the events we're writing about as refracted through a prism. And it allows us to see that even the most unreachable stories—the stories in which truth seems to purposely hide in the shadows—can be written as nonfiction by focusing as much on interpretation as event. In fact, it is these very stories that most need to be written as nonfiction.

USING INTERVIEWS TO ENACT THE PRINCIPLES OF POSTMODERNISM

Remember that standard journalism legend in which two cars crash in an intersection, five people witness it, and, minutes later, all five people tell different stories about what happened? This exercise doesn't tell us anything we didn't know already: people lie, memory fails. But it does confront us with choices. Do we quit asking people for their stories because they're often inaccurate, or do we examine the unreliability, inspect the diverging stories for what they reveal?

When, during interviews or conversation, we ask people, "What happened?"; "Why did this happen?"; "Who was responsible?"; "What does it mean?"—we're asking them to connect cause and effect in a meaningful narrative. We're asking them to construct and create stories. In doing so, they usually tell us less than a transcription of events would—but often they tell us more.

One afternoon, after I'd spent about a year conducting interviews with black people who were living in Walton County, Georgia, at the time of the 1946 lynching, I was driving on a country road when I spotted an older white woman in her front yard raking leaves, and stopped to chat with her.

"What do you remember about the summer of 1946?" I asked after we'd dispensed with introductions.

"I remember that black man stabbed Barney," she said. "That was awful."

The woman remembered accurately; a black man had stabbed a white farmer named Barney Hester during the summer of 1946. And two weeks later, that black man, along with three other black people, was lynched. The lynching of four black people was what most people I'd talked to remember as the tragedy of the summer of 1946; this woman remembers the stabbing of the white man (who later recovered). Standing there that afternoon, I was struck by the profound gap in what people remember as important or surprising or tragic. That gap is the truth; set alongside all the conflicting stories, it offers an accurate portrait of the legacy of racial violence, both in 1946 and today.

The recognition that stories are subjective does not, then, negate the value of the interview, the cornerstone tool of creative nonfiction. Rather, it requires that we view interviewing as a critical—rather than simply a documentary—endeavor. We don't have to interrogate people or accuse them of lying, though both are sometimes necessary. But we have to consider that everybody tells the story "slant." On the one hand, this is unavoidable. Different people see the world differently. On the other hand, people often consciously tell a story a certain way in order to convey a message about themselves/their family/their political party. As creative nonfiction writers, we must bring all sorts of journalistic research—court documents, newspapers, crime reports, and other sources—to bear. Again, recognizing that the truth is subjective doesn't mean that it's OK to print lies. It means that in addition to pointing out inaccuracies in a particular version of a story, the creative nonfiction writer investigates the possible reasons for these inaccuracies.

This opens up fertile and exciting ground. A book about a controversial event—anything that travels contested terrain—then becomes a kind of oral historiography of that event, an examination of the ways people tell that event.

FORGING A STRUCTURE

When I began my book on the quadruple lynching in Walton County, Georgia, I had in mind a nice, neat narrative structure in which a single main character would serve as a kind of guide, leading readers through the chaos of the lynching. But once I began to come to terms with the uncertainty that had to be a part of my account of the lynching, I came to terms with the fact that my structural plan for the book did not reflect the multiplicity and uncertainty that was at the heart of the content.

When I looked around for structural models that could allow for multiplicity and conflict, I found several. In some ways, the most obvious possibility is to fashion yourself—the writer/reporter—as the recipient of all the conflicting stories. In his book *The Other Side of the River: A Story of Two Towns, a Death, and America's Dilemma*, author Alex Kotlowitz positions himself as a stand-in for the reader. He listens closely to people's stories and theories about the death of a black teenager in Michigan, and attempts to arrive at an account of what likely happened. This is not objectivity; it's informed subjectivity. The most famous example of this in nonfiction is, of course, James Agee and Walker Evans's *Let Us Now Praise Famous Men*, in which Agee's struggle to represent the lives of the three tenant farm families becomes the central struggle of the book.

But there are possibilities in other genres. Certainly Akira Kurosawa's film *Rashomon*, which replays the same event four times, each narrated by four different characters, offers interesting possibilities. Translating that to creative nonfiction, the idea would be to place conflicting accounts next to each other, without authorial interpretation, and let the reader puzzle it out.

Documentary theater, as practiced most famously by Anna Deveare Smith, also offers interesting structural ideas. For her pieces—which include works on the Crown Heights, Brooklyn, racial riots; the L.A. riots; and the Clinton White House—she interviews hundreds of people. Then, she edits the transcripts of select interviews to create monologues that she acts out onstage in the character of the interviewee. The effect of the monologues, coming one after another, and clashing with one another, is disorienting—which, of course, is the point.

There are, of course, all sorts of other possibilities. The important thing is to create a structure for your article or book that translates content into form, that allows the structure of a story to serve as a metaphor for the story itself. This struggle to find the literary tools—structure, language, character—is what distinguishes creative nonfiction from purely documentary endeavors, such as oral history or cultural anthropology.

In terms of implementing the principles of postmodernism, the goal is to forge a structure that allows for multiple viewpoints and fragmentation, and a bit of complication and messiness. It would be nice to tell a clean, straight narrative about a highly-charged event, just as it would be nice to be a kid again. But simple stories are for demagogues and their followers. The rest of us need reality, which is that no one has a monopoly on truth.

A NAKED APPEAL TO CREATIVE NONFICTION WRITERS

When I first divulged that I planned to write a book about a lynching that happened more than a half-century ago, some people counseled me to reconsider. It's not a story that can be written as creative nonfiction, they said. All the victims are dead; the members of the lynch mob are either dead or silent; and other people can't be relied upon. There simply aren't enough provable facts. You can never be sure what exactly happened, or who exactly did it. Why not write the story as a novel? others asked.

Every nonfiction writer dreams of the flexibility of fiction at one time or another. Not sure if a person wore a hat on the day he died? Make it up. Not sure what someone thought when she stepped off the bus? Put some thoughts into her head yourself. But, in the end, it was not a suggestion I could consider seriously. So many lynchings—like other instances of violence, like other taboos—have been denied, ignored, and veiled in secrecy. That leaves the victims and their loved ones not only with their loss, but also without any official or public acknowledgment of their loss.

Creative nonfiction writers are in an ideal position to be one-person "truth and reconciliation" commissions, to uncover "the small stories that have gone missing," as one writer put it. Rooted as it is in telling people's stories, creative nonfiction is a particularly well-equipped genre to deal with events that have been forgotten or understudied by official histories, and to unearth lives at the margin of bigger events. Seek out these stories. Listen to them critically. Try to learn as much as possible about what it is to live in this fragmented, contradictory, often incomprehensible world. Then write.

EXERCISES

1. Interview separately two people who were involved in the same event. For instance, interview a married couple about their wedding day. (Use a tape recorder for this exercise.) Transcribe the interviews, and consider the similarities and differences in the two versions. What do they tell you about the event? What do they tell you about the people? Think about how you might write the story of the event using these two interviews.

2. Take a controversial event that has recently occurred in your neighborhood/city/region, and interview three people about it. (Again, use a tape recorder for this exercise.) Ask them to tell you both what happened, in their own words, and how they feel about what happened. Edit your interview transcripts into a monologue for each of your three interviewees, and compare them.

3. Take a historical event you're not familiar with and brainstorm possible interpretations of the event. Make a list of the people you would interview to try to elucidate those interpretations.

Finding a Story, or Using the Whole Pig

ALAN CHEUSE

I left full-time teaching (of literature) for a while in the late 1970s and started writing fiction. In order to support myself and family, I began to take on a number of freelance assignments. The late editor of *The L.A. Times Book Review*, a sweet-natured, chain-smoking, old newsman with a shaven head, named Art Seidenbaum, gave me a piece of advice back then. Sell whatever you're working on to at least three or four places.

When you're first starting out, that's the only way you can make the money you should on writing assignments from most newspapers and magazines.

In those days I was living in Knoxville, Tennessee, and found material all around me that was both interesting to me and potentially interesting to magazine and newspaper editors. The matter of moving from New England to the South became the subject of a personal essay for a Boston Sunday supplement. My wife at the time was teaching at the university, and I was staying at home with the kids (with a little help from a part-time nanny) and helping around the house. That made for an article for *Ladies' Home Journal* on manly me doing housework! A more manly guy, a local heavyweight boxer named John Tate, was fighting for the world's championship in Knoxville. That got me an assignment for *Sports Illustrated*. Watching horror movies at night became the subject of another essay. Wandering around a neighborhood near the University of Tennessee campus in search of the house where James Agee was raised—that was another article.

And the wider world beckoned, filled with potential material for freelance pieces. Visiting those extraordinary engineering sites, the huge dams on the rivers in the region constructed by the Tennessee Valley Authority, made for good copy. A couple of hours' drive across the Cumberland Plateau lay Nashville, where the country music business beckoned as a mecca of potential stories. I wrote a bunch of them, for Sunday supplements and *TV Guide*. So basically I was following Seidenbaum's advice by seeing everything around me as material for a story, using life the way the slaughterhouse uses the whole pig, including hooves and snout and squeal.

(Look at what I'm doing right here on this page, using my own experiences of writing nonfiction to make an article about how a new writer might proceed! Hooves and snout!)

I was reminded of Seidenbaum's words about four years ago when the articles editor of the *San Diego Weekly Reader*, the city's alternative newspaper, called to ask if I were interested in writing for them. They paid, she explained, a good number of thousands for an article whose length was solely determined by the writer. The only stipulation was that the piece had to have something to do with the San Diego region. Although I'd been spending summers in northern California, I had never even visited San Diego, and so had no idea what to do.

"You speak a little Spanish, don't you?" she said.

I did.

"You might want to write about something in Tijuana."

I said the next thing that popped into my head, something that can often get you into a lot of trouble.

"I'd like to write about the Jews of Tijuana," I said.

"Good," she said. "I don't know anything about them."

Neither did I. In fact, I didn't even know if there were any Jews there. One of the pieces I wrote while freelancing out of Knoxville was a story for a now defunct liberal Jewish monthly about the Jewish community of Mexico City. Tijuana was part of Mexico so I supposed that there must be some Jewish life there.

And if there weren't?

Then that would be my story. How Tijuana was a Jewish-free zone.

That's how I lurched into one of the most interesting assignments I've ever taken on, and one that is, in some small way, illustrative, I hope, of how a fiction writer on the freelance trail might proceed.

First of all, you lead as much with your heart as you do with your head. If I were a Protestant I might have said, Well, I'll write about the Protestants of Tijuana. Or Catholic? The Church in Tijuana. Write about something that interests you, yes, or something that you would like to learn about—I recently did a piece on day traders that I found quite fascinating and that taught me a little economics that I hadn't had before—but above all else write about something to which you feel some emotional or psychological tie.

(When, for example, I did the *Sports Illustrated* piece about John

Tate, I came to it with a high school boxer's fascination with the sport and some sense of the pain and triumph that came along with it. When I wrote about Tennessee subjects, it came with the curiosity of someone discovering the new region in which he found himself living.)

So, having grown up Jewish among New Jersey Jews, I moved forward with the Tijuana Jews piece with a certain sense of curiosity and interest. How similar would these people be, how different?

I started making telephone calls, to Jewish religious leaders in San Diego, asking questions about Tijuana. (The Mexican city, whose border meets that of south San Diego County, is in many ways another planet and in other ways the southernmost section of one of our southernmost cities.) It didn't take long for me to learn that there was, in fact, an Orthodox Jewish congregation in Tijuana, many of whose congregants lived in San Diego or had moved there during the past decade or so. I learned that the rabbi of the Tijuana synagogue was a recent immigrant from Argentina, secured for the congregation by the San Diego office of an international organization of "born-again" Jews called Chabad. The story seemed possible—Old World–style rabbi leading a congregation in Mexico's westernmost city, one that bordered on one of California's most advanced economies.

I set up interviews with rabbis and laypeople on both sides of the border. Meanwhile I dove into my research for the piece, refreshing my knowledge of Mexican history, reading histories of Jewish immigration to Latin America and histories of the Spanish Inquisition, which had a Mexican office. A reference in one of these histories led me to an entry in the annals of the Mexican nation, three lines about a Spanish Jew named Hernando Alonso, who shipped to Cuba and then Mexico with Hernán Cortés, and ended up with the dubious honor of becoming the first Jew to be burned at the stake by the Catholic Inquisitors of Mexico.

By the time I arrived in Tijuana, I was fairly well prepared. After a few hours in Tijuana with the Argentinian rabbi, I knew I had a story. After many hours of interviews with members past and present of his congregation, I knew I had a good story. But a name kept cropping up in my conversations with these people, the name of a man who turned out to be a Mexican-born, U.S.-trained Methodist minister who had converted to Judaism, a successful businessman fascinated enough with Old Testament texts to attend the University of Judaism in Los Angeles, and take enough courses to qualify for ordination as a rabbi.

When I heard that this man had built a Jewish temple in one of Tijuana's poorest neighborhoods and was feeding the poor as well as converting dozens of Mexican Catholics to Judaism, I knew I was onto a terrific story.

And when, as luck would have it, the president of the Orthodox congregation, after hearing my refusal to allow him to censor anything I wrote about his group, ordered me out of the synagogue in the middle of Friday evening services, I knew I had a fantastic story, one in which I myself could play a role.

(I'll always remember the story posted from Africa by my friend Darnton, a *New York Times* editor. Having been expelled from Nigeria and he and his entire family put in a boat and sent across the border to Sierra Leone, Darnton included a brief paragraph in which he described his expulsion in the third person.)

The final story, which the editor of the *San Diego Weekly Reader* titled "Tacos and Manna," turned out to be over 12,000 words and nearly fifty pages long. I opened with the narrative of the life of Hernando Alonso, extrapolating on the few details that I knew about him from my knowledge of medieval Jewish life and the life of the Spanish settlers of the Mexican plateau. I also wrote a section on the history of Jewish emigration to South America, and to Mexico in particular. (My research for my previous piece on the Jews of Mexico City came in handy here.) And given the freedom of the assignment, it was possible for me to include myself as a "character" in the piece as well. And when I finished this piece I used the material about the Mexican Inquisition to write a 7,500-word short story called "Hernando Alonso."

These kinds of assignments don't come to you every day. But they do suggest the kind of intensity and juice that you can inject into most any nonfiction reportage that you do. Especially if you're a fiction writer. Because of that, you already have acquired most of the techniques you need in order to write first-rate nonfiction. The only components you may not be familiar with are the research aspect—though anyone who has written graduate research papers can handle that part of it—and the interviewing. For some people, that may be difficult. But there are ways to learn how to become a better interviewer.

So, onward, and don't forget that you can celebrate your fiction-making powers in nonfiction as long as you clearly delineate the border between fact and fantasy. For example, everything I've said in this piece is true to the best of my knowledge, except that my old mentor Art Seidenbaum did not make the following statement, which, in the spirit of his advice, I am about to ascribe to him.

"Remember, use everything, including the squeal."

Writing Personal Essays: On the Necessity of Turning Oneself Into a Character

PHILLIP LOPATE

In personal essays, nothing is more commonly met than the letter *I*. I think it a perfectly good word, one no writer should be ashamed to use. Especially is first person legitimate for this form, so drawn to the particulars of character and voice. The problem with "I" is not that it is in bad taste, but that fledgling personal essayists may think they've said or conveyed more than they actually have with that one syllable. In their minds, that "I" is swarming with background and a lush, sticky past, and an almost too fatal specificity, whereas the reader, encountering it for the first time in a new piece, sees only a slender telephone pole standing in the sentence, trying to catch a few signals to send on. In truth, even the barest "I" holds a whisper of promised engagement, and can suggest a caress in the midst of more stolid language. What it doesn't do, however, is give us a clear picture of who is speaking.

To do that, the writer needs to build herself into a character. And I use the word *character* much the same way the fiction writer does. E.M. Forster, in *Aspects of the Novel*, drew a famous distinction between "flat" and "round" characters—between those fictional personages seen from the outside who acted with the predicable consistency of caricatures, and those whose complexities or teeming inner lives we came to know. But whether the writer chooses to present characters as flat or round, or a combination, the people on the page—it scarcely matters whether they appear in fiction or nonfiction—will need to become knowable enough in their broad outlines to behave "believably," at the same time as free willed enough to intrigue us with surprises. The art of characterization comes down to establishing a pattern of habits and actions for the person you are writing about and introducing variations into the system. In this respect, building a character is a pedagogic model, because you are teaching the reader what to expect.

So how do you turn *yourself* into a character? First of all, you need to have—or acquire—some distance from yourself. If you are so panicked by any examination of your flaws that all you can do is sputter defensively when you feel yourself attacked, you are not going to get very far in the writing of personal essays. You need to be able to see yourself from the ceiling: to know, for instance, how you are coming across in social situations, and to assess accurately when you are charming, and when you seem pushy, mousy, or ridiculous. From the viewpoint of honest essay writing, it is just as unsatisfactorily distorting to underrate yourself all the time, and think you are far less effective than you actually are, than to give yourself too much credit. The point is to begin to take inventory of yourself so that you can present that self to the reader as a specific, legible character.

A good place to start is your quirks. These are the idiosyncracies, stubborn tics, antisocial mannerisms, and so on that set you apart from the majority of your fellowmen. There will be more than enough time later to assert your common humanity, or better yet, to let the reader make the mental bridge between your oddities and those of everyone else. But to establish credibility, you would do well to resist coming across at first as absolutely average. Who wants to read about that bland creature, the regular Joe? The mistake many beginning essayists make is to try so hard to be likable and nice, to fit in, that the reader, craving stronger stuff (at the very least, a tone of authority), gets bored. Literature is not a place for conformists, organization men. The skills of the kaffeeklatsch—restraining one's expressiveness, rounding out one's edges, sparing everyone's feelings—will not work as well on the page.

The irony is that most of us suspect—no, we *know*—that underneath it all we *are* common as dirt. But we may still need to maximize that pitiful set of quirks, those small differences that seem to set us apart from others, and project them theatrically, the way actors work with singularities in their physical appearances or vocal textures. In order to turn ourselves into characters, we need to *dramatize* ourselves. I don't mean inventing or adding colorful traits that aren't true; I mean positioning those that are already in us under the most clearly focused, sharply defined light. It's a subtractive process: You need to cut away the inessentials, and highlight just those features in your personality that lead to the most intense contradictions or ambivalence.

An essay needs conflict, just as a short story does. Without conflict, your essay will drift into static mode, repeating your initial observation in a self-satisfied way. What gives an essay dynamism is the need to work out some problem, especially a problem that is not easily resolved. Fortunately, human beings are conflicted animals, so there is no shortage of tensions that won't go away. Good essayists know how to select a topic in advance that will generate enough spark in itself, and how to frame the topic so that it will neither be too ambitious nor too slight—so that its scale will be appropriate for satisfying exploration. If you are serenely unconflicted when you first sit down to write an essay, you may find yourself running out of steam. If you take on a problem that is too philosophically large or historically convoluted, you may choke on the details and give up.

Still, these are technical issues, and I am inclined to think that what stands in the way of most personal essays is not technique but psychology. The emotional preparedness, if you will, to be honest and open to exposure.

The student essayist is torn between two contrasting extremes:

A. "I am so weird that I could never tell on the page what is really, secretly going on in my mind."
B. "I am so boring, nothing ever happens to me out of the ordinary, so who would want to read about me?"

Both extremes are rooted in shame, and both reflect a lack of worldliness. The first response ("I am so weird") exaggerates how isolated one is in one's "wicked" thoughts, instead of recognizing that everyone has strange, surreal, immoral notions. The second response ("My life is so boring and I'm so boring") requires a reeducation so that the student essayists can be brought to acknowledge just those moments in the day, in their loves and friendships, in their family dynamics, in their historical moments, in their interactions with the natural world, that remain genuinely perplexing, vexing, luminous, unresolved. In short, they must be nudged to recognize that life remains a mystery— even one's own so-called boring life. They must also be taught to recognize the charm of the ordinary: that daily life that has nourished some of the most enduring essays.

The use of literary or other models can be a great help in invoking life's mystery. I like to remind myself, as well as my students, of the tonal extremes available to us. It is useful to know we can rant as much as Dostoyevsky's Underground Man or Céline's narrators, that we can speak—as the poet Mayakovski says—"At the Top of My Voice." That we can be passionate as Hazlitt and Baldwin, or even whine, the way Joan Didion sometimes does, albeit with self-aware humor. It is useful to remind students, enamored of David Lynch or Quentin Tarantino movies, that some of that bizarre sensibility can find a place in their essays—that "outlaw" culture does not have to be left outside the schoolhouse. At the same time, it is necessary to introduce them to the sane, thoughtful, considered, responsible essayists like George Orwell or E.B. White. From both sets of models we can then choose how reasonable or hysterical we want to come across at any time: in one piece, seem the soul of reason; in another, a step away from the loony bin.

Mining our quirks is only the beginning of turning ourselves into characters. We are distinguished one from another as much by our pasts, the set of circumstances we are born into, as by the challenges we have encountered along the way, and how we choose to resolve them, given our initial stations in life. It means something very different to have been born the second-oldest boy in an upper-middle-class Korean family that emigrated from Seoul to Los Angeles than to have been born the youngest female in a poor Southern Baptist household of nine.

Ethnicity, gender, religion, class, geography, politics: These are all strong determinants in the development of character. Sometimes they can be made too much of, as in the worst sort of "identity politics," which seeks to explain away all the intangibles of a human being's destiny by this or that social oppression. But we must be bold in working with these categories as starting points: be not afraid to meditate on our membership in this or that community, and the degree to which it has or has not formed us.

When you are writing a memoir, you can set up these categories and assess their importance one by one, and go on from there. When you write personal essays, however, you can never assume that your readers will know a thing about your background, regardless of how many times you have explained it in previous essays. So you must become deft at inserting that information swiftly and casually—"I was born in Brooklyn, New York, of working-class parents"—and not worry about the fact that it may be redundant to your regular readers, if you're lucky enough to have any. In one essay, you may decide to make a big thing of your religious training and very little of your family background; in another, just the opposite; but in each new essay, it would be a good idea to tell the reader both, simply because this sort of information will help to build you into a character.

In this sense, the personal essayist must be like a journalist, who respects the obligation to get in the basic orienting facts—the who, what, where, when, and why—as close to the top of every story as possible.

So now you have sketched yourself to the reader as a person of a certain age, sex, ethnic and religious background, class, and region, possessing a set of quirks, foibles, strengths, and peculiarities. Are you yet a character? Maybe not: not until you have soldered your relationship with the reader, by springing vividly into his mind, so that everything your "I" says and does on the page seems somehow—oddly, piquantly—characteristic. The reader must find you amusing (there, I've said it). Amusing enough to follow you, no matter what essay topic you propose. Whether you are writing this time on world peace or a bar of soap, readers must sense quickly from the first paragraph that you are going to keep them engaged. The trouble is that you cannot amuse the reader unless you are already self-amused. And here we come to one of the main stumbling blocks placed before the writing of personal essays: self-hatred.

It is an observable fact that most people don't like themselves, in spite of being, for the most part, decent enough human beings—certainly not war criminals—and in spite of the many self-help books urging us to befriend and think positively about ourselves. Why this self-dislike should be so prevalent is a matter that would require the best sociological and psychoanalytic minds to elucidate; all I can say, from my vantage point as a teacher and anthologist of the personal essay, is that an odor of self-disgust mars many performances in this genre and keeps many would-be practitioners from developing into full-fledged professionals. They exhibit a form of stuttering, of never being able to get past the initial, superficial self-presentation and diving into the wreck of one's personality with gusto.

The proper alternative to self-dislike is not being pleased with oneself—a smugness equally distasteful to the reader—but being *curious about* oneself. Such self-curiosity (of which Montaigne, the father of the essay, was the greatest exemplar) can only grow out of that detachment or distance from oneself about which I spoke earlier.

I am convinced that self-amusement is a discipline that can be learned; it can be practiced even by people (such as myself) who have at times a strong self-dislike or at least self-mistrust. I may be tired of myself in everyday life, but once I start narrating a situation or set of ideas on the page, I begin to see my "I" in a comic light, and I maneuver him so that he will best amuse the reader. My "I" is not me, entirely, but a character drawn from aspects of myself, in somewhat the same way (less stylized or bold, perhaps) that Chaplin drew the Little Fellow or Jerry Lewis modeled the arrested-development goofball from their experiences. I am willing to let my "I" take his pratfalls; maintaining one's dignity should not be a paramount issue in personal essays. But first must come the urge to entertain the reader. From that impulse everything else follows.

There is also considerable character development in expressing your opinions, prejudices, half-baked ideas, etc., etc., provided you are willing to analyze the flaws in your thinking and to entertain arguments against your hobbyhorses and not be too solemn about it all. The essay thrives on daring, darting flights of thought. You must get in the habit of inviting, not censoring, your most far-fetched, mischievous notions, because even if they prove cockeyed, they may point to an element of truth that would otherwise be inaccessible. When, for instance, I wrote my essay "Against Joie de Vivre," I knew on some level that it was an indefensible position, but I wanted to see how far I could get in taking a curmudgeonly stance against the pursuit of happiness. And indeed, it struck a chord of recognition in many readers, because lots of us are "so glad to be unhappy," at least as much as we "want to be happy." (To quote two old songs.)

Finally, it would do well for personal essayists to follow another rule of fiction writers, who tell you that if you want to reveal someone's character, actions speak louder than words. Give your "I" something to do. It's fine to be privy to all of "I's" ruminations and cerebral nuances, but consciousness can only take us so far in the illumination of character. Particularly if you are writing a memoir essay, with chronology and narrative, it is often liberating to have the "I" step beyond the observer role and be implicated crucially in the overall action. How many memoir pieces suffer from a self-righteous setup: the writer telling a story in which Mr. or Ms. "I" is the passive recipient of the world's cruelty, the character's first exposure to racism or betrayal, say. There is something off-putting about a nonfiction story in which the "I" character is right and all the others wrong, the "I" infinitely more sinned against than sinning. By showing our complicity in the world's stock of sorrow, we convince the reader of our reality and even gain his sympathy.

How much more complicated and alive is George Orwell's younger self, the "I" in "Such, Such Were the Joys," for having admitted he snitched on his classmates, or James Baldwin's "I" in "Notes of a Native Son," for acknowledging how close he came to the edge with his rages about racism in restaurants. Character is not just a question of sensibility: There are hard choices to be made when a person is put under pressure. And it's in having made the wrong choice, curiously enough, that we are made all the more aware of our freedom and potential for humanity. So it is that remorse is often the starting point for good personal essays, whose working-out brings the necessary self-forgiveness (not to mention self-amusement) to outgrow shame.

I have not touched on some other requirements of the personal essay, such as the need to go beyond the self's quandaries, through research or contextualization, to bring back news of the larger world. Nor have I spoken of the grandeur of the so-called formal essay. Yet even when "I" plays no part in the language of an essay, a firm sense of personality can warm the voice of the impersonal essay narrator. When we read Dr. Johnson and Edmund Wilson and Lionel Trilling, for instance, we feel that we know them as fully developed characters in their own essays, regardless of their not referring personally to themselves.

The need thus exists to make oneself into a character, whether the essay uses a first- or third-person narrative voice. I would further maintain that this process of turning oneself into a character is not self-absorbed navel gazing, but rather a potential release from narcissism. It means you have achieved sufficient distance to begin to see yourself in the round: a necessary precondition to transcending the ego—or at least writing personal essays that can touch other people.

Researching Your Own Life

MICHAEL PEARSON

As strange as it may sound, all memoir is a process of researching one's own life. By that I mean rethinking, of course. I also mean reimagining and perhaps revising—because to see the past anew is often to view it, even at great distances, more clearly. But in the context of these remarks, I mean the word *research* to imply just that— research, a diligent and systematic inquiry into a subject (in this case yourself) in order, as even the most basic dictionaries will say, "to discover or revise facts, theories, or opinions."

I would venture to guess that many of the best recent memoirs demanded that the writers engage in the wonderfully tedious necessities of research. For instance, Doris Kearns Goodwin, with the instincts of the biographer and historian, surely searched spool after spool of microfilm about the Brooklyn Dodgers' 1951 season for her coming-of-age book, *Wait Till Next Year*. As she said, "If I were to be faithful to my tale, it would be necessary to summon to my own history the tools I had acquired in investigating the history of others. I would look for evidence, not simply to confirm my own memory, but to stimulate it and to provide a larger context for my childhood adventures. Thus I sought out the companions of my youth, finding almost everyone who lived on my block, people I hadn't seen for three or four decades. I explored the streets and shops in which I had spent my days, searched the Rockville Centre archives, and read the local newspapers from the fifties."

The kind of research that Goodwin engaged in was something like reliving the past, and her most interesting insight in describing her research process may be her focusing on her belief that it did not merely confirm the "facts" for her but, more importantly, stimulated her memory of the past. For the memoirist, research can bring the story out of the shadows into the light of the present day. Even in a story like Mary Karr's *The Liars' Club*, a book saturated in the changing stream of memory, the author confirmed the veracity of what she had written by having her sister, Lecia, audit the facts. In addition, Karr's mother answered questions and did information gathering for her. As was the case with Goodwin's narrative, Karr's was most assuredly brought to more vivid life because of the research that she did.

It's probable that even a memoir like *Angela's Ashes* by Frank McCourt benefited from some elements of research. The magic of the book, certainly, is McCourt's ability to transform his voice into the evolving child's. As William Kennedy said, McCourt "inhabits the mind of the child he was with such vital memory that boyhood pain and family suffering become as real as a stab in the heart." But there are many moments that McCourt could not have reasonably recollected without some unearthing of documents—the letters written under the name of Mrs. Brigid Finucane or Philomena Flynn, for example. My guess is that McCourt had notebooks and scrapbooks to sift through much as a scholar of early American history will have diaries and family Bibles.

Memory is an archive like any other and can be used as such. The materials stored there can sometimes be tested against other sources. Your memory, after all, is only one person's opinion, and if you can get some evidence to support that opinion, it will make it more cogent, probably more specific and more complex, as well. But rather than speaking for other writers of memoir, let me use my own experience in writing *Dreaming of Columbus: A Boyhood in the Bronx* as an example that may be either representative or anomalous but certainly indicative of what can be true of the relationship between memoir and research.

When the idea for the narrative of *Dreaming of Columbus* first began to germinate, it took root in my imagination as a novel. It wasn't long, though, before I saw that it was a work of nonfiction. The line between memoir and fiction is often blurred, but I'm fairly sure that I know why I stepped across the line from imagining the invented Bronx of the 1960s to describing the historical place and time. I felt that the story had a meaning that was in the actuality of it, in the solidity of the bricks, the smell of the bus exhaust, the existence beyond words of the characters who lived in the stories in the book.

I sensed that the theme had been given to me by the narrative, that the dreams of escape and return, the longing to go and the desire to stay forever, were part of how the "simple facts" had invented a meaning. And that meaning would be there, speaking in its own true voice, only if the stories of the Bronx were both factual and true. Truth, without question, is the ultimate goal, but sometimes truth is not enough. Sometimes the historical reality, even in our deconstructed new world, provides a shape and substance that would otherwise not be there.

In order to write *Dreaming of Columbus*, a recollection of the Irish Catholic Bronx of decades ago, I felt compelled to do various kinds of research. Even though I started writing from the premise that all memoir may be a lie, that Steven Millhauser was probably right when he said, "memory is merely one form of imagination," that memory's highest function may not be to recollect what has happened but rather preserve meaning or make meaning, I still felt obligated to get the facts right. If I didn't make sure that the little details were accurate, then on some important level for me the book would not be speaking the truth that it was intended to tell. So, early on in the writing process it became apparent to me that old-fashioned research was going to be an integral part of reconstructing the Bronx of the 1960s. What I didn't realize until I was far into the story was that, as with Goodwin's, my memory was stimulated by my research into my own past, that the story of the past came alive for me as I engaged in the adventure of going back, of once again searching for what had seemingly been lost.

The first form my research took was into books—but not into history books of the period. Rather, I was drawn back to those books that had shaped my view of the world when I was a youngster. Flannery O'Connor once said that "the writer is initially set going by literature more than by life," and although this may not be the case for all writers, it definitely was true for me. As a young boy, I found my place in the world in books. Therefore, rereading some of the stories that had been important to me then—*The Life of Kit Carson*, *Youngblood Hawke*, *The Catcher in the Rye*, *Catch-22*, *The Adventures of Huckleberry Finn*—was like slipping back in time.

For instance, in rereading *Kit Carson*, which I hadn't looked at since fifth grade, and *Youngblood Hawke*, which I hadn't read since I was fourteen, I found myself recalling vividly what solace books had given me growing up. Rereading those two books allowed me to place myself back in my childhood: "Books became an escape from the present, in the classroom at St. Philip Neri or in the living room at home. Books were a way to forget the world, what Richard Wright called 'a drug, a dope.' And they were addictive. The more I read, the more I wanted to read. For me Kit Carson was a pathfinder. He led me toward Don Quixote and David Copperfield, Pip and Tom Sawyer, the Joads and the Lilliputians. He also led me back to the world, to see how close I could bring my changing vision of possibility to the rigid nature of things. The stories I read made me feel as if I were threading a needle, squinting through whatever aperture the world would allow."

And even though *Youngblood Hawke* was not the same reading experience for me as an adult that it had been for me as a child, I was able to remember what the book had said to me as an adolescent: ". . . a voice in the book told me then to watch and wait; it suggested that living and creating are one and the same, that writing is an act of faith, that, perhaps, all real adventure begins in the imagination."

My research also took a traditional path into the history of the period, particularly the 1960s. I read newspapers, magazines, and books recounting the events of the Vietnam War, the Kennedy assassination, Woodstock, and any other moments that seemed to me to be watershed points in my own life. I watched videos about the times and listened to music that I might not have heard for years.

I remembered that on the day after President Kennedy was shot, my mother took me to Madison Square Garden to see the New York Knicks play the Detroit Pistons. In order to bring that night back to me more tangibly, I read the newspaper accounts of the day after the assassination and the accounts of the Knicks' victory.

Facts can be a catalyst for remembering: "I don't recall much about the game except a feeling that the whole event was surreal. Jumping Johnny Green of the Knicks flew magically into the air for rebounds while gravity held the seven thousand of us in our seats, and our young president had just been shot. Newspapers strewn about the stadium announced, 'Kennedy Killed by Sniper.' News of the assassination had been played over and over again so many times during the twenty-four hours that the murder seemed little more than a nightmare created by the media."

The last shape that my research took was in the form of something akin to time travel. I went back to the Bronx half a dozen times over the course of a three-year period, revisiting places that were landmarks of my youth—St. Philip Neri Elementary School, Mt. St. Michael High School, Fordham University, Villa Avenue, Harris Field, the bars, the pizza parlors, the subway stations, the apartment buildings, and any other spot that held an important place in my memory. Along the way, I spoke with many former teachers, old buddies, a few ex-girlfriends, and some present-day residents of the borough.

In the course of reentering my past, I was checking the details of my memory and igniting new recollections. All sorts of questions were answered. What did the pews in the chapel feel like as I slid my hand across the grain of wood? Was the underpass at Bedford Park Boulevard a tunnel of noise, as I remembered it had been? And what of the apartment buildings, the color of the sky in summer as opposed to winter, the sound of the subway rattling along the Grand Concourse, the way the light broke through the stained glass windows of the church?

Returning to the haunts of my youth gave texture and definition to my memories and created a new dimension to my experience. Such research not only gave me another way of seeing the past but another frame for such memories, as well. The present-day Bronx gave me an access to the past that I might not have had otherwise: "As the heavy doors to St. Philip's creak slowly to a close, I see a young woman standing in the frame. Her face could be my sister's at graduation in 1960. The same blue eyes, looking down as if she is ready to raise them at any moment toward an unexpected guest. The same brown hair, a dark wave crashing to her shoulders. The same smile, the lips tugged together and curving toward laughter. Narrow-shouldered, slim as the slant of door light, ready to leave, she is the image of my sister in the Bronx then. With a few inches of light left, she looks up, her eyes clear and patient, and smiles at me as if she regrets my going, our mutual turning into memory."

For me, the act of writing a memoir became an opportunity to travel backward in time. As Joan Didion said, we write to discover what we think. I read and traveled and gathered notes and in the process discovered what the past meant to me. Disparate lines of research twisted into a thickened cord of recollection. You may not be able to repeat the past, as Gatsby wished, but you may be able, through research, to reenter it, relive it in your imagination, and re-create it for the future.

EXERCISES

1. Choose an event from your past—a confirmation, a birthday celebration, a Fourth of July picnic—for which you have a collection of photographs, and write a narrative of 1,500–2,000 words using the photographs to help you create the scene.

2. Talk to someone else who was also present at the event in number one above, and write a narrative of approximately 1,000 words based on your interview.

3. Reflect on the nature of memory/memoir after comparing the two experiences you had in completing numbers one and two above. Write approximately 1,000 words.

You now have 3,500–4,000 words of memoir—the rough draft of an essay.

Taking Yourself Out of the Story: Narrative Stance and the Upright Pronoun

PHILIP GERARD

Recently, I assigned an advanced class of undergraduate writers to observe a dynamic event and write precisely about what they saw, heard, smelled, and so on. The event could be anything—construction workers framing a wall, a florist arranging a bouquet, the aftermath of a rock concert.

So they wrote of glimpsing the vice-president and his entourage on vacation at Figure Eight Island, watching a rambunctious couple at a movie theater, filming a movie on location, witnessing the protests in Washington, DC, against the World Trade Organization, and so on.

All but two wrote of their own thoughts and feelings about the events—and only secondarily about the events themselves. In many descriptions, it was hardly possible to know what event the writer was actually witnessing. The sensibility of the author was present in virtually every line, but the other people in the stories—the ones the stories were purportedly *about*—were distant and vague.

Factual writers of an earlier generation swore by a code of objectivity: Never let the reporter enter the story. If a reference to the actual person observing events was unavoidable, the writer would duck behind some impersonal shield, referring to himself only as "this reporter" or even "the reporter." As if to admit to the audience that to have a real-live person—full of bias and emotion—on the scene would be to falsify the provable truth of the thing witnessed.

For us, who cut our teeth on the New Journalism of Tom Wolfe and the personal essays of Joan Didion rather than in deadline newsrooms, it seems only natural to participate in the story. And often including ourselves in the story does make it sound more natural, more honest, more real.

But too often these days, I'm afraid we writers of nonfiction fall into the opposite fallacy: We enter the story whether it needs us or not.

For the reader, this can be distracting, even annoying, diverting attention from the real "star" of the piece. The reader perceives us clamoring for attention and rightly resents it. And, as in many of my students' pieces, participation by the author can actually confuse the reader about the literal action of the story.

TWO WAYS FOR THE WRITER TO ENTER THE STORY

There are two ways in which a writer can participate in a story: The first and most obvious is in a direct first-person telling, using "the upright pronoun." It's hard to write a memoir or a personal essay without falling back on the "I." In fact, all nonfiction is really told in the technical first-person point of view: There is always a narrator doing the telling, and the narrator is not some fictional persona but the author.

This single point of view is one of the important—and frustrating— hallmarks that distinguishes nonfiction from fiction.

Yet there are ways to mimic other points of view—and thereby to tell a more natural sort of story.

Listen to the opening lines of Daniel Berguer's *God of the Rodeo: The Search for Hope, Faith, and a Six-Second Ride in Louisiana's Angola Prison*: "When he had finished work—building fence or penning cattle or castrating bull calves with a knife supplied by his boss on the prison farm—Johnny Brooks lingered in the saddle shed. The small cinder-block building is near the heart of Angola, Louisiana's maximum-security state penitentiary. Alone there, Brooks placed his saddle on the wooden rack in the middle of the room, leapt onto it, and imagined himself riding in the inmate rodeo coming up in October."

No sign yet of the author—a strictly third person presentation. But we know exactly where we are, exactly whom to pay attention to—a convict cowboy—and even what he wants out of life: to ride in the rodeo. The author won't enter the story directly for many more lines; he'll duck in once to let us know he's there and then disappear for long stretches, allowing the reader to watch Brooks and the other inmates train for the rodeo in the confines of one of the most remote and fearsome prisons in the world.

But in fact, of course, the author has been with us in every line, in the second way that an author participates in a nonfiction story: *tone*.

Tone is nothing more or less than the attitude of the author, expressed in the words he chooses, the selection and ordering of events, and the rhythms of language. It is the intelligence behind the words, the author's implicit sense of what things mean. Of who is admirable or contemptible, what is important or trivial, how the characters' choices and actions resonate in the author's moral universe.

The moral stance of the piece will be reflected in its tone.

Even without an "I" narrator, we can hear it when an author doesn't approve of something, or finds it humorous, or is awed or confused or skeptical. Tone, as we experience it in the lines and between the lines, tells us the author's sense of right and wrong, his sense of proportion and outlook on the world. It's the reason we either trust a story or don't, either turn away in irritation or remain captivated.

It's not voice, exactly—it's the *tone of voice*.

So in the excerpt above, we hear a subdued admiration in Bergner's tone of voice: Here's a man who's already worked a hard day in the outdoors and now is taking a few minutes to dream. The man is in a hopeless place, but he still has aspirations. And by the way, he can be trusted with a knife—whatever violent acts landed him in Angola, now he seems just another lonesome cowboy.

Later, Bergner will enter the story directly and in earnest—because he will need to. He'll have no choice: The story he thinks he is getting for his first six months inside the prison—the one he can tell in an assured third person—will turn out to be a sham, a reality invented by the inmates to please the warden, who has become for Bergner almost a surrogate father, and who has earned the writer's genuine admiration. But the warden will betray him—ask for a bribe to assure continued access to the prison—and that becomes a huge part of a story that started out to be about a rodeo.

Bergner must actually sue the warden in federal court in order to regain access to the prison, and from that moment on he discovers a very different story: "But now that the staff knew I wasn't his [the warden's] man, they were glad to answer my questions. . . . The inmates, too, felt free to talk. One told me of a rumor that had circulated before the lawsuit: that I was Warden Cain's spy. Why else, the convicts had reasoned, would I be allowed to roam the prison and hold my interviews without anyone listening in?"

So the second half of the book is as much about Bergner's struggle to learn the truth and come to terms with his own emotions in the aftermath of the warden's betrayal as it is about prison cowboys, and this ratchets up the danger, physical as well as emotional, and results in a much more profound insight into the nature of Angola than a feature about the rodeo would have done: Here is a place where even the truth can be controlled by the will of a single man.

The final violence of the rodeo arena becomes a release for long-escalating tensions and a metaphorical spectacle that embodies nearly every aspect of prison life we have come to know: the crowd arrives, hoping for blood, and remains physically segregated from the inmates, who are dressed in prison stripes, as they gamely ride and rope and dodge charging Brahman bulls—and are bruised, thrown, broken, and trampled.

Bergner stands back and lets us watch the rodeo, and we're hardly aware of his presence: It's the spectacle he wants us to watch, not him.

NARRATIVE STANCE

If you combine point of view, tone, and one more element, you create a *narrative stance.* That third element is *psychic distance*: how near or far the writer, and thus the reader, remains from the people and events in the story.

"Tiananmen Square,"[1] from *The Darkness Crumbles* by BBC correspondent John Simpson, begins with an intermediate psychic distance: "It was humid and airless, and the streets around our hotel were empty. We had set out for Tiananmen Square—reporter, producer, cameraman, sound-recordist, translator, lighting man, complete with gear. A cyclist rode past, shouting and pointing, What it meant we couldn't tell."

Simpson is, of course, the "reporter." He's giving us a first-person account, but he's focused on external details, not his own thoughts and feelings. He even presents the BBC crew as if he were an outsider. And he doesn't speculate on what the bicyclist's gesture means.

He continues at this remove, reporting on the "human river" flowing through the Gate of Heavenly Peace into the square, where hundreds of groups of demonstrators have gathered around radios. He observes that these are not students but older, harder workers, "singing, chanting, looking forward to trouble."

The BBC crew starts interviewing and filming—a boy with Coke-bottle Molotov cocktails stuck in his waistband; rowdy workers wearing red head cloths and brandishing knives, spears, and bricks—and Simpson retains his reporter's distance. But soon that detachment dissolves. Caught in the middle of a situation that is fast turning ugly, the crew starts arguing. Against all his professional training, Simpson goes off on his own.

An armored car enters the square, is firebombed, escapes. A second is attacked and crashes into a concrete barrier. The mob swarms over it. Simpson spots his cameraman in the melee around the burning

---

[1] Reprinted in *The Art of Fact: A Historical Anthology of Literary Journalism*, edited by Kevin Kerrane and Ben Yagoda. New York: Scribner, 1997.

armored car, and the psychic distance closes fast: "Now I was the one fighting, struggling to get through the crowd, pulling people back, pushing them out of my path, swearing, a big brutal Englishman stronger than any of them."

We're right there inside his sensibility as he becomes caught up in the chaos and becomes an active participant in it.

As the first crewman of the burning armored car tries to escape, the mob pounces on him and beats him to death in seconds. The second soldier emerges, and the blood-crazed mob literally rips the skin off his face, then beats his skull until his brains spill onto the ground.

As the third and last crewman is dragged out of the vehicle, a bus full of students arrives on the scene—they have come to rescue the soldier from the mob. But the mob is tough, and a deadly tug-of-war ensues, with the soldier in the middle. Simpson realizes how this is going to end: with the grotesque murder of the third soldier. He reports, "It seemed to me then that I couldn't look on any longer, a passive observer, watching another man's skin torn away or his head broken open, and do nothing."

Simpson screams obscenities at a man trying to cave in the soldier's skull with a brick: "The ferocity of the crowd had entered me, but I felt it was the crowd that was the animal, that it wasn't properly human." Simpson then hurls himself bodily at the man, overpowering him, and the students pull the soldier into the bus, and to safety.

The psychic distance has closed in considerably: we are not only inside Simpson's sensibility; we are also acting vicariously with him to change the outcome of the story, and in the process we hear an unmistakable tone of judgment, the moral stance of the writer, implicit in his words and, in this case, exemplified by his actions. Calling himself "this reporter" just won't do. He has entered the story and must account for himself: what he's doing there and why.

And Simpson doesn't conclude there. He relates how he and the crew rushed their film back to the hotel so as not risk its being confiscated by the authorities when the army arrived in force. Then he confesses: "I now feel guilty about that decision; it was wrong: we ought to have stayed in the Square, even though the other camera crews had already left and it might have cost us our lives." The psychic distance has closed in utterly: Now we are not just inside Simpson's sensibility and judgment; we are looking not *out* but *in*. He is no longer judging events but himself. Then he continues the paragraph: "Someone should have been there when the massacre took place, filming what happened, showing the courage of the students as they were surrounded by tanks and the army advancing, firing as it went."

The psychic distance has opened slightly again, like the aperture on a camera admitting more light to expose the film. And the camera is once again aimed outward.

Simpson closes this remarkable journalistic memoir with a metaphor taken from the events of the day. From the balcony of his hotel, which looks down into the Square, he watches as soldiers unroll something and lift it into place: "Soon a great curtain of black cloth covered the entrance to Tiananmen Square. What was happening there was hidden from us."

Now he is restored to his former detachment, his former long psychic distance from the students and the massacre, in an almost cinematic fade to black. But of course, this time the distance is not voluntary, and what lingers in the metaphor is a longing to see behind the curtain, to close the distance again, to be back among the crowd, bearing witness.

WHAT THEY DON'T TELL YOU ABOUT THE "I" NARRATOR

When Hurricane Fran slammed ashore directly into my hometown of Wilmington, North Carolina, in September of 1996, our waterside neighborhood was wrecked: houses smashed and flooded, glorious old live-oak trees torn out by the roots and splayed across wires and speared into roofs, our little harbor transformed into one big shipwreck.

My wife and I spent a long night huddled inside our closet in terror as the eyewall swept over us, and as soon as we emerged in the morning and saw the awesome scale of the damage, I knew I would have to write about it.

What stunned me was not just the physical destruction but also the awful fear I had felt for all those hours, and afterward, the eradication of beauty, the black depression into which it catapulted me, and the depth of my inarticulate anger. With the power out and no running water, in the week following the hurricane, I wrote an essay about enduring the brunt of a major hurricane—longhand, often working by the light of a kerosene lantern.

Instinctively, as I wrote the first line, I made a decision about point of view and narrative stance: "What they don't tell you about hurricanes is the uncertainty." The "I" pronoun was not big enough to do what I wanted it to do. We had suffered during the hurricane, but what I wanted to write about was a whole community of people who had suffered worse, and who had suffered together. The "you" became a way of inviting the reader to become part of that community.

The essay did not get published right away, and even at the time it was being rejected, I knew exactly why—I just couldn't do anything about it: I was still too much in the essay. Or at least, my anger was. I just couldn't get it out. It was a matter of tone: No reader, I felt sure, would suffer through a dozen pages of white-hot anger.

In an odd sense, my research wasn't finished yet.

I needed to get to the other side of the depression brought on by the tremendous destruction, to witness the return of normalcy and beauty, and those things took nearly all of the two years between the time I wrote that first lantern-light draft and the publication of what became a very different piece—different mostly in tone, that invisible, elusive quality.

So it wasn't enough to take out the upright pronoun. I also had to put some psychic distance between me and the experience in order to have the detachment to work my craft.

And even after the piece was in print, I felt a sense of unfinished business. The essay ends with our world destroyed, and that didn't turn out to be the whole story. The ancient Greeks understood that it's not enough to destroy the world; you have a responsibility to rebuild it, to set the stars back in the heavens, to restore order to the universe. So in a second essay, I picked up the story there and recounted how a couple of days after the storm, all the neighbors pitched in during an exhausting twelve-hour day to rebuild our harbor, to salvage what could be salvaged, and how I experienced a sense of absolution, the beginning of a long, slow healing process that came out of that ancient and priceless expression of community. That was the true ending of the story: taking back control of our lives, together.

That was the lesson: It wasn't about *me*; it was about *us*.

EXERCISES

1. Without using any first-person pronouns (*I, me, my, mine, we, our, ours,* etc.), write an accurate scene about an incident you witnessed firsthand.

2. Take the above scene and rewrite it twice, each time expressing a different tone—anger, fear, humor, sarcasm, etc.—between the lines.

3. Take a piece of narrative writing you admire and, in the margins, indicate shifts in psychic distance—in or out. Now take a piece of narrative you have written and do the same.

The Loneliness of the Long-Distance Writer

ROBIN HEMLEY

One of the greatest difficulties for the writer of longer nonfiction is figuring out the structure of the book. For me, this has been one of my major hurdles, why I seem to stew about a book for a year or so before coming to an understanding of what I'm writing about and how to go about writing it. The three works of nonfiction I've struggled with are quite different in subject matter and approach, and perhaps it would be helpful to examine my strategies in terms of figuring out how I put them together and tried to make them seem cohesive.

THE OUTLINE

One of these books, *Turning Life Into Fiction*, a book on writing form, probably can't be categorized as creative nonfiction, and I *was* going to jettison it from the discussion, except that I realize I did some things structurally in the writing of this book that might be helpful to other writers of creative nonfiction.

I am not one to write outlines. I hate outlines. I hate the idea of outlines. I'm one of these artsy types, who, if not relying solely on inspiration, at least tries to allow a book to proceed *organically*. Remember that word. We artsy types use it often. It basically means we don't know what the hell we're doing and it wouldn't take us so long to finish a book if we wrote a simple outline. So . . . organic. Remember this word. If someone asks you what you're writing about, tell her you don't know, that you're going to let the subject matter arise organically.

But with *Turning Life Into Fiction*, the publishers wanted a chapter-by-chapter outline, in which I wrote down more or less what each chapter would contain. The outline helped . . . for a while. And then, about halfway through the book, I realized that the outline was all wrong and I needed to change the chapters and their ordering completely. That's the thing about outlines. As far as I can tell, they don't change the surprises and frustrations in store for you when you're writing a longer work of nonfiction.

And that's probably a good thing, because those surprises and frustrations are an integral part of the creative process. In some ways, writing a book is like putting up a building. There's almost always a disparity between the architect's designs and what is really feasible. No matter what you're doing, if you're not flexible, you can't hope to complete your project. The biggest lesson one can learn about writing a longer work is that one has to be patient with oneself and forgiving of the false starts and turns. The good thing about a longer piece of prose as opposed to a building is that it's a lot easier to revise a memoir than a building. You can take out a chapter that doesn't work, but hey, watch that support beam!

SO MUCH FOR ANALOGIES

OK, so much for analogies. So much for figurative language, for metaphors, similes, you know—you've seen the stuff. What's the point really? Just tell the story from beginning to end, none of these organic flourishes, just a simple story from beginning to end. Just the facts. Boom boom boom.

Of course, it's not that easy.

First of all, what story do you want to tell—before you know it, one story is leading to another and you don't have a book on your hands but The Blob That Ate Up Your Writing Time. Metaphors, if striking enough and handled delicately, can actually provide the structure for a book, or suggest the structure.

This narrative strategy isn't only for writers of nonfiction, of course, but for all writers of prose, including those hybrids, the autobiographical novel, such as Sylvia Plath's *The Bell Jar*, or the fictional memoir, such as Frederick Exley's *A Fan's Notes*. Sylvia Plath, of course, uses the extended metaphor of a bell jar to convey her autobiographical protagonist's solitude and alienation. It works, or else I wouldn't have remembered it lo these many years since reading it at the age of nineteen, when everyone reads Sylvia Plath (I'm forty-two now). It works because it focuses, it orders the longer work into something that the reader can easily comprehend symbolically.

We think really in images and symbols, not words, and what the central metaphor does is reverse the process of turning image and symbol into language. The extended metaphor turns language into symbol and image, which our minds then recognize and go, "Mmmm, now this is something I can recognize. Cool metaphor!" (except, you know, in that mysterious nonverbal way the mind does things).

What we're basically getting at here is the idea of focus, the way we order a story so that the reader can see the book as a cohesive unit and not The Blob That Ate Up Your Reading Time.

GRAND OBSESSIONS

There are other ways, of course, to order the longer work.

Frederick Exley's strategy is to create a version of himself completely obsessed with Frank Gifford. (Now wait! This was written before Kathie Lee, when Gifford was a major football star in the sixties.) I say a version of himself because Exley makes this clear in his subtitle of the book, *A Fictional Memoir*. Perhaps the real Exley was just as obsessed with Gifford as the version of himself in the book, but I doubt it.

The thing about a longer work of art is that it has to sustain a level of tension and focus that life rarely has. Torquing up one's obsessive personality is one way of ordering the longer work.

My friend, the prose writer David Shields, has written a masterful work of nonfiction called *Black Planet*, in which a version of David Shields follows the Seattle Sonics for a season while becoming more and more obsessed with the player Gary Payton. I've known David for twenty years and know that he is not as obsessed with Payton as the persona in the book, but he torques up this mild obsession he has with Payton in order to add focus to the book, at least partly, and to fully explore the ideas behind the book, specifically the ways in which whites worship, condescend, and belittle African-Americans—as seen in the microcosm of the basketball arena. It's a brave and remarkable book, partly due to the hairline fault between fiction and nonfiction that David creates by building his book around a central image.

Of course, none of this happens all at once in a book. One arrives at one's structure piecemeal, and that's why one must be patient. Without a cohesive structure for the longer work, what you will arrive at is a book of essays most likely—if you're lucky. That's fine, but it's not what we're after here.

BRAIDING

When I wrote *Nola: A Memoir of Faith, Art, and Madness*, I wanted to write a book about my sister, Nola, my older sibling by eleven years, who was diagnosed with schizophrenia and died from a prescription drug overdose when I was fifteen.

Trying to figure out the structure of this book was murder for me. If you're writing a memoir, which I see as focused on a discreet part of one's life, as opposed to an autobiography, which deals with the entirety of one's life thus far, you need to figure out a strategy for attack, a way of knowing what to focus on. For me, figuring out the structure told me what to write about and how to write about it.

When I was just beginning the book, a writer friend of mine criticized the straight-on narrative of a very popular memoir. He thought the writer dodged the really interesting issues of his book by stopping the narrative in the writer's late adolescence without giving the reader a sense of who this person was now and how the events of his childhood shaped him. We had no sense of the writer's present life, not a clue. There was no Present Moment.

For me, this was a crucial thing to hear at the formative stages of my book. I decided that in my memoir it was important for me as well as the reader to know why I was telling this story about my sister, why I thought her life could sustain the reader's interest for over four hundred pages. And so, I focused on two stories and wove them together as best I could. I told the story of who my sister was, and who she was to me. And I simultaneously told the story of who I was in this fictional "present" moment of writing the book, who I had become, how far I had drifted from the boy my sister had hoped I would be.

Actually, I told three stories.

I realized that I couldn't tell the story of my sister and myself without telling the story of my mother, herself a storyteller and a powerful influence on who my sister and I were. That doesn't mean I told everyone's story in my family. To tell more than three and try to keep the structure together would have been impossible for me. I consciously avoided saying more than I absolutely needed about my father and brother, not because they were unimportant or uninteresting, but because they were in a kind of separate orbit from my mother, my sister, and me.

So I told my story in alternating chapters, writing a chapter about my mother, followed perhaps by a chapter about my sister, followed perhaps by a chapter about me in the fictional present moment. Then I repeated this sequence, not in lockstep fashion, but in a way that the reader could hopefully comprehend after the first few chapters. I set up a pattern, and allowed for deviation, but kept the pattern more or less throughout the book. In a way, this is similar to what essayist Brenda Miller terms braiding. She writes about the braiding of images, which helps structure the essay. But one can do the same thing with a longer work, braiding separate narratives in a way that makes the placement of each form a kind of silent commentary on the other, simply through juxtositioning them.

THE HUMP

I must warn you about the hump. It comes in any longer work. My rule of thumb is somewhere around page one hundred, when the first flush of excitement of your idea for a memoir has waned and you have no idea what comes next or why what came before came before.

A variation on the hump is the bump. This is the tendency of those who haven't the foggiest clue what they're doing (that's most of us, but some are more persistent than others) and revise their first chapters over and over again until their significant others start to feel like Shelley Duvall in Stanley Kubrick's *The Shining* when she discovers Jack Nicholson has simply written "All work and no play makes Jack a dull boy" over and over for hundreds of pages. In other words, the writer has channeled his obsessiveness not into the work but back into himself, so that he is trapped, unable to go forward or backward in the book. The hump, or the bump, is the point in the book where you have to commit, at least for a while, to a narrative strategy—you have to figure out what you're doing and why, and that often, though not always, comes down to figuring out the structure of the book.

I can't speak for everyone, but many if not most of my writer friends seem to agree that each book for them is like learning how to write all over again. Unless you're writing a kind of formulaic book, and there aren't too many of those kinds in nonfiction—true crime leaps to mind as a possibility—there's probably no getting around the fact that each book will present completely new challenges and frustrations in terms of the way you put it together.

This has certainly been the case for me. After finishing *Nola*, I was visited by my agent who was doing a West Coast swing to visit several of her clients. I took a few days to show her around the area where I live, Puget Sound, and I remember taking a Washington State ferry with her to Friday Harbor, looking out at the water, and telling her I wanted something new to write about, a new challenge. I asked her if there were any writing projects she knew about in want of a writer. She told me there was one she knew about. An editor at Farrar, Straus and Giroux had seen a television program when she was in high school about a purported anthropological hoax, that of the Tasaday tribe in the southern Philippines. This was a group that had been "discovered" in 1971 living in the remote rain forest in what approximated a Stone Age lifestyle. They lived in caves, had no metal, only stone tools, and didn't know anyone else existed besides them. Then, in 1986, a Swiss reporter, acting on a tip, hiked alone to meet the Tasaday and was told that it had all been a setup, that they were merely local farmers who had been forced to pose as "primitives" by a government official.

The story had been a sensation when the group was first discovered and again became a sensation when the hoax reports surfaced. Since then, the mid-eighties, the furor had died down.

I was intrigued by this story, and my editor set up a phone call between the editor and myself. She told me more about the subject and suggested I do a month's research and come back to her with a proposal. So I wrote one. This time, I had no illusions about it. The proposal was written to get the editors intrigued with the book and to assure them that I was the writer to deliver it. We spent the entire summer going back and forth, refining it, until it was presentable to the rest of the publishing house. I'm still a little shocked by my chutzpah in this—I kind of felt like someone in one of those old immigrant stories, a guy who comes from the Old Country and applies for a job as a brain surgeon. You ever do brain surgery in Corsica? Sure, I done it every day, the immigrant says. . . .

The hard part was figuring out how I wanted to tell this story, which turned out to be far more complex than I had initially bargained for. The story of the Tasaday encompassed not just this small group of less than thirty supposed foragers, "The Gentle Tasaday" as they came to be known, but media hype on both sides of the controversy, academic and political rivalries and intrigue, murder, intimidation, Charles Lindbergh, Italian film star Gina Lollabrigida, a Watergate coconspirator, the granddaughter of Francisco Franco, and sexual perversion.

And that's just the tip of the iceberg, to coin a phrase.

After writing an intensely personal book, I wanted to write a book that had nothing to do with me. I wanted to simply tell the history of the Tasaday controversy. This seemed like more than enough, like something that even the best novelist in the world could never imagine in her wildest dreams.

But I couldn't do it. I could do the research. Oh, it was hard, the hardest thing I've ever done, in some ways. In two years' time, I traveled around the world from Texas to San Francisco to Switzerland to Hawaii to the Philippines, sorting through arcane documents and interviewing anthropologists and journalists and linguists, and then trekking down to meet the Tasaday, first with the group that believes them to be a hoax, and next with the group that believes them to be authentic. In the course of this, I was surrounded by armed men, had an M16 pointed at me by a man wearing a Princess Diana T-shirt, interviewed dwarves and midgets at a place called The Hobbit House in Manila, interviewed a man responsible for the deaths of at least two thousand innocent people, met with a former CIA operative about my personal security, avoided kidnappers and Muslim rebels in Mindanao, ate monkey and wild cat, and forded a flooded river on a slippery log.

But this was nothing in comparison to figuring out how to write the book, how to create a cohesive structure.

THE SIMPLEST SOLUTIONS

Sometimes the simplest solutions are right in front of your nose and you don't see them until you're ready to see them. In my case, the thing that was holding me up was this self-imposed restriction that I couldn't include myself in the narrative. I had admired the way Jon Krakauer had written of his subject Chris McCandless in *Into the Wild*. In chapters in which Krakauer was obviously present, he nonetheless backgrounded himself, and he only explicitly entered the narrative toward the end of the book, when he revealed why he was so intrigued with the story of McCandless, a young man from a middle-class family who gave up all of his inheritances, including his name, to live in the Alaskan wilderness, where he died.

The problem was, I'm not that kind of writer, for better or worse. And this story wasn't that kind of story. The story of the Tasaday was as much about who was doing the viewing and from what perspective as it was about whether the Tasaday were a hoax or not. The early chapters I had attempted seemed completely stilted to me. I wrote in a kind of unnatural tone, like a cross between a newscaster and a Hardy Boys mystery, and I tried to tell the story chronologically.

The story of the Tasaday.

But what version of the story? The version that the hoax camp told or the version that the proponents of authenticity told?

Once again, I have David Shields to thank, because he said quite innocently to me one night that I should include myself in the story. Perhaps it was just a matter of getting permission. I realized, of course, that he was right, that the story was as much about my figuring out the story, sorting out the story, as it was about who the Tasaday in fact were, though I think I have a pretty good notion of that now.

And so, once again I have tried to perform a kind of juggling act, putting myself into the narrative in a way that I hope is not too intrusive while at the same time telling a couple of other stories, the story of a mythic tribe and the story of a group of forest dwellers who might have existed in the rain forests of Mindanao. Above all, I realized the story was also about the personalities of the various people who were telling me their sides of the story. What I have hit upon is a story that has a kind of momentum in the fictional present, the detective work of me trying to sort through the complex issues involved, and a kind of mercurial flashing into the past.

EDITING

Undoubtedly, I have overwritten much of the book. At this moment, while I'm writing this essay, I'm 250 pages into the narrative, about halfway through, I think—over the hump, I hope, though I'm loath to say that because of my superstitious nature. But in the fictional present of this essay, I think I've got the structure figured out. It's mostly a matter of seeing it through to the end.

As I said, I'm sure I've overwritten. There will be parts of the book that need substantial editing and revising, or simply cutting of material that might obsess me now but might seem superfluous or boring to others. That's why you show your book to other people. You want what you write to be a book, not a diary.

I've made the conscious decision, as I did with *Nola*, not to show the book to virtually anyone until I've completed this draft. Sometimes you've figured out more than you're aware of structurally, but your knowledge of your own book is fragile and subject to change and self-doubt. You must be aware that you are the only person living in your book—others around you might be living *with* your book, but you're the only one living *in* it, and in a way, you need to acknowledge that and understand that others might not be able to see the whole book in the way that you do.

Of course, this strategy is a gamble. You could fail, as you can fail in anything, but once you have the structure figured out, or you think you have it figured out, once you find the focus, the momentum builds and it's what drives you to the end.

KNOWING WHEN TO BEGIN AND WHEN TO END

Each chapter you write should have an end that feels as right as the ending of the entire book. While each chapter should hopefully build on the other, you also need to think of your chapters as cohesive units with their own structures. Sometimes, thinking in terms of a short story structure is helpful. A chapter should build.

You might start the chapter as you'd start in the middle of a short story, as I did in one chapter in which an anthropologist was recounting how one of the principals in the Tasaday scandal had tried to bribe him. Actually, he wasn't sure he could definitely construe it as a bribe, but it seemed that way at the time. What was interesting to me was not only the attempted bribe but the anthropologist's wrestling with the word *bribe*, his desire to be accurate and not sensational.

As a writer, this seemed like a very good place for me to begin the chapter, though we had talked about other things in the interview before we reached this revelation. Part of writing, part of structure, is a matter of timing and placement, understanding that you want to keep the reader off-balance some of the time in order to sustain the narrative tension.

The same is true of the ending of a chapter. Each chapter has— here's another artsy word that I just love to bandy around—an *arc*. What's an arc? Who knows, but it makes us sound like we know what we're doing, as when we say in our best workshop-ese, "The arc of this narrative seems rather muddled." OK, I admit, *arc* is actually a pretty good word—think of the flight of an arrow. You shoot it so that it arcs, unless you're dumb like I was when I was ten and shot an arrow straight up into the air. I was surprised when it landed an inch from my foot, barely missing my head.

Think of your structure the same way. When you write a chapter, a scene, a book, you want an arc. An arc is a good thing. You don't want to start off in the same place you began and have the damn thing stick you in the head.

Hey, isn't that a metaphor? I thought I was finished with that junk. I guess it just rose organically.

The point is that each chapter should build, should rise and fall, that you should try to build each chapter around a central image, concept, or theme, in the same way you try to construct the overall arc of your book, in the same way you try to focus. There's no formula for ending a chapter, as there is no formula for beginning one. I almost wrote that knowing when to begin and when to end is intuitive, but of course that's hogwash. Nothing about writing is actually intuitive. It's all a learned process the same way language is learned. That's not the same as saying the process is without moments of pure revelation that are so surprising they're almost terrifying. But that's not the same as "intuitive." Writing is a learned process, and the more you do it, the more natural it feels. So, now, even though each book feels like a new beginning to me, I have some perspective. I know what feels right without always knowing why it feels right. Sometimes that feeling can be mistaken for intuition.

EXERCISES

1. Modeling is one way for a writer to figure out the structure of his book. This is what I was doing when I tried to model or pattern

the structure of my most recent book after Jon Krakauer's *Into the Wild*. Never mind that the subject matter is entirely different, though each deals with a mystery of sorts. In any case, look at a book you admire and figure out its structure, chapter by chapter, paying special attention to the ways in which the author balances the various stories and perspectives of the narrative, switching between past and present perhaps. Now, consider the structure of the story you would like to tell and write a simple outline modeled after the book whose structure you so admire.

2. If you have ever started and abandoned a longer work, take it out and dust it off. Where did you abandon the project? Around page one hundred? I thought so. Chances are your project suffered more from a lack of faith and a cohesive structure than it did from the lack of an interesting subject. Now that you've gained some perspective on the work, perhaps you can return to it and regard it with a cool eye. Write down an outline of sorts of what you've already written, and divide the book into two columns, Focused and Unfocused. In the Focused column, note all the characters, chapters, themes, etc., that seem to dovetail. In the Unfocused column, write down those aspects of the story that seem extraneous. Maybe you'll want to go back to the book now—if so, look for simple solutions to your structural problems. It doesn't have to be complex to be right. It needs to feel natural, OK, organic to your book.

3. If you're working on a longer work, think about mixing up the chronology. Telling a story chronologically is often a lazy solution, and a boring one. Flannery O'Connor used to take apart her stories and reorder them backward, or so I've heard, so that she could see how everything fit together. That's really what we're after, both writer and reader. We want to see how things fit together. If you make the effort to throw your story out of order, you can better understand what is necessary to the telling of the story and what you can do without. If you try, on the other hand, to tell the story from beginning to end, it's likely you'll want to include too much.

As Time Goes By:
Creating Biography

PHILIP FURIA

Although biography is one of the most popular forms of creative nonfiction among readers, it attracts relatively few aspiring writers. Young writers say to themselves, "I want to be a poet . . . a novelist . . . a playwright," may even say, "I want to write a memoir," but seldom, "I want to be a biographer."

Certainly, when I look back at myself forty years ago, a high school student pecking out poems, plays, and stories on my father's huge Underwood, writing a biography never occurred to me, even though the books I'd loved most as a kid were biographies of Kit Carson, Daniel Boone, and—before other kids discovered him via Disney—Davy Crockett. When I'd look up from the typewriter, out my bedroom window I could see the towering flames from the blast furnaces of the Pittsburgh steel mills, lighting up the sky, making the huge red, yellow, and purple chemical stains in the bed of the Monongahela River glisten under its oily surface, teasing me into dreams of becoming a writer—signing book contracts with my agent, getting reviewed in *The New York Times*, going on talk shows. Never did I imagine those dreams would come true by writing biography.

Maybe aspiring writers find biography a less attractive form of creative nonfiction because, as I've just shown, we like to write about ourselves, and, unlike memoir, poetry, fiction, and drama, biography seems to offer little chance for self-expression. Philip Levine might prod his students by saying, "Why write about yourself when there are so many *interesting* people in the world to write about?" but still the image of Boswell following Dr. Johnson around London, taking down his every aphorism, makes writing biography look like self-effacing stenography.

I'll come back to the question of what makes a writer want to write biography, but first I want to talk about another reason for the antipathy to biography that is the fault of biographers themselves.

Bluntly put, few biographers treat narrative form with imagination. In my workshops I give students the first and last paragraphs of several randomly chosen biographies, which invariably begin with the subject's birth and end with his death. If students read the intervening pages, they'd probably find the subject's life laid out in monotonous, chronological order.

Instead, I ask them to think about *The Odyssey* as a "mythic" biography that deftly avoids the trap of chronology. It even starts, not with Odysseus, but with his son trying to learn about a father he's barely seen, then uses flashbacks and fast-forwards to weave an intricate, shifting narrative. One of the last things we learn about Odysseus is that he was wounded by a boar as a child; in a chronological narrative, that would have been merely an interesting detail, but when we learn it as his aged nurse confirms his identity by feeling for the scar, the information is riveting.

True, there have been some formal innovations in biography. Jean Stein and George Plimpton in *Edie: American Girl* wove a collage of quotes from people they interviewed about 1960s pop star Edie Sedgwick, never once intruding with a narrative "biographer's" voice. At the opposite extreme, Edmund Morris's *Dutch: A Memoir of Ronald Reagan* creates a fictional character to dramatize the events of Ronald Reagan's life.

EXORCISING THE THREE DEMONS

Yet even these experiments are possessed by three demons that need to be exorcised if biography is to have anything like the narrative innovation of fiction. First, biographers have to resist the impulse to tell the reader *everything* they have learned about their subject.

Second, they need to find the *story* they want to tell about their subject, a story buried under all of that information they've gathered.

Finally, they should create a narrative pattern other than the chronological tick of "and then . . .," "and then . . .," "and then. . . ." I think they can take inspiration from the way biography is handled in theatrical performances and documentary films, but first let's take a look at how the genre of biography has gotten itself into these narrative ruts.

When we think of biography, we think first of all of a *big* book—maybe even several volumes, such as Leon Edel's three-volume biography of Henry James. The implicit contract between reader and writer seems to be that the biography will tell the reader everything the writer has learned about her subject. As a narrative principle, such inclusiveness would be absurd for a novel or play; all the reader needs know about a character is what is important for the story the writer is telling.

But biographers and readers see biography as a massive, all-inclusive form, even though it has only recently assumed such proportions. From Plutarch's *Lives* to Samuel Johnson's *Lives of the Poets*, biography was a compact form that rendered the essential story behind several lives in streamlined, dramatic narratives. It was in the nineteenth century that biography swelled to its current gargantuan size. Biographies of figures such as Thomas Carlyle were routinely issued in two large volumes, as if the life of such an eminent Victorian were too large to be contained in a single book.

In the early twentieth century, modernist writers pared down the huge, literary forms they had inherited from the Victorians. Poets raised on the sprawling, metrical poems of Alfred Lord Tennyson and Henry Wadsworth Longfellow redefined poetry with two- or three-line free-verse Imagist poems that they signed with equal terseness as "W.C. Williams," "e.e. cummings," or even "H.D."

Lytton Strachey similarly tried to modernize the Victorian behemoth of biography by combining several crisp essays about people such as Florence Nightingale into a single book. Instead of telling everything that was known about his subject, Strachey told the story he had found *in* his subject's life and, like a good novelist or playwright, omitted details that did not advance that story. Of course, he could do this because there had already been massive biographies of some of his subjects, and he could sift through their voluminous information to find the "story" and "character" he could re-create.

Yet the massive Victorian tome still haunts our notion of biography. The most recent biography of Hemingway is five volumes long. Such "definitive" biographies certainly serve a purpose: For one thing, they help scholars of Hemingway refine their insights into his work with the most complete information the biographer could find about Hemingway's day-to-day life. But a five-volume work seems so aesthetically wrong for a writer whose own slim novels and minimalist short stories established the aesthetic principle of "less is more"—knowing what information to leave out of a narrative.

Part of the impulse to include everything reflects the fact that biography involves a tremendous amount of research. Until every research lead has been tracked down, you don't feel you can even begin to write about your subject with authority. With a famous subject, there are often archives that hold his papers—correspondence, manuscripts, diaries—and these can be daunting.

Think how many pieces of paper are in your file cabinets, piled on your bookshelves, stored in boxes in your attic or basement. Then think of someone like Irving Berlin, who lived to be 101, owned his own music publishing company and his own Broadway theater, and wrote 899 published songs. When his daughter gave me access to his papers, which had just been deposited at the Library of Congress, I walked among towering stacks in the library's basement that held hundreds of boxes, each crammed with letters, scrapbooks, business documents, sheet music, lyric worksheets, and other papers. I'd have to read all of this before I could even begin my portrait of this complex and extraordinary man. For a moment I wished I'd done what most of my high school friends did after graduation—go to work in the steel mills.

When you do that kind of "hard time" on research, the natural impulse is to try to include as much of it as you can in your book, partly because you found it, partly because you think the reader should know it, too.

But by giving in to that impulse, the biographer works at cross-purposes to a novelist, who puts in only information that contributes to the understanding he wants to give readers of a character. Biographers need to focus their narrative on the research that brought their subject most vividly alive for them, and that can be hard to find.

FINDING GEMS IN UNLIKELY ARCHIVES
When I was working on a biography of Ira Gershwin, I did research at the Gershwin Archive in Beverly Hills, which mostly consisted of Ira Gershwin's own papers; the Gershwin Archive at the Library of Congress, which Ira and his mother established after George Gershwin's untimely death in 1937; and at the Museum of the City of New York, which Ira helped establish in response to pleas from the curator that some Gershwin papers and memorabilia should be deposited in the brothers' hometown.

Traveling expenses to Los Angeles, Washington, and New York quickly ate up my publisher's advance and my university grants, so when I learned that there was another collection of Gershwin papers at the University of Texas, I debated whether it was worth going to the extra expense of a trip to Austin. From what I could tell, the Texas archive had the "manuscript materials" for *The Gershwin Years*, a book about the Gershwin brothers coauthored by Ira's personal secretary and another family friend. Was it worth a trip to Austin to see what might just be notes and drafts for a published book I already owned?

Luckily, I found a cheap flight and spent a week going through a treasure trove of material. There were lengthy, transcribed interviews with people like Irving Berlin about the Gershwins. There were letters from Ira to the authors about his memories of his brother. There were also notes that didn't go into their book, which was published while

Ira was still alive. The notes portrayed Ira as a kindly but insecure man, ruled by a domineering wife (also still alive when their book was published), who had long feared that his brilliant younger brother would strike off musically on his own or find another collaborator. Since Ira managed their collaboration, he directed George into projects, such as working on songs for Hollywood musicals, that would keep their partnership going, even though George had wanted to branch off into other musical directions. When George died suddenly at the age of thirty-eight in Hollywood, Ira carried an excruciating burden of guilt with him until the day he died.

But the real gems in the Texas archive were the manuscripts.

Most songwriters, I'd found, threw away their manuscript drafts of a song once it was published. Lorenz Hart, Irving Berlin, and other lyricists saw no reason to keep the various drafts that had led to the music and lyrics of "My Funny Valentine" or "Cheek to Cheek." But Ira Gershwin's secretary had been an English professor, and when Ira and Harold Arlen worked on songs for the Judy Garland film *A Star Is Born*, in 1954, the author kept fetching their discarded manuscripts out of the trash. In the Texas archive, therefore, were fifteen revisions of one of Ira's greatest lyrics, "The Man That Got Away." As I saw him cutting, changing, recasting the lyric, it was, as Salieri says as he looks over Mozart's manuscripts in *Amadeus*, "like looking into the mind of God."

FINDING THE TRUTH IN INTERVIEWS
Research on biography also involves interviews, particularly if your subject lived recently enough for there still to be people who knew her. If your subject was famous, however, interviewing people will seem deceptively easy. People readily agree to talk about their friendships with a famous person, but you quickly find that what you're hearing are very polished anecdotes that they've probably retold for years. You sometimes have to ask tough questions to get at your subject's character, and people are reluctant to talk about the darker side of someone they admired.

The best strategy I've found is to ask about things you've heard from other interviews.

I'm currently researching a biography of Johnny Mercer, the only Southerner among the great popular songwriters of the mid-twentieth century, most of whom were first- or second-generation Jewish immigrants from New York. As a child growing up in Savannah, Mercer had a black nurse, played with black children, and loved the singing in local black churches as well as what were called "race records"—blues and jazz vocals by black performers. As a singer and songwriter,

Mercer drew upon these roots and some people even thought he himself was black.

I was curious, therefore, about his racial attitudes, particularly during the civil rights movement of the 1950s and '60s. One of the people I interviewed was a black composer who had collaborated with Mercer on several songs during the 1960s. He was full of stories about Mercer's kindness to him as a young composer in Hollywood—how Mercer had him join his table at restaurants, how Mercer fixed "Dagwood" sandwiches for him when they were working at his home, etc. As I listened, I recalled another interview with a woman whose first impression of Mercer had been terrible, though she later became a close friend. When she was introduced to him in the 1960s, Mercer cracked a joke—"Do you know what the NAACP stands for?" he chortled, "Niggers Ain't Acting Like Colored People."

That crack gave me the confidence to push the issue of racism harder with the black composer, and eventually he told me that, yes, Mercer, for all of his kindness for individual black friends like Nat King Cole, had very different attitudes about blacks as a group. When the composer asked for Mercer's help in getting an assignment to write a film score, Mercer said, "Do you think the time is right?" What sounded to me like an ambiguous remark clearly meant to the composer that Mercer didn't think it was appropriate for a black songwriter to do the more prestigious work of scoring a Hollywood film. Now an old man, the composer had never had an opportunity to score a film, and in telling that story about Johnny Mercer his long years of bitterness came out. The time, for him, had never been right.

Sometimes you can ask a tough question without realizing it.

I was interviewing Irving Berlin's oldest daughter, and she was showing me her father's book collection, which filled the shelves of the living room in her New York apartment. As I took down a volume from his complete set of Shakespeare, I asked her if Berlin had a favorite poet. Suddenly her eyes narrowed and I got a sense of Berlin's reputedly icy anger. "My father," she snapped, "liked to read history books and *True Crime* magazine."

Knowing that Berlin had had to drop out of school at age thirteen to help his impoverished family, I realized that my question must have sounded to her like a sneering dismissal of a book collection he probably never read. I explained that I thought Berlin's lyrics, like those of Ira Gershwin, Lorenz Hart, and other songwriters, were quite "poetic," and I was curious about his friendship with light-verse writers such as Dorothy Parker, George S. Kaufman, and other members of the famed Algonquin Round Table.

Her face warmed again, but the exchange had triggered a memory. "There was a famous poet my father admired," she said, and I waited eagerly as she struggled to recall. "Alexander Pope—yes, he admired Pope." Now I was flabbergasted. Of all the great English poets, Pope was such an acquired taste that even few English professors teach him anymore. Then it hit me. Pope wrote all of his poetry, even his translation of *The Iliad*, in the most constricting poetic form imaginable—the heroic or "closed" couplet. Into sequences of two-line units of ten syllables each, he packed the subtle variations of rhythm, phrasing, wit, and rhyme that consistently averted the monotony of other writers of couplets.

Berlin worked within the constrictions of an equally tight form—the thirty-two bar chorus, which gave a lyricist between sixty and eighty words to find a clever and moving way to say, in song after song, some variation of "I love you." Most lyricists fall into cliché and repetition, but Berlin handled this constricting form with deceptive simplicity. Months later, I found a newspaper interview in Berlin's papers in the Library of Congress that confirmed my hunch. Praising Pope's mastery of the strictures of the couplet, Berlin said he thought the poet would have made a great lyricist on Tin Pan Alley. I now had yet another "find" that, naturally, I would want to work into my biography.

BUT WHAT'S THE STORY?

Thus the extensive research that goes into a biography can make for narrative accretion rather than the pruning that makes for good storytelling. That, in turn, begets the second demon that haunts biography. Some biographers amass so much research that they lose sight of what their story, in a nutshell, is all about. After completing the research, they just start writing it up without stepping back and finding where—in all that archival note taking and those hours of taped interviews—the *story* is that they're trying to tell. A biographer should be able to condense the story he is telling about his subject into a couple of sentences, as if he had only a few moments to "pitch" a movie to an impatient Hollywood producer. "You have to make a movie about Ira Gershwin," the biographer has to be able to say, "because he was a man who . . . " (complete in fifty words or less).

It's hard for biographers to take Dorothy Parker's advice to "murder your darlings" by cutting out your best-loved parts of your manuscript—from sentences to whole chapters—if they impede the overall narrative flow.

When I first began writing about popular song lyricists in the mid-1980s, I started a book that became *The Poets of Tin Pan Alley: A*

History of America's Great Lyricists. Nowadays, it would probably be called a "group biography," a subgenre of biography that has become quite fashionable. The book had individual chapters on Cole Porter, Ira Gershwin, Lorenz Hart, Oscar Hammerstein, and other lyricists, placing their lives in the context of the development of popular music, the Broadway theater, and Hollywood musicals in the middle part of the twentieth century.

When word got out that I was working on this book, I was approached by a local jazz musician who wanted to put on a series of theatrical tributes to the great songwriters. He would assemble musicians, singers, and dancers, get a theater, and handle publicity and ticket sales. All I had to do was write a script that would present the songwriter's life through a series of introductions to song performances by members of his company. Then he wanted me to rent a tuxedo (a tux—I hadn't worn one since my high school prom!) and emcee the show.

Our first show was about Irving Berlin, and my first draft of a script seemed to my collaborator like the notes for an interminably long lecture that did what would seem to be the impossible—make the life of Irving Berlin boring.

As my musician friend went through each song introduction, critiquing with a sure instinct, I realized that he, as a jazz musician, was telling me things I had learned long before as a writer—but had forgotten as a biographer. I had to leave things out, no matter how fascinating I had found them in my research; I had to decide on a simple, bare-bones story I was telling about Irving Berlin and not simply amass information about him; above all, I had to make each introduction "set up" the song by telling an anecdote that would make the audience say to itself, "I didn't know *that* about 'Cheek to Cheek,' " just as the curtain was going up to the strains of "Heaven, I'm in Heaven."

There was, I learned, an old theater adage that applies to storytelling as well: "Get in and get out," and that's what I had to do for every song in the show, as well as for shows we did on the Gershwins and Cole Porter.

Every writer ought to have to read her narrative to an audience of three hundred people and learn, by the shuffling of their feet, where the storytelling flags.

A TALE OF TWO STUDENTS

These are lessons I try to pass on to my students in workshops on writing biography. I ask them each to write a biographical essay on some prominent person from Wilmington, North Carolina—where our university is located—for whom we have archival materials and people to be interviewed.

Thus far no student has chosen Michael Jordan, but one student researched the life of Henry Bacon, an architect who, among other things, designed the Lincoln Memorial. Once his research was completed, the student told me he had come across an image that he couldn't get out of his mind: at the dedication ceremony for the Lincoln Memorial, Bacon sat in an elegant barge at the Washington Monument end of the reflecting pool. At the climax of the ceremony, architecture students ceremoniously pulled his barge the entire length of the pool toward the Lincoln Memorial, where President Warren Harding stood to congratulate the architect. As my student pondered that image, he came to see the irony of Bacon, a neoclassical architect, reaching the height of his career just as his style of architecture was being displaced by the sleek modernism of Frank Lloyd Wright and Art Deco. The student then had the kernel for the story he would tell.

Another student had a great "lead" for his essay on a regional artist who achieved an international reputation: The artist was born and died in the same apartment room in downtown Wilmington. But the student needed to find a story to follow that lead. His research showed that the artist had lived with his mother for most of his life, that he had worked with the local railroad company and only painted in his spare time, and that, except for one short trip to France, where he loved painting in the famous light of Provence, he seldom had left Wilmington. Then in an interview with an art historian, my student learned that most of the artist's paintings, prints, and watercolors of local fishermen were based upon a triangular pattern, that most stable of geometric structures.

Stability, clearly, was a driving force in this artist's life, but in the 1960s, when the railroad suddenly pulled out of Wilmington, literally overnight, his life, like those of many other people, fell apart. For the artist, it was doubly shocking, for his mother died at the same time.

What saved him was our university, which invited him to establish its new art department. Working for a university, he found, allowed him time to paint during the day, something his nine-to-five job at the railroad had made difficult. During the afternoons, when he wasn't teaching, he would wander out to Wrightsville Beach, a lovely stretch of the Atlantic coast that lies just four miles east of our campus. There he found light effects as dazzling as he'd witnessed in Provence, and his painting moved into a major phase that established his international reputation.

During his long career, many local people bought his works, so now they hang in many Wilmington homes and even decorate the walls of the local McDonalds. In the tension between stability and airiness, between solid triangular structure and diaphanous shifts of light, between a local life and international acclaim, my student had found a story to tell about his subject. Moreover, he could tell it dramatically, in terms of conflicting forces, rather than in dull chronological order.

BEYOND CHRONOLOGY: LEARNING FROM DOCUMENTARY FILM

That chronological tick is the third demon I would like to exorcise from the writing of biography. Like throwing in all one's research or not bothering to find the simple story behind that research, the day-by-day, year-by-year, narrative pattern of most biography needs to be reimagined. And here we can look to a related genre, that of documentary film, for inspiration.

Many documentary films are really biographies, and the process of shooting footage, which documentary filmmakers do to gather images to edit, resembles the notes a biographer takes in archives and interviews. Both footage and research notes are gathered in nonchronological order. A filmmaker or biographer may, in the same day, learn something about her subject's childhood and something about her old age. So much of the "work" in both genres is sorting out information into its proper chronological order—exactly when *did* Hemingway go hunting in Africa?—that the natural impulse is to use such hard-won knowledge of chronology as your narrative structure.

But the difference for the documentary filmmaker comes in editing a film, where he can exercise his creativity in a way few biographers have done. Particularly with the new digital editing programs, where all the footage that's been shot is simultaneously available to the editor (as opposed to traditional "linear" editing of strips of celluloid film), the creative possibilities of shifting chronology are even more enticing.

Yet documentary filmmakers are prone to the same evils when they make a biographical film. At a recent film festival, there was a screening of biographical documentaries, and, after each film, discussion sessions raised the same points I've been making about writing biography: the filmmaker had not pared down the footage from everything he'd shot to the most essential images for telling the story. He'd not really focused on what the subject's life was about but had simply recounted event after event. And in that recounting, the filmmaker had relied completely upon chronology.

One filmmaker had done a biography of his father that started with birth and proceeded, lockstep, through all of the major events of his life, even using titles such as "Childhood" and "College Years" that only intensified the clock-ticking effect. About halfway through the film, however, chronology led to the filmmaker's own birth, and from that point the relationship between father and son, a relationship that culminated in the very film we were watching, engaged the audience. Had the filmmaker begun with his own birth and then simultaneously moved forward and backward in time, portraying his father as he came to know him as a child, as well as how he learned about his father's earlier life, it would have been a much more dramatic and moving narrative.

The final film in the festival, however, was one of the most "moving" movies I have ever seen—both emotionally moving and adroitly narrated. The filmmaker was fascinated by two elderly, mentally retarded women who had just moved into his neighborhood as part of a community program to take people out of mental institutions and help them live on their own. As he got to know the women as neighbors, he wanted to do a biographical documentary about one of them and, with the help of their social workers, he started filming footage of how she was learning to do the simplest things—making a grocery list, shopping for food, cooking—things that had always been done for her in institutions. As the filmmaker shot footage of these everyday activities, he saw that his "story" was about how this woman was learning to make her own choices for the first time in her life.

In editing his film, which took hundreds of hours, he selected the footage that showed the comic as well as the painful side of that process. For example, the woman, who has always had to eat what the institution served, delights in saying she does not want chicken for dinner, but then she also has to comprehend the fact that chicken is all she has in her refrigerator.

After we see her adapting to everyday community life, the filmmaker and social workers take the woman for a visit back to the mental institution where she'd spent the last forty years. It is a dreary but humane place, with staff people caring for inmates the woman remembers and converses with. Then the camera focuses on a thick manila folder that is the woman's medical file, showing pictures of her that go backward in time until she is a young woman, with a voice-over of comments in the file by doctors and staff that give us retrospective snapshots of her life in this institution.

Although the woman seems calm during her visit, the next morning she is so devastated by the experience she refuses to get out of bed, making us reimagine the scenes we've just witnessed from her point of view. The narrative then returns to the painful process of having her learn again to adjust to everyday life. Gradually, we see her strength return and even triumph in a wonderfully comic encounter with a traveling vacuum cleaner salesman, in which she manages to get her carpets cleaned and receive a complimentary basket of fruit without buying a thing.

At that point, the social workers determine she is strong enough for a return visit to the first mental institution where she was placed as a child. On this visit we see a place that fulfills our worst image of what such institutions were—bars on the windows, bathrooms with no private stalls, virtually a prison.

As the woman walks among the buildings, now used as warehouses, voice-over narration drives home what a terrible place it was when she was committed there in the 1930s. Reports from the director tell of little money to buy blankets, heat, food, or to pay staff. Archival footage of mental patients being jeered in public underscores American attitudes toward the mentally retarded at a time when it was feared they would propagate in epidemic proportions.

After that overview, which places the woman's life in historical context, her personal memories of the place come flooding back to her. She recalls her job of scrubbing the floors in the bathroom, the times she was put in a straitjacket, the times she was beaten.

We then go backward in time again as the camera focuses on her battered manila file folder from this institution, which opens to show a picture of her as a lovely child, and the voice-over narrator reads from the letter her father sent committing her to the place. Far from trying to rid himself of a retarded child, the father clearly loves his daughter and is acting on his doctor's advice, believing that placing her in this institution is her best hope in life.

Coming as it does at the end of the film, this wrenchingly tender letter is far more effective than it would have been if introduced, in chronological order, before we had come to know the woman as she is today.

The movie ends with her walking out of the institution, saying she hated being there but is glad she came back for this visit. She then strides through its huge iron gates, like a child taking her first determined steps, and says, "I just keep on walking," giving the filmmaker his title.

Such documentary films can provide a model for how writers of biography can exorcise the demon of chronology.

CREATING SUSPENSE THROUGH
NARRATIVE ORDERING

After my biography of Irving Berlin was published, the Arts & Entertainment network invited me to New York to tape an interview for a special two-hour *Biography* on Irving Berlin. The director told me he wanted to use my interview for "continuity," then for the next five hours asked me questions that followed strict chronological order:

"Tell us about Berlin's childhood."

"What do we know about his teenage years?"

"What was his first job?"

As I answered these, I feared the documentary would make for a boring two hours, but when it aired I was astounded to see how imaginatively the director had edited the narrative. It opened not with Berlin's birth back in 1888 but at the height of the Jazz Age in 1924. It was then that Irving Berlin fell in love with the daughter of one of the most socially prominent couples in New York, who naturally opposed their daughter's romance with a Jewish immigrant songwriter from the Lower East Side.

Leaving the audience in suspense over whether they married, the narrative focused on the intense "ballyhoo" over the affair in the New York press. Reporters were fascinated by the impoverished origins of Irving Berlin, and the narrative uses that angle to go back into his early life, then follow his meteoric rise to success as a songwriter, bringing us back, after the first hour of the show, to his romance and the ensuing elopement.

As I watched the documentary, I wished that I had handled chronology more imaginatively in my own biography. In my new biography, on Johnny Mercer, I am determined to shake up the chronological form of this staid genre. If biographers can make the genre more formally innovative, it will be more attractive to aspiring writers.

Then we will just have the problem I started with: Most writers like to write about themselves.

WORDS AND MUSIC: THE PASSION TO
CAPTURE OTHER LIVES

What makes a writer want to write about somebody else?

There are probably as many reasons as there are writers, but an intensely passionate interest in righting some kind of wrong often is part of it. The filmmaker who made the film about his mentally retarded friend wanted, without preaching, to let us know how society had treated such people.

A few weeks ago, I read that Hedy Lamar, the Hollywood sex

goddess of the 1940s, had invented an electrical device that was crucial to the development of radar and later was used for the cellular phone. It occurred to me that there ought to be a biography of her, or a group biography of Hollywood vamps who also had little-known brain-power. But the minute it occurred to me, I realized I was not the person who burned to spend the next three years researching, interviewing, and writing such a biography.

It was also that I am still passionately committed to the lives of the people I first discovered as my biographical subjects seventeen years ago. In a way, I had known about them since I was a teenager, but I could not have identified them by name. In that room looking out over the Pittsburgh steel mills where I first dreamed of being a writer, there was always music. By day, I listened to Elvis and Chuck Berry with my friends on little machines that played 45 rpm records. But at night, as I wrote, I would put a stack of LP (long-playing) record albums on my "hi-fi" (high-fidelity record player). I bought my 45s in record stores, but my LPs came in the mail from the Columbia Record Club and the Capitol Record Club. I had joined these clubs, as kids join similar clubs today, because they offered you six "free" albums off the bat.

But being a member meant that you were sent a card each month, announcing the club's "Album of the Month," which would be sent to you automatically unless you mailed the card back saying you didn't want it. Like most kids, I seldom remembered to send back the card, and so I wound up having to buy a lot of "Albums of the Month."

LPs had started out primarily for the classical music audience, but in the mid-1950s, with the advent of rock, they branched into popular songs with vocalists from the Big Band era, such as Frank Sinatra, Ella Fitzgerald, and Doris Day. In the 1950s there weren't enough good new popular songs being written for these singers to fill up the twelve or sixteen tracks needed for an LP, so they turned to the great songwriters of the 1920s, '30s, and '40s—Jerome Kern, Rodgers and Hart, Berlin, the Gershwins. By singing such songs, these performers turned them into "standards" and established what we think of today as The Great American Song Book.

As I wrote my own poetry, stories, and plays, these wonderful songs on my hi-fi burned themselves into my memory. When I went to college, and then on to graduate school, these songs went with me, converted from LPs to cassette tapes. By then, my dreams of becoming a writer had also been converted into the more prosaic life of an English professor. After a few years of teaching modern American poetry at the University of Minnesota, I found that my students' difficulties with experimental poets like Ezra Pound and Wallace Stevens eased a little if I showed them slides of modern paintings by Picasso and Cézanne. They might not understand the poems any better, but at least they could see that modernism had revolutionized other arts as well.

By the early 1980s, I had brought in not only modern painting but photography, architecture, and the music of Stravinsky, Charles Ives, and other composers to create interdisciplinary courses such as "The Jazz Age."

Such courses helped me to get a Fulbright professorship at the University of Graz in Austria in 1983. The university dates back to the Middle Ages—Johannes Kepler taught there—but it prides itself on being a hip school that at the time had the only Jazz (pronounced *yhazz*) Institute in Europe. One day in my course on the Jazz Age, my students asked me what popular songs were like in the 1920s and '30s. I had to confess that I didn't know (and may even have sounded a little condescending that I, as a professor who taught them Hart Crane and Marianne Moore, should be expected to know anything about such a lowly form as the popular song).

Still, the student in me hated not knowing the answer, and I vowed to myself to find it by the next class. As I researched American popular song in the university's excellent library, I discovered that the songs I'd loved since I was a teenager—the songs of Kern and Rodgers and Hart and Porter that I'd listened to on my hi-fi and that I still listened to on tapes—had once been the popular hits of their time. Not only could I *tell* my students about popular songs from that era, I could play them examples from the tapes I'd brought with me. As I listened to my tapes, I learned for the first time which of these songs was by Cole Porter, which by Ira and George Gershwin, and which, like "April in Paris" and "Stormy Weather," were by such unfamiliar names as "Yip" Harburg and Vernon Duke or Ted Koehler and Harold Arlen.

I also realized that my Austrian students, as good as their English was, would have trouble following lines like "You're a rose, you're Inferno's Dante; you're the nose on the great Durante." So I typed up some of the lyrics and photocopied them so my students could follow as I played my tapes. Although I knew most of the lyrics by heart, I played and stopped the tapes over and over to make sure I typed the lyric correctly, and it was then that I began to notice how truly "poetic" they were.

At first I was struck by how a lyricist like Hart would break up the poetic line in brilliant fragments the way William Carlos Williams did or how Cole Porter's catalogs of witty images and allusions resembled the verbal collage poems of e.e. cummings, but then I saw the lyrics in their own right. Most of the lyricists, I learned, had wanted to be writers of light verse. Light verse was so popular in the 1920s and '30s that all the big newspapers carried columns like Franklin Pierce Adams's (F.P.A.) in the *New York World*. When these would-be poets turned to songwriting, they brought the clever rhymes and witty sentiments of light verse to music.

Yet they had to do it the hard way—by writing *to* music. When Gilbert and Sullivan collaborated, Gilbert always wrote his words first as a light-verse poem. Sullivan then set those words to music. But in American songwriting, the importance of jazz that could be danced to always made the music come first. The lyricists, then, had to find syllables, words, and phrases that fit into this musical grid. That writers like Ira Gershwin and Yip Harburg could be as clever as Gilbert when they were writing words to fit the intricate jazz melodies of George Gershwin and Harold Arlen seemed to me a stupefying achievement.

Just as stupefying to my Austrian students were the songs I played for them at the next class. Now they wanted to know more about the people who wrote them—particularly the lyricists. While I could tell them a few things about Irving Berlin, Cole Porter, and the Gershwins, I knew nothing about Dorothy Fields ("On the Sunny Side of the Street"), Leo Robin ("Thanks for the Memory"), or Gus Kahn ("Makin' Whoopee"). As Austrians who had been taught to revere every musical figure in their musical pantheon, they must have been appalled that lyricists of such brilliance were virtually unknown to most Americans.

There is a bit of folklore among Fulbrighters that some of the best books about America have been written by scholars on a Fulbright year abroad. The idea is that if you get a scholar of American culture outside of the United States, she will see America afresh from a foreign perspective. I certainly had a new perspective on American song when I returned to Minnesota, and when I found how little had been written about these brilliant lyricists, I burned to celebrate their lives. What added to my fire was that I found that their musical collaborators were better known than they were. "Gershwin" for most people meant George, not Ira, and "Star Dust" was thought of as a Hoagy Carmichael song even though Carmichael's melody had gone nowhere until Mitchell Parish added words to it.

Like Mrs. Oscar Hammerstein, I had had enough. One night, so the story goes, she was at a party where someone at the piano began singing "Ol' Man River." A guest beside her whispered, "Ah, 'Ol' Man River'—what a great Kern song."

"I beg your pardon," Mrs. Hammerstein said, "But Jerome Kern did not write 'Ol' Man River.' "

"Of course he did," countered the guest, "It's from *Show Boat*."

"Yes," she said, "but Mr. Kern wrote *dum dum dum da*—my husband wrote *Ol' Man Ri-ver*."

I plunged into a book about all of these great lyricists and started teaching courses on American popular song. Students began calling me, "Professor Boom Box," as I trotted off to class with my cassette player under my arm. Colleagues asked me if I ever planned to teach *books* again. But all of the teasing was good-natured, for they, too, I learned, loved these lyrics.

Even one of my crustier older colleagues, a distinguished professor of romanticism known for his scholarly conservatism. One day he confronted me over the departmental photocopier. "I understand," he intoned, "that you are writing a book about people like Ira Gershwin and Cole Porter."

"That's right," I said and started to launch into a defense of my project when he stopped me with a wave of his hand.

"Good," he said. "We need a book about Ira Gershwin and Cole Porter—we don't need any more books about Milton and Pound."

AS TIME GOES BY

I wrote my chapters about lyricists such as Porter, Berlin, and *Ira* (not George) Gershwin as my jazz musician friend produced theatrical tributes to them that helped me write for a popular rather than a strictly scholarly audience. As the book progressed, he suggested I get an agent, and those youthful dreams of becoming a "writer" stirred again after twenty-five years. As we went over the book contract, my agent helped me navigate a problem I hadn't even thought about—getting permissions from copyright holders to quote from hundreds of song lyrics, each one of which normally cost hundreds of dollars. Even though I was given a reduced fee for permissions, the total costs ate up my advance and first royalties. Still, I was feeling more and more like the writer I'd always wanted to be.

One day a student showed up at my office and told me he wanted to be a publicist. Could he try his hand with my book and only charge me if he could increase my royalties? When I agreed, he transformed himself from a mild-mannered Minnesotan into a feisty New Yorker—haranguing book reviewers and pestering producers. In a few weeks, he had gotten the book reviewed in a dozen newspapers from *The Boston Globe* to the *San Francisco Chronicle* (including *The New York Times*) and booked me as a guest on several talk shows, including

Larry King Live. It was fun to see him living out his youthful dreams as I was finally living mine.

So the passion to write biography can feed both your altruism and your ego. If you can find it, or, as in my case, *it* finds *you* from some youthful cranny of your life and gives you subject after subject to champion, I hope you handle the form of biography with imagination. Don't plan to cram all of your research into it. Look for a story underneath all of that research before you start writing. Try to create a narrative pattern that doesn't simply rely upon the chronological tick—and *tic*—of time going by.

On the other hand, remember that, at times, chronology is the best way to tell some stories.

Although most of us know it from the 1944 film *Casablanca*, "As Time Goes By" was actually written back in 1931 by Herman Hupfeld, a songwriter who had few other hits. When it first came out, however, it was not a hit, despite a record by Rudy Vallee. But a college student at Cornell heard it and loved it. When he later wrote a play, *Everybody Comes to Rick's*, he featured the song prominently. The play was bought by Warner Brothers and used as the basis for *Casablanca*, but from the very start of production people objected to "As Time Goes By." They found its lyrics maudlin, its music simplistic, and when Dooley Wilson croakily performed it on the set, just about everyone thought it would never make the final cut. But once Jack Warner learned that Warner Brothers owned the copyright to "As Time Goes By," he insisted it stay in the film. He didn't like it any more than they did, but he knew the movie would plug the song and earn royalties from sheet music and record sales.

Once filming was completed and editing and scoring began, the editor and composer pleaded with Warner to ditch this dreary old song. The scorer even offered to write a new song for the scene himself that couldn't help but be better than "As Time Goes By." Finally, Jack Warner agreed and summoned everyone back for a retake of the scene with a new song. But by that time Ingrid Bergman had cut her hair short for her role in *For Whom the Bell Tolls*. *Casablanca* was stuck with "As Time Goes By." Today, it earns the highest royalties of any popular song ever written.

End of chronological story. Yet within *Casablanca*, "As Time Goes By" introduces one of the most romantic and dramatic of flashbacks. When Sam plays it again, a lost past, an oppressive present, and an uncertain future coalesce in a narrative movement that biographers should try to emulate.

Twelve Years and Counting: Writing Biography

HONOR MOORE

O ne day in the late seventies, a year after the death of my maternal grandmother, I received in the mail a small scrapbook, barely the size of a steno pad, and not terribly thick. I had always been intrigued by this grandmother, whose maiden name was the magic-sounding Margarett Sargent, but it was a misty fascination. She had been an artist and a beauty, but since my mother and she hadn't gotten along and I had grown up hundreds of miles away from where she lived, and since she had suffered from manic-depressive illness all of my life, I came to know her only slightly in the years before she died, years during which her articulation was dramatically impaired by a stroke. I pulled the scrapbook from the package and flipped through it.

An uncredited clipping began

> It will be remembered that one of the prettiest and most dashing girls of the exclusive Boston set broke an engagement just at the end of her debutante year with a Harvard man who boasts one of the most prominent names in the world of finance . . . it was said that a classmate was the cause of the trouble and rumor points to a young man who is at work in the mines.

As if that weren't provocative enough, from the next page, a group of Bohemian-looking young people gazed sullenly from a photograph, among them, my grandmother, young, angular, and gorgeous. Just pages away was glued a letter from one Grace Peabody:

> I send you a few lines on the Keen-Sighted, Untouched, Fair-tressed Artemis—Diana Huntress of men and stags. Curious you should turn to the Goddess so very like yourself in many ways . . .

Who was the man from "the world of finance"? Who was the young man "at work in the mines"? Who were the Bohemians, and who on earth was Grace Peabody? Since I had already considered writing

Margarett's biography, I had a two-pronged reaction. I knew that if I were to write my grandmother's life, I would have to answer those questions. But how? I had no idea I was getting into twelve long years during which I would put preoccupation with someone else's life ahead of attention to my own: It was not *my* relationship with *my* father I was interested in, but Margarett Sargent's; not *my* relationship to *my* art, but hers; not *my* love affairs, but hers. I predicted none of this when I sat down one midsummer day to begin the book that ended my literary novitiate and made me a writer.

I had been invited to write an essay for an anthology called *The Writer on Her Work*. The year was 1979, and I was sick to death of writing about writing, bored with thinking about women writers. But Janet Sternburg's letter was persuasive and evocative. One of her editorial suggestions especially piqued my interest. *Perhaps*, she wrote, *you might write about someone who influenced you*. Margarett, who became a working and exhibiting artist but stopped painting in her forties, had certainly influenced me, but negatively. I was in my early thirties at the time, terrified of inheriting her mental illness, haunted by a fear of being unable to continue to write. Like my grandmother, I had been brought up to marry and have houses and not to work, certainly not to become a working writer. When I sat down to my desk, I often felt fraudulent, and whenever I finished a poem, I was always certain I'd never write another. Was this the beginning of the slippery slope that stopped Margarett painting in her forties, turning her into an alcoholic and a perennial sanitarium resident who endured twenty years of shock treatment? I had always assumed talent endured, but what had happened to that expressionistic blaze that brought forth Margarett Sargent's paintings? I needed to find out. I wrote the essay, called "My Grandmother Who Painted," and soon began the book that a dozen years later became *The White Blackbird*.

As Carolyn Heilbrun has documented in her important book, *Writing a Woman's Life*, the late seventies began a flourishing of feminist biography. These biographies of women, especially of women whose circumstances as women had held them back, were changing the face of the form. I had read Nancy Milford's *Zelda,* about F. Scott Fitzgerald's wife, and Jean Strouse's *Alice James*. These women, writing about women whose lives traversed, with drastically different results, the same terrain as the men whose surnames they shared, opened new avenues of cultural inquiry; their work inspired mine. The importance of deconstructing the social context of a life, pioneered by feminist biographers, applies not only to a woman writing the life of another woman but to anyone who wishes to bring a biographical subject alive on the contemporary page.

My agent asked, *Why not a novel?* My answer was instant: I wanted to know the actual truth.

Although it is axiomatic that fiction can tap a truth deeper than accuracy, fiction is apt to come out of a context established by the way we have lived: A novelist usually plays against what is given. I suspected that even the most powerful of fictional gifts would be at the mercy of cliché when it came to Margarett Sargent: She'd be depicted as an eccentric Boston Brahmin grandmother; the picturesque, privileged victim of mental illness; a bad mother; an upper-class woman who dabbled in the arts. I had an intuition that if I looked at her from my contemporary vantage point, I would find new facts of life hiding in plain view. I had a grandmother whose story was as good as a novel and whom no one had seen clearly while she was alive. I was determined to extract from her life a new way for the culture to see such a woman. Her biography might provide raw material for someone else's fiction, but I planned to write her life.

There are many impulses toward biography, but chief among them I would call *transference*, using the psychoanalytic term for elements in a therapeutic relationship that enable one to work through issues in one's own life. It begins with infatuation. From the first second someone told me I looked like Margarett, I was hooked. When I painted as a child, I thought of her. When I first wore a black dress, I thought of her. When I moved to New York as a young woman, I thought of her. How did she make her way?

Margarett's example was not reassuring. I saw it in simple terms: She had failed at the artistic enterprise for which she had sacrificed domestic harmony. Richard Holmes, the biographer of Shelley and Coleridge, has written eloquently about the psychology of biographical choice; his wonderful *Footsteps: Adventures of a Romantic Biographer* chronicles how, in his own life, certain obsessions became means of focusing on a biographical subject. The intensity of this phenomenon explains partly what sustains a writer through the years it takes to write a biography, what Leon Edel has called the most labor-intensive and expensive of literary forms.

No biography is merely a chronology of the subject's life; witness the number of biographies of Virginia Woolf. Each life can be told in a variety of ways. My concern for my own creative life gave me the focus of *The White Blackbird*: I would write the life of Margarett

Sargent the artist, as distinct from Margarett Sargent McKean, the grandmother and "socialite."

I declared in my original proposal that if I placed this woman in context, a life that had caused much of her family to demonize her would make perfect sense. When I set about the task, I found not one but many, many contexts. Margarett Sargent came from a family. In spite of the fact that she was my relative, I knew nothing about her life in that family, very little about the family as it reached backward into history; I had to learn the Sargent and allied families as if they were not my own. Margarett, like any biographical subject, was born into a particular class in a particular place and time. I had to look at the century she lived, from 1892 until 1978, in America as a whole, to think about that hundred years in terms of women, privilege, sexuality, and art. In order to understand where Margarett came from, I traced both sides of her family back to England and up into the twentieth century, read histories of the building of Boston, of how cataclysms such as World War I impacted the community in which she grew up. Margarett Sargent became an artist of a specific kind at a significant time in the development of American art and in the evolution of American modernism. What was the role in American art of her two chief mentors, George Luks and Gutzon Borglum? How did the transition to modernism play out in New York and Boston? How did it affect the artistic climate in which Margarett came to maturity? I had to find out.

The issue of context is never simple. Let me give you some examples.

The first question many people asked was, Was Margarett Sargent related to John Singer Sargent? Yes, but distantly: no one could tell me the exact relationship. I had to figure it out by making my own genealogical charts. Margarett was born twenty years later than John Singer and was his fourth cousin. Their great-great-great-grandfathers, adults during the American Revolution, were brothers.

Margarett spent time in Paris in the 1920s. "Paris in the Twenties" is the subject of a raft of books, but read them and your head spins! Gertrude Stein and Ernest Hemingway; Janet Flanner and Djuna Barnes; Gerald and Sara Murphy; Picasso and Calder. Which Paris was Margarett part of when she and her husband visited for three months each winter during the late 1920s? I had to find out, and I had to be accurate.

Margarett knew Fanny Brice in New York and she knew Harpo Marx. I pictured the two comics performing in Margarett's Boston living room, but that is not what happened. Fanny Brice lived upstairs in the building where Margarett had an apartment in New York in

1918, and Margarett met Harpo Marx in the late 1920s because he, like her husband, had an interest in Afghan hounds.

But before I could approach those questions, I had to figure out how to proceed.

I was a poet, woefully untrained at research and in art history, not experienced as a prose writer. What did I think I was doing?

I began the summer after I published the essay. I made a deal with my grandmother's estate: I would distribute the paintings family members wanted if I could make slides of the works first. With a friend who knew how to photograph paintings, I dragged lights and equipment to the dark warehouse room where Margarett's work was stored. When I emerged from that week, I sat down at my desk and began my outline. The interviewing and research I had done for the essay and my exposure to the paintings gave me the information and passion to produce an energetic, vivid chronology and outline, which served, along with a brief introduction, as my book proposal. Along with a separate chronology of American art history that a graduate student put together for me from decades of *Art News*, that outline formed the basis of my work on the actual construction of the narrative.

Once I got into the routine of writing and researching, I learned I could save weeks, even months, by taking the time to construct a detailed chronology for each chapter that included incidents not only from Margarett's life and that of her extended family, but also historical events (the assassination of Archduke Ferdinand and the beginning of World War I, the publication of *The Great Gatsby*, Lindbergh's flight across the Atlantic, etc.) and significant moments in art history.

A scholar friend once characterized writing history as a process of placing one event next to another. Here is an example: In 1908 in Paris, Picasso painted his wildly avant-garde *Les Demoiselles d'Avignon*; in 1908 in New York, a group of American artists called The Eight exhibited paintings in New York considered controversial; and in 1908, Margarett Sargent entered Miss Porter's School in Connecticut. *Les Demoiselles* is widely considered a breakthrough in modernism; The Eight's paintings, though avant-garde in that they depicted gritty urban life, were reactionary in technique compared to Picasso's; and though Miss Porter's was a boarding school whose students were all of Margarett's class, Margarett herself was a revolutionary in that she was the first girl in her extended family to go away to school. These juxtapositions lent vitality to my thinking and depth to my narrative. By the time I'd finished a chronology, the material for the relevant chapter was not only in my head but provocatively jumbled; if I had all my sources, I was ready to write.

There were no orderly archives of Sargent letters, no gallery that still represented her work. I had to collect materials from here and there, mostly there, and spend a lot of time on the road. At first I thought that only people who were intimately involved with Margarett were worth interviewing, but I learned that people who were merely of her ilk or generation had contributions to make. Often one vignette or remark was worth a trip of hundreds of miles, as when Margarett's slightly younger contemporary Emily Lodge, with her husband, Henry Cabot Lodge, puttering in the garden nearby, said, "Margarett took to affairs as easily as to brushing her teeth."

Sometimes a scrap of paper or a photograph suggested further investigation; once, to my astonishment, the stamp of Berenice Abbott, the American photographer who chronicled Paris in the twenties, turned up on the reverse of a particularly dramatic portrait of Margarett and suggested an entire dimension of inquiry. I went through attics, discovered forgotten suitcases of drawings and letters, met distant cousins who offered watercolors and paintings, picked through dumps, and haunted museum libraries. With intern help, I scoured newspaper archives in Boston, New York, Chicago, and the Library of Congress for lively details that would characterize an era; sometimes, in art or society pages, I'd even find a flash of reference to Margarett.

In addition, I researched people who had public careers and who were part of Margarett's life, among them Alexander Calder, a friend when they were young artists, who did wire portraits of her two daughters; Gutzon Borglum, sculptor of Mt. Rushmore, for whom she worked; and George Luks, one of The Eight, who was her mentor. Sometimes, leafing through materials about these featured players, I'd find a note or a postcard from Margarett, or much more. The artist and dealer Betty Parsons saved a sheaf of letters Margarett wrote her from a mental hospital, and her executrix passed them on to me. Though by the time I began my book, much had been discarded, my grandmother, fortunately, rarely threw anything out, and so I accumulated an abundance of material—scrapbooks, family photographs, sketchbooks: in biographical terms, a treasure trove.

As I scavenged dumps and attics, I also kept my hand in, looking for documents in more conventional ways. A notice in *The New York Times Book Review* produced a sotto voce informant who announced that Margarett had been an early muse of Archibald MacLeish and that there was a diary to prove it. In succeeding months and years, as my essay about Margarett was published and republished, I began to get letters and drawings in the mail. Soon I became aware that a kind of magic of attraction was operating.

One day, for instance, I was writing about 1919. In despair as to how to determine when Margarett stopped doing academic drawings and began to use the sophisticated modernist line that marked her maturity, I took a break and went to the post office. There in my box was a letter from a gallery in Boston that had "acquired" some drawings from the year 1919, which they found "remarkable for their Modernism."

I leapt into my car, drove to Boston, and purchased the drawings. "Where did you find them?" I asked the young woman who brought out the portfolio.

"They were found in a dumpster," she said with a rueful giggle. Twelve years earlier, when Margarett's house was emptied, neighbors picked through the refuse and saved a group of nudes, signed and dated November 1919.

As the end of Margarett's "life" neared, the momentum speeded up. Even though I lived nowhere near Boston, it began to seem that every time I went to a party, I'd meet someone who'd known Margarett or one of my characters.

As time went on, I began to surrender to this mysterious reverse in dynamic even as I interviewed. When I first began talking to people, I tended to monopolize the conversation, to steer my subject to my own interpretation of Margarett's life. Listening to my tapes, I learned that I often interrupted people just before they were about to tell me something I never would have suspected, so now I tried to let the subject guide the interview and to encourage the interviewee's anecdotes. I came to understand that I was interviewing people not to substantiate my own theories but to learn Margarett's story, a story that was, like its leading lady, full of surprises.

Once, as I was questioning a white-haired octogenarian in a wheelchair, it came to me that he must have been in love with Margarett when he was a young man, something I hadn't suspected, since he was fifteen years her junior. "Did you have a crush on Margarett when you met her?" I didn't have the nerve to be more direct.

"Yes," he snapped, "of course I did!"

In our second interview, when he unexpectedly admitted that he and Margarett had gone to bed together, I didn't miss a beat. "How was it?" I asked.

"I don't know," he said.

"What do you mean, you don't know?" I said.

"She was my first," he answered, turning his face away from my astonished gaze.

By that time I'd learned to ask questions only for clarification or when there was a break in the flow of conversation. "How did it happen?"

"She came upstairs in a negligee, carrying a candle."

I learned to ask a different kind of question, too: "Do you remember anything in particular about seeing Margarett and Shaw [her husband] together?" "What was she wearing when you first met her?" Or, "Did you go to any of her openings?" I might not get an answer to the question I asked, but often a specific inquiry would jog a long-blocked vein of recollection.

I began the process of interviewing with the older people, thinking they were most apt to die first, but ironically important younger ones checked out first, leading me to formulate what I call the biographer's zen: What you have is all you have and all you have is enough to make a book from. The zen was also useful the time my tape recorder erased half an interview for which I had no notes. After that I both taped and took notes on every interview. Eventually I transcribed every interview, then extracted events, which I dated and entered in a log I kept on legal pads so I could quickly find material for chapter outlines and during actual writing.

In the first essay of *Footsteps*, Richard Holmes chronicles a hike he took that his subject Robert Louis Stevenson had taken a hundred years before, also as a young man. Whenever I got bogged down, I'd consider taking another trip to Boston, or to another place where Margarett had lived. Even if I couldn't find an actual building at first, questioning and wandering inevitably brought me closer. Here is an example: Margarett worked for Gutzon Borglum at his country studio in Stamford, Connecticut, then an unspoiled tract of 150 acres. One Saturday, I traveled to Stamford, now a thickly settled Fairfield County suburb, and through what can only be described as divine intervention, found Borglum's stone studio still standing on "Studio Road." The stone floor of the central room where Margarett had sprayed Borglum's giant sculptures was now thickly carpeted in red, but the feel of the space communicated a sense of her time there. And, in an irony she would have appreciated, what had been the workplace of her bombastic and pretentious boss was now the home of the creator of the cartoon "Beetle Bailey."

I had imagined, when I began the book, that I would learn something about the world Margarett had moved through, but I had no idea how deep that connection would become. I thought at first that this was because I was related to her, but I have found it to be true of other biographers. Jean Strouse, who spent a dozen years on a biography of J.P. Morgan, one of the great American tycoons, still reads the business pages in depth even though the book is long finished, and Brenda Wineapple, the author of *Sister Brother*, a dual biography of Gertrude Stein and her brother Leo, is still involved, years after the book's publication, in the disposition of Leo Stein's paintings. I continue to have close friends in the art world whom I would not have met had it not been for Margarett. As I researched, I became friends with a retired French dealer who had been a longtime lover of Margarett's. He and his wife, in her fifties, took me to a restaurant where he had often taken Margarett, got drunk, and began to flirt with me in French, calling me by my grandmother's name, his wife shrieking with horror. Even though he was by then in his eighties, I got a sense of the atmosphere of their relationship.

When I began the book, I was advised to begin writing promptly, cautioned that one could research forever; so once I had material I took the plunge, continuing my research at the same time. Researching can distract from the writing, but returning to primary sources can also be a shot in the arm. On balance, it worked for me: As I wrote, I learned what sort of material I needed and what was superfluous.

I remember the first day I sat down at the typewriter (it was a typewriter!). Naturally I was overwhelmed. I had also been intimidated by my editor, who had said, "Watch it with the fervid prose." I thought that meant that I should write like a "real biographer" and so I did, mimicking the nineteenth-century texts I was then consulting about Sargent genealogy and the origins of American painting. I managed to write nearly 200 pages before Margarett's birth; my editor dubbed me the queen of detail, which I took as a compliment.

A year or so later, I gave a chapter about Margarett's debutante party to Arthur Miller, the playwright, who is my friend and neighbor. Twenty-five pages described the flowers, the decor, everyone's dress; the material was culled from Boston newspaper clippings. It was as though I were writing a poem, every flounce of taffeta or placket of beading exquisitely rendered. Another 10 pages outlined Boston etiquette of the period and the family history of one of Margarett's dance partners. Arthur Miller said, "Throw away the research and write it like a novel." When I recovered from my embarrassment, I understood that I had been taking perfectionist notes, not actually writing. "I've seen your poems," he said. "I know you can write."

Without knowing it, I had been waiting for someone to give me permission to be myself as the writer of this book. I had hoodwinked myself into believing that because I was writing in a different genre, one that veered toward the historical, I couldn't let my voice in.

Actually it was pure fear. The word *author* is not related to the word *authority* by accident. "You're the expert," Arthur said. "We get to her through you."

I came to understand what he meant. All my research, my writing and thinking and leafing through sketchbooks, had given me a sense of who Margarett was. Probably by now no one alive knew more about her than I did. What did I really think? Though I wasn't going to make anything up, I did have to bring my imagination to bear on my sources and wrest a narrative from the evocative debris that vibrated in the paintings, scrapbooks, bankers boxes, and file cabinets that filled my house.

Years later, after hearing me give a reading from *The White Blackbird*, the memoirist and poet Patricia Hampl said, "I think you learned how to write biography by being a poet." When I asked what she meant, she explained that biography makes some of the same demands on a writer that poetry does. The process of making a poem is the process of bringing aspects of experience into a diction that reconfigures them in a new and unexpected way for the reader. Sources for biography come to the writer in many different registers of language and image—historical fact, newspaper clipping, photography, testimony, anecdote, letter, journal, speculation—and require that a writer unify them into a narrative with the biographical subject at its center. Of course Margarett was not the center of American modernism, the history of women artists, or even Boston society, but she was the pivot of her own story and the force that would pull the reader through the events of her century, her geography, and her life.

For an imaginative writer, disparate sources can also offer a rich opportunity to dramatize a narrative and vary its texture. I thought cinematically. The voice of historical context would get interrupted by the voice that related a juicy event in Margarett's life. Attention to the nature of a source also had unexpected results.

When Margarett was twenty-one, she stopped keeping a diary. One day, as I was bemoaning this fact, I looked up at my bookshelf and noticed a row of Margarett's sketchbooks. Hmmm, I thought: She stopped keeping a diary but began to keep a sketchbook! I took one down, went to the computer, and began to write a description of the drawings on one page, then another and another until I had a narrative. Soon these descriptions became what I now call "animations" of her paintings and drawings. Whenever I lacked for a transition or felt disconnected from Margarett, I'd throw one in.

At one crucial point, in describing Margarett's portrait of a woman who may have been her lover, I was able to introduce her bisexuality—something I'd despaired of finding an appropriately sexy way to do. Eventually these translations from image to language became integral to the form of the book, providing a parallel narrative that interpreted and depicted Margarett's inner life.

Writing *The White Blackbird* took twelve years, in part because I had to gather and organize Margarett's work, but an agent who is a friend tells me I am not alone: She never allows a client to sign a contract for a biography with a due date less than five years from signing; she has never represented a biography that hasn't been late; and she has never known a biographer's advance to pay a living wage.

I would say that a biography finished in five years is written by a speed demon or of a subject who died at twenty-five. Writing biography is not for the faint of heart, but it is a great writing challenge and can be as profound a life-changing experience as any deep relationship. It has some of the rewards of parenthood: You bring someone to life and watch her make her way in the world, then observe the world's reactions.

And it has the satisfactions not only of literary endeavor but of scholarship—you've made a contribution, opened the door on a corner of the culture that would otherwise have remained closed. (This is true even if your subject is "famous.") In my case the satisfactions are sweet. There is now another woman artist in the American panoply; in the fall of 2001, an exhibition of Boston women artists called *A Studio of Her Own* will open at the Museum of Fine Arts in Boston, and Margarett Sargent's work will be included, something that would not have happened without the book or the exhibition I curated to accompany its publication.

I began *The White Blackbird* with a big question and finished it with a lot of answers. I learned who the man from the world of finance was and that the man at work in the mines was my grandfather. I learned that Grace Peabody was a divorcée and a classics scholar, that she, too, had poems written to her by Archibald MacLeish, and that she may have been bisexual. I never identified the sullen Bohemians, the woman dressed in a man's suit, the beautiful blonde in the strange hat. Those answers, it seems, will come only if I write a novel.

EXERCISES

Select a much older or deceased person who has meaning for you, someone you know from family stories, history, or the news (e.g. your great-aunt who mysteriously killed herself; your great-grandfather who was mayor of Bayonne, New Jersey; your mother's mother who carried the silver candlesticks across Russia in a cattle-drawn wagon; Richard Nixon; Zora Neale Hurston; Mae West). The point is to find a person to whom you are inexplicably drawn, not a celebrity or necessarily noteworthy person.

1. Find a photograph of that person and study it. Focus with all your imagination on the photograph, and write a description of it. If there is no photograph, imagine what the person looks like, and write down physical attributes as you imagine them. What you write should be the equivalent of a close-up photograph.

2. Write down everything you know about the person in a documentary way: date and place of birth, where she lived, who he married, how many children she had, what he did for a living, what she is famous for, how and when he died, etc.

3. Make a short chronology of the person's life, and then go to the library and insert public events into your chronology. You might look at old newspapers on microfilm in order to find colorful locutions, unusual incidents or a record of the weather.

4. Find a photograph of the person with other people, preferably at a different age than he or she was in the previous photograph. Study the photo and write a short piece from your subject's point of view about what you imagine was happening while the photo was being taken, or before the photograph, or outside the range of the photograph: e.g. "It was a hot day, and the photographer kept asking me to change my expression. . . ."; "My mother was watching as the picture was taken. I'll never forget the look on her face. . . ."

5. Write a short piece describing an experience you had with this person, or an experience with this person that someone described to you. If you choose an experience you have read about, tell it to us in your own words, from your own eccentric point of view.

6. Now, write a ten- to fifteen-page chunk of your subject's biography, using all that you've learned in doing the first five parts of this exercise, even utilizing bits of what you've already written. Be sure to include public as well as private events, and don't forget the sensual reality: light, temperature, sound, etc.

Not the Killing but Why

BEVERLY LOWRY

News is plot, event, what happened last night or this afternoon or is in process right now. News breaks fast, somebody writes it up, the gun's barely fired before the world's clued in. Story's a wider map and involves any number of whys, relating to personal history, family background, the times, place, cultural background, the detached perversity of genes. Story makes a stab at explanation, figuring out how such or another wonderful or terrible thing could have happened. News enjoys a brief shelf life, turns stale fast, grows a quick crust. Story addresses complicated possibilities and reasons, therefore lasts longer, maybe forever.

A magazine called, asked me to write a story about the patricide in Rush Springs, Oklahoma. Three days later, I was there. By that time—October 6, 1993—the story of the killing of Lonnie Dutton was not only two months old; it had been slurped up by every news organization in the country. National newspapers and television newscasters had been and gone. The town was wrung out with being examined, interpreted, sized up, measured, judged. *Good Morning America* described Rush Springs as sleepy. Television newscasters always call small towns sleepy. Instinct told me my first job was to prove to locals I wasn't *USA Today* or Geraldo Rivera.

Journalists call a story that's been widely covered by the media "corrupted." I know a writer who had the inside track on the inner workings of a Montana militia organization *before* the bombing of the federal building in Oklahoma City. He'd sold a well-known magazine on the story and was going down to the Bitterroot Valley on a regular basis, conducting interviews. The men had the same beefs as Timothy McVeigh. The story would break the news of what was going on out in unknown America. Then in a stunning example of bad timing, the famous magazine killed the story. Not timely, said the editor. Or anyway not timely *enough*. And by the time 137 people had been killed and the magazine changed its mind and came back to my friend to ask him to write the story now, the Bitterroot was a war zone of reporters, cameras, monitors, and trailers.

My friend said no. The story he wanted to write had lost its fire. The story he was writing, in fact, was lost. A different story had to be written, not about bombs or extremist groups themselves but the context they'd been placed in. The challenge was no longer to get people to talk and then figure out the import of what they were saying. The job had become one of rehashing, refocus, and deconstruction. And then there was the problem of the interviewees, who by becoming celebrities had turned into heroes in their own eyes.

My friend might still have written a story about the militiamen of the Bitterroot, but this was not the one he wanted to tell.

Every tale has many ways of being told. Arriving after the hoopla's peaked and the band's gone home has its place, and yields its own kind of news, with perspective impossible to come by in the heat of the happening moment.

I'm not a trained journalist, I've never worked on a newspaper, don't have a press card, only last month learned what a nut graf is. When writing feature journalism, I always arrive on the scene wondering, "What am I doing here?" I'm not alone in this. I've talked to career journalists who say the same thing. Walking up to a rank stranger who probably doesn't want to talk to you, introducing yourself cold, then making certain at every turn that you're the one in charge and what you're conducting is not a friendly conversation but an inter-view—these are not natural, or even particularly friendly, ways to behave and not a piece of cake to perform.

But imagination is perverse and the lively mind likes a challenge, and stories based on event and facts drew me from my fictional desk, and I found I loved the work. Liked the road, the unease, the blank pages ahead that other people would help me fill. On the road, you always learn something (though often not what you came for). You meet people you never would otherwise have sat down with in your life (and often never wish to again). Writing a feature story, you have to use all your fiction-writing skills except making things up, then you have to make the fictional techniques work with the information you've gathered and the commentaries you've managed to come up with.

I flew to Oklahoma City, rented a car, drove to Chickasa, the Grady County seat, where I had an appointment with the district attorney. But the DA had changed his mind. His assistant, a sizable young woman with a long yellow braid and many perky stuffed animals on the file cabinet, announced that there was a gag rule, and anyway, he had no comment to make on the Dutton case.

I checked into a motel. The room smelled like a sports bar the morning after. I checked out, found a better room, and drove to Rush Springs. On the way I passed that billboard saying "Socialism is Wrong." In Rush Springs, I drove around then parked, bought a soft drink and some chips, walked down the downtown sidewalk and then back up it.

I'd had a tooth pulled that morning. I'd told the dentist I couldn't interview people with a gap so he inserted a temporary bridge. The bridge poked at my gum. I was on pain pills. At the motel there'd been a phone call from my boyfriend, accusing me of dancing too provocatively with a local poet the night before. And I'd only been in Oklahoma a couple of hours.

I'd been through the state a couple of times going north from Texas to somewhere, but had not spent one night in Oklahoma since high school, when I went with the band to play in a regional concert contest in Enid. I think we did Dvorák, the "New World Symphony." On the way, I sat on the back bench of the bus, got sick from carbon monoxide fumes, threw up on my skirt. Next day, we went on a tour of Oral Roberts University. That was about all I knew of Oklahoma.

Blue ribbons were still tied on the lampposts in support of the Dutton boys. I stood on the sidewalk and pondered possibilities. Who'll talk to me? Who wants to talk to one more outsider? Who *might* want to talk? I stepped off the curb and crossed the street and walked into the offices of the local newspaper, a weekly mostly given to reports of civic club meetings, the PTA, and that week's homecoming football game.

It wasn't much of a paper but odds were the editor had a newspaper background, or came from a newspaper family. And if she did, she'd have a sense of the story yet to be told.

At some point you go with what instinct tells you. You walk in the door—*a* door, some door—with confidence and you introduce yourself; and no matter how well you've prepared—notes taken, questions listed, articles read—you are, at that moment, winging it. You're alone and you're working and the tooth socket doesn't matter and neither does the boyfriend. You're in unknown territory. You marshal your wits, gather up your best imitation of nonchalance, turn the door handle, step in.

You are operating on instinct and the need to know.

One foot in front of the other. Let them do the talking.

One question may or may not lead to the next. You ask it anyway.

Hope for the best, swing with the results, follow up with another.
This never changes.

EXERCISES

1. Set up an interview with someone you don't know. Explain why you want to talk to the person. The story you are after may be an event of some consequence or of little significance at all. Prepare questions. Do your homework. Be ready to explore new territory when unexpected news comes your way. Write the story. Fit the interview into the story, using direct quotes only when they contribute to the story you are telling and move the story along.

2. Go to a neighborhood that is new to you. Describe it. Watch the people. Say what they look like and how they interact with one another. Remain anonymous. Make general observations based on what you see and hear (e.g., if people on this block tend to be especially loud and shrill, why? Can you come up with a theory?). Bring the story to you. Make it yours.

3. Perform the same exercises in third person. The story is still yours and you are still forming theories and suggesting possibilities but you do not speak as an "I."

4. Think of a story that has already been written as news and write it from your own perspective. Make sure it's a story you are drawn to and that, for you, poses unanswered questions, such as, How could this have happened? Talk to people, read articles, stories, or books that have already been written. Try to think of something that happened in a place you can actually visit.

Every Hell Is Different:
Notes on War Writing

CHRISTOPHER MERRILL

W"ar is hell," General Sherman famously remarked. And just as every hell is different—cf. Dante's *Inferno*, Milton's *Paradise Lost*, Sartre's *Huis Clos*—so is every war. There are indeed no rules for writing about war, except that you must survive long enough to put pen to paper. Better still to carve out time to reflect deeply on this fundamental human experience, the cornerstone of the Western literary tradition. It is no accident that our literature is rooted in *The Iliad*. And Homer's ghost hovers somewhere in the back of every war correspondent's mind: How to tell the story in all its complexity? How to sort out fact from fiction? How to honor the dead? These were the sorts of questions I asked myself in researching and composing *Only the Nails Remain: Scenes From the Balkan Wars*, the fifteenth chapter of which is excerpted on pages 283–298.

Keats's praise of negative capability—"that is when man is capable of being in uncertainties, Mysteries, doubts, without any irritable reaching after fact & reason"—seems to me to be a good definition not only of the poet's obligations to his materials and language but also of the writer's responsibilities in a war zone. When lives are at stake, the publication of a factual error or misinterpretation of events can have tragic consequences; when propaganda is the order of the day, writers must take care not to jump to conclusions about the progress of the war. It was my working principle to talk to people, particularly writers and artists, on all sides of the conflict—no small task in the Yugoslav wars of succession, which not only presented a maze of hostilities but also difficult travel conditions. For example, when Croatian authorities refused to let me cross the border into Montenegro, I had to journey an extra two thousand kilometers by bus, plane, and train just to ask the commanding officer of the Montenegrin forces why he had allowed his troops to raze so many villages along the Dalmatian coast—a story the Croats might have wished to read.

I had been traveling in the Balkans for the better part of a year when the events narrated in this chapter occurred. And when in the spring of 1993 I boarded a military transport plane in Split, Croatia, a humanitarian flight bound for the besieged capital of Sarajevo, I had hundreds of pages of notes—and no clear idea of how to write a book on the war, the advance for which I had already spent. *Maybe Airlines* was what the peacekeepers called the airlift destined to eclipse the Berlin airlift in length and scope, and on this C-130 peacekeepers, humanitarians, and journalists were crammed against crates of food and medicine. The plane made an assault landing at Butmir Airport, the front line between government and Serbian forces, then taxied quickly to the terminal, which was surrounded by sandbags and barbed wire.

There we climbed into an armored personnel carrier (APC) for the drive into the city, which had no gas, water, or electricity. It was stifling in the crowded APC, and at each checkpoint the soldiers went through our papers very slowly. Twisted shells of buildings rose above the Milačka River. Cars sped along "Sniper's Alley," where all manner of shields had been raised—dumpsters, slabs of concrete, sheets of rusted iron—to offer some protection to pedestrians, who ran along the sidewalk with their heads down.

A year into the longest siege in modern history, Sarajevo was a shattered place.

Serbian gunners in the surrounding hills rained down a thousand shells a day into the city, damaging or destroying nearly every house and building; snipers shot civilians, especially women and children, with astonishing regularity. For food, Sarajevans relied on the airlift and the black market. It was a desperate situation, not least because the arms embargo the international community had imposed on Yugoslavia prevented the ragtag government forces from defending themselves. Thus gallows humor reigned. One joke making the rounds was particularly dark: What is the difference between Auschwitz and Sarajevo? At least in Auschwitz they had gas.

Nevertheless I had been tipped off that the Bosnians would soon try to break the siege, and when the uneasy calm during my first days in the city ended one Saturday morning in a hail of shellfire, I followed several humanitarians to the basement of the house they were renting: a familiar place for Sarajevans during the siege. No one knew how long we might have to stay, and in my terror I took notes, not because I expected to survive, but because the act of writing calmed me down. I recorded almost every conversation, story, and joke. I described my surroundings in minute detail. I timed the intervals between the rare outgoing *pop* of a Bosnian grenade and the ensuing blizzard of Serbian shells. Thus by the time we went to bed, in makeshift conditions, I had a fairly complete set of notes from one day of life in a basement under fire.

I also had a bad back, having wrenched it during a lull in the bombardment, in a dive away from a sniper's bullet. But my injury turned out to be a blessing in disguise. In the morning, unable to walk, I decided to take a humanitarian flight back to Split, intending to recuperate and then return. No sooner did I reach my hotel, however, than I began to shake uncontrollably.

Nerves, I thought. Typhus, said the doctor who took my temperature the next morning—106 degrees. Maybe dysentery. Indeed I had drunk some bad water in Sarajevo. By then I was delirious, and of the next several days what I remember most vividly is the pleasure the nurses seemed to take in letting my intravenous bottles run dry. I was sharing a room with two convalescing Croatian soldiers, who liked to watch my arm swell, or so I imagined, since only they could convince the nurses to bring me a new bottle, and they sometimes waited as long as an hour to call for help.

My fever was breaking early one morning, when I heard a snatch of music from a radio in another room, the title track of *Brothers in Arms*. "Every man has to die," sang the vocalist from Dire Straits. I sat up in bed. I had heard the song only once before, in the darkening corridor of a hotel in Dubrovnik, after a long day in a village razed by paramilitaries. And now the music struck me with particular force. All at once I had a vision—there is no other word for it—of how to organize my book, and I lay in the dark, buoyantly plotting out a triptych of the Balkan wars: The opening section would be set in Slovenia, the first Yugoslav republic to win independence; the second would recount my journey through Croatia, Serbia, Montenegro, Kosovo, Macedonia, Bulgaria, Turkey, and Greece; the third would tell the story of the war in Bosnia, beginning with one day of life in the basement—where Sarajevans had spent all too many days and nights.

I wanted to give the reader a sense of what life was like under siege. And I imagined that if I devoted one chapter to describing what happened in that basement, I might be able to catch an essential element about this war, which was waged in large part against civilians. (The joke in Sarajevo was that if you were in the military you had a better chance of surviving the siege than anyone else.)

Of course by daylight my euphoria had worn off, and months would pass before I was well enough to return to Sarajevo. My travels in Bosnia had only begun, and I would have to read hundreds of books of history, politics, and literature in order to better understand what I had experienced in these various war zones. But I had glimpsed a way to write the book.

The "New" Literature

CAROLYN FORCHÉ

... while I knew nothing about New Journalism when I was in Africa, I can see now that New Journalism was just the beginning, in liquidating the border between fact and fiction. But New Journalism was ultimately just journalism describing the strangeness of America. I think we have gone beyond that. It is not a New Journalism, but a New Literature.
—*Ryszard Kapuściński*

In September 1978, a young photographer in New York City glimpsed televised news footage of soldiers shooting civilians in the streets of Estelí, Nicaragua, a town he had visited several years earlier while traveling through Central America.

"This was not an imaginary place, nor was it a foreign city I couldn't locate on a map. It was a place I had been, where people I knew still lived. The horror on the screen was, in the literal sense, incredible. I had to see for myself."

He quit his construction job, and within a week, Harry Mattison was one of only two foreigners in Estelí as the city came under aerial bombardment by government forces.

"The high ground, including the church on the central plaza, was controlled by snipers and a single tank. You couldn't move easily because these forces had a direct line of fire down all streets. I was with a group of young Sandinista fighters. Eight of them. They wanted to take me across town to a place where civilians had been killed.

"As each person ran across the street, the others provided covering fire from both sides. The first five or six people made it across. Then it was my turn. With my heart leaping in my chest, I ran the ten-yard distance to the safety of the far wall, but while I ran there was no covering fire. When I reached safety, I turned to the young man next to me and asked 'Why didn't you fire?' He looked at me and smiled.

'We don't waste bullets for gringos.' It took me a while to smile back."

Mattison spoke fluent Spanish, and had traveled and lived in Latin American countries during most of his twenties, but the Estelí bombing was his first experience in a war zone. He showed me the notes he wrote at the time:

"Outside, one concussive explosion after another. People are hiding under sacks of grain, and pulling boxes of supplies over their bodies. A woman soldier with a broken foot sits smoking a cigar. She laughs derisively at a boy who has pulled a great bundle over his torso. 'Those are boxes of tissues, you fool.' Sacks of corn, coffee, and sugar line one wall. Everyone prefers this wall to the wall with the bottles of soda and ketsup.

"Deserted farm houses, dogs barking, fear of open fields.

"The wet ground seems to take my body in—no branches break, no voices. Ten minutes. Fifteen. We agree to move—."

From Mexico City, *Time* correspondent Ed Boyer filed this:

"Estelí. The last remaining rebel stronghold was in flames Tuesday night as photographers Harry Mattison and Hector Carballo made their way from the ravaged city back to Managua. Mattison, on assignment for *Time*, and Carballo from the Argentinian magazine *Somos*, had spent 52 hours in the coffee and tobacco center, 99 miles north of Managua, as heavy arms fire from Nicaraguan National Guardsmen increasingly intensified. . . . Says Mattison: 'The National Guard was firing indiscriminately into the town—rockets, automatic weapons, 50-caliber machine guns, cannons. The rockets made a terrifying swoosh before they exploded. . . . The rockets and 50-caliber machine gun rounds came right through the corrugated metal roofs on some houses, and the machine gun fire tore large chunks of adobe from the walls. . . . Strafing from planes was coming every minute; tiles were flying from the houses. During all this, an old couple who said they had been married sixty years sat in their doorway in rocking chairs. . . . Monday morning. A young mother with an infant child in her arms went out looking for milk near the town's cathedral which was held by the guard. She and her baby were cut down by machine gun fire.' Mattison reports having seen a ten-year-old boy dragged from his house and shot. Another six to eight young teenagers were lined up against a wall and summarily shot by guardsmen. A fourteen-year-old boy was tortured by guardsmen who cut open his chest with a knife. The blood-spattered corpse of another infant lay in the street."

The file went on to explain that "To get into Estelí Sunday, Mattison and Carballo left their car on the Pan American highway about eight miles south of the town. From there, they were guided by rebels around the town to a farm house on its northern approaches. From the farm house an eight-year-old boy guided them into town across an open field where they came under fire from National Guard snipers. 'I didn't get scared then,' says Mattison. 'Fear began the next day.' Three other photographers who had gone in with Mattison and Carballo opted to leave as the fighting intensified. Once in town, Mattison and Carballo were immediately taken to the Sandinista commander, a man dressed 'as I imaged Confederate soldiers were dressed during the Civil War. His clothes were ragged and his frayed boots were held together by string.'

"Heavy rains had fallen in the area during most of the fighting," the file concluded, "and the two photographers, led by a succession of rebel guides, made their way out through ankle-deep mud over rugged mountain terrain. After twelve hours of walking, they made it back to their car to begin the two-hour drive back to Managua, where they arrived drenched and caked with mud."

Forty-eight hours after the bombing, Mattison returned to New York with his photographs, and as he entered the newsroom at Time, Inc., again there were images of Nicaragua flickering on the television monitors. A voice-over reciting the clinical litany of carnage "made the deaths sound like data."

The bombing, carried out by the Nicaraguan Air Force, resulted in civilian casualties in the town of Estelí, among them families attempting to flee . . .

This was the language of the official report, but Mattison had listened for days to the wounded and dying of Estelí, translating and transcribing their testimony in his private notebooks. He became what we have come to call a "bridge person," who moves between cultures and realities, bearing one language into another, the isolated world of brutal experience into the preserved and protected world at once distanced and implicated. Here is one such story:

> The three of us crouched in a corner of the house, trembling and crying all at once, thinking that surely we would die here, as the bullets and shrapnel were destroying our small wooden home. We decided to leave and try to find a safer place to hide, so we went out through the back, through the kitchen, my husband carrying our young daughter in his arms. A plane flew very low; it seemed to be coming directly at us, firing rockets all in a burst, striking my daughter in the back and my husband as he carried her. From where I was, only a few paces behind them, I saw only the heart and entrails of my child. She seemed to have been blown apart. My husband stumbled some thirty

steps with his arms torn away, blood pouring out of him, until he fell dead. There was a great hole in his chest. Part of a still smoking rocket was lodged in one leg; the other was stripped of all flesh to the bone. I wanted to pick up my daughter but there were only pieces of her. I was desperate. I ran and found her arm and tried to put it back on her, tried to put back everything that had spilled out of her, but she was already dead. She was my only child, and it was hard for me to have her. I always dressed her myself for parties and I spoiled her. I don't know what I am going to do . . . I think I am going to go crazy . . .

In the "objective" language of the official story, there would be no human interlocutor; no living and breathing being would have listened to a mother speak about attempting to rejoin her child's arm to her child's corpse. We would not have been told that the rocket in her husband's leg was still smoking, nor that the other leg had been "stripped of all flesh to the bone." If the mother were to be quoted, her story would have been "balanced" by a comment from the Air Force or the Ministry of Defense. A building or an institution would have spoken in the government's defense: The White House or the Presidential Palace in Managua would have issued a "statement." We would not have heard the mother's desperate grief, nor her difficulty with childbirth, much less her concern about maintaining sanity. The reporter would have dutifully produced a language devoid of sentiment, a laboratory language of detached observation, calculated to simulate "fact," as if the family were a statistic diligently recorded in the unfortunate economy of minor warfare. At the very least, the mother would never have been presented as attempting to reassemble her child.

Both this account and the reporter's would have been "accurate." Both would have been factual. One would have been broadcast on the nightly news. One would have appeared in the newspapers of major American cities in the morning.

THE HUMAN TRUTH OF CREATIVE NONFICTION

There is a difference, then, between journalism and the new literature of creative nonfiction. But that genre had not yet recognized itself in its current form, and Mattison kept his nonfiction writings private. He could have written a personal memoir of his experience as a combat photographer, and might have included this dramatic scene, but it would have been presented as an experience in a young photographer's life, framed by a North American's fear and anxiety, his compassion and sensitivity, culminating in speculation about how this incident had been "epiphanic," producing a spark of realization that had transformed his life. The mother attempting to put her child's arm back onto her child's body would have disappeared behind the larger figure of the North American portraying himself as a character in his own— even if interesting—life. Mattison was averse to this. While being interviewed for a book about war photographers, he was once asked how he was able to witness so much horror and yet live a "normal life" in a world apart from it.

"That is a question about a photographer," he said at the time. "Ask me a question about photography.

"The chief of correspondents told me that the war in Nicaragua was a small matter, of no importance unless U.S. interests were at stake. I lacked the experience, he said, to place the bombing of Estelí in an appropriate context. He was a kindly man, and in retrospect, perhaps he was right. But I would not have done what I did had I listened to him."

What he did was to pick up film from *Time*'s photographic bureau, along with an air ticket back to Managua, where he spent the next two years. During the following decade, he worked in El Salvador, Beirut, South Africa, Angola, Zimbabwe, and Northern Ireland.

We met in El Salvador in a makeshift refugee camp in March 1980: a poet and translator turned human rights activist, and a photographer who had moved from the streets of New York to the world's proxy wars. Both of us kept notebooks, but I was "expected" to write poetry and Harry was "expected" to put himself in the line of fire and make newsworthy photographs for world media. Neither of us was comfortable in the work of "manufacturing consent." I joined him in Beirut for the winter of 1984, working as a correspondent to National Public Radio's *All Things Considered*, whose director wanted "prose poems from the front lines." We courted in Beirut, and married before leaving for state-of-siege South Africa during the last days of apartheid. Our son, Sean, was born during the spring and summer of the Paris bombings, and by December we returned to the United States to teach and lecture and work on projects with unemployed mine workers and inner-city housing-project residents.

PRACTICAL ADVICE FOR A SAFE RETURN

The question we are most often asked when speaking before groups of students is this: "How can I go overseas and do what you have done?"

"There isn't really a way to prepare for this kind of work," Mattison admits. We've both found it difficult to advise anyone else, and have also been reluctant to assume responsibility for suggesting methods and itineraries. After advising one young man to go to Chad in the mid-eighties, because it was a country then at peace and I thought he could learn something there without incurring great risk, Chad became a war zone. I have stopped making suggestions.

But had we listened to people who advocate caution, and who err on the side of safe return, we wouldn't have done what we did.

Here, then, is our list of admonitions and advice to people who are now as young as we once were:

• Learn the language spoken in the region or country in which you would like to work. Be aware that language usage may identify you ideologically or give the perception that you are affiliated with one side or another. This also applies to word usage within a language: "guerilla Spanish" is different from "army Spanish." Your vocabulary, jargon, tone, and slang may say more about you than you would wish.

• Read about the history, culture, economics, and politics of the country or region in advance. Don't limit your reading to recent books by journalists.

• Research nonprofits and nongovernmental organizations (NGOs) in advance to determine those that are the most neutral, respected, and trustworthy. Confirm this information when you arrive, and be sure to meet with representatives of these organizations. My recommendations would include Médecins Sans Frontières/Doctors Without Borders, Amnesty International, Helsinki Watch, Oxfam, and The American Friends' Field Service.

• Keep in mind that your nationality, as an American citizen, is not necessarily perceived as "neutral." You arrive with the political baggage of your country's foreign policy, as it is publicly articulated and understood.

• When you arrive, try to meet with cultural and intellectual figures: writers, filmmakers, poets.

• When you analyze media reports, notice which voices are missing or silenced. Talk to the people who have not spoken or been heard.

• There are "official" and "nonofficial" information sources. The latter are often the most interesting.

• If possible, go to U.S. sources last, after you have traveled around the country, and developed your own relationships and impressions.

• Learn about the infrastructure of the country: What are your lines of communication (Internet? telephone? television? radio?)? What are your means of transportation within the country, and what are the available routes out? Know the airports, flight schedules, trains, buses. If you need to leave the country, you might need to have access to more than one means. Within the country, the slowest and cheapest form of transportation is often best; it provides the most contact with the majority.

- Obtain all necessary visas in advance; carry "letters of introduction" with you; have at hand the telephone numbers of lawyers, family, friends, consular officer, etc.
- Be discreet. Do not volunteer information about other people's whereabouts or identities.
- Keep your notebooks, passport, and equipment with you at all times.
- Guard against romanticizing or exoticizing the country, culture, or circumstances. It is dangerous to idealize people under any circumstances, but particularly so during periods of intense political conflict.
- It is not necessary to expose oneself to combat; the most compelling experiences of war are found at the periphery, in the ways people survive and endure despite the violence surrounding them.
- Never handle or pose with weapons.
- Never agree to carry messages, money, or packages.
- See as much as you can, talk to as many people as you can; save research for later. Anything that can be found in a library at home can wait.
- Periodically, make copies of your notes and send them home by reliable means (DHL or courier).
- It is safest to assume that you are monitored, but this does not necessarily indicate that you are being singled out; surveillance is often routine.
- Try not to draw unnecessary attention to yourself: Dress modestly and without ostentation (no expensive jewelry, watches, etc.). Don't carry large sums of money.
- Always let someone know where you are and what you are doing.
- Remember that you are a guest. People don't to have to talk to you; they don't have to help you; they don't have to risk their lives to protect you or to facilitate your project. Comport yourself with humility and grace. What you will learn as an outsider will largely depend on your host's estimation of your seriousness. A Native Athabascan (Alaskan) elder once approached a writer with this question: "Tell me how long you are staying in our village and I'll tell you what you are going to write. One day? Newspaper article. One week? Magazine article. One month? Scholarly article. One year? Book."

JOURNALISTIC ETHICS

The profession of journalism adopted a code of ethics from the American Society of Newspaper Editors in 1926. The Society of Professional Journalists (formerly Sigma Delta Chi) wrote its own code in 1973, which was revised in 1984 and 1987. While literary nonfiction is quite distinct from reportage, it is not exempt from ethical practice and standards. These excerpted provisions of the code might serve to guide the writer of creative nonfiction:

- Test the accuracy of information from all sources and exercise care to avoid inadvertent error. Deliberate distortion is never permissible.
- Identify sources whenever feasible.
- Always question sources' motives before promising anonymity. Clarify conditions attached to any promise made in exchange for information. Keep promises.
- Avoid undercover or other surreptitious methods of gathering information except when traditional methods will not yield information vital to the public. Use of such methods should be explained as part of the story.
- Never plagiarize.
- Tell the story of the diversity and magnitude of the human experience boldly, even when it is unpopular to do so.
- Examine [your] own cultural values and avoid imposing those values on others.
- Avoid stereotyping by race, gender, age, religion, ethnicity, geography, sexual orientation, disability, physical appearance, or social status.
- Treat sources, subjects, and colleagues as human beings deserving of respect.
- Show compassion for those who may be affected adversely [by the publication of your writing].
- Recognize that private people have a greater right to control information about themselves than do public officials and others who seek power, influence, or attention. Only an overriding public need can justify intrusion into anyone's privacy.
- Show good taste. Avoid pandering to lurid curiosity.
- Avoid conflicts of interest, real or perceived.
- Remain free of associations and activities that may compromise integrity or damage credibility.
- Disclose unavoidable conflicts.
- Be vigilant and courageous about holding those with power accountable.

THE AUTHENTIC "I" WITNESS

In an early interview in *Granta*, the Polish writer Ryszard Kapuściński attempted to explain the genre that has come to be called Creative Nonfiction in the United States. "Twenty years ago, I was in Africa, and this is what I saw: I went from revolution to coup d'etat, from one war to another; I witnessed, in effect, history in the making, real history, contemporary history, our history. But I was also surprised: I never saw a writer. I never met a poet or philosopher—even a sociologist. Where were they? Such important events, and not a single writer anywhere? . . .

". . . Why am I a writer? Why have I risked my life so many times, come so close to dying? Is it to report the weirdness? To earn my salary? Mine is not a vocation, it's a mission. I wouldn't subject myself to these dangers if I didn't feel that there was something overwhelmingly important—about history, about ourselves—that I felt compelled to get across. This is more than journalism.

"The traditional trick of literature is to obscure the writer, to express the story through a fabricated narrator describing a fabricated reality. But for me, what I have to say is validated by the fact that I was there, that I witnessed the event. There is, I admit, a certain egoism in what I write, always complaining about the heat or the hunger or the pain I feel, but it is terribly important to have what I write authenticated by its being lived. You could call it, I suppose, personal reportage, because the author is always present. I sometimes call it literature by foot."

If Kapuściński's work diverges from "fabricated" literature, it also diverges from journalism's insistence on the construction of "objectivity" (and also from journalism's current collaboration with its corporate sponsorship).

"You know," he said, "sometimes the critical response to my books is amusing. There are so many complaints: Kapuściński never mentions dates, Kapuściński never gives the name of the minister, he has forgotten the order of events. All that, of course, is exactly what I avoid. If those are questions you want answered, you can visit your local library, where you will find everything you need: the newspapers of the time, the reference books, a dictionary.

". . . You know, sometimes, in describing what I do, I resort to the Latin phrase silva rerum: the forest of things. That's my subject: the forest of things, as I've seen it, living and traveling in it. To capture the world, you have to penetrate it as completely as possible. . . . As a writer, you have experienced this event in your own skin, and it is your experience, this feeling along the surface of your skin, that gives your story its coherence: it is what is at the center of the forest of things. I sometimes call it literature by foot."

CRIMES OF WAR—A HANDBOOK FOR WRITERS

In assembling one's rucksack for this kind of work, it might be helpful to include a copy of *Crimes of War: What the Public Should Know*, edited by Roy Gutman and David Rieff, and published by W.W. Norton and Company in 1999, on the eve of the fiftieth anniversary of the Geneva Conventions.

The book was "conceived as a handbook for reporters," according to its editors, "but just as war is too important to be left to the generals, war coverage is too important to be left uncritically to the news media. . . . Understanding what is going on in the midst of all the havoc, confusion, and disinformation is anything but simple. And almost nothing in their training prepares reporters to be able to make the necessary distinctions between legal, illegal, and criminal acts."

Crimes of War is a guide for writers, human rights activists, relief and aid workers, and others to the intricacies of international law bearing upon human conduct in armed conflict. The entries, in alphabetical arrangement, comprise a litany of horrific if essential knowledge, including aggression, apartheid, biological weapons, blockade as act of war, carpet or area bombing, child soldiers, civilian immunity, combatant status, concentration camps, death squads, deportation, disappearances, due process, ethnic cleansing, executions—extrajudicial, forced labor, genocide, hors de combat, hostages, humanitarian aid, immunity from attack, internal displacement, journalists in peril, just and unjust war, levée en masse, limited war, mass graves, medical transports, mines, nuclear weapons, occupation, pillage, prisoner of war camps, Red Cross, refugees, safety zones, sanctions, siege, starvation, torture, unlawful confinement, victims—rights of, war crimes, willful killing, water supplies and works—destruction of.

AN EXAMINATION OF CONSCIENCE

The final preparation before departure might consist of an examination of conscience: What are my motivations? A work conceived for commercial gain will perhaps provide material enrichment but is unlikely to achieve literary worth. The experience of danger does not build character; it merely exposes it. A journey undertaken for self discovery may lead to a better awareness of self, but the very important "other" may remain hidden.

One writes "by foot" in the world in order to enlarge what Harry Mattison has called "the circle of intimacy," closing the distance between humans in peril and at peace. When one undertakes such a work, one agrees to be forever changed, and henceforth to become a walker of bridges between worlds, a translator of realities, comfortably at ease everywhere and nowhere, in service to others and the word.

Surviving Overseas

BOB REISS

By two in the morning I knew something was wrong. All day I'd been ignoring symptoms. The joint pain had started in late morning, while I was interviewing a gold miner. The abdominal aches had come when I was interviewing a cop. Now, lying in bed in my Amazon hotel, I realized that the night had turned oddly chilly. I covered myself with an extra blanket, but kept getting colder.

Suddenly my body went into convulsions. I was freezing and began throwing up. I made it to the bathroom, but I was losing vision at the edges, and for the next few hours I alternated between bed and toilet, between shaking with cold and burning with fever. The sheets were drenched. I couldn't keep food down. At a Brazilian hospital, the next morning, a doctor drew blood for a malaria test.

"It's negative," he told me. "But we'll never know if you had a single occurrence, and the antimalarial you're taking stopped it. What medicine are you taking?"

"Lariam," I said.

"Good. The malaria strains here are resistant to other drugs."

I thought, at the time, how grateful I was to have taken the right preparations before leaving on that three-month research trip to write about tropical rain forests.

And since then, each time I leave on an overseas trip, I've tried to remember, in the rush of preparations, how important it is to have a checklist in mind when traveling. The list can keep you healthier, aid your work, save you money, and get you home safely. My list has helped me, and I'd like to share it with you.

1. Take the proper medical precautions before leaving on your trip. This sounds fairly basic, but not all doctors know how to prepare you for trips to remote parts of the world. Your doctor should be able to refer to you to the right specialist, or you can

call your local hospital; some travel clinics are even listed in the yellow pages. Make sure you get the right inoculations. Some immunity regimens require a series of shots over several weeks or months to be effective, so give yourself time to complete the regimen. Make sure, if you are going to an area where malaria exists, that you have the proper antimalarial.

Also, always take a medical kit, and stock it with an antibiotic against respiratory disease, another antibiotic to combat stomach parasites, and Flagyl, which kills amoebas. A good travel doctor will supply you with this stuff as a precaution. Don't use it until you are sure you are sick, and if you do use it, follow whatever directions your doctor gave you.

Stay away from uncooked vegetables in rougher parts of the world. Boil drinking water, and carry iodine pills to disinfect water. Eat only fruit you can peel. But be prepared at a certain point . . . when you're in a jungle village . . . when you've not eaten for two days . . . when your poverty-stricken host puts a meal in front of you that he used his last reserves of cash to buy . . . to eat the thing and smile anyway. It *will* happen. If you're heading to a remote part of the earth, assume you *will* get sick.

Many parasites don't show up for weeks after infecting you, so make sure after you get home that you watch for the telltale signs; bloating, gas, unexplained fever, or diarrhea that comes on a month after you've returned from Africa could very well be caused by a parasite you ate. Make sure you have a doctor who understands tropical diseases and will be able to diagnose what you have.

Also, in the medical kit, include vitamin C to supplement diet, aspirin, bandages, a few PowerBars in case the only available food in a place is something you'd better not eat, an antibacterial wash, a good sunblock, and, if you're heading into a jungle, vodka. An old United Press International reporter once told me, "You can drink it, disinfect cuts with it, and use it as a rub to cool off. But watch where you use it, though. Once I rubbed myself down with it before interviewing a bishop. He thought I was a lush."

2. Don't assume people everywhere speak English. And if it looks like no one speaks English, don't assume people do not understand what you are saying.

One of the biggest misconceptions in the world is "everyone there speaks English." Americans often find it hard to believe that elsewhere in the world, people use other languages. You may have to hire an interpreter, so make sure before you go that you can afford one.

The flip side of this, however, is always be careful what you say in English, because you never know who *does* understand. In Brazil, I once visited a cattle rancher named Joao Branco, who was thought to have been the mastermind behind the murder of an Amazon rubber tapper union leader. When I visited Joao Branco's office, Branco and my interpreter began a spirited exchange in Portuguese during which Branco asked what I wanted.

I explained to the interpreter that I didn't want to ask about the murder (which was true at the time) but about ranching. I said I had no preconceived notions about Branco's guilt. I had an open mind. At that point, Joao, a big, imposing man, gazed directly into my eyes and said in perfect English, "OK, fellow, I'll talk to you. What do you want to know?"

3. Try to make contacts in a place before you get there. Going to another country? Do as much reading about it as possible before you go, and try to make a contact at that country's embassy or UN delegation. Phone. Write. Go in person. Contact the press office, explain what you are doing, and ask if they can provide names of people to talk to in their country. It's their job to get favorable publicity for their country, and they are often glad to steer you in certain directions, and even help arrange interviews for you. If they cooperate, your job will be much easier, and you will instantly be accepted as legitimate.

The same goes for opposition groups to a government. They often have spokespeople, offices, or sympathizers in the U.S. Talk to these people before you go.

If the country you plan to visit has a free press, and a newspaper or wire service in the U.S., call the reporters there and ask them for suggestions for sources. I had to go to India while researching a book on climate recently, and Indian journalists in the U.S. provided e-mail addresses of their colleagues in Delhi. The colleagues were of tremendous help in getting stories.

4. Carry journalist ID if possible. The more legitimate you look, the better access you get. It is always good to have a letter from a publisher or magazine saying that you are "writing an article for it" and that "all help will be appreciated." Even if the magazine has not given you an official assignment, and you're funding

the trip yourself, contact a magazine and try to get an editor to provide a letter. The editor might do it if she thinks you may come up with a good piece, and because it guarantees the editor the first look at what you produce. The letter costs nothing to write, but a magazine letterhead gives you instant respectability.

If the story you plan to write about is a conflict, it can help to carry two or three letters of identification, each describing your work in slightly different terms. When I was in Sudan several years ago, covering food relief in a rebel area, during a war, the letter I showed the rebels indicated some sympathy for their position. The one I showed Sudanese government representatives said I had "serious questions" about the rebels. The letter for food relief people indicated I had an open mind. All these statements were literally true but gave different impressions.

If you do manage to get a letter, or better yet, obtain magazine stationery on which you can write your *own* letter, make sure the letter *never* says you are a "freelance writer." To most people, a "freelance writer" is unemployed, a wanna-be, an amateur, a supplicant wasting their time. "Freelance writer" means there's 5 percent chance that anything you write will actually get published.

So if you *are* a freelance writer, and someone asks about it, try like hell to avoid the words. Say you're a "student," if that's true. Or that you're "fascinated with the subject." Tell the questioner, "Very few magazine writers are full-time employees of magazines." Flash your ID letter. Most important, *act* like you're supposed to be there. No matter how insecure you might feel inside, don't show it. If a source senses that *you* are unsure about yourself, *he* will be unsure, too.

5. Obtain free air tickets. It may be hard to believe that an airline might actually give you free air tickets, but it happens. Many national airlines are eager for publicity, and if you have an assignment from a travel magazine . . . or even from a general interest magazine, and your piece might show the country in a good light, *and only if your magazine allows you to do this*, phone the PR department of the appropriate airline. Ask if it makes deals with writers where they exchange free tickets for mentioning the airline.

Over the years I've flown free to Sydney, Nairobi, Hong Kong, Santiago, Johannesburg, and Rio de Janeiro, among other places, in return for this kind of deal. You can seamlessly and accurately insert the airline into most pieces. You write something like, "From the First Class window of the LanChile 747, I looked down on the gorgeous snow-covered Andes," which is true when you fly to Chile. If the service is good, and your magazine allows you, you write something like, "Sipping fine Chilean Merlot as my LanChile Airbus flew south, I gazed down at some of the most lovely peaks in Latin America," which is also true when you fly over that country. The airline is happy. The magazine is happy. You are happy. And you told the truth.

6. Be prepared to use a "fixer," but make sure the "fixer" is the right choice. A fixer is someone you pay in a foreign country to help you get an interview, a car, a document you need. A fixer can be crucial to your work in unstable areas of the world, and if he's the right person, he's worth what you pay. But watch whom you pick.

Several years ago, on assignment from a magazine, I faxed Somali clan leader Hussein Aidid asking for an interview in Mogadishu, at his residence. Aidid's father had been responsible for the death of U.S. soldiers. Aidid the son had lived in California and been a U.S. Marine.

Two days later someone called me from Toronto, Canada, claiming to be Aidid's cousin, clearly having read my fax, and offering to arrange the interview. So far everything sounded good. But then the "cousin" wanted me to pay for his airfare to Somalia. When I refused, he started bargaining. Would I pay half his airfare? Would I pay at least for his hotel rooms on the way?

At the magazine, we decided not to do it. The "fixer" clearly had connections to Aidid or he never would have read my fax. But the money demands were excessive and suspicious. I located Aidid's sister in Italy and routed the request through her, and when Aidid said yes I flew to Nairobi, the jumping-off point for Somalia.

So far things looked good again.

But the "fixer" turned out to be in Nairobi, too, as part of Aidid's staff. Apparently he had been scheduled to fly to Somalia anyway on Aidid's money but had planned on cashing in the ticket and keeping the money if I bought him another one. Now, on my first night in Kenya, I landed up in a five-star hotel room where the fixer sat barefoot, chewing kat leaves (a drug) and telling me it was his job to schedule my interview. This meant, by inference, that he could block the interview if I didn't pay off.

Was he telling the truth? As he spoke, I realized that the other man in the room, his roommate, was the former Somali ambassador to the UN. I thought, pay the guy.

So when the ambassador left I told him, meaning it, that I'd pay *after* the interview. And every day for the next week the fixer told me to wait in the lobby for Aidid. Every day nothing happened. Finally, on the seventh night, the ambassador got drunk and said in the lobby that I shouldn't trust the fixer.

Which man was lying? Who was telling the truth? A magazine had paid thousands of dollars to get me to Africa. If the fixer got angry, and *could* block an interview with Aidid, I'd fly home empty-handed, and never get an assignment from that particular magazine again.

Discreetly, I approached Aidid's private secretary and, not mentioning the bribe requests, tried to arrange the interview. It worked.

I never paid the fixer, who kept calling my hotel and asking for money until I left. He had turned out to be the wrong fixer.

7. Never assume you know a story until you've finished researching it. Always be prepared to change your preconceived ideas, even though it was on the *basis* of those ideas that you got your assignment.

In Antarctica, several years ago, I spent a few weeks on a U.S. research base. *Esquire* magazine had assigned me to write about the Antarctic Treaty, under which the continent is managed. It's a pretty unique treaty. It keeps any country on earth from owning any part of the place. It holds all territorial claims in abeyance. But that year, some countries wanted to change the treaty and allow commercial development.

Before arriving, I "knew" that Antarctica was a frigid, barren, inhospitable place, and that the people working there were in constant danger from weather, and moving ice, and isolation.

When I got there, though, I found a base filled with happy, fun-loving, hardworking men and women scientists. They went skiing every morning. There was a hot tub on the base. The food was terrific. There was a pub, and dances, and video movies, and frankly, the place felt more like a great resort.

For the first two weeks I went crazy trying to find the hardship. But finally I realized that the story *was* the level of comfort that humans had achieved in Antarctica, because in treaty negotiations, the forces favoring developing the place were claiming that the continent was so inhospitable that even if a treaty *permitted* development, it would not occur for decades. Clearly their claims were not true. If a treaty opened Antarctica to development, it could begin immediately.

The ease with which people could live on that U.S. base turned out to *be* the story.

These days, if a book or assignment takes me overseas, I try to keep my list in mind. In the rush of preparation, it's easy to forget a simple precaution, and if that happens, I tend to regret it later. As you can see, much of the list is common sense, but there's a difference between knowing something intellectually and incorporating it into a more instinctive part of your mind.

So remember before you go: Pack the damn insecticide. Don't wait until you're being eaten up by Amazon sweat bees before you realize you forgot to bring any. Pack the sunblock. Don't wait until the back of your neck starts to burn to find out there's no drugstore within five hundred miles.

Carry some U.S. dollars, because you may not be able to cash traveler's checks, and because U.S. dollars often go further than local currency. Always know where the U.S. embassy is. Try to keep your valuables in a safe instead of in your pocket. Don't walk around looking like a rich American when you're in a poor country. And remember, a middle-class American *is* rich in most countries.

Just because you're aware of things that might go wrong, it doesn't mean any of them *will* go wrong. Your trip might be perfect, easy, seamless, a delight. Either way, though, in the end, when you come home, your memories will be richer, your knowledge broader. You'll have more to write about. You'll have made new friends.

You may never have needed to use the alcohol pads at all, the whole time.

So good luck.

Good hunting.

But did you remember to pack the antibiotics?

EXERCISES

1. Devise an assignment that will take you to a remote foreign place. Make a list of everything you need to do before you leave, and of

everything you need to carry with you: money, documents, special clothing or tools, medical kit, etc. Make a timetable to go with the list: how long it will take to obtain a visa, how long you'll need for obtaining a series of vaccinations that may require weeks between shots, how much travel time you need to allow to and from the place where the story lives, and so on.

2. Through your doctor or the yellow pages, locate the nearest travel clinic in your locale and investigate what services it offers and at what fees.

3. Check your passport: Is it up-to-date? Will it likely expire while you're overseas? It can take three months to renew a passport in the U.S.; overseas in the wrong country, it may be nearly impossible.

The Comfortable Chair: Using Humor in Creative Nonfiction

DINTY W. MOORE

You want a chair that makes you comfortable, isn't that right?"

My wife and I, blundering into a furniture showroom just slightly smaller than the state of Delaware, found ourselves ambushed by a chipmunk of a man. He was barely over five feet tall, stooped by age. His dark hair was thinning in patches, and his robin's egg blue blazer was as unstylish and unattractive as any blazer I've ever seen. But he had clear, direct eyes, and quite the smile.

That was *my* initial assessment. What *he* saw, perhaps, were two shy, middle-class pigeons with "easy sale" tattooed on their foreheads.

The gentleman introduced himself as Howie, "your furniture consultant for today," pumped my hand and winked at my spouse. "You want a comfortable chair, yes? One you can sit in and relax?"

He was, it seemed, not just a furniture consultant but a mind reader as well, having intuited by my mere explanation "we're looking at chairs" that Renita and I had absolutely no interest in an uncomfortable chair that made us squirm and kept us endlessly tense.

"I'm going to take you around," he announced, a trace of Brooklyn in his voice. "We have over three thousand chairs in our showroom today. I'm going to show you all of them."

Later, after I had turned up my nose at the first few offerings, he really said this:

"I only want to make you happy."

Even my wife has never said that to me. Howie did, however, and I began to believe him. He was pushy, slick, odd, and yet it became somehow impossible not to like the little man. His gaze was warm and neighborly. He had that slow, spreading smile. I don't understand how it works, but within moments of entering Howie's magnetic field, I wanted to befriend him. I wanted him to be my grandfather, even though I suspected that if he *were* my grandfather, the piece of butterscotch candy he would pull for me from his pocket would be ten years old and lint covered. I would love him anyway.

Howie told me he was top salesperson for the entire Mid-Atlantic region. I didn't doubt him for one second.

A little later still, when I rejected the whole category of chair that I call "marshmallow-puffy recliner," Howie turned, extended his hands palms upward and promised:

"I'm not going to make you buy something you don't want."

It didn't make sense to me at the time—why ever would I buy something I didn't want?—but after an hour with Howie, I understood that I might have done just that.

He had that certain power.

HUMOR AND NONFICTION

The world of nonfiction has come a long way recently in letting down its hair, but the truth is, the genre of fact-based literary writing still stands awfully close at times to its cousin, journalism. With that proximity comes the latent baggage of objectivity, leading all too often to a dreadful, deadening seriousness.

This seriousness is not necessarily bad. As nonfiction writers, much of what we describe and illuminate is indeed grave—the ravages of disease, war, or perfect storms, the inequities of society, the desolation of family—and in many cases it is entirely appropriate, maybe crucial, that our style and voice reflect this reality. But it needn't always, and often it is the case that a light touch of the pen can afford the reader a welcome breath of fresh air.

Novelists and short story writers have always known this. Even the most serious novel is helped along by a moment of levity; just as, of course, even the funniest work of fiction is infinitely stronger if there is a core of serious truth underlying the joke. In nonfiction, however, these two realms are often held separate.

But not always.

A loose tradition exists of American literary nonfiction humor, starting certainly as far back as Benjamin Franklin and including, of course, Mark Twain. It was the latter gentleman who once said, "Get your facts first, and then you can distort them as much as you please."

What you make of that quote probably depends on your definition of *distort*, because a fact is a fact, and if you change the facts, you aren't writing nonfiction anymore; you are writing something else. But maybe Twain was pulling our leg—he had that habit. Maybe what he meant was, "Get your facts first, and then you can present them however you wish."

The manner of presentation—the way a truth is packaged—is often all that differentiates what makes us wince from what makes us chortle. Every successful comic and humorist knows that the line between an uncomfortable truth and a good belly laugh is remarkably thin.

And then there are those occasions when even the most serious subjects seem to demand a comic presentation. In some cases, humor is perhaps the only sane way to really get at them.

Take Frank McCourt. His best-selling and widely praised memoir *Angela's Ashes* describes as bleak a childhood as any Dickens could imagine. McCourt's memoir presents a world of painful poverty, parental abandonment, infant death, alcoholism, and class prejudice. These are not light subjects.

But McCourt's wonderful book is hilarious at points, simply wry at others, and if it had needed a subtitle (it didn't), that subtitle might be "grinning through the sadness."

McCourt could conceivably have presented his memoir without humor (hard to believe, actually, given McCourt himself, but let the premise ride for a moment), but it would have been a very different book. I'm convinced it would not have been as widely read, and in truth, I think it would have only been half the story. Humor was what brought McCourt and his siblings through their dismal early years. Humor is a large part of the tale.

And humor needn't be limited to memoir.

Any fan of Susan Orlean's *New Yorker* pieces, or her classic nonfiction work *Saturday Night*, can see where a little levity, a sly wit, translates directly into style and voice. Yet Orlean is still, basically, a reporter.

Joan Didion, too, is a humorist by my definition, not because she presents knee-slapping frivolity or cracks conventional jokes, but because her writer's eye cannot help but to pick out the ironic detail.

Gay Talese's classic of literary nonfiction, *Fame and Obscurity*, is a serious book, dense with closely observed description, but full, too, of gently comic moments: the wig-bearing woman, for instance, in Talese's essay "Frank Sinatra Has a Cold."

Bill Bryson presents a broader style of humor in his travels across England, America, and Australia, as do Ian Frazier in *Great Plains* and Jonathan Raban in *Hunting Mr. Heartbreak*.

People are funny. For some of us, it is hard to write about them without pointing that out.

Why do these writers use humor, and why do we read their work?

Human nature. When I get together with my friends, one of the first things we do is to look across the coffee table and try to make one another laugh. That's what a lot of friends do, I think, and my favorite writers are no different. The experience of reading a writer like McCourt, Orlean, Bryson, Twain is like spending time with a friend. A comfortable friend.

These friends keep me grinning through every page. We laugh, and we laugh, because it is all so true.

"YOU NEED A FENCE?"

Also true is the fact that Howie tried to sell me his fence.

We passed through the giant circular showroom, rejecting chair after chair. "You like this one?" Howie would ask. He would pause then, study my face, and before I could form an answer, he would say, "Of course not, I knew you wouldn't!"

Along the way, my wife and I let it slip that we had just moved into town. Howie, it turned out, was about to leave our new town, for a better furniture consultant job down South. We mentioned our small, untrainable pup.

"You have a small dog? *I* have a small dog!"

Howie could not have been more delighted had I just revealed that I was his long lost son, orphaned at birth.

"You need a fence? I'm selling my fence."

I didn't need a fence, but had I needed one, or had Howie been just slightly more insistent, I would probably be in his backyard right now, taking his fence down, stuffing it into the back of my station wagon, instead of writing this essay.

WHAT MAKES A STORY FUNNY?

Have you ever heard someone try to explain a joke? It seldom works. Explaining how to "write funny" may be just as futile an endeavor, but that is what I've been asked to do, so here goes.

There are a few basic elements that make a story funny—sometimes.

Juxtaposition

For some reason (probably because he had a book contract), Bill Bryson decided to hike the Appalachian Trail from Georgia to Maine, despite the fact that he was middle-aged, out of shape, and not a seasoned hiker. That might have been funny enough, but Bryson lured a friend along—Stephen Katz.

Katz, as the following passage from *A Walk in the Woods* shows, was as improbable a companion as Bryson could likely have found, and that juxtaposition provides much of the engine of the ensuing story.

Here is how Bryson introduces his friend, exiting a plane at a small New England airport:

> Katz was arrestingly larger than when I had last seen him. He had always been kind of fleshy, but now he brought to mind Orson Welles after a very bad night. He was limping a little and breathing harder than one ought to after a walk of twenty yards.
>
> "Man, I'm hungry," he said without preamble, and let me take his carry-on bag, which instantly jerked my arm to the floor.
>
> "What have you got in there?" I gasped.
>
> "Ah, just some tapes and shit for the trail. There a Dunkin Donuts anywhere around here? I haven't had anything to eat since Boston."

Irony

Bryson's juxtaposition of Katz and the trail was intentional, but juxtaposition is often unintentional, and that we call irony.

Irony underlies countless good stories. Gay Talese's essay "Frank Sinatra Has a Cold" holds the central irony in the title itself: Sinatra's throat was worth millions, yet a simple germ could shut it all down. James Thurber's essays hold irony in every line. In his classic "The Night the Bed Fell," Thurber opens with this line: "I suppose that the high-water mark of my youth in Columbus, Ohio, was the night the bed fell on my father."

Thurber's father decided to sleep in the attic "to be away where he could think." The bed falls, no one sleeps, no one experiences any quiet at all.

That's ironic, and hilarious, at least the way Thurber tells it.

Satire

Frank McCourt's memoir is filled with irony, some of it tragic. But he is also a master of Dickensian satire: the skewering of the pompous man.

A case in point—the following passage. One damp Limerick morning, McCourt's mother takes young Frankie and his brother Malachy to the St. Vincent de Paul Society, in search of charity. There, they encounter the sarcastic, but effective, Nora Molloy.

The boots are all gone. Nothing I can do. What's this? Who's smoking?

Nora waves her cigarette. I am, she says, and enjoying it down to the last ash.

Every puff you take, he starts.

I know, she says, I'm taking food out of the mouths of my children.

You're insolent, woman. You'll get no charity here.

Is that a fact? Well, Mr. Quinlivan, if I don't get it here I know where I will.

What are you talking about?

I'll go to the Quakers. They'll give me charity.

Mr. Quinlivan steps toward Nora and points a finger. Do you know what we have here? We have a souper in our midst. We had the soupers in the Famine. The Protestants went around telling good Catholics that if they gave up their faith and turned Protestant they'd get more soup than their bellies could hold and, God help us, some Catholics took the soup, and were ever after known as soupers and lost their immortal souls doomed to the deepest part of hell. And you, woman, if you go to the Quakers you'll lose your immortal soul and souls of your children.

Then, Mr. Quinlivan, you'll have to save us, won't you?

Exaggeration

Comic novelists have always used exaggeration to bring out the humorous in characters—think Dickens again.

But some people out there don't need to be exaggerated. Some people just seem to naturally exaggerate themselves. Howie the chair consultant was certainly one. He was the consummate salesman. He was, in all senses of the word, a perfect character.

So was Katz. And Nora Molloy.

All a writer had to do was capture the truth.

A FEW ADDITIONAL RECOMMENDATIONS

Juxtaposition, irony, satire, and exaggeration are everywhere. Developing an eye for life's truly comic moments is part of what a writer must do to bring humor into the writing of nonfiction. If you find it honestly funny, then write it down.

But in truth, it is not *that* easy.

The trick is often in the presentation, the way in which the facts are packaged. Though there are no firm rules in this matter, there are some approaches I feel comfortable offering as suggestions.

The first is to avoid seeming to look down at the subjects of your writing. You can probably skewer a politician or personal injury lawyer with abandon, but you should be gentle when mocking the common man. If you seem mean-spirited, if you take cheap shots, we aren't so willing to laugh.

Secondly, you need a story. Just setting up a joke is not enough to keep the reader interested. If your goal is to write compelling nonfiction, the story always comes first: What is it you are meaning to show us, and why should the reader care? It is when the humor takes a backseat to the story being told that humor is most effective, and the finest writing is done.

Finally, there is nothing wrong with the occasional punch line, but remember that nothing kills a joke more than the joke teller slamming a bony elbow into your ribs, winking, and saying, "Wait until you hear this joke, it is going to be hilarious."

The best humor sneaks up on you.

THE REAL SECRET TO BEING FUNNY

The real secret is this:

I believe that Howie really wanted me to have a comfortable chair. Putting my middle-aged bottom in a soft, commodious seat brought him a sort of pleasure. He wasn't *just* trying to sell me something, and as such, he could probably sell me the world.

Humor is like that. Don't ever try to tell a joke. Don't ever force humor. You have to be amused yourself, and you have to take honest pleasure in your amusement.

I want to tell my story of Howie, relay his dialogue, describe his person, because frankly, I am sitting here grinning just thinking about him. Really, truly, not sort of. Howie struck me as hilarious the moment I met him, and he still does. And I like him.

Humor has to be honest. Funny writers can make us smile, which is a good thing in and of itself, but the best comic writers make us smile, laugh, guffaw, and then, maybe just for a moment, see something that is true, about ourselves, about our prejudices, about the silly world we inhabit. That is the power of humor, and the power of humor in the service of truth.

THE PERFECT CHAIR

"Tell me," Howie eventually asked, "when you think of a chair, what are your first thoughts?"

We were nearing the end of the showroom, and he was clearly

worried. I had explained my stubborn dislike of busy fabric, my abhorrence of gratuitous puffiness, my disdain for Queen Anne, and we had come up empty.

"Wait. You'll like this one."

He pointed to a maroon recliner at the end of a row, not puffy in any way, a simple, understated pattern.

"Sit down, relax."

I did.

It was the perfect chair.

We left that day with a comfortable chair, and additionally, with orders for a new loveseat, and a home entertainment cabinet—one where you can close the doors and not look at your ugly television and stereo. We didn't know we needed this until Howie told us so.

My budget for the day was seven hundred dollars. Howie kept us within that budget, give or take an extra eighteen hundred dollars. The man could sell anything to anyone. We were in the presence of a true master.

Howie left town before the new furniture arrived, but it was delivered, as promised, and it fits perfectly in our new home.

I never bought his fence.

I never saw him again.

EXERCISES

1. Think of someone who makes you laugh, not just because of what she says, but because of who she is, how she walks, the way she moves her eyes, what she wears, the way in which she eats a piece of chicken. Try to describe this person in fewer than five hundred words, through simple observation. Try to make us believe that you love this person, despite the individual's comic attributes.

2. Use yourself as the subject. What is an entirely improbable thing for you to do, an improbable place for you to go, an improbable subject for you to encounter? Go there, try it, and then write a first-person account of your (honest) experiences. Like Katz on the trail, the juxtaposition is bound to be funny.

Getting Published

STANLEY L. COLBERT

Your journey to the best-seller list begins with a single reader.
That reader is an agent or an editor. More accurately, that reader is probably an editorial assistant (at some agencies and publishing houses a euphemism for an underpaid but titled-glorified secretary). If the gods are smiling on you that day, and despite the weeks or months you've poured into your project, that person probably will take no more than a few minutes or so to decide your fate. If you can say all that you have to say, all that's important to say, in a few minutes' worth of reading time, you may be on your way.

If that sounds harsh and insensitive, it's intentional. Getting an agent or an editor to pay attention to you and your work isn't as much a long shot as having Ed McMahon knock on your door—it only seems that way. And yet, some people become winners.

When you're ready to begin soliciting interest from either an agent or an editor, there are a few things you should have at hand. You'll need a small notebook in which to log your submissions, with the obvious information of when you sent them, to whom, and the responses. If a notebook seems like a step back into the world of paper, you can create a folder on your computer and a separate file for each submission. You'll need blank envelopes and lots of stamps since every inquiry you send should be accompanied by a self-addressed, stamped envelope. That isn't going to guarantee you a response; it just makes the recipient a little more inclined to get some word back to you. And you'll need a gallon-size jug of Patience and Tolerance since unsolicited inquiries and submissions rarely impel prompt replies.

Most of all, you'll need a clear idea of what your book is about, and the ability to distill it into the fewest, most provocative words possible. Richard Balkin, whose book *A Writer's Guide to Book Publishing*, published by Plume, is one of a handful of worthwhile how-to books on the subject, acknowledges the value of the query letter but suggests bypassing it in favor of submitting a full proposal. "Why waste time in adding another step to your contact with an editor?" he asks. Others, and include me among them, believe a good query letter is easier for an editor to handle, can be more inviting in fewer words, and, if successful, can open the relationship and help ensure a more positive reaction to the proposal when it arrives. Since this is my take on the subject, let's look at the query letter a bit further.

First, some basics that need stating, just for the record. Address your letter to a real person and not to "Editor," or "Publisher," or "Agent," and be certain you've determined, to the best of your ability, that this is the right editor/agent at the right company for your project. The simplest way to determine this is to hie yourself to your favorite bookstore and check the books in your particular genre on display there. Odds are, overwhelmingly, that there's an acknowledgments page where you can find the names of both the agent and the editor, "without whose assistance/inspiration/unswerving support, etc." this book could never have been written. Handle the book gingerly so you can return it, unblemished, to the stack without the burden of actually buying it (if such is your current financial circumstance), and make note of the publisher's name on the spine as well as the names of the agent and the author.

Correct addresses are best found in a reference book called *The Literary Market Place*, which some booksellers have behind the counter, for their own use, and most public and university libraries have in their reference sections. There's an index of names in the back so you can track the relevant people to their current places of employment and find the right addresses. Don't get thrown by the publisher's listing that gives multiple addresses. Make sure you're writing to the editorial offices and not the warehouse or some other branch that has absolutely nothing to do with the place where the company's creative juices flow. If you can't find this book, try the Web page for the publisher or the listings of agents contained on www.bookwire.com on the Internet.

The purpose of the query letter is, simply, to attempt to open a dialogue with a real person and pique some curiosity in your proposed work and you. Think of it as a kind of flirtation, and not a full-fledged dinner date. Reveal just enough, and not a word more. Remind yourself of how little there is about a book on the inside dust jacket, how it is written, and how effective it was in getting you, at best, to buy the book, and at the very least, to open it and scan a few pages.

When it comes to describing yourself, and why you're the best person to write the book you're proposing, include only what's important and relevant and not a whit more. The reader, if she's gotten that far, is looking for some reassurance that the subject and the ability to develop it into a book are within your range of skills and knowledge. And while you're justly proud of the extent of your education, your grades, and the occasional awards you may have won, literary or otherwise, include only those things that are directly relevant to the subject you're proposing as a book.

Taking on a book project is, at best, a crapshoot, and agents/editors are always looking for ways to reduce the odds of failure. One traditional and effective way to make this work for you is to make clear that you are writing "at the suggestion of" or "encouraged by" a name that is known to the letter's reader. It may be a published author (it helps if the author is published by the same publisher), a prominent person in the genre your book falls into, or, best of all, a friend or acquaintance of the person to whom you are writing. One of the few virtues of a college alumni publication, which you may receive whether or not you want to, is that it keeps you current on the literary activities of classmates who, for old time's sake, may be willing to recommend you to their publishers or agents. Another option is to contact a former teacher or professor who has published and make the same pitch for a recommendation.

If you can get such a recommendation, by all means use it at the top of your letter. It does not help, however, to suggest you are writing because "several friends," or "a number of people to whom I've shown the manuscript" have urged you to send it.

The final paragraph of the query letter—your query letter, incidentally, should be trimmed to fit on one single page—should ask if the recipient would like to see more. You can offer an outline, a proposal, or the full manuscript, if it exists.

Once you've devised this letter and have honed it as finely as you can, feel free to send it to as many recipients as you can find who are potential buyers. This is called "multiple submission," and while many editors and agents deplore the practice of offering something to more than one place at a time, they aren't you, with your needs and hopes and dreams.

So what have you got? An accurate and appropriate name and address of a relevant person and entity, an opening sentence that identifies someone of consequence who suggests you write to the recipient, a paragraph or two (if they're short) designed to describe the nature of your proposed book and to leave the reader wanting to know more, a paragraph about yourself that reassures that you're capable of producing the book, and a sentence asking for permission to send more: These are the basic components of a query letter.

Once you've mastered the form (not as easy as it sounds!) you can work out your own variations and query to your heart's content. Somewhere, along with all the "no, thanks" you'll undoubtedly receive, you're bound to hit a responsive chord if you've chosen your recipients wisely. After that, success or failure depends on the effectiveness of the material you're asked to send.

Past experience leads me to suggest that agents are more susceptible to a good selling letter than editors. Perhaps, that's because salespeople—which is what agents are underneath their Armani suits—are generally easier to sell, with only their time at stake if they're wrong. Whether you send a query letter to agents or editors (I suggest, initially, you solicit both), don't expect an immediate response. While some of these people are compulsive, or just plain efficient, in dealing with unsolicited correspondence, the bulk of them have developed their own rhythms regarding such mail. In the summer they may be dependent on extended weekends at rented summer cottages; in the winter they may be in direct relation to the availability of taxicabs on a snowy morning. What's important to you is that you develop a regular procedure for keeping the letters in motion—always sending out a batch on a regular basis, whether you've gotten responses or not.

Earlier, it was noted that your query may end up on the desk of an assistant, rather than the person you intended. Don't be dismayed. The best way for an assistant to move up to agent or editor status is through discovery and sponsorship of a worthwhile project, perhaps yours. So don't be discouraged if a response you receive, asking for a little more information, comes from an unfamiliar name. That person may turn out to be your in-house champion, who hopes to hitch her star to yours. Almost everyone who chooses publishing as a career is a compulsive reader. They read everything, from books, to jokes on cocktail napkins, to matchbook cover ads for art courses. They read until they are bored. So don't bore them; tease them.

From Betsy Lerner, whose book *The Forest for the Trees*, subtitled *An Editor's Advice to Writers*, published by Riverhead Books, is outstanding and enormously informative, and who has been both editor and agent, comes this final advice: ". . . do not use colored paper (it doesn't copy well) or scented paper; and no joky attention-getting opening lines, no sob stories, no crazy fonts, no overly long explanations of what follows, and no ridiculous threats or overstated marketing statistics. . . ."

A successful query letter can be useless if you don't have something in hand and ready to send when the mail brings that hoped-for response and request to see more. It's rare, but not totally uncommon, for a writer to have a finished nonfiction manuscript at the ready. Most professionals are properly unwilling, or unable, to complete a full nonfiction manuscript with neither encouragement nor support. What they do have, however, is a proposal at hand, and so should you, preferably before the first query letter is sent.

The proposal should have started to take shape in your mind, and on your page, after you've slept on the idea for the book over several days and then done some general research. One of my favorite writers says it's time to start writing the proposal when it begins to write itself in your mind, or when you will need an advance in order to delve any more deeply into your subject, whichever comes first. Another favorite writer puts it somewhat differently: "I stop the general research when the best structure for the book has been revealed. Then, after writing the proposal, I do focused research for the sample section."

Tuck away that reference to a "sample section." We'll come back to it.

Your proposal is where the promise you displayed in your query letter is now reinforced. It's also where you first reveal your "voice" and your skills as a writer. "I wish I could write a whole volume that read with the briskness of a proposal and am sure my editors wish I could, too," a writer told me. Another writer noted that, to some extent, writing the proposal should lead one to the voice for the book. He added, still referring to voice, ". . . a proposal can be slightly more knowing than the book itself, since it is, in essence, an extended advertisement from one industry insider to another."

If you're jumping ahead of me and wondering, now, how long the proposal should be, let me put your mind to rest: I don't know, and I don't know any sure rule of thumb. As an agent, and as an editor, I've been attracted by and successful with proposals that were five or ten pages long and with those that were thirty or fifty pages long. Short or long, however, a proposal should encompass certain elements. Generally, it should create some degree of excitement with an opening page or so that ends in a short, memorable summary of the idea of the book. It doesn't hurt in this section to include a couple of quotations from some heavy hitters on the subject, courtesy of your preliminary research.

Keep in mind the process that occurs in the average publishing house. It's a rare editor, indeed, who is attracted to a book project and is able to commission it and issue a contract and an advance without some form of peer consultation. It may take the form of a weekly editorial meeting where potential projects are discussed and recommended, or an editorial form that contains a synopsis of the project, the qualifications of the author, and the editor's expectations of potential sales and accompanying costs, such as advance and production. In either event, having a quotable precis of the project makes the editor's task, and your chances of being accepted, a lot easier.

After your brisk, memorable summary, it makes sense to follow with a chapter-by-chapter breakdown of the contents of the book. Aside from what this obviously reveals about what you have in mind, it also begins to give an agent or editor an idea of how much, or little, skill you possess in structuring a full-length book. Battle-scarred editors know how important a good sense of structure is to the eventual success of the writing venture. Here, too, is where the editor begins to get a sense of the size and scope of the project and begins to form an opinion on how long it might take to complete the work. If it looks like a two-year writing project, for example, with another year or so added for the usual editorial time and often snail-like estimates from the production department to produce the book, will the subject still be of interest? Will another book, on the same or a related theme, be published in the interim by someone else?

An editor in chief who shall remain nameless, for obvious reasons, once told me in a drunken moment that the reason he held his position for dozens of years, despite the efforts of some within the house to topple him, was that he could always find a reason to be negative about books his junior editors were sponsoring for publication. Having expressed himself against publication of a manuscript, however, he left the door open for the young editors to move forward anyway, if they really felt impelled to, on their own. "I was usually 99 percent right," he said, "and in those cases where the editor went ahead on his own and the book was successful, I could always point out to management the brilliance of the staff I had assembled and the benefits of my liberal editorial policy."

After the chapter breakdown, cite and describe any existing and competing works on the same subject, and then, dismiss them, with plausible explanations. The question is sure to arise in the editor's mind and in the ensuing editorial meeting and you should anticipate it.

Next, include a sample from the book, either part or all of a chapter. Whatever you choose, it should sing. It should also, if you will forgive me, reinforce the fact that you are a writer, and not just a purveyor of words. Finding the proper piece to include, however, doesn't mean you have to have written the entire manuscript. Somewhere in that preliminary research, one hopes, you've found enough material to allow you to produce a chunk of text that pleases you and captures the voice and approach you plan to use in the entire book. Remember, you're still creating a "selling piece" and whatever you've written for this sample, should the project go forward, will undoubtedly be rewritten and revised, either by you or the editor, or both of you, beyond recognition. For my taste, and comfort level, I always preferred a sample that was longer rather than shorter, clear and exciting instead of a compendium of facts and figures, and, generally, something of real interest that I might not have known before about the subject. If that turns out to be the opening of the book, fine; if not, use whatever works best.

Finally, and this is especially important for new or as-yet unpublished writers, explain who you are and how you will help sell the book. If you've been published, by all means provide the details. What's important to convey here is why you are the person who should write this book, more than anyone else. If you lecture, teach, have a dozen cousins, all of whom manage large bookstores and will support book signings, have made numerous television appearances, and do anything else that sounds like it can be translated into promotion possibilities or sales, this is the place to say so. The sad fact is that publishers, generally, are still in the Dark Ages when it comes to marketing and promoting their product. They need all the help they can get. That's not to say they want your suggestions about what they can do for you in promoting the book; what they want to know is what *you* can do for them.

What does the opening of a successful proposal look like, read like? Here's an example of one that brought a six-figure advance for the author and resulted in a book that became, among other things, a book club main selection.

Eyewitness to America

Tell me what happened . . .

Everyone wants to hear what the eyewitness says.

To know what really happened, and how it happened, we want the eyewitness to describe it as it happened.

An eyewitness story sparks an immediacy and energy that no historian's cold analysis can capture. The correspondent on the scene, sharing the shocking jolt of joy or horror in watching the world change in an instant, never fails to imprint the event on our memory and imagination.

The eyewitness may not even fully understand what happened. No matter. History begins with people caught in the minute-by-minute rush of events. *Eyewitness to America* offers a picture of American history drawn from vivid firsthand accounts that give each event a freshness and urgency no historian could duplicate.

Tell me what happened . . .

- an early settlement is almost wiped out by a mysterious plague, until a Native American arrives and concocts an herbal cure . . .
- a fiery Southern belle rides a train home at the close of the Civil War and witnesses the devastation left in the wake of Sherman's March . . .
- an earthquake and fire level San Francisco, forcing eyewitness Jack London to wander through the chaos and rubble . . .
- a Navy worker speeds on his motorcycle to the Pearl Harbor base, watching plumes of fire and smoke rise from the burning ships . . .
- fresh from the internment camps that still hold their families, troops from the "Go for Broke" Brigade advance up a mountainside in Germany, under heavy fire, to rescue 200 trapped Army Rangers . . .
- the Chicago police fire tear gas on student protesters, and Studs Terkel, at the Democratic National Convention . . .

The book starts with accounts from the early European voyagers, and continues to the present day. Among the entries:

- Nathaniel Hawthorne takes a government job (1839)
- Cy Young throws baseball's first perfect game (1904)
- Mark Twain and Jack London on San Francisco earthquakes (1868 & 1906)
- A run on the Bank of California (1875)
- The first car in Detroit (1898)
- The first view from the Empire State Building (1931)
- The assassination of Bobby Kennedy (1968)
- Student protests in Chicago (1968)
- Traffic jam at Woodstock (1969)
- A homicide investigation in Baltimore (1988)

This book was inspired by a similar volume, *Eyewitness to History* (originally published in Britain as *The Faber Book of Reportage*), which offers accounts of world events. It is a real, reading history book, with great writing, some surprising entries, and a simple, formal design. Yet, from first glance, it is accessible and entertaining.

The U.S. trade paperback of the Faber & Faber book, first published by Avon in 1991, has sold over 120,000 copies after nine printings (at $12 retail). The U.S. hardcover was a sleeper bestseller for Harvard University Press, netting about 30,000 copies after publication in 1988.

Eyewitness to America offers the same immediacy and surprise that delighted readers of *Eyewitness to History*. It is aimed at those readers, and also the many more whose particular interest in American history accounts for the great success of *Don't Know Much about History* (now in its 33rd printing) and *Legends, Lies and Cherished Myths of American History* (210,000 trade paperbacks). It can also be used as an American history reader at junior colleges and universities.

It is arranged chronologically. I am keeping editorial introductions to a minimum. If a piece needs a long intro, it's probably the wrong piece. Regarding dates, the editor of *Eyewitness to History*, John Carey, set an appealing rule which I plan to follow. Wherever possible, he chose events that could be pinned down to a specific date—rather than simply a year or month. The few other chronological collections I've found—*American Datelines: One Hundred and Forty Major News Stories From Colonial Times to the Present* (Facts on File, 1990), *Mirror for Gotham* (NYU Press, 1956)—didn't press this point. As a result, they feel less immediate.

I have arbitrarily defined America as the United States of America, including the early history of the territory that eventually became an official part of the republic. Admittedly, I have broken my own rule on a few occasions. For example, I have included the fall of Havana, which altered domestic politics and led to an important wave of Cuban immigration.

The final collection will include well-known events, such as the Salem witch trials, the New York City draft riots, the Last Spike, the Johnstown flood, the Triangle Shirtwaist Company fire, the suffragettes, the executions of Sacco and Vanzetti, Prohibition, the flying adventures of Amelia Earhart and Chuck Yeager, and the internment of Japanese-Americans. It will also include some lesser known events, such as a meeting of ships in mid-ocean so the captain's wives could visit, the battle between Texas fishermen and the Vietnamese immigrants who wanted to work the same waters, and a look inside Bellevue.

In every case, the quality of the writing will be the overriding concern. Not every author will be famous. Some pieces will even be anonymous. Yet famous authors will certainly be included. Among them will be Ernest Hemingway, Studs Terkel, Greil Marcus, H.L. Mencken, Theodore H. White, John Gregory Dunne, John Dos Passos, Richard Tregaskis, Ernie Pyle, Michael Herr, Mary Chestnut, John Muir, George Templeton Strong, Ralph Ellison, Red Smith, Joan Didion, Tom Wolfe. I am avoiding newspaper stories that were clearly assembled from several eyewitness accounts. I am also avoiding newspaper stories that were more influenced by a paper's politics than by facts, for instance, most stories about labor unrest written before the 1930s.

However, I am selecting some accounts that are clearly subjective, including several that may offend the politically correct. Eliza Andrews's account of returning to a family plantation in southern Georgia is unrepentantly patriotic—for the Confederacy. Howard Smith's view of the Stonewall riot is hardly compassionate, but it reflects the tone of 1969. Some selections describe an important part of the everyday American experience, rather than a famous event. Frontierswoman Helen Marnie Stewart's meeting with the Sioux did not shape American history.

But Stewart was part of the great wave of "emigrants" to the West in the 1850s, most of whom were obsessed with meeting the various Native peoples, and her account is especially vivid.

Some of the pieces were written years after the event; yet one, Relman Morin's Pulitzer prize–winning story of the Little Rock school riots, was dictated to the Atlanta Associated Press office from a phone booth as the event occurred.

I plan to select about 300 accounts, averaging perhaps 1,000 words, for a book of 550–600 pages.

I don't believe the book should include illustrations, but I'm open to other views. (I think illustrations would make it look like a Bonanza Book instant remainder, rather than a full-priced backlist staple.)

The book will include an introduction from a prominent historian with appeal in both general and college markets.

The book can be complete, with permissions cleared, by December 1995.

Straightforward, confident, authoritative, and with an accessible voice, the proposal made for an easy decision for an editor and an abundance of quotable information for the editor to use in an editorial conference. It worked. Since then, the author has used the same basic format for proposing, successfully, two follow-up books—*Eyewitness to the American West* and his current book, *Eyewitness to Wall Street*. I've followed his career avidly, with enormous admiration, since David Colbert, the author, is not only my son, but a former agent/editor/publisher who learned his lessons well and has successfully put them into practice.

Now it's your turn.

I'm grateful to David for permission to include this portion of his proposal, as well as for his comments, which have helped shape this piece. I'm also grateful to Stacy Schiff, a writer of extraordinary talent and a Pulitzer prize winner, for taking the time from her own writing to offer a few suggestions as well. Finally, let me again recommend the books to which I've referred earlier, by Richard Balkin and by Betsy Lerner, as being invaluable in learning, not how to write, but how to be a writer.

Avoiding Self-Censorship: A Guide to the Detection of Legal Land Mines

NICHOLAS S. HENTOFF AND HARVEY A. SILVERGLATE

INTRODUCTION

In the summer of 1902, a young journalist named Jack London disguised himself as a member of the underclass and went undercover to expose the horrendous living conditions in the slums of London's East End. The resulting book, *The People of the Abyss*, is widely regarded as one of the greatest works of nonfiction in the past one hundred years.

Almost a century later, in the tradition of writers such as Jack London, television journalists in the United States went undercover to expose unsanitary food preparation conditions in a chain of supermarkets. The resulting story revealed the sale of rat-gnawed cheese and spoiled chicken washed in bleach. The resulting lawsuit led to a multimillion-dollar jury verdict for fraud—not against the supermarket, but against the journalists, because they lied to obtain their jobs at the supermarket. In another recent case, the publisher of a nonfiction book purporting to be a how-to manual for hit men was successfully sued, in spite of a vigorous First Amendment defense, because someone who bought the book followed its directions, resulting in the murder of a young woman and her child.

While society has changed a great deal in the one hundred years since Jack London practiced his craft, it is important to remember that the legal landscape facing nonfiction writers today is still in its adolescence. It is just over thirty years since the United States Supreme Court, in *New York Times v. Sullivan* (1964), first extended First Amendment protections to journalists and other writers defending against civil suits alleging defamation and other torts. In the past three decades, the legal pitfalls facing nonfiction writers have increased, rather than decreased, along with the number of lawyers and lawsuits that have fueled this country's litigation explosion.

The sad truth is that even frivolous lawsuits cost money to defend, and even the mere threat of a lawsuit is often enough to achieve the goals of those seeking to keep embarrassing facts hidden from the light of day. As one turn-of-the-century British humorist described the balance of power in such a situation:

> If a man stopped me in the street, and demanded of me my watch I should refuse to give it to him. If he threatened to take it by force, I feel I should . . . do my best to protect it. If, on the other hand, he should assert his intention of trying to obtain it by means of an action in a court of law, I should take it out of my pocket and hand it to him, and think I had got off cheaply.

It is important for nonfiction writers to realize that perhaps the greatest pitfall that they face is the self-imposed obstacle of self-censorship. Nothing can put a damper on a work in progress faster than a threat from a law firm with a half a dozen names on its letterhead. The ultimate question facing the nonfiction writer in such a situation is do you hand over your watch, or do you call the bully's bluff?

Author John Bear, an expert on fraudulent diploma mills, documents the example of the American Council on Education, which, in 1982, had announced an impending hard-hitting book on fake schools selling fraudulent college degrees. According to Bear, by the time the book was published in 1988, it didn't name a single operating school. The authors apologized for their lack of specificity by citing "the present litigious era." The respected academic journal *Lingua Franca* did publish a hard-hitting article on what it claimed was a fraudulent diploma mill and was thanked for its public service with an expensive lawsuit that was ultimately thrown out of court. Bear himself has survived eight lawsuits brought by different schools that didn't appreciate his writing about the diploma mill industry. Although only one of the lawsuits ever got to court, and was quickly dismissed by the judge, he still notes that the litigation was not without cost, "both in dollars and, [as] my wife will confirm, despondency."

The point of the diploma mill saga is that your research can be unassailable, your fact checking perfect, you can have the law on your side, and you can still be sued. Unfortunately, there is no way to prevent anyone from filing a frivolous lawsuit against you. Changes in the rules of procedure enacted over the past thirty years, along with the permissive attitude of most trial judges, have resulted in a climate where defendants in even frivolous lawsuits may have to go through expensive discovery procedures before they are able to get the lawsuits dismissed.

The purpose of this essay is to serve as an "issue-spotting" exercise to alert the writer to when he or she is entering problematic territory, and when a potential threat should be considered serious. An attorney's threat of a lawsuit can amount to little more than a thunderstorm that you can hunker down for and wait out, or it can be a typhoon that will capsize your boat. By vetting your work for potential legal problems in advance, you can know when it is prudent to call an attorney's bluff. This essay will therefore attempt to help nonfiction writers detect legal land mines before they explode, thereby eliminating the fear of uncertainty that too often leads to self-censorship. However, the information provided here is not legal advice and is not a substitute for consulting a qualified attorney when specific problems arise.

While the constitutional defenses used to fend off civil lawsuits are generally uniform throughout the country, the elements of the individual torts that form the basis of these lawsuits, and even their availability, often vary from state to state. The Reporters Committee for Freedom of the Press maintains a Web site with legal information and a hot line for legal advice and referrals (http://www.rcfp.org). The committee's online publication *The First Amendment Handbook* forms the basis for some of the analysis provided in this essay.

FOUR FUNDAMENTAL CAVEATS

There are four fundamental caveats that should always be kept in mind by nonfiction writers facing a legal challenge.

First, consent is almost always a defense to a civil lawsuit.

Second, personal notes and other documents created while preparing your work may become public during the course of any lawsuit. The destruction of this material after a suit has been filed, or a refusal to produce it in response to a valid request, may result in the loss of the lawsuit.

Third and most important in protecting yourself against either a civil lawsuit or a criminal charge, never ever admit fault before consulting an attorney.

Finally, the First Amendment is almost never a defense to the commission of criminal activity. If you commit a crime, the prosecuting attorney will usually not be sympathetic to your claim that you did so in furtherance of the First Amendment, particularly where the crime involves child pornography or the transmission of obscene materials to minors. At least one writer is currently serving a very long prison sentence after both a court and jury rejected his claim that the child pornography found in his possession was part of an article he was writing on Internet pedophiles.

Obscenity, which is measured by a three-part test using contemporary community standards, falls outside of the protection of the First

Amendment. However, society has evolved to the point where even nonfiction writers who focus on sexually explicit themes usually have little to worry about from local obscenity statutes. A work of nonfiction, taken as a whole, must completely lack any serious literary, artistic, political, or scientific value before it can even be considered to have violated a local obscenity statute.

PRIVACY TORTS

Depending on the state you live in, there are four fundamental torts based on an individual's right to privacy:

1. appropriation
2. intrusion
3. public disclosure of embarrassing private facts
4. false light

There are other torts, such as fraud or intentional infliction of emotional distress, that are distinct from the right to privacy but usually flow from a similar set of facts.

Unlike defamation, where substantial truth is usually an absolute defense, a writer can be liable based solely on his or her actions without regard to whether the facts he wrote about are true or not. There are numerous cases where writers have exposed corruption, a risk to public health, and other newsworthy information that was obtained in such a way as to expose them to civil lawsuits and even criminal prosecution. How you play the game is more important than whether you win or lose when it comes to avoiding a privacy tort lawsuit. Most importantly, always remember the fundamentals. While truth may not be a defense to privacy torts, consent is almost always a defense to all privacy torts.

Appropriation

The tort of appropriation applies exclusively to the unauthorized use of a person's likeness or identity for commercial purposes. When applied to a private citizen, appropriation usually involves the violation of a personal right of the individual to be let alone, with resulting damage. When applied to a celebrity, courts usually approach the case as involving the recovery of lost profits from a violation of his or her right of publicity. Some federal appeals courts have even held that the common law right of publicity protects a celebrity from appropriations of his or her "identity" not strictly definable as "name or picture."

Consequently, a court has allowed Johnny Carson to sue the manufacturer of portable toilets labeled with his famous catchphrase:

"Here's Johnny." In another case, television personality Vanna White recovered for the unauthorized depiction of a robot turning letters on a set simulating her television show *Wheel of Fortune*. A race car driver has even recovered for the unauthorized use of an image of his well-known and highly recognizable race car.

Courts have ruled that the tort of appropriation does not apply to the use of a person's likeness to promote sales of a newspaper or magazine that contains the likeness in a valid news story, as long as the use doesn't imply endorsement. Courts have also distinguished such promotional uses in news, artistic, or literary context, from a purely commercial use. Consequently, it is permissible to use Fred Astaire's likeness in a documentary on dance, but not in a commercial for vacuum cleaners. Nevertheless, the use of a person's identity may still be protected in a purely commercial context, depending on the circumstances, if it involves the incidental use of newsworthy or historical facts. Uses constituting parody or satire are also usually protected.

Intrusion

The tort of intrusion involves the unauthorized physical, electronic, or mechanical intrusion into a person's private space. Once again, consent is an absolute defense to any lawsuit based on the tort of intrusion as long as you don't exceed the scope of that consent. Allegations arising under this subset of intrusion are among the most dangerous facing a nonfiction writer. Many of the improper information-gathering techniques that can give rise to civil liability for intrusion can also give rise to criminal liability.

Common sense tells us that you can't break into a person's home, open her mail, or hack into his computer files without the person's permission, no matter how noble the underlying purpose. In one recent case, a reporter investigating a large corporation was prosecuted after he used a password he obtained from a source to access an executive's voice mail system.

Being in the presence of a public official, such as a police officer or emergency worker, doesn't necessarily protect you from liability for invasion of privacy and may even expand your potential liability if you are perceived as acting jointly with the public official. CNN found this out the hard way when its crew worked closely with federal agents to film the search of a private citizen's home. The court allowed the private citizen to sue CNN, along with the federal agents, for federal civil rights violations. Jurisdiction against CNN under the federal civil rights statute was predicated on the finding that CNN had "acted jointly" with the federal officials. Curiously, while the federal agents escaped liability by asserting the defense of qualified immunity, CNN could not rely on a qualified immunity defense and therefore became the only defendants found liable for damages.

Tape-recording conversations is a more difficult matter. Thirteen states require that both parties to a conversation must consent before it can be tape-recorded. If two or more parties are in two or more states it is prudent to check the law of all states before proceeding. The Reporters Committee for Freedom of the Press Web site maintains a list of individual states and their laws with respect to tape-recording telephone conversations. Federal law prohibits a third party from recording a conversation without first obtaining the consent of all parties. Such an interception, without valid consent, would be considered a "wiretap" under federal law. However, federal law does allow a participant to record the conversation without the consent of the other parties.

Be aware that in many states that require consent by all parties to a conversation, law enforcement officers are authorized to record the conversation with just the consent of a single participant (who will later appear in the police report as "the cooperating individual," also known as "the informant"). Court wiretap orders typically are required only when law enforcement does not have the cooperation of any participant to the conversation.

Finally, if you are in a jurisdiction that has a two-party consent law, and if you decide you want to tape the conversation, it would be prudent to obtain that consent at the very beginning of your conversation so that your request for permission to record, and the other party's consent, appears at the beginning of the tape. Writers who fail to check the laws in their states prior to tape-recording without the other parties' consent risk being prosecuted by local law enforcement authorities, particularly in high-profile cases.

An intrusion claim can also give rise to a claim for fraud where the intrusion is accompanied by deception. News media defendants have not had a good track record in fraud suits, several of which have resulted in large damage awards even where the information that was obtained by deception resulted in the exposure of serious wrongdoing on the part of the plaintiffs. Consent is not a defense to a fraud claim since any consent obtained by fraud is invalid. In certain circumstances, obtaining information through fraud can also result in criminal liability.

Public Disclosure of Embarrassing Private Facts

The torts of public disclosure of embarrassing facts involves the publication of true facts that are not of public concern and are so intimate that publication outrages the public's sense of decency.

However, there are broad "fair use" privileges that usually protect writers in these cases, particularly where the private facts are obtained from official reports or court documents. This tort will not be available to anyone who voluntarily thrusts himself or herself into an issue of public concern, even if the private facts have nothing to do with the underlying public issue. This was discovered by a Vietnam veteran from San Francisco who saved President Gerald Ford from an assassination attempt only to have his heretofore-secret status as a homosexual rights activist broadcast to his parents in the Midwest. His lawsuit for public disclosure of private facts was dismissed by the trial judge who cited the newsworthy and voluntary nature of his heroic actions.

False Light

False light invasion of privacy occurs when information is published about a person that is false or places the person in a false light, is highly offensive to a reasonable person, and is published with knowledge or in reckless disregard of whether the information was false or would place the person in a false light. Although this tort is similar to defamation, it is not the same. The report need not be defamatory to be actionable as false light.

Examples of false light include publishing a photograph of the plaintiff in a legitimate news story in such close proximity to an unrelated article on local child molesters that readers are confused as to which article the photograph relates to. Another example might be publishing true facts about a plaintiff while ignoring other facts that would help mitigate the harmful impact of the statement, or intentionally deleting portions of a quotation that would place a harmful statement in context. A number of states no longer recognize the tort of false light, preferring to deal with such torts within the context of defamation claims.

Defamation Torts

Libel involves the publishing of a falsehood that harms someone. *Slander* is the same doctrine applied to the spoken word. Collectively, they are referred to as *defamation*. As a general rule, in order to be sued for libel you must have (1) made a false defamatory statement about (2) an identifiable person that is (3) published to a third party and (4) causes injury to reputation. Although libel law varies from state to state—including the elements a plaintiff must prove and the defenses available to a defendant—the Supreme Court has established that the degree of fault that the plaintiff will be required to prove will depend largely on the legal status of the plaintiff as a public or private figure.

If the plaintiff is a public figure or public official, he or she must prove that the publisher acted with *actual malice*. Actual malice is not ill will or intent to harm. In order to satisfy the actual malice requirement, the plaintiff must prove that the defendant knew that the statements were false or acted with reckless disregard for the truth.

Editing or paraphrasing attributed quotations so as to change their meaning will usually satisfy the actual malice requirement. However, courts have held that even extreme deviations from professional standards will not, by themselves, constitute actual malice. Consequently, while carelessness is not usually considered a reckless disregard for the truth, ignoring obvious ways of substantiating allegations could be. The mere failure to investigate facts is therefore not necessarily actual malice, while a purposeful avoidance of the truth is usually sufficient to constitute actual malice. For instance, if a writer is told by a third party that the writer's brother saw a famous Christian evangelist go into a motel with a prostitute, and fails to call his brother to verify the facts before publishing the story, he might have problems defending against a lawsuit by the evangelist if the facts prove to be false.

The surest way of meeting the actual malice requirement is to simply make up the information relating to a public figure. Consequently, writers should scrupulously avoid the urge to "tweak" a story by fabricating facts or quotations attributed to public figures. Those writers who feel such advice is so self-evident that it does not bear repeating should note the unfortunate example of the Society of Professional Journalists, who recently settled a defamation lawsuit arising out of its widely distributed textbook, *Doing Ethics in Journalism*.

Mike Snyder, a well-known television anchor in Texas, was mentioned in a chapter of the textbook titled "Conflicts of Interest" about journalists who have been disciplined by their employers for supporting politicians. The textbook described Snyder's experience of being disciplined for regularly introducing George W. Bush at rallies during his 1994 campaign for governor and included statements purporting to be from Snyder regarding the incident. The settlement agreement includes an admission from the authors that Snyder never introduced Bush at any event, that they never interviewed Snyder, and that they attributed quotes to Snyder that he never made.

Private plaintiffs usually need not prove much more than that the publisher was negligent in failing to ascertain that the statement was false and defamatory. However, if the story in question involves a matter of public importance, courts will hold the private figure to a higher standard of fault. Some courts have carved out a fourth category of plaintiff, the limited public figure, and imposed an intermediate standard of fault that approaches that of the public figure or public official.

A good rule of thumb is to never *assume* that someone is a public figure, because you can't always be sure that a judge will agree with your assessment of the plaintiff's status. In addition, always be sensitive to the fact that other people who are not public figures may be involved in your story. You may be preparing a profile on a recognized public figure that will necessarily involve references to other people, such as the subject's friends and family, who are not public figures. It is also a good idea to have a standard procedure in place for verifying the truthfulness and accuracy of your work that you use on a regular basis regardless of whether your subject is a private figure or a public figure. Treating everyone as if they were private figures will go a long way toward immunizing yourself from liability in lawsuits threatened or brought by public figures and public officials.

Libel is perhaps the only tort that doesn't even require that the wrongful conduct injure a person. A corporation can sue for libel if the allegedly defamatory statements relate to the honesty, credit, efficiency, or prestige of its business. Libel lawsuits can also be brought on behalf of food products. As Oprah Winfrey found out, disparaging comments about hamburgers in the context of a discussion of mad cow disease resulted in a multimillion-dollar lawsuit by cattle ranchers in the state of Texas. Although Oprah won a jury verdict in her favor, the trial court did not invalidate the food disparagement statute as being unconstitutional. In another Texas case, emu ranchers sued Honda in federal court for a 1997 tongue-in-cheek TV commercial in which a character said: "Emus, Joe. It's the pork of the future."

Texas is not alone, however, in protecting the honor and dignity of food products. At least thirteen states now have statutes that authorize lawsuits against anyone who disparages a food product with information unsupported by reliable scientific data. In Colorado, the state legislature has passed a *criminal* law designed to punish those found guilty of disparaging farm products.

Luckily, these statutes were not in force when Upton Sinclair published his groundbreaking novel *The Jungle* in 1906, or Rachel Carson published *Silent Spring* in 1962. *The Jungle* contained graphic descriptions of slaughterhouses that resulted in America's first food safety legislation. *Silent Spring* carefully documented the damage to the environment caused by pesticides, challenged the practices of agricultural scientists, and is credited with the creation of the Environmental Protection Agency. Many commentators have noted that in today's climate both of these authors would have been subjected to costly libel lawsuits.

These statutes present tremendous problems to those wishing to write about genetic alteration of agricultural products or explore the excesses of the food production industry. Since what constitutes "reliable scientific data" is subject to debate, any lawsuit brought on behalf of the dignity of food products will likely be resolved by a jury following a battle of expert witnesses. Writers who based their work on thorough scientific research will be in a strong position before a jury, but will still have to defend against a lengthy and costly legal onslaught. Solo scientists wishing to publish their research and consumer journalists in small media markets are particularly vulnerable.

As Ronald K.L. Collins and Paul McMasters noted in a 1998 article in *Legal Times*:

> The net effect of the Oprah ruling may well be to silence those who cannot endure the time and expense demanded by a seven-figure lawsuit. In that respect, the food disparagement laws encourage lawsuits designed to intimidate food critics by the mere threat of we-can-bankrupt-you litigation, replete with gag orders from cooperative judges. . . . Finally, the sword of Damocles still hangs over the media as well. For as long as food critics must satisfy a high burden of scientific proof, the media will be understandably hesitant to publish stories in this area lest their names be added to a legal complaint.

It is hopeful to keep in mind that a favorable ruling invalidating these food disparagement statutes might still be expected in the event that an appellate court, particularly the United States Supreme Court, has the opportunity to decide an appropriate case.

Proving the Elements of Defamation

As a general rule, defendants in a libel lawsuit will prevail if it is established that the allegedly defamatory statement is substantially true. The Supreme Court has held that public figures, public officials, and even private citizens in cases involving matters of public concern all bear the burden of proving that the statements were false. The statement must also be defamatory, which is closely linked with the element of harm or injury to reputation. Consequently, falsely stating that someone was an Eagle Scout when he was not may be false but it is not defamatory and therefore could not form the basis for a libel suit.

In order to satisfy the publication element in a libel action, the plaintiff must establish that the allegedly defamatory information was negligently or intentionally communicated to someone other than the person defamed. An author or publisher can be held liable for the republication of a libelous statement made by another person. Consequently, if someone steals your private diary in which you question the academic credentials of a colleague, you will most likely not be held responsible if that information is later published. However, if you edit an academic journal and publish a letter accusing a colleague of plagiarism, without investigating the facts, you might find yourself on the wrong end of a libel lawsuit. Internet publishers have special protections provided by the Communications Decency Act of 1996 that insulates Internet service providers (ISPs) from liability based on the actions of their users unless the ISPs exercise editorial control of the users' content.

The element of identification requires that the plaintiff prove that the defamatory statement refers to him. While the element of identification may seem an obvious requirement, occasions arise where the defamatory statements are sufficiently oblique that a question arises as to which individual the statements refer to. If a statement defames a small group of individuals, any member of that group may sue. Members of large groups do not enjoy this privilege.

For instance, if someone publishes an account of a sexual assault by a male nurse at a local nursing home that proves to be false, and there are only two male nurses employed at the nursing home, both nurses would be allowed to sue for libel. On the other hand, if someone published a statement alleging that all members of the Teamsters Union are mobsters, individual teamsters would not be able to sue for libel.

In order to prevail in any slander or libel suit, the plaintiff must also establish that his reputation was harmed. A defense to any action can be that the plaintiff doesn't enjoy a reputation that is capable of being injured. For instance, if someone accused O.J. Simpson of being a drug dealer, he would have a hard time establishing that his reputation was capable of being injured.

Most states have created a statutory presumption of harm for certain categories of defamatory statements based on the common law distinction between slander or libel *per se* and *per quod*. In per se cases, a plaintiff is usually not required to establish proof of actual harm where the defamatory statement in question involves a criminal offense, a loathsome disease, a female's unchastity, and matters pertaining to a person's business, trade, profession, or office. In per quod cases, plaintiffs are required to prove actual harm. Some states have done away with the common law distinction between per se and per quod damages and have ruled that a plaintiff must prove actual damages in all defamation cases.

PRIVACY AND DEFAMATION DEFENSES

There are a variety of defenses that are available to writers facing lawsuits based on either privacy or defamation torts. As has been previously discussed, the most surefire defense to any lawsuit is *consent*. If the plaintiff clearly and unequivocally consented to that which he now complains, it is likely his lawsuit will be thrown out of court. Another strong defense is what has come to be known as the "fair reporting privilege." The fair reporting privilege provides that certain public and official statements can be disclosed by the media without fear of liability. In most states, reports of arrests, civil and criminal trials, official statements made by and about law enforcement officials are all absolutely privileged providing the reports are accurate and fair. It is highly advisable for writers to explicitly attribute the information to the official sources in order to fall within the protection of the fair reporting privilege.

Most states also have a strict statute of limitations within which any lawsuit must be brought. Failure to file a lawsuit within the statute of limitations will result in its quick dismissal. The precise time period varies from state to state, but the time period usually begins to run at the time of the first publication.

Although there is no separate privilege for an expression of opinion, opinion statements require special consideration. Whether someone can be held liable for a statement of opinion will depend on whether it is based on, or presumes, underlying facts that are false or defamatory. A statement of opinion with no "provably false factual connotation" will usually be protected. Similarly, parody and satire are also usually protected. Parody and satire are frequently calculated to inflict discomfort and shame on the target, but are not meant to be taken seriously as literal factual representations.

A growing trend in the discouragement of constitutionally protected First Amendment activity is the initiation of the SLAPP-suit. SLAPP stands for Strategic Lawsuit Against Public Participation. Based on traditional theories of tort law, these lawsuits are designed to deter expressive activity regarding matters of public concern. Although the lawsuits are usually frivolous, and most are ultimately dismissed, they are costly to defend and are directed at individuals and organizations with little or no money and insufficient resources to mount adequate defenses. They are frequently used against citizen advocacy groups. Powerful plaintiffs are also beginning to use federal civil rights and fair housing statutes to mount attacks against individuals who express politically incorrect opinions or petition their government for a redress of grievances concerning issues ranging from affirmative action to low-income housing. Fourteen states now have anti-SLAPP laws that require courts to dismiss frivolous lawsuits quickly in cases where a citizen's First Amendment rights are implicated. It is always wise when sued for activity that is arguably protected by the First Amendment to check to see if your state has an anti-SLAPP statute.

Intentional Infliction of Emotional Distress

Lawsuits containing claims of invasion of privacy or defamation also frequently contain claims based on the torts of negligent or intentional infliction of emotional distress. These torts require a showing that the defendant acted in an extreme and outrageous manner, causing the plaintiff to suffer severe emotional damage as a result. In those states that recognize the tort, the elements of such a claim will vary. Some states require a showing that the emotional distress was accompanied by physical symptoms before the plaintiff can recover.

In *Hustler Magazine v. Falwell* (1988), the United States Supreme Court expanded the actual malice requirement to include cases where a public figure or public official seeks to recover damages on a theory of intentional infliction of emotional distress. The lawsuit arose out of a Campari liquor ad parody in *Hustler* magazine that contained a purported interview with Jerry Falwell in which he states that his "first time" was during a drunken incestuous rendezvous with his mother in an outhouse. The jury found against Falwell on the libel claim, holding that the parody could not "reasonably be understood as describing actual facts . . . or events," but ruled in his favor on the emotional distress claim, stating that he should be awarded compensatory and punitive damages. The Supreme Court reversed, holding that the First Amendment prohibits public figures and public officials from recovering damages for the tort of intentional infliction of emotional distress without showing that the publication contains a false statement of fact that was made with "actual malice." The Court concluded that the state's interest in protecting public figures from emotional distress is not sufficient to deny First Amendment protection to speech that, although patently offensive and intended to inflict emotional injury, could not reasonably have been interpreted as stating actual facts about the public figure involved.

PRIOR RESTRAINTS, GAG ORDERS, AND SUBPOENAS FOR CONFIDENTIAL SOURCES AND UNPUBLISHED WORK PRODUCT

A lawsuit for damages following publication is not the only legal action that can threaten a nonfiction writer. Writers can also become subject to prepublication legal actions, such as prior restraints and gag orders, as well as efforts to force disclosure of confidential sources and other unpublished work product. Prior restraints and gag orders constitute an effort in a civil or criminal case to prevent the publication and dissemination of information that is the object of the order in question. These orders can be sought by attorneys for civil litigants, a criminal defense attorney, a prosecuting attorney, or by the court itself on its own motion.

The Supreme Court has repeatedly held that there is a strong presumption against the constitutional validity of any prior restraint on expression. In order to overcome this presumption, a trial court must first find that irreparable harm to a substantial government interest would occur if a temporary restraining order did not halt publication of the story.

Even in the case of prior restraints requested to protect national security, the courts have held that the government bears a heavy burden to establish a sufficient showing of harm. Prior restraints directed at the advocacy of force or criminal activity are invalid unless the targeted advocacy is directed to inciting or producing imminent lawless action *and* is likely to incite or produce such action.

Civil litigants in privacy cases have not fared well in their efforts to prevent the publication of embarrassing or unwelcome projects. For instance, Paula Jones, the woman who sued President Clinton for sexual harassment, was unsuccessful in her attempts to restrain publication of an issue of *Penthouse* magazine containing nude photographs of her taken by a former boyfriend. The Court noted that Mrs. Jones had inserted herself in a matter of public interest and the photographs related to an editorial in the same issue of the magazine that took issue with her credibility. Frank Sinatra was just as unsuccessful in his efforts both to restrain Kitty Kelley from conducting interviews and to prevent the publication of her unauthorized biography on his life.

Those civil cases in which restraining orders have been obtained usually involve both an injunction against the dissemination of proprietary information, such as trade secrets, as well as a special relationship between the company seeking the injunction and the party being enjoined. A corporation's mere assertion that publication of private information will put it at a competitive disadvantage, standing alone, will almost never be sufficient to overcome the heavy presumption against prior restraints.

Litigants in criminal cases who have sought the imposition of prior restraints and gag orders have fared somewhat better than their counterparts in civil cases. In 1976, the United States Supreme Court overturned a lower court order prohibiting the publication of information obtained in a pretrial criminal proceeding holding that "[p]rior restraints on speech and publication are the most serious and least tolerable infringement on the First Amendment."

Since 1976, there appears to have been a gradual erosion of the Supreme Court's heavy presumption against gag orders in criminal cases, fueled in part by the increasing impact of media coverage on a defendant's ability to get a fair trial.

When a writer's First Amendment right to free expression conflicts with a defendant's Sixth Amendment right to a fair trial, courts are required to apply a three-part test in evaluating the validity of a requested gag order. The party seeking the order must show that the nature and extent of publicity about the case would impair Sixth Amendment rights, that no alternatives are available to protect the fair trial right, and that a gag order will protect the individual's interest.

Appellate courts reviewing gag orders have generally required that less restrictive alternatives—such as changing venue, postponing a trial, carefully screening prospective jurors for prejudice, and even sequestering the jury—must be exhausted before a trial court resorts to a gag order.

In two recent cases where federal appellate courts have upheld gag orders on the press arising out of criminal trials, the materials subject to the prior restraint were confidential communications between high-profile criminal defendants and their attorneys. One of the cases involved the broadcast by CNN of secretly recorded conversations between deposed Panamanian ruler Manuel Noriega and his attorneys. After defying the federal court's gag order, CNN was found in criminal contempt and ultimately agreed to pay $85,000 in attorney's fees and broadcast an on-air apology to the trial judge who issued the order.

Some attempts at a prior restraint are based on state statutes that prohibit the release of certain information, such as a rape victim's identity or a juvenile's criminal record. However, the United States Supreme Court has refused to punish journalists for publishing truthful information they have obtained from public records or official sources. As a general rule, a court's prior restraint or gag order is unconstitutional if it prohibits the publication of either (1) information obtained during a court proceeding attended by the reporter or (2) information obtained legally from a source outside the court.

If you are faced with a temporary restraining order or gag order, *consult an attorney immediately*. Be aware that courts disagree on whether you may still be fined, and even jailed for criminal contempt, if you disobey a court order that is later found to be unlawful by an appellate court. Remember that time is of the essence. Many courts will consider the speed with which the order was appealed in assessing sanctions for violating the order if it is not overturned on appeal. Make no mistake about the fact that many judges are quick to impose sanctions on those who willfully disobey their orders. Consequently, writers who are facing a gag order must engage in serious soul-searching as to whether the principle at issue in exercising their First Amendment rights, and the importance of the information they are seeking to publish, outweigh the very real risk of heavy fines, criminal records, and even jail if they disobey the court's order.

The image of a crusading reporter willing to risk jail time by defying a judge's order to reveal a confidential source has become a part of American popular culture. The reality of a threat of jail time to a working writer is somewhat more intimidating than watching the scenario play out on television. First and foremost, writers should be aware that thirty-three states and the District of Columbia have enacted "shield laws," which protect reporters from disclosing confidential sources and unpublished work product. Shield laws generally do not apply to reporters who witness criminal activity. Qualified privileges, which offer somewhat less protection, are generally available under the laws of those states without shield laws. It is important to consult an attorney familiar with the laws of your state as soon as possible after service of the subpoena.

In addition to the various state shield laws, the First Amendment also provides journalists with a limited privilege not to disclose their sources or information to litigants who seek to use that information in court. In *Branzburg v. Hayes* (1972), the Supreme Court held that reporters did not have a privilege to refuse to answer a grand jury's questions that directly related to criminal conduct that the journalists observed and wrote about. However, a majority of the Court recognized a qualified constitutional privilege spelled out in a three-part test that requires judges to inquire whether (1) the information sought by the subpoena is clearly relevant and material to the pending case, (2) it goes "to the heart of the case," and (3) the information could be obtained from other sources.

In the case of a reporter called to testify in a criminal case, the court applies the three-part Branzburg test to determine whether the defendant's Sixth Amendment right to mount a defense and confront all witnesses against him outweighs the reporter's need for confidentiality. The decision usually comes down to whether the information sought is clearly essential to the proof of the crime, to the defendant's defense, or to the charge and/or the sentence.

Writers will enjoy the most success invoking the qualified constitutional privilege in civil cases in which they are not a party. Even in libel suits in which the writer is the defendant, many courts will not require the disclosure of confidential sources unless the plaintiff is able to establish by substantial evidence that the published statement is both factually untrue and defamatory. The plaintiff is also usually required to prove that reasonable efforts to discover the information from alternative sources have been made, that no other reasonable source is available, and that the identity of the confidential source is necessary to properly prepare the case. Once a court has ordered production of the disputed information, failure to comply with the court's order can result in a variety of evidentiary sanctions, including the possibility of a directed verdict in favor of the plaintiff.

CONCLUSION

The old adage that "the pen is mightier than the sword" has become a tired aphorism with little meaning to underpaid writers struggling to meet a deadline. Nevertheless, it is undeniable that the ability to communicate clearly and effectively to a large audience can be more powerful than the ability to make money or to wage war. Consequently, nonfiction writers should not be surprised that projects devoted to matters of public concern will result in opposition to their efforts by powerful interests with lots of money at their disposal.

While this may not be particularly encouraging advice for nonfiction writers, the conclusion of this essay is that if you want to be absolutely safe from legal liability you should write about gardening and try to avoid criticizing the pesticide industry. The privilege of using your gifts in the exercise of your First Amendment rights does not come without a cost. In some cases, this cost can be measured in having to defend against a frivolous lawsuit, or in facing the prospect of jail time for defying the illegal order of an abusive judge. However, if writers refuse to fight these battles and succumb to self-censorship, the real cost to society will be measured in the gradual loss of our liberties and freedoms, which will have withered like a useless appendage from apathy and disuse.

II

Aftershocks— Responses to the Genre

Learning to Breathe
After the Memoir

E. ETHELBERT MILLER

Note: Fathering Words: The Making of an African American Writer *is about the journey every poet undertakes. It is a journey that begins in the heart. Moving beyond the loss of both his father and brother, E. Ethelbert Miller tells the story of how love survived in his family. When Miller was about ten years old, his father told him how he could have left his mother. Years later, now a writer and a father, Miller looks back on that simple remark and how it shaped him. In* Fathering Words, *Miller explores his development as an African-American writer, the responsibility of his chosen career, and his ambitions to raise the consciousness of black people. Miller's poetry often relies on the voices of women. In* Fathering Words *he has chosen to write his memoir in two voices. He places his sister's voice on the page next to his own. The result is a duet that tells two stories woven together into one.*

Well, it's done and I'm still alive.

My memoir, *Fathering Words: The Making of an African American Writer*, rests on the bookshelf next to my desk. Now and then I look at it like it's one of those artificial flowers or plants. I think a number of my friends were surprised to see this book published. I can't recall how often I was accused of being too young to write a memoir.

Some of these comments were made by people who just don't take care of themselves. They look much older then I. I turn fifty this year. It's something many black men living in the United States often don't achieve. I remember all the black poets who died in their youth, never reaching middle age. I have a hole in my heart where the friendships of Essex Hemphill and Garth Tate once were. It was losing two men I loved that opened the door for me to another genre. The deaths of my brother and father in the 1980s made the decade a period I wanted to forget. It forced me, however, to remember. I wanted to keep the memories of my father and brother alive. I also needed to understand their lives. How much were we similar? On those dark evenings when my mood changed, how much of it was being directed by the blood beneath my flesh? My father and brother were men who had their dreams broken. Growing up, I saw the sharp pieces of hope that left scars on their hands.

I wrote *Fathering Words* in much the same manner prophets receive revelations. One becomes a medium for a visit from the spirits. I wrote while embracing mystery. I felt guided by an inner light that permitted me to see around the corners of my past. I wrote from memory. I decided not to read old journals or letters. I didn't want to talk to anyone in order to obtain an opinion or insight. I needed to trust my memory. I also knew I wanted to make the men in my family heroic. On the second page of my memoir I compared my father to God.

As I told my story, I felt I was weaving. It is not an accident or coincidence that the cover jacket to *Fathering Words* is a textile from Mali. In many African societies, it is men who do the weaving. I like to link weaving to the creative process of writing. The creation of fabric and design. Within the tapestry of my life there is music, so the narrative I created contained the elements of jazz. Riffs, improvisation, and actual names of jazz musicians I placed throughout the text. I was interested not only in telling my story but also in how I sound telling it.

It was because of sound that I wrote *Fathering Words* in two voices: my own and my older sister Marie Hunter's. Our voices create what I see as a duet on the page. In terms of texture the narrative is both masculine and feminine. The idea of including my sister's voice occurred when I tried to imagine what my family was like before I was born. It was not a difficult challenge. For many years, I've been exploring the female voice in my poems.

Stepping outside of oneself can be risky. The poet Ai had an early influence on my work. Her collection of poems *Cruelty* opened a door to new possibilities. I liked how she experimented using different voices. Writing in my sister's voice permitted me to look at my family from a different perspective.

It helped with writing about my mother. Creative nonfiction should provide the writer with a blueprint for examining complex personalities. My mother is a complex person. I knew that as I attempted to understand her response to key events and incidents that involved our family, I would be uncovering a pile of secrets. My memoir encouraged me to look at my mother as my father's girlfriend. I also looked at her as being a woman coming of age in the 1940s and 1950s.

My mother was the daughter of a West Indian man who came to America to find his dream. My father's family also had West Indian roots. These facts meant my story was linked to the history of a geographical region. How many Sunday afternoons had I spent in Brooklyn brownstones listening to stories told by aunts, uncles, and cousins? I grew up not really knowing these people. What was their relationship to me? I lived with these questions hidden inside my heart. The problem I encountered while writing my memoir was the shortage of information I had access to. Being the baby of the family (the third of three children) I was never taken aside and told things. I was kept in the dark and outside the room of family secrets. This was compounded by the quiet demeanor of my father. He was a man who said few words. A string of letters could have been purchased for him from a corner store.

They could have been mints for his breath. In writing about my family I had to "father" words. There was just too much space inside the Bronx apartment I called home.

I was instructed by my parents not to let people know your business. When I was little this advice meant hiding money in one's sock. Someone might steal from you. I have no idea what my mother is thinking about right now. All I know is that I had to tell my own story.

Many critics and reviewers of my memoir have focused on my relationship to my father and my own ties to my two children.

Although this is an important theme in *Fathering Words*, it is not the primary one. It's amazing how many reviews contain factual errors about my life. While reading a few of them I kept looking for those old carbon copies that would leave ink on my hands. Why do people read creative nonfiction and make up their own fiction? It's disappointing to read a review in which a person has not paid careful attention to the text.

Writing my memoir forced me to defend my work in a way I never had to do with poetry. A poem has many open windows for interpretation. Fresh air is always blowing in. I don't want to sweep the errors under the rug.

One reviewer claimed my brother was a drug addict, another thought my sister's name was Denise (my wife's name). Of course someone might believe these errors are minor. But what if a review is placed online? This means other writers and scholars might continue to pass on incorrect information. One runs the risk of being introduced at a reading by an organizer who prepared his or her remarks from searching for information on the Internet. One is talking about misreading a memoir, not a novel.

It's another reason for opposing the death penalty. What if the jury is wrong?

While *Fathering Words* was in production, I convinced my editor to include my e-mail address on the inside of the cover jacket (at the end of the biographical note). I have been fortunate to receive wonderful feedback and comments from people who have read my book. I have saved e-mail letters from friends and strangers. These documents I view as an "extension" of my memoir. They complement what I've written as much as a sideman sitting in on a jazz jam. My friends also mention what they felt was missing in the book. They want to know why I left certain things out. For example, a Jewish friend wanted to know why I had not included the political work I had done with the Jewish community. There are places in my book where I omitted the names of certain individuals. This was a political decision and one I made in order for the narrative to flow. I wrote in a language that was poetic. I was working outside my genre. I read sections of my memoir aloud in order to uphold the rhythmic nature of speech.

Prior to completing *Fathering Words* I encountered some concerns voiced by my agent. After sending the manuscript off to several major publishers she began to receive a few interesting rejection letters. A couple of editors recommended I drop my sister's voice. They felt it intruded into the narrative. What did my sister's story have to do with mine?

We might write as individuals, but our words often become fruit and bread for others. In my family there were no writers.

My journey is therefore one of departure. In many ways I needed to talk to my family through the memoir. I was often ignored and told to keep quiet while a young boy. This is how it was in a small Bronx apartment. My sister and brother playing together before my birth. My father placing his arm around my mother's waist. A small gesture that might have been the beginning of my breath.

My sister's voice is a witness to my beginnings. It is also a measurement of the distance traveled from Eugene Miller to E. Ethelbert Miller. A memoir is a photograph. It captures the pose, the way we wish to see ourselves and how others see us. My life has been a way of learning how to push back the darkness in this world. One struggles to be good and when one fails, one struggles again. This is how I write. Starting over meant writing my memoir. I needed to know more about the writer I am, and the writer I am becoming. *Fathering Words* was a self-portrait with my sister playing with the paint.

EXERCISES

1. Why write a memoir? List five things a person can learn from your life. What family secrets do you plan to tell? List two. Why do you feel you must reveal these secrets?

2. You're about to write the last page of your memoir. Where do you want to end your story? Why?

Excerpts From
Fathering Words: The Making of an African American Writer

E. ETHELBERT MILLER

I could leave your mother and be like everyone else," my father says to me during a commercial. It doesn't matter how old I am, his words will find a place in the cuff of my pants, in the corner of my coat pocket, or as I turn a corner on a cold winter afternoon and turn my collar up against the wind. My father is blowing down my neck like Coleman Hawkins, and someone says, "The Hawk is blowing," and the notes from my father's life are rushing at me and the composition is as complex as anything Thelonious Monk could imagine. Yes, "Ruby My Dear."

Two bodies in the dark, one talking and the other listening to a strange sound coming from where pain and hurt is mixed with depression and the blues, and if you cry for everyone and not just yourself, this is where you discover the Middle Passage, the Holocaust, the plantation, the concentration camps, the bombing of cities, and whatever is left. This is the howl Allen Ginsberg described for an entire generation. That spoken unspokenness. Those moments between father and son that are not the simplicity of playing catch with a ball and glove. It is the moment when your father lets you touch the nakedness of his back. The place where the weight of his own sex and identity meets your own. And the mirror you were afraid to look into is the face of your own father, and this is also the face of history.[1]

I always wanted to have children, and when I couldn't, I couldn't find anyone to talk to about it. When I had my surgery, I slowly came to realize that I was the only person in that bed, room, and hospital. I was lying there looking at nothing and knowing that nothing would ever come out of me. I was holding on to being whole by a slender

---

[1] Excerpt from chapter four.

thread. I tried to talk to my husband about what I was going through, but he looked at me as if I had contracted a disease. His male mind just wanted to see himself in a small body. He wanted a little boy. Was that not the unspoken agreement at the altar when we took our vows? I was to be a mother by any means necessary.

Giving birth is the beginning of life and beauty. Sometimes I walk through the hospital where I work and I need to leave the emergency ward, so I take the elevator up to the floor where the babies are. Behind glass, or in arms, the newborns sleep, their eyes too new for this world. I like to inhale the joy and smell of motherhood, watching the first drops of breast milk falling into sheets and the space between us.

I am different from other women. I believed this for many years. When my mother called on the phone and whispered something about my brother in Washington living without rules, I wanted to join him. Who made the rule so that I couldn't have children? I cried many nights listening to my tears fall down the back steps of my heart.[2]

---

[2] Excerpt from chapter fourteen.

One Nation,
Under the Weather

LAUREN SLATER

July 05, 2000. I am self-centered. I am an exhibitionist. I pose when-ever possible in public places. I have a billy club (Watch out!) and it would not be beyond me to flog you on your tender head, just to get my point across, my point across, my point across. Immature and whiny, constantly ill, a voluble bellyacher, not to mention derivative in all pursuits artistic, I still, at the ripe old age of 36, blame my mother for it all.

It is Thursday, June something, and this is what I wake to, the points above, written, alas, in a huge newspaper, *The New York Times*, a newspaper as wide as the world, with print as black as an old bruise. My new book—the book I love best of all my books, my baby—has been *panned* by a woman named Maslin, named Janet. She hates it. She hates me. Her dislike seems to seep from the spaces between the words, and my first response, after reading it twice—"*Lying* flogs these important things to the point where they cease being important . . . though she has already cataloged a full litany of com-plaints including depression, anorexia and self-mutilation, Ms. Slater now locates a whole new vein of illness to mine . . ."—after reading the review twice, no, three times, I do what any good illness memoirist would do. I reach for the shelf and take my meds.

I take, to be specific, two Valium, which I keep on hand for emergen-cies such as these. The drug is fast-acting and sweet, and soon I am calm enough to eat a corn muffin. I sit at my kitchen table and think. How could she say I'm so self-absorbed? Me? ME? Self-absorbed? I'm so nice that the mice I catch in sticky traps I later free in the woods, five miles from my home. I don't eat meat. I don't eat chicken. I personally palpate my dog's anal sacs because he's so afraid of the vet. Me? ME? Self-absorbed? I love animals and people, and to top it off I'm a psychotherapist, goddamit, I'm in the helping profession; I don't whine, I listen to other people whine, me? ME? ME?

I call my husband at work. "I got a terrible review in the *Times*," I say.

"I'm sorry," he says.

"The reviewer basically accuses me of being narcissistic, solipsistic and writing too much about illness. That's not true," I say. "Don't you think?"

He doesn't say anything.

"Listen, sweetie," I say, "Today is not the day I want your honest response. Lie to me."

"Honestly," he says, "you do write a lot about yourself, and yourself as ill, but I like your books."

"I don't believe you," I say.

"Really," he says.

"I'm going to call her," I say.

"Call who?" he says.

"The reviewer," I say, "Janet Maslin."

"I don't think that's a good idea," he says. "Why don't you calm down first?"

But I am calm. And it suddenly occurs to me, or the me-on-Valium, that this is exactly what I need to do. I need to call Ms. Maslin up on the phone and have a heart-to-heart.

Exactly what my heart will say to her heart is not clear to me, but the urge to hear her voice is. I feel, I suppose, a little like a jilted lover. A very powerful person has rejected me, and there is nothing like rejection to stir that little crimson clementine in our chests. I am stirred. I hang up with my husband. I imagine Ms. Maslin as very tall, with handsome hair and a freshly sharpened pencil tucked behind a compact ear. I imagine her briefcase, well-worn and Coach; her Manhattan apartment, where a cat curls on top of a sleek black stereo set. She is impeccable, powerful and beautiful, with a brain like a blade. I must redeem myself in her eyes. I must reason with her. I must persuade her to write another review. I must make her feel guilty. I call her.

I'm surprised by how easy it is to find her. All you have to do is call information and get the main number for *The New York Times*. Then you tell the gum-snapping operator on the other end of the phone that you'd like to speak with Janet Maslin. It's as though they've been waiting for my call. Not a second's hesitation, the operator ferrets me through.

I hear Janet's phone ring once, twice. I imagine her desk, with my book on it, the margins marked up. Click click. "Your call is being answered by Audix," I hear, and then a pregnant pause, and then what I know is Ms. Maslin's voice saying, "Janet Maslin is busy right now." I am taken aback by Janet's voice. I am surprised by its sound, soft, tentative in its tone, a voice without the vim and vigor of her muscular writing style. She must be short. I am shocked to think that Janet Maslin might be short, and that she has such a human sound. Suddenly, her deeply critical review of me is much harder to dismiss. Maybe I am self-centered. And why do I write so ceaselessly about being ill? I replace the phone. There is sweat on the receiver where my hand has been. Damn hand. Ugly hand. Derivative hand. Ms. Maslin has it right. I am a part of, alas, the once-fashionable, now-fading brat pack of illness memoirists, and we can be a tiring bunch to read.

So there. As a memoirist I am very good at making confessions. I concede Ms. Maslin her points. I now have three, count them three, books on the market in which psychiatric illness figures significantly. To make matters worse, I have a fourth on the way. This is an embarrassment.

Illness as an artistic or narrative device is cheap, easy to sensational-ize, obvious in its plot. Illness is not subtle, and so the illness memoirist need not grapple with the problems of how to render those fleeting poignant moments of being, those Woolfian wisps that disappear in mid-formation, the quarks of emotion or perception, like how she touched her forefinger to her lip, or how the couple, rendered omni-sciently, argued at the restaurant without ever saying a word. The illness memoirist need not struggle with all the possibilities of point of view—first person, close third person, alternate voices—because her tale is relentlessly singular. And how much easier it is to dramatize the syringe or the psychosis than it is to conjure up the haunting emptiness of Don DeLillo suburbia or the poverty of Jean Toomer's inner city.

Most disturbing of all, perhaps, is how the illness memoir can be reductive in its approach to the hugeness of human problems. At its worst, by framing everything as a syndrome, as diagnosis, the illness memoir underscores medicine's dangerous but alluring stranglehold on our understanding; existentialism, love, spirituality, even nihilism fade away as explanatory models, and we are left with only this: our-selves, myself, sick, staring at the singular wound, endlessly penning it bright, penning it black as an old bruise.

The day is bad. I speak to my agent. She says, "Well a review like this won't kill the book," which leads me to believe that, although the book will still be breathing, it will need some serious life support. My illness memoir has now become ill itself. It needs to be in the hospital, and I long to find a very special bed for it. My friend Lisa, who is very savvy about the publishing world, says, "I hate to say this, but other reviewers take their cues from *The New York Times*."

There is, of course, nothing I can do. Except think. And I am a reasonably good thinker, even on Valium. I think about all the problems with the illness memoir as a genre, its tendency toward artistic cheapness, its obsession with syndromes, its brass Oprah-ness. I think about whether or not I really *am* an illness memoirist or if I have just capitulated to the market forces that have shaped the image of work. After all, although my first book, *Welcome to My Country*, was promoted as a book about me, it was actually a series of portraits of six schizophrenic men whom I treated as a psychologist. I think about the time I went on *Roseanne*, when my second book, *Prozac Diary*, was published.

I tried to write a nuanced book about the complexities of the Prozac cure, but, ultimately, I wound up on *Roseanne*, my face caked with makeup, my hands gesturing wildly, hopefully (I saw a tape of it later), as I admitted, on air, to having this and that mental problem, and the audience clapped, and my Amazon.com number rose oh so briefly into the 80s. I will never forget Roseanne. She herself was nice, and plump and very feminist, and she seemed to feel secure enough in what she was doing.

But I will never forget myself on *Roseanne*, the six-minute segment when my writing sank to its lowest point as I allowed myself to be seen as simply sick and cured, sick and cured, trotting out on TV and showing off my war wounds—for what? For fame? Of course not for fame. I am not so naive as to think a six-minute segment on a faltering talk show would bring fame. No. I did it simply to stay in print. I did it because, if you write about illness, there seems to be no other way of marketing it except to sensationalize it, or to let it be sensationalized by certain celebrity readers. You can't go on a talk show and discuss nuance. You have to bray, or say nothing and sell no books and lose your publishing house and your editor, who is very important to me, my editor is. In a way I even love her.

So I think about Roseanne, and whoring, on this bad day. And because even on a bad day I am a reasonably good thinker, I muse also on why the hell I keep writing these whorish books. Am I simply a whore? Is the illness memoir as a form just a crooked cheap shot by writers who can't conjure up a novel? This is what I think: Sometimes yes. But sometimes no.

As a psychologist, one of my favorite theorists to read is Irvin Yalom. He writes beautifully about existential psychotherapy and group psychotherapy, and he's one of the few in the field who has really been able to articulate what the healing principles of group therapy might be. Yalom claims that universality is a core healing component of the group therapy process. In other words, patients in group therapy learn that they are not the only ones who feel this way, that they are not aberrant, or perverse, and this in itself is deeply healing.

The best of the illness memoirs, especially those dealing with psychiatric illnesses such as depression, are offerings in this spirit. They were written, I believe, not for the purpose of a peacock display, but to offer solace, to forge connection in times of trouble. I, for one, expect that my readers will be troubled; I envision my readers as troubled, as depressed, as guilty, mourning, maybe, a medication that failed them. I write to say, you are not the only one.

I write with the full faith that the reader I envision is hungry for my tale. I know it, because, having suffered psychiatric illness myself, I am always hungry for tales from the trenches, stories in which I can see myself, stories that might help me map my way. We must consider the illness memoir not only as, or solely as, an *Oprah* bid, but also as this: a gift from me to you. A folk cure, a hand held out. I look into my heart and I see a whore there. But I also see something else. I can, if you are hurting, keep you company.

Perhaps, however, the purpose of literature is not social, or therapeutic. That may be, in which case, I suppose we should house these memoirs, my own included, on the self-help shelf. But that seems a little too easy. The illness memoir, after all, is not a prescription but a description, offered not to cure but to accompany.

Furthermore, shelving the whole lot of us in the self-help section would remove us from public discourse and, if anything, the illness memoir as a social phenomenon is worthy of public discourse. Why are there so many? What might they mean, not only about their singular authors, but about the collective culture in which we all live? Remember this. No author authors alone. Every text is a joint construction of meaning. Every illness memoir came from the world that you and I co-created, and thus we all, together, Janet Maslin included, write and continue to write this long story of sickness? For what?

Let me begin by saying that in every age there has been a prevailing explanatory grid that the myriad writers of that time have used to frame or explain their lives. The 17th-century spiritual autobiography is a perfect example of this. So is the 1960s political memoir or the 1970s feminist memoir.

Beneath these grids, however, the same essential story prevails; the grid is merely the conduit through which the tale flows. From Augustine's *Confessions* to *The Autobiography of Malcolm X* to Nancy Mairs' *Remembering the Bone House*, the tale, if it is done well, is always the classic heroic journey, the Dantean descent into the hell of sin, or oppression, or sickness, the long night of the soul, the gradual redemption, partial or complete. This is the story we, as humans, tell ourselves over and over again, and an illness memoir, if it is done deeply, will put its own signature on the transcendent tale, and will be, thus, transcendent.

It is a mistake, therefore, to dismiss illness memoirs out of hand. The worst of them are showy and whiny. The best of them are tussling with the great human themes in an utterly contemporary context; here, modern diagnosis and the ever-present pill are just jazzed-up versions of polytheistic gods teasing with mere mortals, the aching Achilles' heel, Sodom, Gomorrah, burning, cities and salt.

And yet. Are there not other ways of getting at these great themes than through the relentless use of disease? So the critic argues. So might Ms. Maslin say. I say no. Not for me. Not for now. This might be my great limitation as a writer, or this might mean I'm onto something the crazy optimists just can't see.

The fact is, or my fact is, disease is everywhere. How anyone could ever write about themselves or their fictional characters as not diseased is a bit beyond me. We live in a world and are creatures of a culture that is spinning out more and more medicines that correspond to more and more diseases at an alarming pace.

Even beyond that, though, I believe we exist in our God-given natures as diseased beings. We do not fall into illness. We fall from illness into temporary states of health. We are briefly blessed, but always, always those small cells are dividing and will become cancer, if they haven't already; our eyes are crossed, we cannot see. Nearsighted, farsighted, noses spurting bright blood, brains awack with crazy dreams, lassitude and little fears nibbling like mice at the fringes of our flesh, we are never well.

Science proves me right, the great laws of the universe, the inevitability of entropy. So there. The illness memoir is so many things, a kindly attempt to keep company; a product of our culture's love of pathology, or of our sometimes whorish selves; a story of human suffering and the attempts to make meaning within it; and finally, a reflection on this awful and absurd and somehow very funny truth, that we are rotting, rotting, even as we write. *Salud.*

Becoming the Godfather of Creative Nonfiction

LEE GUTKIND

What is it about the term "creative nonfiction" that makes people want to attack or make unfunny jokes about it—or anyone having any connection with it? Over the past ten years, I have discussed the genre and the meaning of the term at colleges and universities and conferences in the U.S., Europe, and Australia. But wherever I go, there are the inevitable questions and complaints, especially about that first word—*creative*—which seems to insult or infuriate academics and scare journalists to death. "Why can't my work be creative, too?" they whine. Why are their essays on Milton or postmodernism or their articles concerning the local water authority considered criticism and reportage, respectively, while my prose about cross-country motorcycling or the medical world is artistic and literary?

People sometimes become so indignant that they entangle the terms they want to criticize or attack, confusing, for example, creative nonfiction with "noncreative fiction" or talking with great intensity about the "nonfiction essay"—as if there's an alternative. Those who are especially clever will observe that creative nonfiction is an oxymoron. Some will realize that nonfiction is also an oxymoron. A couple of months ago, a woman who spotted me at Ronald Reagan International Airport in Washington, DC, began pointing and yelling, "Hey, it's the uncreative fiction guy!"

The fact that I was recognized by a total stranger in a city hundreds of miles from where I live stems from a four-page October 1997 feature in *Vanity Fair*, "Me, Myself, and I," by James Wolcott, who had some snide and nasty observations about the term "creative nonfiction" and about me. Wolcott boiled all creative nonfiction down into what he called "confessional writing" and took to task as "navel gazers" nearly any writer who had been the least bit self-revelatory in his work. (Captions read "Never have so many [writers] shared so much of so little," and "No personal detail is too mundane to share.") His definition of creative nonfiction? A "sickly transfusion, whereby the weakling personal voice of sensitive fiction is inserted into the beery carcass of nonfiction . . . to form a big, earnest blob of me-first sensibility."

Inexplicably, Wolcott zeroed in on the memoir and made it seem as if that was creative nonfiction in its totality, while ignoring the significant information-oriented work done by John McPhee, Annie Dillard, Tracy Kidder, Gay Talese, and many others.

Wolcott reserved an especially interesting title and role for me as "the godfather behind creative nonfiction." He abhorred the fact that I traveled and talked about creative nonfiction all over the world, that I wrote books about creative nonfiction (He called me a "human octopus"), publish a journal (*Creative Nonfiction*), direct a creative nonfiction writers' conference, edit a series of books for new writers in creative nonfiction, and teach creative nonfiction in a creative writing program, which, collectively, he maintained, ruined the audience for fiction. Because of the proliferation of these courses, "The short story has become a minor arts-and-craftsy skill, like Indian pottery," he stated.

It was unfortunate that Wolcott had so much to say in such a major publication concerning a subject about which he knew so little. (He had never been involved in a writing program or a writing course.) In truth, creative writing programs have actually legitimized literary nonfiction—made it more important in the literary world than ever before by acknowledging, albeit belatedly, the awesome challenge and intrinsic art of the genre—and indirectly affected, in a very positive way, *Vanity Fair* and Wolcott, himself. Without the new appreciation for (creative) nonfiction as an art form as significant as fiction and poetry, Wolcott's opinions would be less important, while magazines like *Vanity Fair*, *GQ*, and others might not wield the influence and attract the advertising that enhances profits and prominence.

THE ORIGINS OF CREATIVE NONFICTION IN THE UNIVERSITY

When I started teaching in the English Department at the University of Pittsburgh in the early 1970s, the concept of an "artful" or "literary" nonfiction was considered, to say the least, unlikely. My colleagues snickered when I proposed teaching a "creative" nonfiction course, while the dean of the College of Arts and Sciences proclaimed that nonfiction in general—forget the use of the word *creative*—was at its best a craft, not too different from plumbing.

As the chairman of our department put it one day in a faculty meeting while we were debating the legitimacy of the course: "After all, gentlemen [the fact that many of his colleagues were women often slipped his mind], we're interested in literature here—not writing." That remark and the subsequent debate had been precipitated by a contingent of students from the school newspaper who marched on the chairman's office and politely requested more nonfiction writing courses—"the creative kind."

One colleague, aghast at this prospect, carried a dozen of his favorite books to the meeting—poetry, fiction, and nonfiction—gave a belabored mini-review of each, and then, pointing a finger at the editor of the paper and pounding a fist, stated: "After you read all these books and understand what they mean, I will consider voting for a course called Creative Nonfiction. Otherwise, I don't want to be bothered."

Luckily, most of my colleagues didn't want to be bothered fighting the school newspaper, so the course was approved—and I became one of the first people to teach creative nonfiction on a university level, anywhere. This was 1973.

Over the next quarter century, creative nonfiction courses in creative writing programs began to grow both on graduate and undergraduate levels. Being awarded tenure in the English Department at Pittsburgh in 1979 was another milestone—perhaps another first for literary nonfiction. Now there are many tenure-track positions for writers whose specialty is nonfiction, exclusively. This was no small feat. The practice in English departments and writing programs then was to appoint writers who had "legitimized" themselves by becoming accomplished in fiction or poetry—a recognizable literary art—but who could also teach nonfiction. As the job market tightened in the early 1980s and a few nonfiction positions were posted, an amazing transition occurred: Poets, short-story writers, and composition Ph.D.s who had written articles for newspapers and scholarly journals and who had previously concealed or ignored their journalistic backgrounds, however slight, were suddenly reinventing themselves as creative nonfiction writers.

Some very accomplished poets and fiction writers were taking nonfiction more seriously, however, by actually practicing what others were pretending. John Updike published his first collection of essays, *Assorted Prose*. Diane Ackerman began involving herself in the natural world and writing spellbinding articles for *The New Yorker*, while W.S. Merwin's first memoir, *Unframed Originals*, became a bestseller.

Prominent writers crossing genres and adding their talent and prestige to nonfiction was a significant part of the process of legitimizing creative nonfiction as an entity beyond journalism and on the same general level as fiction and poetry.

Vanity Fair wasn't alone in attacking the genre in the late 1990s, however. *The New York Times*, *The New Yorker*, and other major newspapers and magazines made it clear that even though they recognized an explosion in the nonfiction form (mostly memoir) they also predicted a quick demise. And by the way, they hated the term, preferring narrative nonfiction, literary journalism, expository writing, among others. In its precious and traditional simplicity, *The New Yorker* called the creative nonfiction it published by John McPhee, Roger Angell, Jane Kramer, etc., "fact pieces."

Anything but creative nonfiction.

THE CREATIVE STORYTELLER

What does it really mean to be creative? And what is so difficult or terrible to contemplate about the term? Why is it bad to acknowledge that you are trying, as a writer, to show imagination and to demonstrate artistic or intellectual inventiveness? Nonfiction writers aren't boasting or bragging by utilizing the word in describing what we do—and it is not a term or a concept that I or others have coined out of the air. Creative nonfiction—writing nonfiction using literary techniques such as scene, dialogue, description, allowing the personal point of view and voice rather than maintaining the sham of objectivity—is hardly a new idea.

Hunter Thompson (*Hell's Angels*), Gay Talese (*Fame and Obscurity*), Norman Mailer (*The Armies of the Night*), Tom Wolfe (*The Electric Kool-Aid Acid Test*) were introducing literary techniques and personal voice into their nonfiction work in the 1960s—a style then called the "New Journalism." Earlier work by Lillian Ross—and much earlier by George Orwell—could clearly be situated under the creative nonfiction umbrella.

The term was eventually adopted by the National Endowment for the Arts to represent the different styles within the genre (memoir, immersion journalism, etc.), an "official" acknowledgment of the distinction between the way in which the literary or creative essay is written compared to the traditional essay or news report.

This difference has to do with storytelling—employing real-life experiences of the writer or people they know or people they learn about through the techniques of immersion or involvement in a dramatic, often suspenseful sequence—in order to communicate information or establish a special meaning or idea. Creative nonfiction is different because writers aren't constrained by traditional academic or journalistic straitjackets. Literally or symbolically, we can dye our hair blond, wear earrings in our navels, and allow our own personalities to appear on the page with our ideas and observations—a seemingly special violation to the journalist, who has been locked into the inverted pyramid 5W (who-what-when-where-why) format over the past half century and beyond.

I am not disputing the overabundance of "navel gazers," as Wolcott put it—writers who are primarily inward and self-obsessed—or the notion that there hasn't been an overemphasized craze for this sort of personal (sometimes too personal) writing as of late. But there's also an explosion of altogether brilliant nonfiction prose being written today by people who can reveal their feelings or the feelings of the people about whom they are writing while communicating compelling information and striking some sort of universal chord. What about *Angela's Ashes*, *A Natural History of the Senses*, *Autobiography of a Face*, *The Professor and the Madman*, *A Heartbreaking Work of Staggering Genius*, to name a few?

Journalists have, over the years, been so stifled from being creative that they don't exactly understand what the word *creative* might signify beyond the parameters of fiction. William Zinsser, author of the highly respected text *On Writing Well*, has acknowledged his uneasiness with the phrase *creative nonfiction* because he associates "creative" either with fiction or with writers who "fudge the truth."

Young writers, he fears, will take the word *creative* as a license to fabricate.

Zinsser agrees that nonfiction can be creative when "a writer raises the craft to an art by imposing an interesting shape or organizing idea on it," which to me is one of many ways in which writers can write with style without sacrificing substance. But clearly he doesn't have much confidence in the intelligence of our young people, if he thinks that students will take creativity as a license to lie.

YOU DON'T MAKE IT UP

In the past couple of years, a number of journalists have been discovered and disgraced for, literally, fudging the truth. In 1997, Stephen Glass admitted to fabricating parts of twenty-seven articles for *The New Republic*, where he worked as a reporter, and for *The New York Times*, *George*, and *Harper's*. He even provided fake supporting material, including self-created Web sites, to outfox his fact checkers. And a columnist for the *Boston Globe*, Patricia Smith, a Pulitzer prize finalist, admitted to fabricating the people and the quotations in four of her columns in 1999. In one case she made up an entire column about a woman dying of cancer. These reporters, only two examples among many, weren't claiming that they were trying to be creative; they took liberties that were blatantly dishonest. The journalism community must learn to police themselves more carefully—rather than fantasize about the potential damage that can be done in other glass houses.

Unfortunately, however, with so many new people discovering creative nonfiction from so many different orientations (especially in the areas of psychology, literature, and composition), the journalistic, fact-oriented roots of creative nonfiction are often forgotten—or ignored. Writers can become too enamored with the creative part of the term, paying precious little homage to the nonfiction part.

There must be a delicate balance between style and substance. Whether writing memoir or dramatic reportage, creative nonfiction writers must always work as hard as necessary to be true to the facts; there are some creative nonfiction writers who don't care about accuracy or who consider it unimportant. These writers lose credibility when they are writing nonfiction and not paying attention to verifiable information.

I recently participated in an Associated Writing Programs panel in which one woman, writing about a town in Germany during the Nazi era, stated that she wouldn't employ the name of the town because, she said, she was keeping her options open just in case she wanted to change what she was doing to fiction. What is that all about, one wonders? If she doesn't know if she's writing fiction or nonfiction, then she is writing fiction. Readers don't appreciate or deserve such sleight of hand.

John Berendt, author of the best-selling *Midnight in the Garden of Good and Evil*, admitted to making up saucy dialogue for a real-life character and creating situations in order to more easily manipulate his narrative. "I call it 'rounding the corners,' " he explained, adding that he has no regrets because, by doing this, he feels he is giving his readers "a better story." But it is not a true story and it denotes inexcusable laziness. When confronted with a character who might not have exactly scintillating things to say, a good writer, rather than making up better stuff, will work harder to discover other aspects of the subject that are interesting, like by talking to other people about the character in question, or make better connections between one part of an essay to another, or simply work on getting the character to talk more and reveal himself, rather than resorting to fiction.

At the same time, while facts can be checked and confirmed, all truth isn't verifiable. This is especially important to acknowledge for those writing memoir. Ideas and feelings fished out of a person or unearthed from memory can't be fact-checked. Scenes that are re-created, conversations that have been recalled and recounted from the distant past, will be highly personal and subjective.

But in creative nonfiction we draw the line: We do not make up out-of-the-air information of any kind—for any reason. We do our best to replicate with truth and accuracy exactly what we believe has happened, even if, in the real world, there is a possibility that it hasn't happened in exactly the way we describe it or if other people disagree with our interpretations.

THE SHIFT TO STORYTELLING VALUES

This is not a new idea, historically, but many journalists have become so cemented into the traditional 5W form of reporting that they are often afraid and/or unable to try anything different—afraid that they simply don't have the talent or the energy to write and report in a creative manner. The timidity of their editors and the narrow range of their literary perspective have devastated their potential as serious writers. Many of the newspaper reporters who enroll in my M.F.A. classes experience great difficulty writing longer essays—twelve pages or 3,000 words or more, or focusing on one theme. Intellectual investigation is an unmined concept in daily journalism. Reporters have been trained for so long to write short, to dumb down their ideas to a sixth-grade level—and to think in quotes and sound bites—that they can't introduce real characters with intelligent perceptions. It is ironic that journalists like to refer to what they are doing as "stories,"—but they aren't stories; rather they are reports, with a few scenic elements sometimes included.

Which is not to say that the journalistic community hasn't recognized the inevitable shift to a more creative concept of journalism; they are simply not advertising it. Through much of this year I have been mentoring reporters and editors at National Public Radio, teaching a style of journalism in which story or narrative is given much more attention, without a loss in substance, integrity, or verifiable facts. Up to this point, most journalists have maintained that a concentration on story (style) endangered the journalistic integrity of the final product—which is a legitimate danger if the reporter devotes the same amount of time and effort to style and story as in her traditional work. The problem is that most journalists devote most of their efforts to the information-gathering process.

Then they sit down and write their "stories," basically relying on their skills as writers to be clear, concise, and compelling. It's good when a natural narrative emerges—but not unusual when it doesn't.

By enlisting my help, NPR has symbolically and literally endorsed its commitment to the story form. The organization is authorizing and encouraging reporters to invest extra time and effort to understand and integrate dramatic, suspenseful, compelling story structures within the reports they file. NPR hasn't backed away from the term "creative nonfiction," while, ironically, *The New York Times*, while pretending that we don't exist, has endorsed virtually every idea that creative nonfiction stands for in an all-encompassing way.

Quite literally, front-page news is now often told in a story-oriented fashion in the *Times*. Here's the beginning of just one story, selected at random, from its brilliant twelve-part series "How Race Is Lived in America," but you can find them on any day of the week:

> It must have been 1 o'clock. That's when the white man usually comes out of this glass office and stands on the scaffolding above the factory floor. He stood with his palms on the rails, his elbows out. He looked like a tower guard up there or a border patrol agent. He stood with his head cocked.

Here we have specificity of description and intimacy of detail, written in the cold staccato rhythm of the poet, while a character has been created and an inner (the character being written about) point of view is established. A few sentences later, the conflict telegraphed in this paragraph is launched:

> The white man stood and watched for the next two hours as the blacks worked in their group and the Mexicans in theirs. . . . At shift change, the black man walked away, hosed himself down and turned in his knives. Then he let go. He threatened to murder the boss. He promised to quit. He said he was losing his mind, which made for good comedy since he was standing near a conveyor chain of severed hogs' heads, their mouths yoked open. "Who that cracker think he is?" the black man wanted to know. There were enough hogs, he said, "not to worry about no fleck of meat being left on the bone. Keep treating me like a Mexican and I'll beat him."

So here we have the other anchors of creative nonfiction—dramatic, compelling story energized by electrifying dialogue. Call it what you want, but it is the epitome of creative nonfiction.

DARING THE LIMITS

It is particularly interesting that creative nonfiction has experienced such an amazing renaissance in the past decade—one that has been dominated in the United States by President Bill Clinton. This is a man who, in my mind, is to politics as creative nonfiction is to literature. In the past half century, no one has charmed and ignited the spirit of Americans as has Clinton, and no one has presided over such an incredible and ongoing economic boom. The Clinton economic miracle has been reflected in the publishing world, which has witnessed an unparalleled profitability—driven by nonfiction in many forms, especially memoir. Clinton's ethics and morals have been questioned and his reputation demeaned—both legitimately and not.

So, too, with creative nonfiction. Memoirists, writers who have accelerated the pulse, expanded the barriers, increased the dimensions of the previously more confining and traditional publishing world, have become characters the media loves to lambaste—also without complete authority. Creative nonfiction writers are "out there," highly visible, sometimes obnoxiously so, walking the line between truth and reality, style and substance—just like Bill Clinton. So we can make people, especially those traditionalists anchored in the past, feel resentful and angry, as in the case of James Wolcott. We can and often do handcuff emotions to manipulate feelings, not subtly like the poet, but in a very obvious and titillating way.

In this regard I am thinking of Lucy Grealy's poetic and powerful self-deprecation in *Autobiography of a Face* and Kathryn Harrison's humiliating confessions of sleeping with her Presbyterian minister father in *The Kiss*. These writers are walking the edge, testing literary and societal norms, and, for good and for bad, creating excitement and controversy, as did Clinton. I don't condone Clinton's actions nor the liberties of writers anxious to excoriate themselves for personal gain. But I appreciate the spirit of their revelations, their willingness to test boundaries rather than sitting comfortably in the safe spaces of respectability, whining about their lack of prominence, criticizing others who have daringly ventured forth with new ideas and concepts. I would not myself do what Edmund Morris did in creating a fictional narrator in his biography of Ronald Reagan, *Dutch*, to illuminate the dead fish of the man he was struggling to capture, but I admire his resourcefulness. He created unprecedented interest and stimulated intellectual discourse about a man people revered but knew nothing about. He also made a lot of money.

At its purest form, creative nonfiction is, similarly, nothing else but real—with all of the potential flaws and warts of any real human being. The media seems to attack Clinton and creative nonfiction writers because he and we are both too difficult and too complicated to figure out. And we can become much too embarrassingly public. We don't fit into the traditional form of reportage. But how can you apply the inverted pyramid 5W formula to a three-dimensional saxophone-playing, politically astute animal like Clinton? Who would want to? That's not the inherent challenge of literature—minimizing larger-than-life characters for the sake of brevity and space.

Journalists have difficulty thinking in more than twelve column inches—a narrow format for an outsized subject. Creative nonfiction writers visualize a world in three multicolored, multiconflicting dimensions.

In a subsequent interview in *The Chronicle of Higher Education*, Wolcott said that he had learned most of what he had picked up about writing working in the classified ad section of the *Village Voice* rather than studying in a creative writing program, and that today all of these writing programs are producing creative writers who are "coddled and swaddled" and who will never get jobs. I am not certain that he is wrong about the value of creative writing programs, which I think are ill-suited for many of the students who support them. But his attitude in the face of ignorance is indicative of the two-dimensional, surface-skimming orientation inherent in magazine and newspaper journalism.

Wolcott also told an interviewer that he was "distrustful of memory," which is why he would never write a memoir. But perhaps he and others who are so critical of creative nonfiction are more distrustful of what they might, in fact, remember when they actually started to search their souls and think about their lives with an open and analytic perspective. This is a frightening concept to people unable to face and/or reveal their innermost feelings—or who just don't recognize the value or understand the method in doing so.

That, in fact, is the essence and the meaning of creative nonfiction: the ability to capture the personal and the private and to make it mean something significant to a larger audience, and to provide intellectual substance that will affect readers—perhaps even incite them to action or to change their thinking—in a compelling and unforgettable way.

My thinking was changed by my experience with Wolcott and *Vanity Fair*—incidentally, in a way that James Wolcott might not find great pleasure in discovering. For weeks after "Me, Myself, and I" was published, our subscription inquiries at *Creative Nonfiction* shot up. We got phone calls from Hollywood producers seeking new stories for their movie mills. People were recognizing me in airports, restaurants—and congratulating me. Although Wolcott's attack caught me by surprise and might be described as mean-spirited, I believe, in retrospect, that the attention he generated and the controversy it triggered actually fortified the cause and elevated the discourse surrounding high-quality creative nonfiction literature, which is why it is important to remember it now.

In the end, I discovered the truth in Oscar Wilde's observation, found in the first chapter of *The Picture of Dorian Gray*: "There is only one thing in the world worse than being talked about, and that is not being talked about." And I have James Wolcott to thank for it.

III
Creative
Nonfiction Reader

The Woman Who Slept
With One Eye Open

JUDITH ORTIZ COFER

As a child caught in that lonely place between two cultures and two languages, I wrapped myself in the magical veil of folktales and fairy tales. The earliest stories I heard were those told by the women of my family in Puerto Rico, some of the tales being versions of Spanish, European, and even ancient Greek and Roman myths that had been translated by time and by each generation's needs into the *cuentos* that I heard. They taught me the power of the word. These *cuentos* have been surfacing in my poems and my prose since I decided to translate them for myself and to use them as my palette, the primary colors from which all creation begins.

The stories that have become the germinal point for not only my work as a creative artist but also my development as a free woman are those of two women. One is Maria Sabida, "the smartest woman on the whole island," who conquered the heart of a villain and "slept with one eye open." And the other is Maria Sabida's opposite, Maria La Loca, the woman who was left at the altar, the tragic woman who went crazy as a result of a broken heart. Once a beautiful girl, Maria La Loca ends up, in my grandmother's *cuento*, a pitiful woman who retreats into insanity because she is shamed by a man, cheated out of the one option she allowed herself to claim: marriage.

The crude and violent tale of Maria Sabida, which I have found in collections of folktales recorded from the oral tellings of old people at the turn of the century, revealed to me the amazing concept that a woman can have "macho"—that quality that men in certain countries, including my native island, have claimed as a male prerogative. The term "macho," when divested of gender, to me simply means the arrogance to assume that you belong where you choose to stand, that you are inferior to no one, and that you will defend your domain at whatever cost. In most cases, I do not recommend this mode as the best way to make room for yourself in a crowded world. But I grew up in a place and time where modesty and submissiveness were the qualities a girl was supposed to internalize. So the woman who slept with one eye open intrigued me as a possible model in my formative years as a creative artist. Of course, it would be a long time before I articulated what I knew then instinctively: Maria Sabida's "macho" was what I myself would need to claim for my art. It is almost bravado to say "I am a writer" in a society where that condition usually means "I am unemployed," "I live on the fringes of civilization," "I am declaring myself better/different," and so forth. I know writers who will put anything else under "occupation" on a passport or job application rather than call up a red flag of distrust that the word "writer" has come to have for many people

When I feel that I need a dose of "macho," I follow a woman's voice back to Maria Sabida. I have come to believe she was the smartest woman on the island because she learned how to use the power of words to conquer her fears; she knew that this was what gave men their aura of power. They knew how to convince themselves and others that they were brave. Of course, she still had to sleep with one eye open because when you steal secrets, you are never again safe in your bed. Maria Sabida's message may be entirely different to me from what it was to the generations of women who heard and told the old tale. As a writer I choose to make her my alter ego, my *comadre*. In Catholic cultures two women otherwise unrelated can enter into a sacred bond, usually for the sake of a child, called the *comadrazgo*. One woman swears to stand in for the other as a surrogate mother if the need arises. It is a sacrament that joins them, more sacred than friendship, more binding than blood. And if these women violate the trust of their holy alliance, they will have committed a mortal sin. Their souls are endangered. I feel similarly about my commitment to the mythical Maria Sabida. My *comadre* taught me how to defend my art, how to conquer the villain by my wits. If I should ever weaken my resolve, I will become Maria La Loca, who failed herself, who allowed herself to be left at the altar.

Comadres y compadres, let me tell you the *cuento* of Maria Sabida, the smartest woman on the whole island.

Once upon a time, there was a widower merchant who had no other children, only a daughter. He often had to leave her alone while he traveled on business to foreign lands. She was called Maria Sabida because she was smart and daring and knew how to take care of herself. One day, the merchant told her that he would be away on a

183

trip for a long time and left Maria Sabida in the company of her women friends.

One moonless night when she and her *companeras* were sitting on the veranda of her father's house talking, Maria Sabida saw a bright light in the distance. Because the house was far away from the pueblo, she was very curious about what the light could be. She told her friends that they would investigate the source of light the very next morning.

As planned, early the next day, Maria Sabida and her friends set out through the woods in the direction where they had seen the light. They arrived at a house that seemed to be unoccupied. They went in and peered into each room. It looked like a man's place. But they smelled cooking. So they followed their noses to the kitchen, where an old man was stirring a huge cauldron. He welcomed them and asked them to stay and eat. Maria Sabida looked in the pot and saw that it was filled with the arms and legs of little children. Then she knew that this was the house of a gang of killers, kidnappers, and thieves that had been terrorizing the countryside for years. Sickened by the sight, Maria Sabida picked up the pot and poured its contents out of the window. The old man screamed at her: "You will pay for this, woman! When my master comes home, he will kill you and your *companeras!*" Then at gunpoint he led them upstairs where he locked them up.

When the leader of the thieves arrived with his gang, Maria Sabida heard him conspiring with his men to trick the women. Bearing a tray of *higos de sueno,* sleep-inducing figs, the *jefe* came up to the bedroom where the women were being kept. In a charming voice he persuaded the women to eat the fruit. Maria Sabida watched her friends fall deeply asleep one by one. She helped the *jefe* settle them in beds as she planned. Then she pretended to eat a fig and lay down yawning.

To test how well the potion in the fruit had worked, the *jefe* of the caves lit a candle and dripped a few drops of hot wax on the women's faces. Maria Sabida bore the pain without making a sound.

Certain now that the women were deeply asleep, the *jefe* went to the second-floor veranda and whistled for his comrades to come out of the house. Maria Sabida leaped from the bed as he was leaning over the rail, and she pushed him off. While his men were tending their injured leader, Maria Sabida awakened the women and they followed her to safety.

When Maria Sabida's father returned from his journey days later, she told him that she had decided to marry the leader of the thieves. The father sent a letter to the man asking him if he would marry his daughter. The *jefe* responded immediately that he had been unable to forget the smart and brave Maria Sabida. Yes, he would marry her. The wedding took place with a great fiesta. Everyone in the pueblo hoped that Maria Sabida would reform this criminal and that they could stop fearing his gang. But as soon as the couple had arrived at the thieves' house, the new husband told his bride that now she would pay for having humiliated him in front of his men. He told her to go to the bedroom and wait for him. Maria Sabida knew that he was going to murder her. She had an idea. She asked her husband if he would let her take some honey to eat before she went to bed. He agreed. And while he drank his rum and celebrated her death with his gang, Maria Sabida worked in the kitchen making a life-size honey doll out of burlap sacks. She filled the doll with honey, cutting off some of her own hair to affix to its head. She even tied a string to its neck so that she could make the doll move from where she planned to hide under the marriage bed. She took the honey doll upstairs and placed it on the bed. Then she slid underneath the bed where she could see the door.

It was not long before the husband came in drunk and ready for blood. He struck the honey doll, thinking that it was Maria Sabida. He insulted her and asked if she thought she was smart now. Then he plunged a dagger into the doll's heart. A stream of honey hit him on the face. Tasting the sweetness on his mouth and tongue, the assassin exclaimed: "Maria Sabida, how sweet you are in death, how bitter in life. If I had known your blood contained such sweetness, I would not have killed you!"

Maria Sabida then came out from under the bed. In awe that Maria Sabida had outsmarted him again, the leader of the thieves begged her to forgive him. Maria Sabida embraced her husband. They lived happily together, so they say. But on that night of her wedding, and every other night, Maria Sabida slept with one eye open.

I have translated the tale of Maria Sabida several times for different purposes, and each time the story yields new meanings. Time and again the words I use to roughly equate the powerful Spanish change meanings subtly as if the story were a Ouija board drawing letters out of my mind to form new patterns. This is not hocus-pocus. It is the untapped power of creativity. When a writer abandons herself to its call, amazing things happen. On the surface the *cuento* of Maria Sabida may be interpreted as a parable of how a good woman conquers and tames a bad man. In the Spanish cultures, with their Holy Mother Mary mystique, the role of the woman as spiritual center and guide in a marriage is a central one. Men were born to sin; women, to redeem. But as a writer, I choose to interpret the tale of the woman who outmaneuvers the killer, who marries him so that she does not have to fear him, as a metaphor for the woman creator. The assassin is the destroyer of ambition, drive, and talent—the killer of dreams. It does not have to be a man. It is anything or anyone who keeps the artist from her work. The smartest woman on the island knows that she must trap the assassin so that he/she/it does not deprive her of her creative power. To marry the killer means to me that the artist has wedded the negative forces in her life that would keep her from fulfilling her mission and, furthermore, that she has made the negative forces work for her instead of against her.

Her sweetness is the vision of beauty that the artist carries within her, that few see unless she sacrifices herself. Does she have to be destroyed, or destroy herself, so that the world can taste her sweet blood? Woolf, Plath, and Sexton may have thought so. I would rather believe that the sweetness may be shared without total annihilation, but not without pain or sacrifice: that is part of the formula for the honey-filled burlap sack that will save your life. The transaction that took place between Maria Sabida and her assassin-husband was a trade-off on macho. She took on his macho. He understood that. So they embraced. The artist and the world struck a compromise, albeit an uneasy one on her part. She had to sleep with one eye open and watch what was offered her to eat. Remember the sleep-inducing figs.

Some women eat sleep-inducing figs early in their lives. At first they are unwitting victims of this feminine appetizer. Later they reach for the plate. It is easier to sleep while life happens around you. Better to dream while others *do*. The writer recognizes the poisoned fruit. She may pretend to sleep and bear the pain of hot wax as she prepares herself for battle. But she knows what is happening around her at all times. And when she is ready, she will act. Occasionally my *comadre* will try to save other women who have eaten the *higos de sueno*. She will try to rouse them, to wake them up. And sometimes, the sleepers will rise and follow her to freedom. But very often, they choose to remain unconscious. They rise briefly, look around them. They see that the world goes on without them. They eat another fig and go back to sleep.

There is another kind of woman that my *comadre* cannot save: Maria La Loca, the woman who was left at the altar. I first heard my grandmother tell this *cuento* when I was a child in Puerto Rico. Later I wrote this poem:

The Woman Who Was Left at the Altar

She calls her shadow Juan,
looking back often as she walks.
She has grown fat, breasts huge
as reservoirs. She once opened her blouse
in church to show the silent town
what a plentiful mother she could be.
Since her old mother died, buried in black,
she lives alone. Out of the lace
she made curtains for her room,
doilies out of the veil. They are now
yellow as malaria.
She hangs live chickens from her waist to sell,
walks to the silent town swinging her skirts of flesh.
She doesn't speak to anyone. Dogs follow
the scent of blood to be shed. In their hungry,
yellow eyes she sees his face.
She takes him to the knife time after time.

Again this is a tale that is on the surface about the harsh lessons of love. But even my Mama knew that it had a subtext. It was about failing oneself and blaming it on another. In my book *Silent Dancing*, I wrote around my Mama's *cuento,* showing how she taught me about the power of storytelling through the tale of Maria La Loca. Mama told it as a parable to teach her daughters how love can defeat you, if you are weak enough to let it.

There is a woman who comes to my *comadre* and complains that she knows that she has talent, that she has poetry in her, but that her life is too hard, too busy; her husband, her children are too demanding. She is a moral, responsible person and cannot in good conscience allow herself the luxury of practicing art. My *comadre* takes the time to tell this woman that she can choose to "learn to sleep with one eye open," to conjure up some female macho and claim the right to be an artist. But the woman is always prepared with an arsenal of reasons, all bigger than her needs, as to why she will die an unfulfilled woman, yearning to express herself in lyrical lines. She will, if pressed, imply that my *comadre* cannot possibly be a nurturing mother or caring partner, if she can find the time to write. In my culture, this type of woman who has perfected one art—that of self-abnegation, sometimes even martyrdom—is called *la sufrida*, the suffering one. There is much more admiration and respect for *la sufrida* in our society than there is for the artist.

The artist, too, suffers—but selfishly. She suffers mainly because the need to create torments her. If she is not fortunate enough to be truly selfish (or doesn't have enough macho in her to do as men have always done and claim the right, the time, and the space she needs), then she is doomed to do a balancing act, to walk the proverbial line that is drawn taut between the demands of her life—which may include choices that were made *before* she discovered her calling, such as marriage and children—and her art. The true artist will use her creativity to find a way, to carve the time, to claim a kitchen table, a library carrel, if a room of her own is not possible. She will use subterfuge if necessary, write poems in her recipe book, give up sleeping time or social time, and write.

Once I was asked to teach an evening writing class for a group of working-class Latinas who had taken the initiative to ask a community arts organization for a workshop they could attend. These women toiled at mind-numbing jobs eight or more hours each day, and most of them had several small children and a tired husband at home waiting for them to cook at the end of the workday. Yet somehow the women had found one another as artists. Perhaps on a lunch break one of them had dared to mention that she wrote poems or kept a journal. In any case, I met a determined group of tired women that first night, many nervously watching the clock because they had had to make complex arrangements to leave their homes on a weeknight. Perceiving that the needs of this class would be different from those of my usual writing students, I asked these women to write down their most pressing artistic problem. I read the slips of paper during the break and confirmed my intuition about them. Almost unanimously they had said that their main problem was no time and no place to write. When we came together again, I told them about my method of writing, how I had developed it because, by the time I knew I had to write, I was a young mother and wife and was teaching full-time. At the end of the day, after giving my child all of the attention I *wanted* to give her, grading papers, and doing the normal tasks involved with family life, I was done for. I could not summon a thought into my head, much less try to create. After trying various ways of finding time for myself, short of leaving everyone I loved behind for the sake of Art, I decided on the sacrifice I had to make—and there is always one: I had to give up some of my precious sleep time. In order to give myself what I needed, I had to stop eating the delicious sleep-inducing figs that also make you good at finding excuses for not becoming who you need to be. I started going to bed when my daughter did and rising at 5:00A.M. And in the two hours before the household came alive and the demands on me began, I wrote and I wrote and I wrote. Actually, I usually had just enough time, after drinking coffee and bringing order to the chaos in my head, to write a few lines of a poem, or one or two pages on my novel—which took me, at that pace, three and one-half years to complete. But I was working, at a rate that many unencumbered writers would probably find laughably slow. But I wrote, and I write. And I am not left at the altar. Each line that I lay on a page points me toward my *comadre* Maria Sabida and takes me farther away from falling into the role of *la sufrida*.

The first assignment I gave that group of women was this: to go home and create a place to write for themselves. It had to be a place that could be cordoned off somehow, a place where books and notes could be left without fear of someone disturbing them and ruining a thought left unfinished, and, also important, a place where no one would feel free to read a work in progress—to ridicule and perhaps inhibit the writer. Their second assignment: to come up with a plan to make time to write every day.

As I expected, this latter injunction caused an uproar. They each claimed that their situation was impossible: no room, no privacy, no time, no time, no time. But I remained firm. They were going to write their versions of Virginia Woolf's "A Room of One's Own" to fit their individual lives.

Two evenings later I met them again. I recall the faces of those weary women on that night. They were tired but not beaten, as they were used to challenges and to dealing with nearly impossible odds. I had dared them to use the strength of character that allowed them to survive in a harsh world of barrio and factory and their endless *lucha*. The struggle for survival was familiar to them. One by one they read their *cuentos* of how they had made a writing corner for themselves, the most fortunate among them having a guest room that her mother-in-law often occupied. She turned it into her study and bought a lock; permission for other uses would have to be requested. Others had appropriated a corner here and there, set up a table and a chair, and screened off a space for themselves. The *No Trespassing* rules had been discussed with family members; even mild threats had been issued to nosy teenage children: You mess with my papers, I'll make free with your things. It was a celebration, minor declarations of independence by women used to yielding their private territory to others.

That night I saw that the act of claiming a bit of space and time for themselves was the beginning of something important for some of these women. Of course, not all of them would succeed against the thief of time. Some would find it easier to revert to the less fatiguing norm of the usual daily struggle. It takes a fierce devotion to defend your artistic space, and eternal vigilance over it, because the needs of others will grow like vines in your little plot and claim it back for the jungle. Finally, we came to the last writer in the circle. This was a young woman who always looked harried and disheveled in her old jeans and man's shirt. She had two sons, little hellions, both under six years of age, and an absent husband. The story she had brought to class the first night had made us cry and laugh. She had the gift, no doubt about it, but had been almost angry about the writing space and time assignment. She lived in a cramped apartment where the only table had to be used to store groceries, change babies, and iron. The story she had read to us had been written during a hospital stay. What was she to do, cut her wrists so that she could find time to write? We waited in respectful silence for her to begin reading. She surprised us by standing up and announcing that she had brought her writing place with her that night. Out of the back pocket of her jeans she pulled a handmade notebook. It had a sturdy cardboard covering, and within it was paper cut to fit and stitched together. There was also a small pencil that fit just right in the groove. She flipped the notebook open and began to read her essay. She had nearly given up trying to find a place to write. Everywhere she laid down her papers the kids had gotten to them. It became a game for them. At first she had been angry, but then she had decided to use her imagination to devise a way to write that was childproof. So she had come up with the idea of a portable room of her own. Because she could not leave her children and lock herself up in a room to write, she constructed a notebook that fit her jeans' pocket precisely. It had a hard back so that she could write on it while she went around the house or took the kids to the park, or even while grocery shopping. No one thought anything of it because it just looked like a housewife making a laundry list. She had even written this essay on her son's head while he leaned on her knees watching television.

Again there was laughter and tears. We had all learned a lesson that night about the will to create. I often think about this woman carrying her writing room with her wherever she went, and I have told her story often to other women who claim that the world keeps them from giving themselves to art. And I have put this young woman, who knew the meaning of *being* an artist, in my little pantheon of women who sleep with one eye open, the clapboard temple where I visit my storytelling *comadre*, Maria Sabida, to seek her counsel.

There are no altars in this holy place nor women who were left at one.

Basha Leah

BRENDA MILLER

You are here to kneel
Where prayer has been valid. . . .
—*T.S. Eliot*

I.

In Portugal I walk slowly, like the old Portuguese men: hands crossed
behind my back, head tilted forward, lips moving soundlessly around
a few simple words. This posture comes naturally in a country wedded
to patience, where the bark of the cork oak takes seven years to mature, and olives swell imperceptibly within their leaves. Food simmers
a long time—kid stew, bread soup, roast lamb. Celtic dolmens rise
slab-layered in fields hazy with lupine and poppies.

It's very late. I've drunk a lot of wine. I don't sense the cords that
keep my body synchronized, only the sockets of my shoulders, my
fingers hooked on my wrist, the many bones of my feet articulating
each step. I'm flimsy as a walking skeleton; a strong breeze might
scatter me through the eucalyptus.

A few days ago, in a 16th-century church in Évora, I entered the
"Chapel of the Bones." Skulls and ribs and femurs mortared the
walls, the bones of 5,000 monks arranged in tangled, overlapping
tiers. A yellow lightbulb burned in the dank ceiling. Two mummi-
fied corpses flanked the altar. A placard above the lintel read: *Nos
ossos que aqui estamos, Pelos vossos esperamos.* "We bones here
are waiting for yours." Visitors murmured all around me, but not
in prayer; none of us knelt in front of that dark shrine. What kind
of prayer, I wondered, does a person say in the presence of so many
bodies, jumbled into mosaic, with no prospect of an orderly resurrection? A prayer of terror, I imagined, or an exclamation of baffled
apology.

191

II.

On Shabbat, the observant Jew is given an extra soul, a *Neshama Yeterah*, which descends from the tree of life. This ancillary soul enables a person to "celebrate with great joy, and even to eat more than he is capable of during the week." The Shabbat candles represent this spirit, and the woman of the house draws the flame toward her eyes three times to absorb the light.

In California, one rarely heard about such things. We grilled cheese-burgers on the barbecue, and bought thinly sliced ham at the deli, ate bacon with our eggs before going to Hebrew School. Occasionally we visited my grandparents in New York; they lived in a Brooklyn brownstone, descendants of Russian immigrants, and they murmured to each other in Yiddish in their tiny kitchen. They reflexively touched the mezuzah as they came and went from their house. When I watched my grandmother cooking knishes or stuffed cabbage, I imagined her in *babushka* and shawl, bending over the sacred flames while her husband and daughters gazed at her in admiration. So I assumed my mother must have, at some time, lit the Shabbat candles and waited for the *Neshama Yeterah* to flutter into her body like a white, flapping bird.

But when I ask my mother about this, she says no, she never did light the candles. "I didn't really understand," she says. "I thought the candles were lit only in memory of your parents, after they died." She remembers her mother performed a private ceremony at the kitchen counter every Friday evening, but didn't call for her daughters to join in the prayers. My grandfather worked nights, as a typesetter; he might have worked on Shabbat, doing whatever was necessary to feed his family in Brooklyn during the Depression, and so my grand-mother stood there alone, in her apron, practicing those gestures that took just a few moments: the rasp of the match, the kindle of the wick, the sweep of the arms. She did this after the chicken had roasted, the potatoes had boiled, and the cooking flames were extinguished. But my mother, this American girl with red lips and cropped hair, was never tutored in the physical acts of this womanly ritual.

The *Neshama Yeterah* departs with great commotion on Saturday night. To revive from the Shabbat visitation, a person must sniff a bouquet of spices "meant to comfort and stimulate the ordinary, weekday soul which remains." The ordinary, weekday soul? Does he pace through the arteries and lungs, hands behind his back, finding fault with the liver, the imperfect workings of the heart? "Some cinnamon is all I get?" he mutters. "Some cloves?" In my family, the word soul was rarely mentioned, but my mother, and my grandmother, chanted the Jewish hymn, "eat, eat," as if they knew our ordinary, everyday souls were always hungry. As if they knew we had within us these little mouths constantly open, sharp beaks ravenous for chicken liver and brisket, *latkes* and pickles and rolls.

III.

Outside the spa town of Luso, in the Buçaco woods, in a monastery built by the Carmelite Monks, the shrine to Mary's breast flickers inside a tiny room. I open the cork door, sidle in sideways, and face a portrait of the sorrowful Mary who holds her naked breast between outstretched fingers, one drop of milk lingering on her nipple. The baby Jesus lies faceless in her arms, almost outside the frame, the lines of focus drawn to the exposed breast and the milk about to be spilled. Hundreds of wax breasts burn on a high table, and tucked among these candles are hundreds of children—faded Polaroids of infants in diapers, formal portraits of children with slicked back hair, stiff ruffles, and bow ties. The children's eyes, moist in the candlelight, peer out from among the breasts and the bowls of silver coins.

The tour guide describes the shrine in Portuguese, using his hands to make the universal symbol for breast. I catch the word *leite*; of course the milk is worshipped here, not the breast itself, that soft chalice of pleasure and duty. I want to ask: what are the words of the prayer? Is the prayer a prophylactic or a cure? But my language here is halting and ridiculous. Whispers linger in the alcove, *Por favor, Maria, Obrigada, Por favor.*

I want to kindle the wick on Mary's breast, but I don't know the proper way—how much money to drop in the bowl, or the posture and volume of prayer.

At home, in Seattle, I volunteer once a week on the infant's ward at Children's Hospital. I hold babies for three hours, and during that time become nothing but a pair of arms, a beating heart, a core of heat. I'm not mindful of any prayer rising in me as we rock, only a wordless, off-key hum. Most of these children eat through a tube slid gently under the skin on the backs of their hands; pacifiers lie gummy on their small pillows as they sleep. I'm sure there's a chapel in the hospital where candles stutter, and a font of holy water drawn from the tap and blessed. Maybe a crucifix, but more likely secular stained glass illuminated by a wan bulb. Mary's breast will not be displayed, of course—the distance between these two places is measured in more than miles—but the succor of Mary's milk might be sought nonetheless.

It will be quiet. The quiet is what's necessary, I suppose, and an opportunity to face the direction where God might reside. I imagine there's always a few people in the chapel, their lips moving in various languages of prayer, including the tongue of grief.

IV.

Our synagogue was near the freeway in Van Nuys, California, and it looked like a single-story elementary school, with several cluttered bulletin boards, heavy plate-glass doors, gray carpet thin as felt. White candles flickered in the temple; the Torah was sheathed in purple velvet; gold tassels dangled from the pointed rollers. Black letters, glossy and smooth as scars, rose from the surface of the violet mantle. When the rabbi, or a bar-mitzvah boy, brought the Torah through the congregation, cradling it in his arms, I kissed my fingers and darted out my hand to touch it, like the rest of the women.

In Hebrew School, we learned the greatest sin was to worship a false idol. "God is not a person," my teacher said, "but God is everywhere." The Torah, though we respected it, was not God. The alphabet, though it was a powerful tool, was not God. Abraham and Isaac and Moses were great men, not God. "God is everywhere," my teacher said. "Like the air." I learned about Exodus. I learned about Noah's ark. I learned about the Burning Bush. These miracles were played out by faceless figures smoothed onto the felt-board. The 22 letters of the alphabet paraded like amiable cartoons across the top of the classroom wall, and I was called by my Hebrew name—*Basha Leah,* which over time was shortened to *Batya.* I preferred the elegance of *Basha Leah,* enfolded by lacy veils, while *Batya* turned me into a lumpy dullard, dressed in burlap, switching after the mules.

In the temple, the drone of the prayers rose in a voice close to anger from the men, nearer to anguish from the women, then ebbed into a muttered garble of tongues. I tried not to look too hard at the rabbi, lest I should worship him. I averted my eyes from the face of the cantor. I ended up staring at my feet, squished and aching in their snub-nosed shoes. My mother's hand fell like a feathery apology on the back of my neck, and I swayed uncomfortably in place. The ache in my feet rose through my body until it reached my eye sockets.

"I've had it to up here," my mother sometimes cried, her hand chopping the air like a salute at eye level, grief and frustration rising in her visible as water. In the synagogue, waters of boredom lapped through my body, pouring into every cavity, like a chase scene from *Get Smart.* I imagined my soul as a miniature Max, scrambling away, climbing hand over hand up my spine to perch on the occipital ridge until the waters began to recede.

V.

There's another kind of soul that enters the body—a *dybbuk*, "one who cleaves." A *dybbuk* speaks in tongues, commits slander, possibly murder, using the body of a weak person as a convenient vehicle. If roused and defeated, this soul will drain out through the person's little toe.

The word *dybbuk* is in me, part of my innate vocabulary, though I don't know how. Perhaps from the murmured conversations of my relatives in Brooklyn and their neighbors, the women with the billowing housedresses and the fleshy upper arms. I was only an occasional visitor to these boroughs saturated with odors of mothballs and boiled chicken, soot and melted snow. I may have heard the Yiddish words in the exchanges between my paternal grandmother and the customers in her knitting shop; I blended into a wall of yarn, camouflaged by the many shades of brown, in a trance of boredom, as the women clustered near the cash register. "That one's a *golem*," they might say, nodding in the direction of a simple-minded man in the street. A *golem* meaning a zombie, a creature shaped from soil into human form, animated by the name of God slipped under the tongue. Or, "He's possessed of a *dybbuk*," they might whisper of a neighbor's child gone bad. They gossiped about *nebbishes* and *schlemiels*, the bumbling fools who never quite got anything right, swindled from their money or parted from their families through ignorance or bad luck.

Sometimes I sat next to my grandfather after he woke in the afternoons, and he explained the transformation of hot lead into letters, the letters into words, the words into stories. I held my name, printed upside down and backward on a strip of heavy metal. My grandmothers pinched my cheek and called me *bubeleh*—little mother. They cried "God Forbid!" to ward off any harm. On Passover I opened the front door and hollered for Elijah to come in; I watched the wineglass shake as the angel touched his lips to the Manishevitz. I closed my eyes in front of the Hanukkah candles and prayed, fervently, for roller skates.

VI.

In the central chapel of the Carmelite monastery in the Buçaco woods, dusty porcelain saints enact their deaths inside scratched glass cases. Above each case the haloed saint, calm and benedictory, gazes down on the lurid scene below: a small single bed, a man's legs twisting the bedclothes, his thin arms reaching out in desperation. The witnesses (a doctor called in the middle of the night? A maid, nauseated by the bloody cough of her master? A scribe, summoned to write the last words?) recoil from the bed in a scattered arc.

And the saint? Somehow he's beamed up and transformed into the overhanging portrait, the eyes half-closed, the halo pressing into place the immaculately combed hair. One finger touches his lips as if to hush the tormented figure below. His arms have flesh; the lips are moist; the background is lush and green.

We have our heaven, too, though I don't remember the mention of Paradise at Temple Ner Tamid. Paradise, I thought, was for the Gentiles; when my Christian friends asked me if I would go to heaven, I sorrowfully shook my head no. They looked at each other, and then at me, touching my shoulder in sweet-natured commiseration. "We don't believe in Jesus," I said, my voice trailing off. I thought our religion was about food. It was about study, hard work, persecution, and grief. But I've since learned there is a Paradise for the Jews; it is, in fact, the Garden of Eden, where the Tree of Life grows dead center. "So huge is this tree that it would take five hundred years to pass from one side of its trunk to the other." We even have a hell: *Gehinnom*, where "malicious gossip is punished by hanging from one's tongue, and Balaam, who enticed the Israelites into sexual immorality, spends his time immersed in boiling semen." Of course, such things weren't mentioned when I was a child.

But my mother covered the mirrors with black cloth when her father died. She sat in mourning, with her mother, for seven days. She may have even spoken the Kaddish for twelve months, since my grandfather had no sons. Certainly she lit the Kaddish candle on Yom Kippur. But I was a child. I didn't listen, or I didn't understand, that the soul remains attached to the dead body for seven days, and takes twelve arduous months—ascending upward, flopping downward, cleaning itself in a river of fire—to enter Paradise. I didn't realize the soul needs our help, in the form of many and repeated prayers.

Before me now, a saint is dying in his rectangular case, on a narrow bed covered with a single woolen blanket. I surreptitiously cross myself, the way I've seen people do. The gesture, so delicate, touching the directional points of my body—my head, my heart, my two arms—seems far removed from the passion of Christ. It doesn't feel like a crucifix I inscribe on my body, but the points of a geometrically perfect circle. I curl one fist inside the other, and I kiss my knuckles, I bow my head. I don't know if I'm praying. It feels more like I'm talking to myself.

VII.

Swaying in prayer is "a reflection of the flickering light of the Jewish soul, . . . or it provides much-needed exercise for scholars who spend most of their day sitting and studying." I get out my yoga mat; I sway down into a forward bend and stay there a long time, breathing, and then roll up, one vertebra on top of the other until I stand perfectly straight, aligned. I think about moving a little, and I do, like the oracle's pendulum that swings to and fro in answer to an unspoken question.

VIII.

When I was 16, I became president of my Jewish Youth group, and we set out to create *meaningful* Shabbat ceremonies, feeding each other *challah* on Friday night, reading passages from Rod McKuen, holding hands in a circle and rapping about our relationships. We petitioned for and received permission for a slumber party, properly chaperoned by our counselors—college students in their early 20's. The minutes from the planning meetings illustrate our real concerns: "It was decided no one under the age of 20 can sleep on the couches." "*Challah* will be split equally before anyone begins to eat." "Ronnie says no wine. So Mike's in charge of the grape juice." We rented spin-art machines. We got a Ping-Pong table. We decided to give Ronnie a bar-mitzvah.

Ronnie had a black mustache and dreamy brown eyes. He wore tight jeans and read Dylan Thomas. When he confessed that he'd never been bar-mitzvahed, we clucked over him like a gaggle of grandmothers. We made plans in the bathroom. We took out every prayerbook we could find. We found him a *yarmulke* and a dingy tallis to drape across his shoulders. "*Baruch Atah Adonai,*" we chanted in unison, "*elohanu, melach ha'olum. . . .*" We closed our eyes, and the prayers trailed off when we didn't know the words; we moved our lips in the parched, desperate way of the old people in synagogue. We swayed back and forth; we felt mature, and very wise. Someone gave a speech enumerating all of Ronnie's strong points. Ronnie gave a speech telling us how he expected to improve in the coming years. We improvised a Torah with pillows, and we made him walk among us, beneath an arch made of our intertwined hands.

I think he cried then, his lips scrunched tight together, a Kleenex in his hand. I remember his thanks, and I remember us sitting in a circle around him, our eager hands damp with sweat, our satisfied faces aglow.

IX.

I call home from a post office in Lisbon. My booth, number four, is hot and dusty, my hands already clumsy with sweat, and I dial the many numbers I need to connect me with home. Like the Kabbalists, manipulating the letters of the alphabet, I work this dreary magic. Travel has not agreed with me. I have a fever, and I want to lie down, but my pension has a dark, steep staircase and soggy newspapers in the windows holding back the rain.

My mother answers the phone. I picture her at the kitchen counter: the long wall of photographs tacked together on a bulletin board— all the children, my two brothers and I, peering out at my mother from our many ages. She sits in the green vinyl chair, reflexively picking up her ballpoint to doodle. The lace *Shalom* hangs motionless in the entry. A red-clay Menorah sits on the mantel, the candle holders shaped like chubby monks, their hands uplifted.

"How's everything?" I ask. We talk in a rush. "How are *you*?" she asks again and again. Not until I'm almost ready to hang up does she mention: "Well there is a little problem."

"What?"

"Everything's a little *meshuga*," she says, and her voice gets that catch; I can see her biting her lower lip, pushing her hand up into the hair at her forehead. "I'll put your father on," she says, and I hear the phone change hands.

"Your mother," he says.

"What?"

"Your mother had to have a hysterectomy. They found some cancer."

"What?"

"She's okay," my father says. "Everything's okay."

"A hysterectomy?"

"They got it all, the cancer. They found it early enough. Don't worry."

I'm breaking out in a damp sweat across my face, under my arms. I can't think of anything to say but, "Why didn't she tell me herself?"

"Don't worry," my father says. "Everything's fine."

I decide to believe him. After a few more distance-filled exchanges, our voices overlapping with the delay, I hang up. I push my way past the people waiting for my booth, I pay my *escuedos*, I walk out on the *Avenida Da Liberdade* among the taxis and the busses. I start walking to the north, but I don't know where I'm going, so I turn around and head to the south along the busy, tree-lined boulevard. I stumble past the National Theater, past a vendor selling brass door-knockers the shape of a hand. What am I looking for? A synagogue? Or another shrine, this one to Mary's womb?

"In the womb a candle burns," the Kabbalah tells us, "the light of which enables the embryo to see from one end of the world to the other. One of the angels teaches it the Torah, but just before birth the angel touches the embryo on the top lip, so it forgets all it has learnt, hence the cleavage on a person's upper lip."

I want to light a candle, the flame sputtering in a bed of salt water and blood. If I had the lace scarf my grandmother gave me when she died, I might slip into a stone synagogue, cover my head, and follow the words of the Torah. But I don't know how. I don't know to whom I'd be praying; I thought we weren't allowed to worship a human God, so I eradicated the concept of God entirely. *It was all a mistake*, I want to say now. *I wasn't listening.*

There is a Kabbalah tale about an illiterate man who merely uttered the Hebrew alphabet, trusting that God would turn the letters into the necessary words. His prayers, the story goes, were quite potent. But I can hardly remember the alphabet. *Alef, Gimmel, Chai* . . . I don't remember the Hebrew word for Please. I remember the words *Aba, Ima*, Father, Mother. I remember the letters tripping across the ceiling, the letters minus their vowels, invisible sounds we needed to learn by heart.

X.

A touch of the angel's finger, and knowledge ceases. I touch my lip, the cleavage. *Do you remember?* I ask myself. *Do you?* Something glimmers, like a stone worn an odd color under the stream, but my vision is clouded by a froth of rushing water. Perhaps knowledge exists in the amnion; the fluid is knowledge itself, and the angel's fingernail is sharp; his touch splits the sac, and drains us dumb.

The *mikveh* is a gathering of living waters—pure water from rain or a natural spring. This public bath was the center of any Jewish village; the water refined the body, washed off any unclean souls residing there. A woman stepping into these baths purified herself before marital relations with her husband; on emergence the first object she spied determined the kind of child she might conceive. If she saw a horse, this meant a happy child. A bird might equal spiritual beauty. If she saw an inauspicious omen—a dog, say, with its ugly tongue, or a swine—she could return to the bath and start again.

"The Talmud tells how Rabbi Yochanan, a Palestinian sage of handsome appearance, used to sit at the entrance to the mikveh, so that women would see him and have beautiful children like him. To those who questioned his behavior, he answered that he was not troubled by unchaste thoughts on seeing the women emerge, for to him they were like white swans."

What do I see when I step from my tub? My own body, lean and young in the mirror, kneeling to pull the plug and scrub the white porcelain. What do I see when I step from the baths of the Luso spa? Water arcing from the fountain, and all the Portuguese women gathered round its many spouts: bending forward, kneeling, holding out cups and jugs to be filled. A grandmother—in black scarf, wool skirt, and thick stockings—turns to me and smiles.

XI.

At my cousin Murray's house, brisket and matzoh balls and potato kugel lay heavy on the oak table. The curtains were drawn; I think of them as black, but they couldn't have been. They were probably maroon, and faintly ribbed like corduroy. I remember an easy chair; and my cousin in the easy chair looking too tense to be reclined; he should have been ramrod straight, the murmur of relatives lapping against him. My memory is hazy with the self-centered fog of childhood, the deep boredom, my eyes at table height, scanning the food.

"If only she'd gotten the dog," someone murmured, not to anyone in particular. This must have been a funeral. I remember my cousin Anita being "found." I didn't understand what that meant, but my cousins were sitting in the living room, covering their faces with their hands. Their *yarmulkes* slipped sideways off the crowns of their heads. I remember the gesture, that's all—three grown men, slumped in chairs, their hands covering their eyes as if they couldn't bear to see any longer. As if they had already seen too much.

I don't think I went to the service. All I remember clearly is the food on the table: platters of chicken, congealing; baskets of knotted rolls; tureens of yellowish soup. And the men in the living room, so contorted in their grief. When I think of my cousins, I see them framed between the legs of adults, in a triangle of light, frozen. No one ate. All that food: for the extra souls, the one extra soul who wouldn't leave the room, even though the burial must have taken place according to Jewish Law, as soon as possible. Someone must have washed the body, anointed her with oil, wrapped her in a shroud. But a soul hovered in the corner of the room, a darkness smudging the corners of my vision. Eat, someone said, it is good to eat, and a plate was brought into my hands.

XII.

"One who cleaves." The definition of the word "cleave" is two-fold and contradictory: to cleave means both to split apart and to adhere. Perhaps one is not possible without the other. Perhaps we need to break open before anything can enter us. Or maybe we have to split apart that to which we cling fast.

In yoga class, my teacher tells us to "move from the inner body." We glide our arms and our legs through a substance "thicker than air, like deep water." We swim through the postures. The Sphinx pose. Sun Salute. Tree. I generate intent before the muscles follow. I breathe deeply, I stretch sideways, I reach up, I bring my hands together at my heart. *Namasté,* I whisper. *Namasté.* I know my access to composure is through attention to the pathways and cavities of my body, so I sit cross-legged, my forehead bent to the ground in a posture of deep humility. Sometimes, then, I feel whatever *dybbuks* cling inside me loosen their hold; they begin the long slide down my skeleton to drain out through my little toe.

XIII.

I have a snapshot taken of me when I was eighteen. I've got long straight hair, and I'm wearing a Saint Christopher medal around my neck. It falls between my breasts. On another, shorter chain, I wear a gold "chai," the Hebrew letter for "life." It clings to the bare skin between my collarbones.

The medal was given to me by my first boyfriend—a boy I cleaved to, a boy by whom I was cleaved, split apart. I was *crazy* for him. I wanted the medal because I had seen it on his chest; I had gripped it in my fingers as we made love. He draped the pendant over my head, and kissed me between the eyes.

Eighteen years later, I still have Saint Christopher—a gnarled old man carrying a child on his shoulder, a knotted staff clutched in one hand. He dangles off the edge of my windowsill, next to a *yad* amulet inset with a stone from the Dead Sea. I have candles on the windowsill, their flames swaying to and fro, like little people in prayer.

A Catholic friend tells me that Saint Christopher is no longer a saint; the Vatican has declared him a non-entity. His life is now mere fable about the Christ child crossing a river on the ferryman's shoulders, growing so heavy he became the weight of every bird and tree and animal, the combined tonnage of mankind's suffering. But the ferryman, being a good man, kept at his task, his knees buckling, his back breaking, until he had safely ferried the small child to shore. "It's just a story," my friend says, but I don't understand how this tale differs from the other Biblical accounts: the walking on water, the bread into body, the wine into blood. "It is different," my friend assures me. "Saint Christopher never existed."

But I know people still pray to him. They believe he intervenes in emergency landings, rough storms at sea, close calls on the freeway. Words of terror and belief form a presence too strong to be revoked. I still take him on the road; *it couldn't hurt*, as my grandmother used to say, with that small Jewish shrug, an arch of her plucked eyebrows. All this, whatever you call it—superstition, religion, mysticism—do what makes you happy, *bubeleh*.

XIV.

Alef, Gimmel, Chai . . . I recite the letters I know, and they grow steady as an incantation, a continual flame. The Kabbalists manipulated the letters into the bodies of living animals and men. They know an alphabet behind the alphabet, a whisper that travels up the Tree of Life like water.

White swans. I dream I am wrapped only in a white sheet, and the Chasidic men turn their square shoulders against me; they will not touch me, they will not talk to me, because I am a woman. I am unclean and dangerous. If I do not follow the law—if I do not light the Sabbath lamp, if I touch the parchment of the Torah, if I look at a man while I'm menstruating—I will be punished by death in childbirth. Punished when I'm most vulnerable, during the act that makes me most a woman. But what about Miriam? I plead. What about Rachel, and Leah, and Ruth? They were women. They saved us. It is a woman who brings the Sabbath light into the home. It is a woman who resides as a divine spirit in the Wailing Wall. But the men, in their black coats, their black hats—the men turn away. They ignore me. I grip the white sheet tighter against me as the men file into the synagogue, muttering.

XV.

I'm staying in a pink mansion on a hill overlooking Luso. It used to be the residence of a countess, and the breakfast waitress makes fun of my halting Portuguese. "*Pequeno Leite*," I say in my submissive voice as she raises the pot of warm milk. I only want a little, but she drenches my coffee anyway, laughing.

In the evening I stroll down a winding street, past two women waiting at their windows, their wrinkled elbows resting on the sill. I don't know what they're waiting for: children to come home, or perhaps the pork to grow tender in the stew. They wave to me, amused. Another woman splashes bleach outside her doorway and kneels to scrub the already whitened stone. Bougainvillea, bright as blood, clings to her windowsill. Men are nowhere in sight; this appears to be a province maintained entirely by women. I make my way to a stone bridge and watch the sun sink beyond fields of flowering potatoes.

In the distance, women harvest vegetables in a field. I think they are women, but I can't be sure; all I see are the silhouettes of their bodies bending, and lifting, and bending again. These women—are they the ones who walk to the monastery and tuck pictures of their children between Mary's breasts? Do they pray before that altar? I don't know; they seem always to be working, or resting from their work.

Back in the square, the Portuguese men emerge to sit in clusters, wearing hats and wool vests; they walk down the lanes, their hands behind their backs, or they stand together, leaning on wooden canes. I sit on a bench facing the fountain, and the men converse around me, all inflection and vowels, grunts and assents. I'm silent as a hub, turned by words without meaning, without sense.

XVI.

The *luz* bone is a hub, unyielding. "An indestructible bone, shaped like an almond, at the base of the spine, around which a new body will be formed at the Resurrection of the Dead." The *luz* bone feeds only off the *Melaveh Malkah*, the meal eaten on Saturday night to break the Sabbath. It's a bone without sin, taking no part in Adam's gluttony in the garden; so, our new bodies on the day of judgement will be sweet and pure.

For proof of its durability, three men in a Jewish village tested a *luz* bone. (Like magpies, did they pluck the bone out of the rubble of an old man? or of a woman dead in childbirth? or of a child?) They smuggled the *luz* bone to the outskirts of their village, to a blacksmith's shop, the fires glowing red in the stove. They thrust the vertebra in the coals; they plunged it under water; they beat upon it with sledgehammers. I can see them, these men dressed in ripe wool, sweating, their black hats tilted back on their heads. They hold it up to the light of the moon, the bone glossy from its trials, but intact. It's smooth as an egg, oval and warm.

XVII.

". . . those who bow to God in prayer are thought to guarantee themselves a resurrected body, because they stimulate the *luz* bone when they bend their spine."

Downward-Facing Dog: the sit-bones lifted upward. Forward bend. Triangle. Warrior I, II, III. Sphinx. Cobra. Cow. These words come to me like directives, and my body twists and bends and turns, gyrating in a circle around the *luz* bone.

The Tree. I balance on one foot, the other pressed into my thigh. I put my hands together in front of my chest. I breathe. I look past my reflection in the window; I focus my gaze on the trunk of a holly. I grow steady and invisible. The alphabet hangs from my branches like oddly-shaped fruit.

Child's pose. I curl into a fetal position on the mat.

Nu? I hear my mother's voice across a great distance. *Nu, bubeleh?* She pats one hand on her swollen abdomen, and holds it there. I want to answer, but from my mouth comes a watery language no one can understand.

Excerpt From
"Tacos and Manna"

ALAN CHEUSE

The Story of Hernando Alonso

Ciudad de Mexico, 1528—A bell clangs and he, with the great difficulty of an old man with stiff limbs and creaking bones, sits up in the dark, awakened from a sleep that had taken him far away from the high stink of his own urine and the stench of his own ordure in the far corner of the cell, away from the shouts and cries of madness and pain in the night.

Hernando Alonso is back.

He had been dreaming a strange and fluent dream, an excursion to far places to which he had found himself flying like a bird, at one point soaring over an entire fleet of brigantines and knowing, even as he looked down, that it had been his own armada, the very ships that had so long ago carried him and all of the troops of Hernán Cortés from Hispania to Cuba and then to the shores of this territory that he had called home for nearly ten years.

There had been battles along the way, and there had been forests, and the conquerors on horseback had won the battles, with some help from tribes angry with the ruling Aztecs, and, after winning, the soldiers had cut down many trees so that the plain would look more like home and set the pigs to rooting, which had the double effect of feeding the troops and destroying more trees. In the rising noise of the prison in early morning he could still hear the barks and screams of those early wars.

He had been born in Condado de Niebla and grew up in Cadiz, a city of water and sails, one of three sons of a carpenter named Joseph.

How ironic, yes! The same name as the father of the Savior. And it was his father who had taught him beginning at an early age his trade, carpentry, and then working with metal so that he had become a smithy. And initiated him into the secret religion of their forefathers, one of whose rules was that he should eat no pork.

The old rules had made for a lot of trouble in the old land. The times in which Hernando Alonso grew into manhood were filled with stories of funeral pyres piled with burning logs and Jews on fire! Not until he was in his thirties, still unmarried, his father having died and left him the shop and the tools, one of his brothers disappeared in the middle of a voyage to Africa, the other brother a success in the ships-handling trade, that good news arrived. It came from across the water. An expedition mounted by the Crown had returned with word about New Lands, new territories on the other side of the great ocean.

Ever since Hernando had been a small child he had listened avidly to the stories of the voyages around the coast of Africa made by Portuguese explorers, and then after he came into his manhood to news of the Spanish voyages to the New World. In his heart, he felt a deep longing, more like a tingling that worked through his chest when he thought such things, to sail away from this place of subterfuge, silence, and the fearful flames.

But in the end, it hadn't been his heart that had taken him across the sea to the new world, it had been his hands. When the call went out along the docks, he was a man in mid-age but still it seemed natural for him to sign up as a ship's carpenter on the royal expedition led by Hernán Cortés. His brother had known for years the ship's captain who would pilot one of the galleons in Cortés's fleet and had made it possible for Hernando to sail west with the would-be conquerors. Gonzalo stood weeping at the dockside and Hernando's own eyes turned wet, but he did not let the tears flow, fearful that the rough sailors who passed along the rail would take it as a sign of weakness. When the land sank down beneath the waters to the east, a large part of his heart felt that it was sinking, too.

The passage was rough, the ships meeting awful, heaving seas. Alonso, along with many others, suffered moments of cold and disabling fear. With the winds blowing hard and the great waves breaking across the bows of the brigantine, he dropped to the planking and put his hands to his face, saying quietly, "Please, Dear Lord, Lord of Abraham and Isaac, spare me a watery death! Oh, spare me, spare me, I pray You." And then, just to be sure, he would reach for the crucifix that he wore about his thick neck and hold it cupped in his hands as the salt waves broke over his feet. The wind howled about the tops of the mast, the voice of evil hell-hounds chasing after his soul.

"Spare me, Oh, Lord," Alonso prayed, "and I will dedicate my life to the duties of your Holy Person."

* * *

Hernando Alonso is the first Jew to have his presence in the New World set down in a historical record. Some historians speculate that other Jews came as Hernando Alonso did, on board one of the Spanish oceangoing ships, a few of them, it is presumed, with the early expeditions of Columbus and others with Cortés's fleet, but Alonso is the first to be noted. There are also some romantic-minded interpreters of history who would argue that Columbus himself was a hidden Jew, but no one has ever proved this. As for Hernando Alonso, he had signed on as a ship's carpenter. But once the need became apparent, during the year of war between the Spaniards and the various eastern Mexican tribes, he put to use his skill as a blacksmith, repairing the steel of weapons, reshoeing the horses so necessary to the victories over the Indians.

On the night of the great battle in the city in the middle of the lake against the Aztec rulers of Tenochtitlan, the night the Mexicans have come to call the Noche Triste, Hernando Alonso's talents served the army well. The ship's carpenter oversaw the construction of the thirteen bridges to the city so that the Spanish troops could enter in force. He had crossed the main bridge himself just behind the archers, and a few days later he was present in the crowd of troops when they heard that Moctezuma, the Indian King and God, now a captive of the Spaniards, had died, killed by a stone thrown by one of his own people.

For his part in the conquest of the Aztec capital, Alonso was awarded land and cattle and some Indian captives to be used as slaves. These he set to work clearing a ranch where he raised imported cattle and, forgive him, Oh, God of Abraham and Isaac, hogs for sale to the army for meat. His brother had come to join him. Only two years after Hernando had sailed for the New World, the Spanish Court issued the Edict of 1523, forbidding Jews, Moors, or other heretics from taking up residence in New Spain. So his brother had used his friendship with another sea captain and a forged document in order to gain entry to these new lands under the name of Morales.

Morales: "And do they know you are a Jew?"

Alonso: "I am what I am. I have never hidden anything. I believe what I believe and I have gone to Mass in the church that we have built on the place where the Aztec temple stood."

Morales: "It is a crime for a Jew to cross the border into New Spain. We are both criminals in the eyes of the Crown."

Alonso: "I have helped the Crown win mighty victories."

Morales: "You raise swine for the soldiers of the Crown. And in turn they would call you a hog."

Alonso: "No one calls me anything but my own name."

After the victory, Mass had been served in that church where the pagan temple had stood; few of the old soldiers attended. But Alonso became enamored of one of his female slaves and freed her and married her in this same church. His first child was baptized there, although when he returned home after the ceremony, Hernando, much to the dismay of his wife, who feared that one of the servants would see him, dipped his fingers in wine, splashed it on his child's brow, and then drank the rest of the wine in the cup. Staring down at the child's naked body, he thanked the old Hebrew God that a daughter had come to him instead of a son, because he did not have to worry about the problem of circumcision. If the child had been a boy, would he, Hernando, have to had made the cut himself? No, no, he would have asked his brother. But would he have done it?

Nights on the ranch on the high plateau, skies filled with burning stars, the sound of the animals lowing in the corrals—he thought himself so fortunate that he had removed himself from the turmoil back home. Once the army had defeated the Indians here, a great calm had settled over the center of the territory. He himself had given all of his own servants their freedom, all of them staying on to work at the ranch. But when he and his wife strolled in the center of the city he noticed the conquerors, turning fat and grey some half dozen years after the end of the war, shouting at Indians, kicking at them, in one instance punching one to the ground for not getting out of the way quickly enough. He had come to love his wife, and it disturbed him to see her fellow Indians, her family, treated in such a manner.

But there was nothing he could do except behave in the best way he knew how toward his own servants. In the quiet of their bed he would tell her stories from the Five Books of Moses, stories he had learned as a child, and gradually she understood that, though they both attended Mass, he still valued the old ceremonies of the Jews. Although the news from Spain had it that the Inquisition's fires were burning brightly, fed by the bodies of unrepentant Jews, here on the high plateau of Mexico Alonso felt so distant from such matters that he scarcely gave them a thought. Here was a place where he could grow old in peace. The Franciscans were avidly attending to the business of converting the Indians. They didn't seem to have time to worry about the faith of the old soldiers and their retinues.

When the second child came, again he dipped his fingers in wine and dripped some of the liquid onto the girl's forehead—oh, yes, Thank the Lord, another girl!—saying some old but newly recollected words in the Ladino tongue. Other memories jittered flamelike in his mind. One

Sunday just before Mass, with his wife in her monthlies, he told her to stay at home.

"Señora," he is reported to have said, "in your present Condition thou wouldst profane the Church."

His wife replied, "These are old ceremonies of the Jews which are not observed now that we have adopted the evangelical grace. . . ."

When the priest inquired about her, leaning down to pat one of the children on the head, Alonso said, "She is ill." It became his custom, asking her to stay away from Mass when she was in that Condition. Whether or not the priest noticed, he never said anything more about it.

Another few years went by, all those ink-black nights passing beneath the hot and burning stars, the children grew, he and his brother increased their cattle and swine herds ten-fold. Alonso had competition in the bidding, but the city council recognized his seniority by accepting his bids over some lower proposals. It didn't hurt that the acting governor of New Spain was an old ship-mate, Alonso de Estrada.

Did his rivals speak badly of him? Did they make clear that they knew he was a secret Jew and thus undeserving of special privilege? It didn't matter to him. He was getting to be an old man and thought that he deserved such deference. Think back to the Noche Triste and how it might have been if he hadn't built those bridges to the center of the city. Now and then he would see his old commander at Mass. The greying warrior looked over at him, as if to ask, Why does a Hebrew man like yourself suffer this inscrutable pageantry? Old soldiers still kept up their brawling in the taverns and the streets, sometimes even right up to the steps of the churches. The priests spoke to Cortés, but he pleaded for his men. Would the Church Itself be here in Mexico without these soldiers?

And then came the spring of 1528, and the arrival in the city of the Dominican Friar San Vicente de Maria, sent to Mexico to act in all matters against the Faith as well as to establish the first monasteries. A number of conquistadores were hauled in before a church tribunal to answer for blasphemies and other insults. Still, Hernando Alonso did not worry about himself because his old commander would look after him. Then in May Cortés returned to Spain to plead some grievances before the Crown and Alonso was left without a protector.

It didn't take long before they came for him in the night, leaving behind his sobbing wife and sleeping children. His priest-confessor stood to one side while a Dominican friar conducted the proceedings. The charges against him were composed of three counts: (1) that his children were baptized twice, once by a Franciscan friar and then again "according to the ritual of the law of Moses"; (2) that he refused to permit his wife to attend Mass when she was having her menstrual period. The third charge: a witness, one of his own former slaves whom he had freed, stated that Alonso poured water over the head of one of his children and then drank the water in mockery of baptism. According to the records of the archives of the Mexican Inquisition, the witness stated also that Alonso sang a psalm that referred to Israel's Lord God of Egypt, "o una cosa de esta manera. . . ." Thus he was found guilty of "Judaizing," the punishment for which was death by fire. Days went by and then his brother was thrown into the same cell with him.

"The fire that burned in Spain," Gonzalo said. "It has almost caught up with us."

"But why?" Alonso asked. "I have made a good life here and I have done good things for the territory."

"It is a matter of blood," his brother said.

"Do they want blood? I'll give them some of my blood in exchange for life."

"Our blood is no good to them," his brother said. "They say it is different from theirs. It sullies their veins. They want to purify the bloodlines of New Spain just as they have in the old country."

"Why is our blood impure?" Alonso said. "Why?" he said when they came for him on the last morning and slipped the ritual garment over his head. He walked slowly along the route to the pyre, his head bowed with that question weighing heavily on his mind. Surely they were not going to execute him just for being who he was? He, who had crossed the ocean sea border to help defeat the pagan Aztec? **And my children, my children, what of them, what will become of them?** Such questions haunted him until the very instant that he smelled his own flesh burning.

More Fuel for the Flames

Hernando Alonso was the first Mexican Jew, and, as the records of the Mexican Inquisition reveal, the first Jew to be killed in the New World. But not the last. By the end of the sixteenth century so-called conversos, or people with Jewish family roots who converted to Catholicism, were going to the fires with some regularity in the Kingdom of New Spain, with the greatest number of people accused as Jews burned at the stake in the Great Auto de Fe of 1649. Merchants, monks, pharmacists, doctors, actors, weavers, constables, jewelers, shoemakers, handymen, mostly men, some women, nearly a hundred in number. According to the records of the time, one woman was the sister of a Jesuit priest and mother of a Dominican monk. As historian Judith Elkin has written, though the woman was raised in a Catholic household and having raised her own children as Catholic, she still had not sufficient warranty that as a converso she could take her place in Mexican society.

From the lowest to the highest in society, few escaped the scrutiny of the Inquisiton. Take the case of Luis de Carvajal y de la Cueva, the first governor of the province of Nuevo Leon, recently glorified in the San Diego Opera production of *The Conquistador*. Carvajal was not a Jew, nor were his parents, though his maternal grandmother and his wife were Jewesses. While never found guilty of being Jewish, he was convicted by the tribunal for not reporting to them that his nephews and niece observed Jewish rites. As historian Samuel Liebman has noted, their Judaism stemmed from their father, and their mother adopted or was converted to Judaism by her husband. Dishonored, stripped of rank and office, Carvajal escaped the flames but died in jail. Others like him went to prison for extended terms or spent years as galley slaves, their lives ripped asunder by the wrath of the Inquisitors, whose task, as they saw it, was to establish the purity of the bloodlines of the Kingdom. The chemistry of the Inquisition seemed apt. Flames were a good instrument for purification. Those who escaped into the countryside or left for the north were burned in effigy. Others who had died in their cells before they could be turned over to the secular authorities for execution had their bones disinterred and roasted in the pyres, their names inscribed on the church walls and in Church ledgers, which is how we have such a precise record of just how many Jews went up in flames: Alonso, Carvajal, Castro, Fernandez, Garcia, Gomez, Gonzalez, Leon, Lopez, Machado, Mendez, Nuñez, Paz, Pena, Pereira, Perez, Rodriguez, Rosa, Suarez, Tinoco, Torres, Villegas, Zarate. A few of the names of the hordes of so-called crypto-Jews or hidden Jews or Judaizers of the New World who went to their deaths by fire. On the same locations where once the Aztecs sacrificed thousands of victims to their old gods, the Church now burned hundreds of old believers for the sake of the new God.

Meditations on a Myth

The story of the death by fire of Hernando Alonso is a powerful thing to consider. The Jew in flames! With those bonfires fed by Jewish fuel, the great golden age of triadic Spanish culture—Catholic, Jewish, Muslim—came to an end. And you can say that such a run of destruction as the Inquisition presaged the destruction of European Jewry by the Nazis in the twentieth century, or you can just notice the similarities. After a great period of peace and intercommunal benificence, an age of great art and music and literature, the nation, like some magnificent edifice built on unsteady soil, came crashing down into a boiling pit of race hate and murder.

Could it happen again in Mexico? More pyres? More Jews thrown into the flames? There are some who fear the worst. There are some who, pondering the current high profile of Jew-hating militias and so-called Christian Identity churches that preach a doctrine of racial "purity," say that it could happen in the United States, the stereotype of the high-minded dark-robed Spanish Inquisitor or the neatly tailored Gestapo officer, his nails well manicured, turning off the Beethoven on the Victrola to settle down to serious questioning of his Jewish captive, replaced by the image of a lanky, long-jawed Yank in camouflage clothes, squatting over a latrine hole, his drawers down about his ankles, an unfiltered cigarette dangling from his narrow lips, defecating on the Jew in the pit.

Disgusting! The nightmares, I say, of a neurotic-depressive imagination, and not a useful thought to consider when meditating on the millennial prospects of the Jewish immigrant. There is, in fact, a much more evocative New World story to consider, an ur-story, a myth, we have to call it, that has persisted for centuries that puts the Jew as the *first* to arrive on New World soil. In North America, for example, in the theology of the Mormon Church, the story persists that the Lost Tribe of Israel emigrated by ship from the Middle East to the American continent. Some early U.S. chroniclers of the mores of the North American plains Indians wrote of the amazing similarities between the rituals of certain tribes and Jewish ritual. Anthropologists dig all over Mexico even as you read this, some of their work sponsored by the Mormons, inspired by this old story of the tie between the Biblical lands and the territory of the New World, the myth that the Lost Tribe of Israel sailed from the Holy Land to Mexico, carrying with them the ancient scrolls of the Law, in the same way that Aeneas in Virgil's great poem of the founding of Rome carried the hearth gods from the city of Troy to the shores of Italy.

Certainly a number of legitimate anthropologists and researchers have based their work on the possibility of such a voyage. Thor Heyerdahl made his famous raft "Kon-Tiki" to show that a reed boat could survive such a trip. Ivan Van Sertima, a Rutgers University scholar, has written extensively on the oceangoing traffic between Africa, the Near East, and the Mexican coast where the mysterious Olmecs thrived and left behind the huge stone heads with inexplicably African features. And if we can skate for an instant to the furthest rim of the links between mythology and history, consider the story of Quetzalcoatl, the Plumed Serpent, God of the Aztecs, whom theology proclaimed would arrive in the flesh from over the great waters to the East, and bring to a conclusion one of the great cycles of time. As the Spanish chroniclers of the period suggest, the Aztecs mistook Cortés for Quetzalcoatl. But what if the Plumed Serpent had already arrived and the working out of the myth in the time of the conquistadores was a faint replay of an early Advent on American soil? What if the Plumed Serpent, Quetzalcoatl Himself, had been a Jew?

All these speculations, fantasies, myths and dreams! A far cry you may say from the life of the Jews of contemporary Mexico, with their ties to Europe, either Spain or Germany, Poland, and Russia. And yet there are those Mexican Jews—people who call themselves Jews, as the Orthodox would say—who claim an inheritance that goes far enough back in time to link them to the period of the Conquest, people who claim that their ancestors miraculously survived the period of the Mexican Inquisition and passed along their rituals from generation to generation, these indigenous people, native in appearance, who read and write Hebrew and participate in all of the rituals of the faith, some of whom I met myself that Sabbath morning in 1976 in the synagogue on Calle Caruso in Mexico City. In the agricultural village of Venta Prieta, in fact, there are a thousand such families who make these claims, people whose ancestors apparently went underground during the Mexican Inquistion instead of fleeing north across the border to territory that we now call the state of New Mexico, families whose grave markers display small Stars of David along with the crosses and whose lives are filled with the rituals—blessings of bread and wine, observance of the Sabbath, sacramental marriage—that have bound Jews together as co-religionists over millenia.

The story that the Lost Tribe of Israel sailed to Mexico may remain always a myth. But it opens a door onto fabulous thoughts of historical continuity and raises provocative questions about the nature of religious identity. The Indian Jews I met, and those thousands more gathered in the village of Venta Prieta, may be the apparent descendents of the Mexican Judaizers long lost to the flames of the Inquisition, the children of Hernando Alonso, and a kind of Lost Tribe themselves, whose time may possibly have come around again.

Portrait of My Body

PHILLIP LOPATE

I am a man who tilts. When I am sitting, my head slants to the right; when walking, the upper part of my body reaches forward to catch a sneak preview of the street. One way or another, I seem to be off-center—or "uncentered," to use the jargon of holism. My lousy posture, a tendency to slump or put myself into lazy, contorted misalignments, undoubtedly contributes to lower back pain. For a while, I correct my bad habits, do morning exercises, sit straight, breathe deeply, but always an inner demon that insists on approaching the world askew resists perpendicularity.

I think if I had broader shoulders I would be more squarely anchored. But my shoulders are narrow, barely wider than my hips. This has always made shopping for suits an embarrassing business. (Françoise Gilot's *Life with Picasso* tells how Picasso was so touchy about his disproportionate body—in his case all shoulders, no legs—that he insisted the tailor fit him at home.) When I was growing up in Brooklyn, my hero was Sandy Koufax, the Dodgers' Jewish pitcher. In the doldrums of Hebrew choir practice at Feigenbaum's Mansion & Catering Hall, I would fantasize striking out the side, even whiffing twenty-seven batters in a row. Lack of shoulder development put an end to this identification; I became a writer instead of a Koufax.

It occurs to me that the restless angling of my head is an attempt to distract viewers' attention from its paltry base. I want people to look at my head, partly because I live in my head most of the time. My sister, a trained masseuse, often warns me of the penalties, like neck tension, that may arise from failing to integrate body and mind. Once, about ten years ago, she and I were at the beach and she was scrutinizing my body with a sister's critical eye. "You're getting flabby," she said. "You should exercise every day. I do—look at me, not an ounce of fat." She pulled at her midriff, celebrating (as is her

214

wont) her physical attributes with the third-person enthusiasm of a carnival barker.

"But"—she threw me a bone—"you do have a powerful head. There's an intensity . . ." A graduate student of mine (who was slightly loony) told someone that she regularly saw an aura around my head in class. One reason I like to teach is that it focuses fifteen or so dependent gazes on me with such paranoiac intensity as cannot help but generate an aura in my behalf.

I also have a commanding stare, large sad brown eyes that can be read as either gentle or severe. Once I watched several hours of myself on videotape. I discovered to my horror that my face moved at different rates: sometimes my mouth would be laughing, eyebrows circumflexes in mirth, while my eyes coolly gauged the interviewer to see what effect I was making. I am something of an actor. And, as with many performers, the mood I sense most in myself is that of energy-conserving watchfulness; but this expression is often mistaken (perhaps because of the way brown eyes are read in our culture) for sympathy. I see myself as determined to the point of stubbornness, selfish, even a bit cruel—in any case, I am all too aware of the limits of my compassion, so that it puzzles me when people report a first impression of me as gentle, kind, solicitous. In my youth I felt obliged to come across as dynamic, arrogant, intimidating, the life of the party; now, surer of myself, I hold back some energy, thereby winning time to gather information and make better judgements. This results sometimes in a misimpression of my being mildly depressed. Of course, the simple truth is that I have less energy than I once did, and that accumulated experiences have made me, almost against my will, kinder and sadder.

Sometimes I can feel my mouth arching downward in an ironic smile, which, at its best, reassures others that we need not take everything so seriously—because we are all in the same comedy together—and, at its worst, expresses a superior skepticism. This smile, which can be charming when not supercilious, has elements of the bashful that mesh with the worldly—the shyness, let us say, of a cultivated man who is often embarrassed for others by their willful shallowness or self-deception. Many times, however, my ironic smile is nothing more than a neutral stall among people who do not seem to appreciate my "contribution." I hate that pain-in-the-ass half-smile of mine; I want to jump in, participate, be loud, thoughtless, vulgar.

Often I give off a sort of psychic stench to myself, I do not like myself at all, but out of stubborn pride I act like a man who does. I appear for all the world poised, contented, sanguine when inside I may be feeling self-revulsion bordering on the suicidal. What a wonder to be so misread! Of course, if in the beginning I had thought I was coming across accurately, I never would have bothered to become a writer. And the truth is I am not misread, because another part of me is never less than fully contented with myself.

I am vain about these parts of my body: my eyes, my fingers, my legs. It is true that my legs are long and not unshapely, but my vanity about them has less to do with their comeliness than with their contribution to my height. Montaigne, a man who himself was on the short side, wrote that "the beauty of stature is the only beauty of men." But even if Montaigne had never said it, I would continue to attribute a good deal of my self-worth and benevolent liberalism to being tall. When I go out into the street, I feel well-disposed toward the (mostly shorter) swarms of humanity; crowds not only do not dismay, they enliven me; and I am tempted to think that my passion for urbanism is linked to my height. By no means am I suggesting that only tall people love cities; merely that, in my case, part of the pleasure I derive from walking in crowded streets issues from a confidence that I can see above the heads of others, and cut a fairly impressive, elevated figure as I saunter along the sidewalk.

Some of my best friends have been—short. Brilliant men, brimming with poetry and worldly ideas, they deserved all of my and the world's respect. Yet at times I have had to master an impulse to rumple their heads; and I suspect they have developed manners of a more formal, *noli me tangere* nature, largely in response to this petting impulse of taller others.

The accident of my tallness has inclined me to both a seemingly egalitarian informality and a desire to lead. Had I not been a writer, I would surely have become a politician; I was even headed that direction in my teens. Ever since I shot up to a little over six feet, I have had at my command what feels like a natural, Gregory Peck authority when addressing an audience. Far from experiencing stage fright, I have actually sought out situations in which I could make speeches, give readings, sit on panel discussions, and generally tower over everyone else onstage. To be tall is to look down on the world and meet its eyes on your terms. But this topic, the noblesse oblige of tall men, is a dangerously provoking one, and so let us say no more about it.

The mental image of one's body changes slower than one's body. Mine was for a long while arrested in my early twenties, when I was tall and thin (165 pounds) and gobbled down whatever I felt like. I ate food that was cheap and filling, cheeseburgers, pizza, without any thought to putting on weight. But a young person's metabolism is more dietetically forgiving. To compound the problem, the older you get, the more cultivated your palate grows—and the more life's setbacks make you inclined to fill the hollowness of disappointment with the pleasures of the table.

Between the age of thirty and forty I put on ten pounds mostly around the midsection. Since then my gut has suffered another expansion, and I tip the scales at over 180. That I took a while to notice the change may be shown by my continuing to purchase clothes at my primordial adult size (33 waist, 15½ collar), until a girlfriend started pointing out that all my clothes were too tight. I rationalized this circumstance as the result of changing fashions (thinking myself still subconsciously loyal to the sixties' penchant for skintight fits) and laundry shrinkage rather than anything to do with my own body. She began buying me larger replacements for birthdays or holidays, and I found I enjoyed this "baggier" style, which allowed me to button my trousers comfortably, or to wear a tie and, for the first time in years, close my top shirt button. But it took even longer before I was able to enter a clothing store myself and give the salesman realistically enlarged size numbers.

Clothes can disguise the defects of one's body, up to a point. I get dressed with great optimism, adding one color to another, mixing my favorite Japanese and Italian designers, matching the patterns and textures, selecting ties, then proceed to the bathroom mirror to judge the result. There is an ideal in my mind of the effect I am essaying by wearing a particular choice of garments, based, no doubt, on male models in fashion ads—and I fall so far short of this insouciant gigolo handsomeness that I cannot help but be a little disappointed when I turn up so depressingly myself, narrow-shouldered, Talmudic, that grim, set mouth, that long, narrow face, those appraising eyes, the Semitic hooked nose, all of which express both the strain of intellectual overachieving and the tabula rasa of immaturity . . . for it is still, underneath, a boy in the mirror. A boy with a rapidly receding hairline.

How is it that I've remained a boy all this time, into my late forties? I remember at seventeen, drawing a self-portrait of myself as I looked in the mirror. I was so appalled at the weak chin and pleading eyes that I ended up focusing on the neckline of the cotton T-shirt. Ever since then I have tried to toughen myself up, but I still encounter in the glass that haunted uncertainty—shielded by a bluffing shell of cynicism, perhaps, but untouched by wisdom. So I approach the mirror warily, without lighting up as much as I would for the least of my acquaintances; I go one-on-one with that frowning schmuck.

And yet, it would be insulting to those who labor under the burden of true ugliness to palm myself off as an unattractive man. I'm at times almost handsome, if you squinted your eyes and rounded me off to the nearest *beau ideal*. I lack even a shred of cowboy virility, true, but I believe I fall into a category of adorable nerd or absentminded professor that awakens the amorous curiosity of some women. "Cute" is a word often applied to me by those I've been fortunate enough to attract. Then again, I attract only women of a certain lopsided prettiness: the head-turning, professional beauties never fall for me. They seem to look right through me, in fact. Their utter lack of interest in my appeal has always fascinated me. Can it be so simple an explanation as that beauty calls to beauty, as wealth to wealth?

I think of poor (though not in his writing gifts) Cesare Pavese, who kept chasing after starlets, models, and ballerinas—exquisite lovelies who couldn't appreciate his morose coffeehouse charm. Before he killed himself, he wrote a poem addressed to one of them, "Death Will Come Bearing Your Eyes"—thereby unfairly promoting her from rejecting lover to unwitting executioner. Perhaps he believed that only beautiful women (not literary critics, who kept awarding him prestigious prizes) saw him clearly, with twenty-twenty vision, and had the right to judge him. Had I been more headstrong, if masochistic, I might have followed his path and chased some beauty until she was forced to tell me, like an oracle, what it was about me, physically, that so failed to excite her. Then I might know something crucial about my body, before I passed into my next reincarnation.

Jung says somewhere that we pay dearly over many years to learn about ourselves what a stranger can see at a glance. This is the way I feel about my back. Fitting rooms aside, we none of us know what we look like from the back. It is the area of ourselves whose presentation we can least control, and which therefore may be the most honest part of us.

I divide backs into two kinds: my own and everyone else's. The others' backs are often mysterious, exquisite, and uncannily sympathetic. I have always loved backs. To walk behind a pretty woman in a backless dress and savor how a good pair of shoulder blades, heightened by shadow, has the same power to pierce the heart as chiseled cheekbones! . . . I wonder what it says about me that I worship a part of the body that signals turning away. Does it mean I'm a glutton for being abandoned, or a timid voyeur who prefers a surreptitious gaze that will not be met and challenged? I only know I have often felt the deepest love at just that moment when the beloved turns her back to me to get some sleep.

I have no autoerotic feelings about my own back. I cannot even picture it; visually it is a stranger to me. I know it only as an annoyance, which came into my consciousness twenty years ago, when I started getting lower back pain. Yes, we all know that Homo sapiens is constructed incorrectly; our erect posture puts too much pressure on the base of the spine; more workdays are lost because of lower back pain than any other cause. Being a writer, I sit all day, compounding the problem. My back is the enemy of my writing life: if I don't do exercises daily, I immediately ache; and if I do, I am still not spared. I could say more, but there is nothing duller than lower back pain. So common, mundane an ailment brings no credit to the sufferer. One has to dramatize it somehow, as in the phrase "I threw my back out."

Here is a gossip column about my body: My eyebrows grow quite bushy across my forehead, and whenever I get my hair cut, the barber asks me diplomatically if I want them trimmed or not. (I generally say no, associating bushy eyebrows with Balzackian virility, *élan vital*; but sometimes I acquiesce, to soothe his fastidiousness). . . . My belly button is a modest, embedded slit, not a jaunty swirl like my father's. Still, I like to sniff the odor that comes from jabbing my finger in it: a very ripe, underground smell, impossible to describe, but let us say a combination of old gym socks and stuffed derma (the Yiddish word for this oniony dish of ground intestines is, fittingly, *kishkas*). . . . I have a scar on my tongue from childhood, which I can only surmise I received by landing it on a sharp object somehow. Or perhaps I bit it hard. I have the habit of sticking my tongue out like a dog when exerting myself physically, as though to urge my muscles on; and maybe I accidentally chomped into it at such a moment. . . . I gnash my teeth, sleeping or waking. Awake, the sensation makes me feel alert and in contact with the world when I start to drift off in a day dream. Another way of grounding myself is to pinch my cheek—drawing a pocket of flesh downward and squeezing it—as I once saw JFK do in a filmed motorcade. I do this cheek pinching especially when I am trying to keep mentally focused during teaching or other public situations. I also scratch the nape of my neck under public stress, so much so in fact that I raise welts or sores which then eventually grow scabs; and I take great delight in secretly picking the scabs off. . . . My nose itches whenever I think about it, and I scratch it often, especially lying in bed trying to fall asleep (maybe because I am conscious of my breathing then). I also pick my nose with formidable thoroughness when no one, I hope, is looking. . . . There is a white scar about the size of a quarter on the juicy part of my knee; I got it as a boy running into a car fender, and I can still remember staring with detached calm at the blood that gushed from it like a pretty, half-eaten peach. Otherwise, the sight of my own blood makes me awfully nervous. I used to faint dead away when a blood sample was taken, and now I can control the impulse to do so only by biting the insides of my cheeks while steadfastly looking away from the needle's action. . . . I like to clean out my earwax as often as possible (the smell is curiously sulfurous; I associate it with the bodies of dead insects). I refuse to listen to warnings that it is dangerous to stick cleaning objects into your ears. I love Q-Tips immoderately; I buy them in huge quantities and store them the way a former refugee will stock canned foodstuffs. . . . My toes are long and apelike; I have very little fellow feeling for them; they are so far away, they may as well belong to someone else. . . . My flattish buttocks are not offensively large, but neither do they have the "dream" configuration one sees in jeans ads. Perhaps for this reason, it disturbed me puritanically when asses started to be treated by Madison Avenue, around the seventies, as crucial sexual equipment, and I began to receive compositions from teenage girl students declaring that they liked some boy because he had "a cute butt." It confused me; I had thought the action was elsewhere.

About my penis there is nothing, I think, unusual. It has a brown stem, and a pink mushroom head where the foreskin is pulled back. Like most heterosexual males, I have little comparative knowledge to go by, so that I always feel like an outsider when I am around women or gay men who talk zestfully about differences in penises. I am afraid that they might judge me harshly, ridicule me like the boys who stripped me of my bathing suit in summer camp when I was ten. But perhaps they would simply declare it an ordinary penis, which changes size with the stimulus or weather or time of day. Actually, my penis does have a peculiarity: it has two peeing holes. They are very close to each other, so that usually only one stream of urine issues, but sometimes a hair gets caught across them, or some such contretemps, and they squirt out in two directions at once.

This part of me, which is so synecdochically identified with the male body (as the term "male member" indicates), has given me both too little, and too much, information about what it means to be a man. It has a personality like a cat's. I have prayed to it to behave better, to be less frisky, or more; I have followed its nose in matters of love, ignoring good sense, and paid the price; but I have also come to appreciate that it has its own specialized form of intelligence which must be listened to, or another price will be extracted.

Even to say the word "impotence" aloud makes me nervous. I used to tremble when I saw it in print, and its close relation, "importance," if hastily scanned, had the same effect, as if they were publishing a secret about me. But why should it be my secret, when my penis has regularly given me erections lo these many years—except for about a dozen times, mostly when I was younger! Because, even if it has not been that big a problem for me, it has dominated my thinking as an adult male. I've no sooner to go to bed with a woman than I'm in suspense. The power of the flaccid penis's statement, "I don't want you," is so stark, so cruelly direct, that it continues to exert a fascination out of all proportion to its actual incidence. Those few times when I was unable to function were like a wall forcing me to take another path—just as, after I tried to kill myself at seventeen, I was obliged to give up pessimism for a time. Each had instructed me by its too painful manner that I could not handle the world as I had previously construed it, that my confusion and rage were being found out. I would have to get more wily or else grow up.

Yet for the very reason that I was compelled to leave them behind, these two options of my youth, impotence and suicide, continue to command an underground loyalty, as though they were more "honest" than the devious strategies of potency and survival which I adopted. Put it this way: sometimes we encounter a person who has had a nervous breakdown years before and who seems cemented over sloppily, his vulnerability ruthlessly guarded against as dangerous; we sense he left a crucial part of himself back in the chaos of breakdown, and has since grown rigidly jovial. So suicide and impotence became for me "the roads not taken," the paths I had repressed.

Whenever I hear an anecdote about impotence—a woman who successfully coaxed an ex-priest who had been celibate and unable to make love, first by lying next to him for six months without any touching, then by cuddling for six more months, then by easing him slowly into a sexual embrace—I think they are talking about me. I identify completely; this, in spite of the fact, which I promise not to repeat again, that I have generally been able to do it whenever called upon. Believe it or not, I am not boasting when I say that: a part of me is contemptuous of this virility, as though it were merely a mechanical trick that violated my true nature, that of an impotent man absolutely frightened of women, absolutely secluded, cut off.

I now see the way I have idealized impotence: I've connected it with pushing the world away, as a kind of integrity, as in Moliere's *The*

Misanthrope—connected it with that part of me which, gregarious socializer that I am, continues to insist that I am a recluse, too good for this life. Of course, it is not true that I am terrified of women. I exaggerate my terror of them for dramatic effect, or for the purposes of a good scare.

My final word about impotence: Once, in a period when I was going out with many women, as though purposely trying to ignore my hypersensitive side and force it to grow callous by thrusting myself into foreign situations (not only sexual) and seeing if I was able to "rise to the occasion," I dated a woman who was attractive, tall and blond, named Susan. She had something to do with the pop music business, was a follower of the visionary religious futurist Teilhard de Chardin, and considered herself a religious pacifist. In fact, she told me her telephone number in the form of the anagram, N-O-T-O-W-A-R. I thought she was joking and laughed aloud. But she gave me a solemn look. In passing, I should say that all the women with whom I was impotent or close to it had solemn natures. The sex act has always seemed to me in many ways ridiculous, and I am most comfortable when a women who enters the sheets with me shares that sense of the comic pomposity behind such a grandiloquently rhetorical use of the flesh. It is as though the prose of the body were being drastically squeezed into metrical verse. I would not have known how to stop guffawing had I been D.H. Lawrence's lover, and I am sure he would have been pretty annoyed at me. But a smile saying "All this will pass" has an erotic effect on me like nothing else.

They claim that men who have long, long fingers also have lengthy penises. I can tell you with a surety that my fingers are long and sensitive, the most perfect, elegant, handsome part of my anatomy. They are not entirely perfect—the last knuckle of my right middle finger is twisted permanently, broken in a softball game when I was trying to block the plate—but even this slight disfigurement, harbinger of mortality, adds to the pleasure I take in my hands' rugged beauty. My penis does not excite me in nearly the same contemplative delight when I look at it as do my fingers. Pianists' hands, I have been told often; and though I do not play the piano, I derive an aesthetic satisfaction from them that is as pure and Apollonian as any I am capable of. I can stare at my fingers for hours. No wonder I have them so often in my mouth, biting my fingernails to bring them closer. When I write, I almost feel that they, and not my intellect, are the clever progenitors of the text. Whatever narcissism, fetishism, and proud sense of masculinity I possess about my body must begin and end with my fingers.

What They Don't Tell You About Hurricanes

PHILIP GERARD

What they don't tell you about hurricanes is the uncertainty.
First it's *whether*. As in *Weather* Channel. There's been a rumor of storm off the coast of Africa, and it's turned into a tropical depression. It churns across the Atlantic into the Caribbean and is upgraded to a Tropical Storm, winds at forty or fifty knots, and the person in charge of such things gives it an androgynous name: Fran.

Will it hit us here on the south coast of North Carolina?

They can't tell. The experts. We've been through this before—Hugo, Felix, Marilyn, Edouard, Bertha. My wife, Kathleen, who grew up with California earthquakes, bridles at the lingering uncertainty, the waffling, a whole season of emergency. She wants it quick, bang, and over. But it doesn't happen that way. Hurricanes are big and slow and cyclone around offshore for a few thousand miles.

So the radar scope on the Weather Channel becomes familiar, part of the nightly ritual before going to bed, like taking out the dog and locking the front door. It becomes the first thing you do every morning, even before coffee. Watching the swirls of red and orange, a bright pinwheel of destruction. Checking the stats—wind speed, barometric pressure, latitude and longitude. We are at 34 degrees 12 minutes north latitude, 77 degrees 50 minutes west longitude. A degree of latitude equals sixty miles north or south. The arithmetic isn't hard.

Fran bangs into some islands from the vacation brochures and it's heading toward the U.S. mainland. But here in Wilmington, we just had Bertha, a direct hit. The eye sat over our backyard—you could look up and see the actual sky wound into a circular wall, like being down inside a black well, watching the stars out the top.

Surely, not twice in one season—what are the odds?

What they don't tell you is that hurricanes, like lightning, can strike exactly the same spot time and again. Fran is not the first storm. It's the second slam from a hurricane in eight weeks, and in the meantime it's rained torrentially almost every day. It's been a whole summer of violent storms, of lightning fires and local floods, of black line squalls that knock down fleets of sailboats racing off the beach. The ground is so saturated we have had the lawn sprinkler system turned off all summer. Starved of oxygen, tree roots are rotting in the ground.

The longleaf pines that ring our property stand sixty and seventy feet high, two feet in diameter, precarious upright tons of wet wood, swaying already in the breeze. Their roots are soft in the spongy ground.

We've been set up. It feels like there's a bull's-eye painted on the map next to the words "Cape Fear."

So it's *when*. Fran is moving at 14 knots, then 16, then wobbling slowly into a kind of hover. It's a monster storm, darkening the whole map of the Atlantic between Cape Fear and Bermuda, sucking up warm water and slinging it into windy horizontal rain. It's too big to miss us entirely.

It's Monday, the beginning of a long week. We fill up the bathtub, stockpile batteries and canned goods, locate flashlights and candles and matches, fill the truck with gas. Then we load all our important documents—passports, mortgage papers, insurance policies, marriage license—into a single attaché case and keep it handy. We take lots of cash out of the automatic teller.

Landfall of The Eye expected Wednesday night, late. Wednesday is good for us, because Wednesday means south. Good for us, bad for Charleston. Hugo country.

We wish it on them. Me, Kathleen, the neighbors who drift back and forth between houses just to talk out loud, just to look at the sky. We feel bad about it, but we wish it on them anyway. If we had real magic, we would make it happen to them, not to us.

But Fran wanders north, following Bertha's path, and on TV they change the *when*: Thursday night, after midnight. Because our Beneteau sloop *Savoir-Faire* is moored in a tidal harbor, we pay attention to the tides. Low tide will be at 9:34 P.M. From then on, the tide will rise one foot every two hours until 3:29 A.M. By mid-afternoon all of us whose boats remain in the community harbor at the end of our street are lashing on extra fenders, strapping lines to the pilings, watching the water lap at the bulkhead separating the marsh from the harbor.

I'd take the boat out of there, drive her to safety, but where? It would take eight hours to get down the waterway and up the Cape Fear River, and I don't know the hurricane holes there. I'd be stuck on the boat, away from my wife, in the low-country wilderness, with a three-to-five knot current pushing dangerous debris down the river at me all night long.

Full-force Fran aims for coast says the local newspaper front-page headline.

Everybody is thinking the same thing: *don't let it come ashore at high tide.*

We speculate nervously about how much the tidal surge will actually be in this protected harbor, blocked from the ocean by a large, developed barrier island—Wrightsville Beach—a channel, a spoil island, the Intracoastal Waterway, and finally a hundred yards of marsh that is dry land at low tide.

Nobody knows.

Our docks are the floating kind—they can float up on their pilings another nine feet, and all will be well. All of our boats made it through Bertha without a scratch—eighty-five knot winds and a tidal surge of six feet.

There's the standard hurricane drill: strip all sails, remove all windage-making gear—horseshoe buoy, man-overboard pole, lifesling. We all help one another. Nobody has to ask. While unbending the large full-battened mains'l, I bang my new racing watch on the boom gooseneck and break it. A bad portent.

We retreat across the causeway to our homes, where the power has already gone off, as the rain becomes torrential and the wind begins to blow in great twists of energy. It has started. So we have an answer to *when*. An hour later, when Fran comes howling down on us out of the ocean, it's *how hard*. As we huddle indoors and listen to the roaring, the question becomes *how long*.

When, How Hard, How Long: the trigonometry of catastrophe.

The answer is 8:05 P.M., almost dead low tide.

The answer is sixteen feet of surging water anyway and winds of 105 knots.

The answer is 15 hours.

Some of the clichés turn out to be true.

The rain really is *torrential*, as in *torrents*.

A hurricane *does* sound like a freight train. Exactly like. If you were lying between the rails and it went roaring along over your head all night long. It really does *roar*. Like whatever is holding the world together is coming apart, tonight, this minute, right here, and you're smack in the middle of the program.

225

And your mouth really does go so dry with fear you can hardly talk.

The great trees cracking and tumbling to the ground in the roaring darkness really do sound like an artillery barrage—*crack! crack! whump! whump!* It takes italics, exclamation points, boldface clichés to tell about it. The house shudders again and again. Our house has too many large windows, so we run next door to wait out Fran with our neighbors. We're sitting up with them in their living room drinking any liquor we can get our hands on—vodka, beer, wine, rum—and each shudder brings a sharp intake of breath, a little cry. You can't help it. You laugh and make jokes, but it feels bad and the feeling gets worse every minute. The kerosene lanterns don't help. They make Halloween light. Eerie, spooky light.

There are times when you have to dodge out into the maelstrom of wind and flying debris and back across the lawns to check the outside of your house, to clear the storm drain and prevent flooding of the lower story. It's stupid, especially in the pitch blackness, but it feels like something you have to do. The world is way out of control, but you're still responsible.

There are freaky contradictions of nature. Paradoxes of chance. A massive oak tree that has weathered three hundred years of storms is ripped apart by the wind, literally twisted out of the earth by the roots. The next lot over, a pair of forgotten work gloves left to dry on the spikes of a picket fence are still there in the morning, and so is the fence. Dry.

The wind blows strips of new caulking out from between the casement windows but leaves intact the plastic tarps you nailed over the open sides of the upstairs porch.

There are amazing feats of heroism and survival. A man on one of the beach islands sends his wife and kids to the shelter, remains behind with their dog to finish boarding up the house, then the only road off the island overwashes, and he's cut off. He grabs his dog in his arms and ropes himself to the house, and all night long he and the dog are bashed against the house by water and wind, but they make it through. The dog was a boxer.

Lightning strikes the home of an old couple and it catches fire. Two young men appear out of the storm, attack the fire with a garden hose and keep it from taking the house until the fire trucks arrive, then disappear. Nobody knows who they are or where they came from. The old couple believes they are angels.

There are tales of death. Another man is seen stepping onto his front porch as the hurricane hits. They find him in the morning miles away, floating face-down in the Intracoastal Waterway. A woman rescued from a mattress floating in the marsh dies anyway.

For a week afterward, urban rescue workers prowl the wrecked homes along the beach with dogs, sniffing out the bodies of the ones who wouldn't leave.

It's also true, the cliché about the capriciousness of nature and about blind luck. Three Marines in a Mustang are swept off the road by the rushing water. One is washed to the far shore and stumbles into a shelter. The second clings to a tree limb for nine hours until he is rescued. The third drowns.

There are things that are outrageously unfair. A family down the street gets flooded out on the ground floor. They scramble upstairs ahead of the surge. But the battery of their brand new car shorts out in the rising water, and it catches fire. The garage underneath the house burns. Soon the whole house is burning. Incredibly, at the height of the hurricane, the volunteer firemen arrive. They maneuver their pumper through waist-deep water. But they can't get the electric garage door open and have to axe it down. And by then the family is smoked out, the house is partly destroyed, the car is a hulk.

Hurricane, flood, fire, all at once.

Thunder and lightning come in ahead of the hurricane. Tornadoes spin off the leading edge like missiles, knocking out bridges, tearing holes in houses, twisting trees out of the earth and flinging them into power lines.

Biblical stuff.

Furious Fran unforgiving, the local newspaper says, again on page one, unable to let go of the corny habit of alliteration.

What they don't tell you about hurricanes is the heat.

The oppressive stillness of the stalled atmosphere the day before the winds start. The hundred degrees of swampy humidity the day after, before the torrential rains resume. The air-conditioning is off, the windows are latched down tight. An hour into the storm, everything you touch is greasy. You put on a fresh shirt and sweat it through before you can fasten the buttons.

And then the bees arrive. Swarming, disoriented, stinging, bees gone haywire. Bumblebees, wasps, yellow jackets, hornets. I'm no entomologist—they all sting.

After a hurricane, the radio warns, that's when the injuries start. Beestings are number one, followed by poisonous snakebites and chainsaw cuts.

When the rains resume a day and a half after Fran passes, the yard is jumping with frogs and toads. Little bright green tree frogs with suction cups on their feet, smaller than a penny. Black toads the size of your fist. Giant croaking bullfrogs that splash around like rocks. Rat snakes. Water moccasins. Copperheads.

What's next—locusts? Well, not exactly: crickets. By the millions. All over the debris, the backyard deck, the wrecked boats.

But the birds are gone.

The water is off.

After sweltering hours clearing the tree limbs out of the road, pulling limbs off cars and shrubs, dragging downed trees off the driveway, raking the mess off the steps and walks and deck, my wife and I shower by pouring buckets of cold water, saved in the bathtub, over our soapy heads and bodies. We are scraped and cut and bruised and stained with pine resin that does not wash off. Every pair of shoes we own is wet and muddy and will not dry. The house is tracked with mud and debris, and a lethargic depression sets in—part physical exhaustion from relentless manual labor in the heat, from two sleepless nights in a row. Part emotional exhaustion. Grief.

We were luckier than many. It just doesn't feel that way.

When the power comes back on, it's like a religious experience. Everything becomes possible again—bright lights, cool air, television news, ice.

Then after a few hours it goes off again.

What they don't tell you about hurricanes is that the Big Hit is the beginning, not the end. Fran has swept on up the coast, taking the Weather Channel and CNN with it. On the networks, things are happening in Bosnia, Chechnya, Indonesia.

Here in Hurricanelandia, it's raining eight inches in three hours on top of ten inches that came in with Fran. They predict it will rain for another week. All the low-country rivers are cresting, shouldering through the wreckage of human cities toward the sea.

Our house is an island surrounded by rushing water two feet deep, and it's back out into the storm wearing Red Ball boots, clearing out clogged gutters on an aluminum ladder, counting the seconds between lightning and thunder, counting how long to dare such foolishness. Then slogging out onto the muddy access road behind the house to rake out the clogged storm culvert, trying not to get carried into the muddy water.

On the local radio, the jocks are chatting about this and that and the other, but for hours nobody gives a weather report. When will it stop raining? *Will* it stop raining? The phone is working. A friend from across town, where they have power, calls. Look out your window—is it raining there? The edge of the cloud is moving over us now, she says, and there's sun behind it.

The water recedes, and now it's time to clean out the flooded garage. At dusk, the generators go on. It gets dark and noisy. We will wake to the lumber-camp sound of chainsaws.

For weeks and weeks.

What they don't tell you about a hurricane is that it just seems to go on and on.

But the worst of it is not captured on the awesome helicopter videotape of destruction. The worst of it is waking up to the new stillness of the morning after, when the wind has finally quit and the rain has slacked and the sun may or may not be up yet, the sky is just a gray slate of clouds.

Overnight, the world has changed in some important, irrevocable way. You can just feel it.

My neighbor John is standing outside waiting. "You ready?" he says, and I nod.

Half a mile away, the approach to the harbor is littered with dock-boxes, paddles, small boats, lifejackets. Like a shipwreck has happened to the whole neighborhood. The houses by the harbor have taken a beating. A 44-foot sportfishing boat lies on its side on a front lawn, and my stomach turns. That's how high the water rose.

A few nights earlier, I had stood on our dock talking quietly with an old friend, admiring the sleek, trim lines of *Savoir-Faire* under starlight, feeling lucky. Thirty-two feet of beautiful racing yacht, a dream of fifteen years of saving come true. I'd take *Savoir-Faire* out onto the broad back of the Atlantic and race her hard, rail down, or just jog along in mild breezes, clearing my head, sharing her with friends, or filling up with the good strength that comes from working a yare boat alone.

The harbor was demolished. Boats and docks were piled up like a train wreck. Boats were crushed, sunk, broken, smashed, aground. Some were simply gone.

Out in the middle of the harbor, alone, *Savoir-Faire* lay impaled on a piling, sunk by the bows, only her mast and transom rising above the dirty water.

What they don't tell you about hurricanes is how many ways they can break your heart.

Excerpt From
Irving Berlin: A Life in Song

PHILIP FURIA

O ne evening in May of 1924, Irving Berlin wandered down to
Jimmy Kelly's, a bar where he had once worked as a singing
waiter. Throughout his life he had a habit of returning to his old
haunts in Union Square, Chinatown, and the Bowery, a habit easily
indulged in a city where no matter how far up—or down—the ladder
of success you had climbed, you could reach your antipodes by walking a few blocks. On this particular night, Berlin may have been more
than usually reflective about the course of his career. While he was
undoubtedly the premier American songwriter, his hold upon that
position was tenuous. It may have already been clear that he could
not maintain it by writing scores for revues at his own Music Box
Theatre, and he was not ready to plunge into the newly emerging
genre of the integrated musical comedy, where songs had to grow out
of story and character.

Already, younger songwriters were vying for his mantle. On February 24, 1924, Paul Whiteman presented a concert at Aeolian Hall
that purported to fuse jazz with the classics. Much of that program,
however, including a "Semi-Symphonic Arrangement" of Irving Berlin's songs, proved drearily monotonous; only when young George
Gershwin strode to the piano, nodded to Whiteman, then plunged
into *Rhapsody in Blue*, did it become clear that jazz had found a new
spokesman.

If Berlin could not clearly foresee his future in American song, a
look backward at his past seemed to suggest that his stunning career
had reached a plateau. His friend Alexander Woollcott was writing a
biography of the songwriter—an enormous tribute yet one that suggested that sense of closure. Woollcott traced Berlin's rise from the
immigrant Lower East Side to the heights of American success, romanticizing his subject as an untutored genius who drew upon his melancholy heritage as a Russian Jew. Woollcott predicted that his music

would endure only after a trained composer had transmuted it, as Liszt and Chopin had taken anonymous folk melodies and lifted them into the realm of classic art. While Woollcott acknowledged that it was unusual to write the biography of a man in his mid-thirties, his book implied that Berlin had come as far, creatively, as someone like him possibly could.

What may have made Irving Berlin especially reflective on this particular night, however, was that he had not come to Jimmy Kelly's alone. With him was a lovely and sophisticated young lady named Ellin Mackay. Earlier that evening, they had met at a fashionable dinner party. She had charmed him by saying, "Oh, Mr. Berlin, I do so like your song, 'What Shall I Do' " And, he, after correcting her about the title of his latest hit, "What'll I Do?," graciously acknowledged the propriety of her distinction between *shall* and *will*: "Where grammar is concerned," he said, "I can always use a little help." After dinner, he invited her to accompany him to Jimmy Kelly's, which had become, in the parlance of the Prohibition era, a "speakeasy." Kelly had also moved from his old Union Square location to Sullivan Street in Greenwich Village, the heart of artistic experiment, social protest, and Bohemian lifestyles in the Jazz Age.

The transformation of Jimmy Kelly's was indicative of the vast changes in American social mores that had taken place since Berlin had worked as a singing waiter. The coming of the cabaret around 1910 had threatened to break down the barriers between the social classes, to place young girls from the highest echelons of society next to men from the lower and even immigrant classes. Dancing, dining, and the intimate floor show invited the expression and exploration of private experience, once confined to the homes of a closely knit society, into the open, public domain. The redefinition of the American girl that had started out with Irene Castle as the healthy, active, fox-trotting playmate of 1914 had, ten years later, transmogrified into the Jazz Age flapper, kicking up her stocking-less legs in the Charleston.

The encounter between Irving Berlin and Ellin Mackay was the most dramatic upshot of these changes in American society. Barely twenty-one, the lithe, blonde Ellin came from the highest reaches of New York society. Her father, Clarence Mackay, on the strength of a family fortune spawned by the fabled Nevada Comstock silver mines, had invested in the telegraph system and was known as "The Cable King." Ellin had grown up at his estate on Long Island, gone to the finest private schools, and, in the year before she met Irving Berlin, made her debut into society at a ball at the Ritz-Carlton. Later that fall, she would dance with the Prince of Wales, who was destined to become King Edward VII of England until he, in an even more scandalous crossing of class barriers, gave up the throne to marry a divorced commoner.

Ellin, however, had literary aspirations and found herself drawn to Greenwich Village and to her aunt, Alice Duer Miller, a member of the Algonquin Round Table. The Round Table itself exemplified social mixing among people like Woollcott and Franklin Pierce Adams, who came from solid gentility, George S. Kaufman and Dorothy Parker, who stemmed from wealthy Jewish families, and Jews like Berlin and Herbert Swope, who had struggled up from poverty. For a flower of New York society like Ellin Mackay to mingle with such a mongrel group, however literate, testified to the breakdown of class distinctions. Ellin knew it and capitalized upon it. In 1925, she would write a two-part essay, "Why We Go to Cabarets: A Post-Debutante Explains," for *The New Yorker*, the new magazine founded by Round Tabler Herbert Ross to set a standard of wit, insouciance, and urbanity.

Ellin's essay gleefully satirized the dreaded influence of cabarets on American society:

> Our Elders criticize many things about us, but usually they attribute sins too gaudy to be true. The trouble is that our Elders are a trifle gullible; they have swallowed too much of F. Scott Fitzgerald . . . They believe all the backstage gossip that is written about us . . . Cabaret has its place in the elderly mind beside Bohemia and bolshevik, and other vague words that have a sinister significance and no precise definition. . . . We have privacy in a cabaret . . . What does it matter if an unsavory Irish politician is carrying on a dull and noisy flirtation with the little blonde at the table behind us? We don't have to listen; we are with people we find amusing.

In just such a cabaret Ellin Mackay had fulfilled the worst of those fears by finding companionship with an immigrant Jewish songwriter. In Ellin, Berlin found the high spirit of his first wife, Dorothy, together with the literate sophistication of his current friends from the Algonquin Round Table.

When he learned that his daughter was involved with Berlin, Clarence Mackay was incensed. The fact that his family was Catholic made him even more virulent in guarding his social standing, and Mackay was especially wary of Jews who were pushing at the edges of society where his own family had only recently entrenched itself. His hold on his social position had already been challenged when his wife, Katherine Duer, became entangled in an affair with the family doctor shortly before World War I. Mackay refused, on Catholic tenets, to grant his wife a divorce, and spirited Ellin and his other two children off to Europe. Katherine, in turn, traveled to Paris, where her lover, Doctor Joseph Blake, headed an American Red Cross hospital. After a scandalous remarriage, she left Mackay to Harbor Hill, his magnificent Long Island estate, and to his bitterness.

That bitterness flared anew over his daughter's association with Irving Berlin. Although he himself had taken a mistress, Anna Case, she was from the upper echelon of the musical world, a star at the Metropolitan Opera, where Mackay was a member of the board of directors. When he learned that Ellin and Berlin were seen together at parties, including one at Harbor Hill, he hired private detectives to investigate the songwriter. When he could turn up nothing damaging, he reverted to the tactic he had used when his own marriage had collapsed, whisking his daughter off to Europe in the hope that other suitors would expunge the memory of Berlin.

What Mackay did not realize was that removing his daughter from New York would only intensify Berlin's feelings, which do not seem to have been as committed to the relationship, until that point, as Ellin's were. Later, she admitted that in those early days she had been the pursuer. However, in her absence, Berlin seems to have felt his mid-life emptiness all the more keenly. A newer, youthful era was emerging as epitomized by the success of the Gershwins' *Lady, Be Good!*, while Berlin, along with the revues to which he had committed himself and his theater, seemed to be ebbing into the past. In his first marriage he had hoped to find an escape from the demons that drove him to maintain the success he had achieved with "Alexander's Ragtime Band." As he contemplated this new commitment, it may have seemed a bulwark against the vicissitudes of time and fortune.

By the end of 1924, songs such as "What'll I Do?" and "All Alone" had become enormously popular, and newspapermen would later ascribe them to Berlin's longings for his departed Ellin. While "What'll I Do?" had been written before they met, "All Alone," according to the account of their oldest daughter, Mary Ellin Barrett, in her exquisite memoir, *Irving Berlin: A Daughter's Memoir*, was "clearly written for my mother during their courtship (however often the composer might try, self-consciously, to deny this)." In December, Berlin took out a song he had been working on, on and off, for two years. Originally, it was called "Don't Forget to Remember," but now he revamped it to the more minimalist "Remember," and took great pride in "the little musical phrase that is coupled with the word 'remember' in the song." The word begins the chorus on a syncopated upbeat, so that the waltz rhythm is slightly out of kilter, reflecting the singer's consternation. The second syllable of "remember" then climbs up three notes, an unusual rising interval that leaves the question—and the chord—unresolved. When the word is repeated at the end of the A-sections, it stretches over a full octave, intensifying the singer's despair. Then, at the beginning of the release, "remember" traverses four intervals beyond the octave, yet still follows that haunting pattern of the rising third. Only when "remember" recurs at the very end of the song is the chord resolved, though the effect is more one of resignation than resolution: "You promised that you'd forget me not, but you forgot to remember."

It was when this final "turnaround" phrase came to him as a "tag line" that Berlin felt his two years of work had reached an end. That line "made the song," illustrating his conviction that "it's the lyric that makes a song a hit, although the tune, of course, is what makes it last."

If "Remember" was inspired by Ellin Mackay's absence, the song also registers Berlin's gnawing sense of insecurity, always present in him but particularly so as he entered such a critical period in his professional as well as his personal life. With "Remember," he recalled, "I tried to express a feeling or an emotion that had been embodied in me," and he was "a bit sensitive and enthusiastic concerning it."

> On Christmas morning I called Max Winslow and Saul Bornstein, my publishing associates, to my studio room in the Music Box Theatre to hear the new song I had composed. I sang it, certain I had a hit. When I finished . . . Bornstein said that it was not so good. Winslow said it was terrible. I told them I thought the song was good and would be a hit. They tried to persuade me from publishing it and suggested I throw it into the wastebasket and forget about it . . . During the spring and summer I remembered "Remember" and worried about it. I thought I had lost my skill, my talent. I was afraid to write anything for fear Winslow would say it was terrible. I was developing an inferiority complex, which is the greatest hindrance a writer can have . . . I worried so much that I was becoming a bundle of nerves . . . That Christmas Day was the worst one I had ever spent in my life. Every time I felt worried or troubled I remembered that day and felt worse.

Berlin had always worried about how long his talent would endure, and part of his drive reflects his fear that one day he would find he could not come up with another successful song. Earlier he had speculated that while his ability to concoct tunes was safe, he feared that lyrics would one day be his downfall. Now, in the creation of a single song, he seemed to be at a dead end. If the song reflected the absence of young Ellin Mackay, Berlin's loss was doubly poignant.

"After much worrying and thinking," Berlin decided to "publish the song against the advice of Winslow and Bornstein and let the public judge." Its success buoyed Berlin's confidence, and, though Ellin still remained abroad, his professional life seemed to revive when an opportunity presented itself to work on a genuine "book show." His collaborator would be George S. Kaufman, yet another of his Round Table friends and already recognized as one of the finest playwrights of his era, the comic counterpart to Eugene O'Neill. Kaufman approached playwriting with as business-like an attitude as Irving Berlin approached songwriting. Although he once quipped, "Satire is what closes on Saturday night," Kaufman had a brilliant sense of the excesses and foibles of the Jazz Age.

The show he envisioned would send up one of the decade's biggest fads, the Florida real-estate boom which reached its peak in 1925. In that year in Miami alone there were 2,000 real estate offices and more than 25,000 agents (or, as they preferred to be called in typical 1920s grandiosity, "realtors"). The city, which had grown from 30,000 residents in 1920 to 75,000, had to pass an ordinance forbidding the sale of property—even the showing of maps—in the street to try to stem congestion. Kaufman's satire targeted the wildest get-rich-quick-schemes that the most megalomaniacal American could want. The success of Coral Gables spawned other developments, some sunny and some shady, and people around the country wrote out their checks for unseen lots. Stories of fabulous profits abounded. Lots that cost $800 in 1920 were selling for $150,000 in 1924. People began to buy land solely with the notion of reselling it at such enormous profits, but by early 1926 the bubble began to burst. By that summer, people who had put all their money into "binders" on lots found they could not sell them and could not make the payments. Then in September a hurricane hit Florida and, in the words of Frederick Lewis Allen in his delightful history of the 1920s, *Only Yesterday*, "piled the waters of Biscayne Bay into the lovely Venetian developments, deposited a five-masted schooner high in the street at Coral Gables, tossed big steam yachts upon the avenues of Miami, picked up trees, lumber, pipes, tiles, debris, and even small automobiles and sent them crashing into the houses."

The zaniness of the Florida boom made Kaufman's script a perfect vehicle for the Marx Brothers. Harpo Marx, also a member of the Algonquin group, solicited Berlin's help in persuading producer Sam Harris to use him and his brothers in the show. Berlin prevailed upon Harris who, with some trepidation, agreed to use the unpredictable foursome in *The Cocoanuts*. The Marx Brothers ensured the success of the show, but at the expense of Berlin's songs and Kaufman's script. Groucho, Harpo, Chico, and Zeppo threw in their own routines, ad-libbed lines, and treated songs as "throwaway" comic material. "I never knew that musical comedy was so difficult to produce," Irving Berlin said, "until we began working with the Marx Brothers on *The Cocoanuts*":

> When we started to rehearse we had our plan well-formulated. But 'ere long suggestions began to come in from the Marx Brothers, from Kaufman, from Harris—in fact, from everybody—and before we knew what had happened the general scheme of things had been turned topsy turvy. My well laid score was opened up and I wrote new songs, new lyrics and eventually we had an entirely different production than had been planned.

When the show ran long in rehearsals and out-of-town tryouts, Kaufman had to cut his script and Irving had to drop songs. But when the show opened in December 1925, the Marx brothers convulsed audiences with their comic *shtick*. Groucho at one point tries to bamboozle Chico into buying real estate at an auction. "I know an auction," Chico pipes up, "I come from Italy on the Atlantic auction." When Groucho shows him a map of a development with levees, Chico says he knows a family of "Levis," but when Groucho points out a "viaduct," Chico is stymied. "Why a duck?" he demands and the two are off on another verbal rollercoaster. How could mere songs follow an act like that?

The only Berlin song that might have become a hit from *The Cocoanuts* had been cut from the score early in the "doctoring" process. It had started out rather inauspiciously as a syncopated waltz for a young woman named Mona, who was the girlfriend of Berlin's musical secretary at the time, Arthur Johnston. One day, so the story goes, she asked Berlin and Johnston to write a song about her. Berlin hummed a melody, Johnston jotted it down, then Berlin added a lyric that began, "I'll be loving you, Mona." The story is reminiscent of the legend that George Gershwin had a private song that he used to impress whatever young lady he happened to be interested in at the time; the lyric was designed to allow the insertion of any girl's name to convince her that she had inspired Gershwin's spontaneous flight of creative fancy. Working on the score for *The Cocoanuts*, Berlin resurrected the song, changed "Mona" to "Always," and devised a complex version of the standard thirty-two bar AABA chorus. The first three sections start off with the same syncopated waltz phrase but then each section goes a different melodic way to create an unusual ABCD pattern. Berlin not only shifts melody but even shifts keys. Each of these innovative variations, however, returns to the title word, "Always" but always on a different pair of notes. Only in the fourth and final section did Irving Berlin return to the same two notes on "Always" that had concluded the initial phrase of the chorus.

Such melodic invention Berlin dismissed as easy—"but not the lyric," Berlin affirmed. "Off and on, I spent a year on it. If I'd hurried, the melody would have been the same, but the words wouldn't have been so plain and simple. That's what I aim at—always." Once again, it was the "tag line" of the lyric that bedeviled him. "I just couldn't get the last three lines, so I ad-libbed—'Not for just an hour, not for just a day, not for just a year—but always.' And there it was—exactly what I wanted to say." Where the earlier sections had two or even three rhymes (including the subtle "*Days may* not be fair al*ways*"), this last had none. Such simple artistry was lost on Kaufman, who admittedly knew nothing about music. His cynical wit, however, turned on the sentimental lyric. " 'Always' was a long time for romance," quipped Kaufman when Berlin demonstrated the song for him. As someone who thought romantic love one of the silliest of cultural artifices, Kaufman suggested "the opening line might be a little more in accord with reality—something like 'I'll be loving you— *Thursday*.' " Another Tin Pan Alley songwriter, Buddy DeSylva, parodied the sentimentality of Berlin's lyric:

> I'll be loving you always, both in very large and small ways,
> With a love as grand as Paul Whiteman's band
> And 'twill weigh as much as Paul weighs—always.

For a songwriter as insecure as Berlin was in those times, such scorn was probably twice as cutting, but he soon had a better use for his waltz than as grist for the Marx Brothers comic mill.

In September 1925, Ellin Mackay returned from Europe; after almost a year abroad, her ardor for Berlin had not abated, and the two resumed their courtship. As they did, they were caught up in a new phenomenon, then called "ballyhoo," now, less poetically, "publicity" or "media blitz." "Ballyhoo" was the result of the consolidation of newspapers into national chains, such as the Scripps-Howard and Hearst systems. Instead of newspapers developing local coverage and features, the syndicate office in New York now provided their chains "editorials, health talks, comic strips, sob-sister columns, household hints, sports gossip, and Sunday features prepared for a national audience and guaranteed to tickle the mass mind." This consolidation helped solidify New York as the cultural center of America and had people across the country delighting in Dorothy Parker or Robert Benchley's latest quip at the Round Table.

Helped by the increase of national magazines with their large circulation and advertising revenues, as well as by radio broadcasting, the newspaper chains began to play upon the national mind with a series of riveting stories that for a time dominated the headlines. The Scopes "Monkey Trial" in Dayton, Tennessee; Charles Lindbergh's flight across the Atlantic; the athletic feats of Babe Ruth, Red Grange, or Bobby Jones—these events, as Allen noted in *Only Yesterday*, were "hurled at one in huge headlines," so that the reader "waded through page after page of syndicated discussion of it, heard about it on the radio, was reminded of it again and again in the outpourings of publicity-seeking orators and preachers, saw pictures of it in the Sunday papers and the movies, and (unless one was a perverse individualist) enjoyed the sensation of vibrating to the same chord which thrilled a vast populace."

The courtship of Ellin Mackay and Irving Berlin was fodder for this new mass-media machine. Even before Ellin returned from Europe, newspapers rumored they were engaged, and Broadway shows featured skits of the lovelorn songwriter pining for his missing high-society beauty. Naturally, reporters were there to greet Ellin's ship when it docked in New York. The biggest ballyhoo, however, came on January 4, 1926, when Ellin eloped and married Irving Berlin at City Hall in a civic ceremony. The couple was dogged by reporters to Berlin's apartment, from there to Penn Station, then to Atlantic City, where they spent a tense week until they sailed to Europe. During that week, they were besieged by reporters, sometimes fifty at a time, who asked about their relations with Clarence Mackay. *Variety* reported that Clarence Mackay had vowed their marriage would only happen "over my dead body," and *The New York Mirror* even invented an angry exchange between the telegraph magnate and his songwriter son-in-law.

The most poignant aspect of the marriage was one that did not get to the newspapers. While Clarence Mackay's statement to the press was simply that his daughter had married without his "knowledge or approval," he quietly took more forceful steps, cutting Ellin out of his will and depriving her of $10 million (although he could not touch her substantial trust). Irving Berlin's response was to take his ballad "Always" and dedicate it to his bride as a wedding present, signing over its copyright so that the royalties would go to her. It was the sentiment, rather than the royalties, that Berlin tendered in his lyric that envisioned "caring each day more than the day before." " 'Always' was a love song I wrote because I had fallen in love," he said simply. What Kaufman and other sophisticates dismissed as maudlin sentimentality, however, was Berlin's heartfelt musical and lyrical expression of his marriage vow, and his life with Ellin would quickly displace his intimacy with the Algonquin Round Table.

The Berlins spent nearly a year abroad, but the ballyhoo rekindled when they returned. Reporters hounded them with rumors that Berlin planned to convert to Catholicism and that the whole marriage had been a publicity stunt to promote his songs. Berlin grew more testy under the pressure and Ellin more withdrawn, responses heightened by the fact Ellin was expecting a baby. When Mary Ellin Berlin was born in November of 1926, the frenzy of reporters reached its climax. As the couple left the hospital, reporters crowded around snapping flashbulbs and shouting questions. "No, no. I won't go out there," Ellin shrieked, "I won't!" She then fainted and had to be taken back into the hospital only to have to brave the throng again later. The Berlins were one of the first couples to be subjected to ballyhoo, but they soon learned that its saving grace was brevity—it could concentrate on only one headline story at a time. When other events grabbed the public's attention—the death of Valentino, the Dempsey-Tunney fight—the spotlight mercifully turned from Mr. and Mrs. Irving Berlin.

It was a time of hope,
that was the thing
(1927–1930)

HONOR MOORE

Excerpt from *The White Blackbird:*
A Life of the Painter Margarett Sargent by Her Granddaughter

Margarett at Prides, c. 1928

Her line rushes as if attracted to each object in the room: the dark wood bed frame, its tall, ornamental headboard; a small American bedside table—on it, telephone, tumbler, pocket watch; a child's chair at bedside; pictures on the wall; a woman's shoes askew on the floor; the bed itself, linens rumpled, a hat hurled on mussed pillows—all sketched with charcoal. Then, as if composing a variation, she lays in pastel: white-green striates walls, buff paper shows through where light doesn't reach; sky-blue, white-green to model one pillow, heavy cream etching curves of another, bright white for the creases of sheets, all leading the eye to two garments—one rose, the other robin's-egg blue—slung on a bedpost toward the lower right of the drawing. Below, on the slightly tilted floor, the shoes—black with rose insides.

If you enter the room, you see something else: an artist at work, tray of pastels set out beside her, paper on a small easel. This was the bedroom Margarett shared with Shaw, but his bed is not in the picture. In this room, its walls lined with silk, there were two Venetian beds, one unlike the other; Margarett has left out her husband's. What you see is a woman's sleeping room, sunlight falling across the voluptuous shapes of an unmade bed, sheet, pillow, beautifully made nightclothes.

"There were five, six, or seven remotely happy years," Margie said of her parents' marriage. "It was a terribly abnormal, strained, difficult, tenuous relationship," said young Shaw. And Harry, his twin: "I never knew any happiness between them, ever."

At the end of her life, Marjorie did not believe Margarett had ever loved her, and when she described Isabel Pell, the woman whose visits to Prides supplanted hers, she used the word "wicked." Margarett would never have admitted she treated Marjorie callously, would have described herself as "devoted"—"incredulous" at her friend's indignation. In 1926, leaving out the tension in their friendship, she did a watercolor called *The Quilt*—Marjorie asleep, beautiful and dreamily rendered in pale washes, both hands resting carefully on her chest, the quilt covering her a splash of vividly painted squares, an opening path.

Margarett's second New York exhibition, at Kraushaar in March 1927, included a group of large watercolors, *The Quilt* among them. "Though slight, their note is clear and fresh," the progressive critic Forbes Watson wrote in the *New York World*. "Her attack is not in the least literal," he continued, "and where a hint will do she does not, so to speak, insist upon writing a chapter." Margarett also showed three new plaster panels, to be the last she'd exhibit. Life at Prides pulled her from the studio and its solitude. What had been confined to her sketchbooks—the vitality of the household—she began to treat in large pastels.

Marjorie sits at a dressing table, hands in her lap, having her hair washed by Miss McNamara from Manchester. Margarett puts Margie behind her; in short underwear, spindly legs bare, she scrutinizes a book. Jenny looks up from a book on her lap; and a small black-and-white dog, slash of red for his collar, poses on the floor.

A woman, reclining on a green chaise longue, wears a rose peignoir, its ostrich collar languorously open. Margarett uses colors as dusky as those Lautrec painted Paris prostitutes, so the little girl is a surprise. In short dress and hair ribbon, she sits on the edge of the chaise, hand resting on the woman's. Marjorie, wearing Margarett's peignoir, hair dark around her face, could be Margarett, if Margie, who was the child, did not remember it was Marjorie's hand she held and her mother who quickly and quietly drew.

The announcement of Margarett's third Kraushaar show, in February 1928, was illustrated by the pastel of the unmade bed. For the first time, she did not show sculpture, just pastels and watercolors. In the *Brooklyn Eagle*, Helen Appleton Read remarked on her "newfound vivacity and interest in reality," and Henry McBride, in the *Sun*, noted her search for "free expression and simplicity. . . . Occasionally in the effort for the last named quality she misses a direct contact with life, but occasionally also, she gets it precisely."

Although Margarett was showing in New York, she had become a presence in the Boston art world. Kraushaar advertised her New York shows in the *Transcript*, and in December 1927, she was included in a group exhibition of American portraits at the Boston Art Club. "It is here that a Bostonian, Margarett Sargent, makes her first local appearance in a general exhibition," Harley Perkins wrote in the *Transcript*, "saying the essential things with the fewest of means."

By showing at the Art Club, Margarett allied herself with the group of insurgent painters, Perkins among them, who were turning the venerable organization into a venue for artists who looked toward what was new in New York and Paris. Though Margarett was more interested in work that distorted the recognizable than she was in abstraction, and though her temperament was more "avant-garde" than her taste, it was in modernism that she found her aesthetic home. Its expressiveness reassured her; it seemed natural to be more interested in color than in fidelity, to experience distortion as revelation. Her rage at "those dreadful hunting prints," transformed to a hunger to see things in her own way, would soon change her art.

Easily and naturally, she sought the like-minded. "Modernists respect the past," she snapped to a reporter in 1928, "but why copy it?" Two years later, when Florence Cowles of the tabloid *Boston Post* came to interview her, Margarett was more diplomatic. Smiling, she said she understood why her work was considered modernist: "We must be called something. If you say a girl is pretty or ugly, I know what you mean, but literally of course, we are not 'modern' as many of the painters who belong to the school were painting 60 or 70 years ago. It is that the public is just becoming aware of us."

The sketchbook is eight by ten inches. On its mottled black-and-white cover is the date, 1927. On its first page, Margarett draws a young man, half of him. Her line is thick as a wire hanger not meant to bend. She gets what's gentle about his mouth, the tentative angle of his head, then contradicts with a swagger of lapel. On the reverse page is his other half: bottom of jacket, hand, crayon-jagged legs crossed at the ankle. If an entire face does not hold her, she excerpts. Of an anguished man, she draws just a balding brow and eyes that don't balance.

There are pages of men drawn with that hanger line. They wear ties. Their hair is slicked back. They are weak and weakly drawn, don't look up from their reading or out through their glasses. Then, abruptly, Margarett is no longer bored. She draws a man in a tuxedo, places him at an angle on the page. Poker-straight lines as random as pick-up-sticks cohere as his jacket, and above the tall starched collar and the black tie, a densely drawn swarthy face. He looks up—dark hair, bristling eyebrows, sunken eyes, turned-down mouth, gutted cheeks. This in charcoal, then across the surface, like bird tracks in sand, the odd delicate line exposes the pain beneath: a quick moment, like certain silences in conversation.

The drawing is of Roland Balay, a French dealer, member of the Knoedler family and director of its galleries. Margarett met him in London, walked with Shaw into an exhibition of old-master flower paintings, asked to see the person responsible. Roland came forward— a small, quietly witty man with a spark behind his eyes, no sign of the darkness Margarett later got in the drawing. They had dinner immediately, talked in French and English, talked about, among other things, Donatello and Della Francesca. Roland was, by his own account years later, undone. "Surrealiste," he said of his new friend. "The essence—aristocracy, intellectuality, vulgarity."

Roland was married, but in the French way he continued his amorous adventures. When he got to go to New York, he did not hesitate to telephone Margarett. He was coming to Boston, he said, to deliver a Braque; perhaps she might like to see it. They had lunch at the Ritz, and afterward when he rose to go up to his room to get the picture, Margarett stopped him. "I'll come with you," she said.

"No, no," Roland said, "I'll bring it down."

"I'd like to come with you—"

"But no, Margarett, I—"

She insisted. Telling the story, Roland shrugged and, disingenuously, blushed.

It was the beginning of a long affair. "In and out," Betty Parsons said, "as the wind blows." Afternoons at exhibitions and evenings in hotel rooms in Paris and New York, the tango at El Morocco, nights in Harlem at the Cotton Club. Roland understood Margarett in a way she wasn't used to. She had "fantaisie," he said, purposely avoiding an English word. Soon he and his wife were visiting Prides, and Roland was hunting and fishing with Shaw. One night, hours after Roland and Mimi had gone to bed, Margarett appeared in the garden outside the guest room. Roland was not surprised, just eager she not wake Mimi. "Roland!" Margarett said in a stage whisper.

"Shhhhhhh." He gestured through the window, putting on his robe.

"I have something extraordinary to show you," she said, leading him to the pool. There, by the light of the moon and its reflection, calmly floated a Canada goose. Again Roland was not surprised, as he had come to expect from Margarett a confusion of life with dreams. The next day, he took her aside. "That was certainly one of the most interesting things I've ever seen." "Well," she said, "I tied it there for you to see."

If Margarett was to move on entirely from sculpture, she would need a medium to accommodate and amplify what had such force in the drawing of Roland. The face with gutted cheeks burned through pages of children, nursery twins, tentative young men and a woman beautifully drawn with a supple, fluid line. "George Luks met me and told me I should be a painter," Margarett said. Her old friend had guided her through every transition she'd made as an artist, but the urgency had always been her own. The shift to oil was swift. In February 1928, she had shown pastels and drawings. That summer, she began to prepare for a January show at Kraushaar, in which she would exhibit twenty-four oil paintings.

"Your photograph irks me that I did not seize your face in paint," she wrote me once. Seize: Margarett's most characteristic paintings took possession with the unapologetic directness of that work. Her bravado was another gift from Luks. In 1927, he visited Prides, and Margarett commissioned a portrait of Jenny, who was then four, dressed as an infanta. Little Jenny stood as with frenzied dispatch. Luks laid in brocade with a housepainter's brush, muttering, "Velazquez, he was the baby," and producing a delicate and vital likeness.

Margarett took from the older painter, sixty that year, what served her—spirit, nerve, speed, an emotional approach—but not color or brush technique. His palette evoked the Spanish or the Dutch: colors rich and dark, lighter hues emerging from darkness like light in a night fog, figures modeled with an abundance of paint. Margarett painted with bright, clear colors, diluting pigment so the color became almost transparent, or modeling a faint impasto across the canvas.

She began to use oils in Vermont the summer of 1927, the family's first in Dorset, the village where Marjorie Davenport lived. In the countryside, large working farms interrupted a landscape of mountains, meadow marshland, and abandoned quarries. In town, the sidewalks were slabs of white Vermont marble, and in the clapboard farmhouse Margarett and Shaw bought for four hundred dollars and moved to a plateau on West Road, everything that could be was marble—bathtub, windowsills, thresholds, the terrace out back.

For a month, the McKeans lived, as the Sargents had at Wareham, a life that could be described as simple. Everyone ate at a big table at one end of the open living room, then sat around after supper on furniture Margarett picked up at farmyard auctions and draped with patchwork quilts. Margarett and Shaw shared a room that adjoined the only full bath; the girls and Senny the only other bedroom. The twins slept in a loft above the big room.

Margarett often left the house at six in the morning. She took ink, charcoal, and watercolor, made sketches, then, at home, enlarged and enhanced the images with oil paint on canvas. She painted Vermont people without sentimentality: country women, whose gaunt faces showed both their intelligence and the harshness of their lives; a tall thin man in a dark, derelict doorway; Annie, a neighbor girl who played with Margie and Jenny, wearing a white dress, bent over sewing, too large for her chair.

When Margarett returned at dusk, Shaw was often at the stove. He had learned camp cooking in his copper-mining days, and he and Senny split the job in Dorset. "I imagine you painting boys with apples, or women with arms covered with soap suds," Dan wrote Margarett. "Shaw has a white chef's cap on when he cooks. He heats up the sauce in a blue sauce-pan, stirring it with a wooden spoon. 'Taste this' he says."

There had been artists in southern Vermont for decades, and painting was in the air. Margarett got the children to paint, and in the ease of the country even Shaw set up an easel. In the 1928 summer annual at the Equinox Hotel in Manchester, Margarett showed paintings, Jenny McKean a portrait in the children's division, and Shaw McKean a group of oils—colors faithful, edges definite, contours restrained: the bone china tureen on a table between two windows in the big room; little Shaw, blond, sitting neatly on a chair.

In a photograph, Margarett stands grinning on the marble-slab terrace behind the house. "She loved it there," Margie said.

By the autumn of 1928, back in Boston, Margarett was painting with assurance. If you looked for American resonance, you saw the women Alfred Maurer painted in hot Fauve colors; the stylized, chic restaurant habitués of Guy Pene du Bois; the 1920s figures of Walt Kuhn. Or you saw Paris: the abrupt, committed intensity of her own Picasso, the unnerving challenge in the gaze of that woman in the yellow hat. Margarett brought this directness to her most compelling subjects, women and men of social Boston who like herself chafed against its suppression of sensual will, its curb on the demonstration of feeling, its social requirements. How this conflict came through a face was what she painted.

At first, the portraits were ironic. Like Margarett, her subjects rebelled with charm and wit, a tossed-off light-touch arrogance, as in a 1928 portrait of a woman in a cloche hat, devil-may-care "Whoopee!" scrawled across the top of the canvas. As she became more experienced, the paintings challenged and deepened, leaving behind the pale lyricism with which she'd made watercolors of Marjorie Davenport, the buoyant entertainment of her Prides pastels. When she first used oils in Boston, Margarett hired a round-faced model named Edna, of whom she painted disengaged, placid portraits, but there was nothing, it seemed, in Edna's presence to knot the elements of composition into a tough, energetic whole. In 1928, when she began to paint her cousin Bobo's widow, Maria, all that changed.

The wall behind the woman is pale pink. Next to her, loosely painted, a table; on it, a large Chinese lamp, white porcelain and white silk shade swirled light and dark blue. Visible behind the lamp is the edge of a gilt frame, and in the foreground, a vase of pink flowers cropped at the right edge of the canvas. It is a background for a lyric Cupid or a languishing Venus, but Margarett has introduced a modern Diana. Sitting tall, the dark-haired woman holds a dog, a fox terrier that sprawls across her lap. The dog looks at us; we see the woman in profile. Her alabaster skin shimmers with faint undertones of blue, pink, and yellow and the effect is luminescence, paleness that shocks in contrast to the black of her hair, short and pulled behind her right ear. Her nose is slender, aquiline, her long neck elegant, chin delicate. Her shirt with its flipped-back man's collar is deep cornflower blue; its faint purple glow sets off a luscious violet jacket. All of this would recede in pleasing harmony if it weren't for the bright-red hat, close to the head—a crimson crown—not modest or restrained.

Maria deAcosta was born in New York, one of eight children of a Cuban father of Spanish ancestry and a Castilian mother whose noble birth, beauty, and inheritance eased the deAcostas to the center of New York society. Their daughters became unreluctantly famous: "Oh, she was one of the deAcostas," people would remark. The youngest, Mercedes, was an intimate friend, possibly a lover, of Greta Garbo, and in her 1960 autobiography published photographs of herself with Garbo, Cecil Beaton, Stravinsky, and Marie Laurencin. The oldest, Rita, was a famous beauty, whose portrait by Boldini is in the collection of the Louvre.

Maria was a dozen years older than Margarett, who met her when she was married to Charles Sprague Sargent's only son, Robeson. After Bobo's death, of flu in 1918, Maria lived in Harvard, Massachusetts, with her son and a woman named Miriam Shaw. "A Boston marriage," a niece explained: Maria flamboyant, effusive, and Spanish in her picador hat; Miriam a bluestocking and, though younger, "more like Maria's governess than anything else."

In another of Margarett's portraits, Maria wears a plum-colored beret. Her right hand rests on her knee, her left is half hidden in a pocket. Her sharp Spanish features are animated. One eyebrow is nearly obscured by the angle of her beret; the other is raised, bemused and disdainful. Her expression is mischievous, her mouth about to laugh. The taupe suit she wore for this portrait could be called "mannish," an effect accentuated by the tawny vest, the pale-blue ascot. "Oh, I'm sure she was a lesbian," exclaimed another niece, telling a story—Maria greeting her from bed, wearing a black lace slip, holding a glass of whiskey, the two of them alone in the house. At lunch once at a women's club in Boston, Maria malapropped: "I wouldn't be in town at all, but I needed a new pair of bisexual glasses." Margarett called the portrait *Tailleur Classique*.

"Oh," said Betty Parsons, looking at a slide. "That was Maria deAcosta. She had a *passion* for Margarett."

What sort of passion? If the red hat were a faded letter in a torn envelope, a page from a journal, it might answer that question. If *Tailleur Classique* were a short story, one might find clues to the mysteries of a half-hidden eyebrow, a hand almost concealed in a pocket. What passed between the two women when Margarett wasn't painting, when Maria wasn't posing with a dog or, as in a third portrait, sporting a bright-red smock and holding a cigarette, its ash hot and live?

Margarett and Maria may have had an affair or they may not have, but Margarett's lovers were not all men. More than one woman testified to having been approached, to having reciprocated with confidence. "Margarett had love affairs with women, there's no doubt about that," Betty said. But, also, "Margarett was a very subtle woman. She wouldn't tell you." When Margie was in her late twenties and curious about her mother's life, she sat Margarett down and recited a list of certain women who had come to stay at Prides for weeks at a time. "They were all lesbians. Surely you had affairs . . . !" Margarett faced her daughter down. "I've only known one lesbian in my life," she declared, and mentioned a woman with whom she had no particular friendship. She knew that as long as she was discreet, she could do as she pleased. If she was a lady in her behavior, her secret life, however well known it was, would not interfere with invitations to dinner.

Margarett had admired—had even had a crush on—Eleo Sears when she was a child and Eleo and Alice Thorndike were Amazons of the pony rink at the New Riding Club. Eleonora Sears had never married. She was the first national women's squash champion, four times the national women's tennis doubles champion, and the first woman to play polo, and was famous for the long walks she took from Providence to Boston accompanied by Harvard undergraduates, escorted by a chauffeured limousine stocked with refreshments. Eleo was both open and discreet. Protected by great wealth, her mystique enhanced by tall good looks, she lived a proper Bostonian life and, apparently, loved women. "Everyone knew it, but it was never spoken of," said Nancy Cochrane, one of Vivian Cochrane's daughters.

Miss Sears, as she was known to servants and children, was eagerly received by every North Shore and Boston hostess, and invitations to the famous dances she gave in the ballroom of her house in Prides Crossing or, in the winter, in Boston were prized. "She was such fun," said Margie. "I loved Miss Sears," said Paul Moore, who would marry Jenny. "Even a stuffy banker like my father loved her!" On a Thursday afternoon, Eleo might play bridge with a group of North Shore wives, on the weekend receive her particular friend, a young French actress who'd take the train up from New York. "Mother would take us to tea at Miss Sears'," Nancy Cochrane said, "and there she'd be, Mademoiselle. Eleo was madly in love with her, gave her a Duesenberg. Oh, they were so glamorous!"

The young actress had displaced another woman in Eleo's life. Isabel Pell, of New York, London, and, later, Paris, was tall, lean, and, Margie said, "handsome, *wonderfully* handsome." By the late 1920s, Isabel was visiting Prides three or four times a year for weeks at a time, and she and Margarett were seeing each other in New York. It was she whom Marjorie Davenport had characterized as "wicked." Among other lesbians, Isabel had a reputation as a sexual predator, and in her dominating character even those who admired her found a streak of duplicity.

Like Margarett, Isabel had broken an early engagement, and like Eleo, she lived an independent life unprotected by marriage or a married name. She was also an adventurer. Margarett pasted clippings of her exploits in her scrapbook, one of which recounts the rescue, sometime in the early thirties, of two "sporting" women off the coast of Denmark by a German freighter. Isabel had taken a seaplane voyage with Mrs. Henry T. Fleitman, an attractive brunette and "habituée of London's Mayfair equally with Long Island's Hamptons." Mr. Fleitman had not heard from his wife since she'd sailed for France months before, and "knew nothing of the crash."

Shaw seemed to be no more aware of the nature of Margarett's relationship with Isabel than of the erotic element in her association with Roland Balay. He and Isabel talked about golf. The children loved her so much they asked to call her "Cousin" rather than "Miss" Pell. They'd never seen a woman wearing anything but a nightgown to bed until Cousin Pell appeared in pajamas cut from heavy silk crepe, "exactly like a man's." She drove a succession of maroon Duesenbergs named Olga, her perfume—Tabac Blanc—was musky and sexy, and she wore her honey-colored hair smooth and short. She was reputed to own forty pairs of riding boots, and if she abandoned jodhpurs or slacks for a skirt, she wore, Margie said, a "marvelously tailored" suit.

Nothing documents what Margarett and Isabel said to each other, the defiant wit they apparently shared, or what they actually did behind closed doors, but Margarett made one ink drawing after another of a woman with bobbed hair and prominent eyebrows who always wore pants. Her first painting of Isabel was of a mannish woman in leather jacket and necktie, cigarette hanging from her mouth, background fire-engine red. In a second portrait, she enthroned Isabel in an arched chair of pale gray and painted the wall behind her almost lavender. Her jacket is the color of flesh; her white shirt, which must be silk, is open at the collar, its shadows watery gray. She has large hands, and the look on her face is surprisingly tender. Pepe, her black Scottie, sits in her lap.

Soon after Isabel appeared, Marjorie Davenport challenged Margarett about the nature of her new friendship, but Margarett would tell her nothing. Marjorie, at last standing up to her, accused her of betrayal. "You've changed," Margarett retorted, "ever since you inherited that money from your uncle. . . ." It was dark, a late afternoon at Prides, and they shouted until Marjorie threw down her glass, shattering it on the tile floor. "She and Isabel deserved one another," she said bitterly at eighty-eight. "Finally Margarett got someone whose cruelty matched hers."

Thirty years later, not having seen her since the afternoon of the broken glass, Margarett arrived at Marjorie's house in Vermont, bringing flowers. Marjorie open the door, and Margarett gave her the bouquet. They stood there at the door for a few minutes but said very little. It was the last time they saw each other.

When Margarett's first oils were exhibited, in 1929, two portraits of Maria deAcosta Sargent were among them. The walls at Kraushaar bristled with color, Margarett's strongest work since the sculpted heads of Luks and Chaffard, her freest since the model walked naked in her studio in 1919. A cigarette hung from the mouth of a woman in a striped sweater; a cook and a kitchen maid played cards at a table; two blond children mixed with a pattern of vivid red-and-blue pinwheels. Maria as *Tailleur Classique* bore little resemblance to the woman washed in watercolor who, dressed like a Greek suppliant, had raised a draped arm to obscure her face.

This, Margarett's fourth Kraushaar exhibition, allied her with other American modernist and Post-Impressionist painters whose works were on display in New York that month—Marsden Hartley, Jane Peterson, and Edward Hopper. Henry McBride considered her in the context of her famous relative: "Miss Sargent seems more than careful not to let a suggestion of the relationship extend to her art. She burns her incense before the later gods." *Art News* noticed the shift in her work and found a way to patronize: "Miss Margarett Sargent has quite evidently grown a trifle weary of the sedate muse she used to follow and has mounted a more fiery Pegasus who has taken her for a somewhat breathless ride among the colorful phenomena of modern art."

But many reviews wholeheartedly affirmed Margarett's work in the new medium. "Her subjects," Forbes Watson wrote, "seem ready to step from their frames and become really alive." And *Vanity Fair*, whose editor, Frank Crowninshield, himself a collector of modern art, was a distant cousin and friend, reproduced three paintings: "Unfortunately the black and white reproductions fail to convey their beauty and importance."

The revolution in painting that exploded in Paris before the war had resumed in a shifting international community of artists in Montparnasse, some of whom, like Alexander Calder, Max Jacob, Jean Lurçat, Jean Pascin, and Isamu Noguchi, Margarett knew, collected, or came to know. She was also aware of the American expatriate writers Janet Flanner reported to be "richer than most in creative ambition but rather modest in purse" and had read their work in émigré journals like *Transition* and *Broom*.

In the years after the war, navy surplus and shipping yards hot with a new capacity to build had swelled the count of great ocean liners from 117 in 1918 to 328 four years later. Daily columns in the Paris editions of *The New York Herald* and the *Chicago Tribune* reported arrivals and departures of notable and moneyed Americans. The impoverished crossed in steerage for fifty dollars; the prosperous strolled first-class decks and drank champagne at captains' tables. Each season, Paris couture emblazoned American magazines, beckoning women of fashion to its source, and American men like Shaw, who had fallen in love with France during the war, returned with their wives in pursuit of pleasure and the postwar business opportunities that waited all over Europe.

It was not unusual to read of the arrival of thirty-five hundred tourists in one day or of the railroad's scramble to schedule seven extra trains for transport from Cherbourg or Le Havre to Gare Saint-Lazare. It was less expensive to sail to Le Havre than to take the train to California, and France was cheap. In 1926, the exchange rate peaked at fifty Frances to the dollar; later, it leveled off at twenty. A meal *haute cuisine* might be had for a dollar or two, a suite in a first-class hotel for six dollars a night. The *bar americain* was devised to quench the thirst of those in flight from prohibition: "10,000 Yankee Cocktails 'Go' in Nice Daily," exulted a *Herald* headline in 1924, the year Margarett and Shaw made the first of their trips abroad.

"In those days you met anybody anywhere," wrote Gertrude Stein. Margarett and Shaw were as likely to run into friends from New York or Boston at the Ritz in Paris as they were at the Ritz in New York or Boston. Dan and Louise Sargent stayed at the Hotel de Cambon; the MacLeishes had an apartment on rue Las Cases; and Dickie Ames took two rooms at the Ritz, the second to store his paintings. In 1927, the *Herald* reported Marjorie Davenport at the American Women's Club, and on Easter Sunday, 1928, the marriage of Margarett's cousin Hollis Hunnewell to Mary Frances Oakes at the American Cathedral on avenue George. "Paris has now frankly become an American suburb," wrote the American Elizabeth Eyre in *Town and Country* in 1926. "One warm night, Paris suddenly turned American."

When Margarett first visited Paris in 1924, she found her friend Betty Parsons hungrily living the life of an artist, sharing a house on rue Boulard in Montparnasse with the painter Adge Baker, an Englishwoman, with whom she would live for six years. The exchange rate multiplied her alimony to a small fortune, and marriage had convinced her that her sexuality was inspired more by women than by men. She was twenty-four years old and burned, as she put it, with a "love for the unfamiliar."

On her arrival in Paris, she had enrolled in Antoine Bourdelle's sculpture class at the Grande Chaumiere. There she met fellow Americans Caresse Crosby and Alexander Calder and shared their teacher's most enthusiastic encouragement with a tall, quiet sculptor named Alberto Giacometti. She canoed the Seine with Caresse's husband, Harry, and went dancing with Sandy Calder, "twice a week," she said, "for exercise." She was invited to the Saturday lunches Natalie Barney gave for young people at her salon on rue Jacob, where "All the men were homosexual, all the women were lesbian, and the conversation was brilliant. Brilliant."

She had tea with Gertrude Stein and Alice Toklas, and she met Janet Flanner, who would soon begin to write her "Letter From Paris" for Harold Ross's new magazine, *The New Yorker*. Flanner, eight years older, took her in hand, guided her to theater, concerts, and exhibitions. In the galleries of Paris and the studios of Montparnasse, Betty

began to develop the eye that fifteen years later made her a revolutionary dealer in the history of American art. "After years of knowing
only people who did what they were supposed to do, I suddenly knew
people who did nothing whatsoever that was conventional," she said.

When she and Betty met in 1919, Margarett was an unmarried
daughter defying family expectation by pursuing art in a great city.
Now it was Betty who lived and worked with heady excitement, meeting everyone, allowing herself to be changed by a city at the center of
the world. Betty took Margarett to hear *les diseuses*, "those *fantastic*
woman singers," and to Le Boeuf sur le Toit, Cocteau's jazz club,
hung with Picabia's paintings and Man Ray's photographs, where the
Montparnasse model Kiki sang and artists gossiped and drank.

If Margarett had been ten years younger and still unmarried, she might
have gone to Paris to seek her fortune as an artist. As it was, she
checked into a Right Bank hotel with a businessman husband who
played squash at the Travellers Club with his friends from Morgan's
Bank. As Madame Q.A. Shaw McKean, she plied the glistening shops
along the phalanx of Place Vendôme. She bought handkerchiefs,
"crêpe uni couleur," the latest accessory, "to be caught in the exact
center and carried with all four points waving," had several mono-
grammed "Maria" and "Vivian." She bought lingerie and gloves at
Le Grande Maison de Blanc on the Place de l'Opéra, and at Goupy,
under the arcade on rue Castiglione, a dress of raw silk. For the children, left at home with Senny, she shopped at "Fairyland."

The earliest Paris document I have, a bill of sale for a Mary Cassatt
aquatint, *Mère et Enfant*, places Margarett and Shaw in Paris in February 1924. The following month, Cassatt, going blind, would offer for
sale "those of her works which she had guarded with jealous care."
A receipt for an unidentified Cassatt from the venerable dealer Hode-
bert, had Margarett and Shaw back in Paris on May 5, 1925, in time
for L'Exposition des Arts Décoratifs, the first international exhibition
of Art Deco. Though there are no documents for 1926 or 1927, "They
went every year," Margie said, "and stayed three or four months."
And Betty, sentences racing as Margarett must have—from taxi to
shop, luncheon, galleries—said, "Yes. Oh, yes. They did the life of
Paris in the spring." Expensive restaurants, horse races at Long-
champs, Maurice Chevalier at Casino de Paris, Mistinguett at the
Moulin Rouge, and then on to Monte Carlo, London, or Berlin.

They visited the Princes at their foxhunting estate in the mountains
at Pau. Margarett liked Freddie Prince, who was one of Shaw's Myo-
pia polo friends—"he was far more aesthetic in his business," she

wrote once to Betty, "than most painters are on canvas." In Paris, they dined with Hope Thacer, Margarett's childhood playmate, and her husband, "Bunny" Carter, head of the Paris office of Morgan's Bank. At Harry and Caresse Crosby's parties on rue de Lille or at their converted mill outside Paris, they mixed with guests as likely to include Bunny Carter as D.H. Lawrence, Kay Boyle, or Hart Crane.

The novelist Louis Bromfield became a great friend. Because of two best-sellers and a Pulitzer prize at thirty, he was celebrity enough that when he accidentally tore up his steamer ticket on his way to the pier, *The New York Times* reported it. Janet Flanner declared his "the finest flower garden of any American in the Île de France territory, except Mrs. Edith Wharton, whose white garden was celebrated." He was such a gracious host, it was remarked that in another life he might have run a great hotel. At the Bromfields' converted monastery outside Paris, Margarett and Shaw met Gertrude Stein and Alice Toklas, and Edith Wharton. There is no record of Margarett's response to Gertrude and Alice, but as an old woman she yelped with scorn at the mention of Wharton, whose books she admired but whose approach to decorating she found extremely dreary.

More than once Margarett pulled Betty from class at the Grande Chaumiere for the morning auction at the Hotel Drouot. She bought one of Betty's sculptures—a red clay cat—and took her to meet Marie Laurencin. She went to Durand-Ruel for Cassatt and Morisot and, at Georges Aubry, bought *Women and Children* by Bazille, whose work was so scarce—he had died in the Franco-Prussian War—that any acquisition was a coup. When she got to Paris in April 1928, an exposition of one hundred lithographs by Toulouse-Lautrec had just opened; she would eventually own two of his drawings and eleven lithographs—among them three of Yvette Guilbert, one of Jane Avril.

Check stubs dated 1928, checks made out to Betty Parsons, Harry Crosby . . . I am leafing through a messy stack of papers: pages torn from a 1930s sketchbook—"Île de France, 1931." A man with a funny fat face slouches in a deck chair; a figure in a green coat climbs a gangway; then a photograph, dusky with age, creased and bent. It takes a moment to recognize her. Her irises rest above the horizon of her lower eyelids; the stare fixes me. This was not the Margarett who glittered in a silver Poiret gown, fragrant with Le Bleu, out for the evening with Shaw, who walked with Frederic Barlett along rue La Boétie, or drank with Betty and Sandy Calder at le Boeuf sur le Toit. This was Margarett, by herself, at the age of thirty-six. On the back of the photograph, the inky stamp: *"Photographie de Berenice Abbott."*

Abbott left a darkroom job with Man Ray in late 1926 and in

January 1928 moved to a "big old daylit studio" near the Palais Lux-embourg. It was to this studio, a top-floor room with a large north-facing skylight, that Margarett went to have her portrait made by the talented, unusual young woman, an Ohio refugee in Paris. In 1926, Abbott's first exhibition of portraits, invitation card designed by Jean Cocteau, had opened at Au Sacre de Printemps, where André Kertesz had shown photographs, Kiki of Montparnasse paintings, and Calder sculpture. A month after she photographed Margarett, in April 1928, twelve of her portraits, exhibited with work by Kertesz, Man Ray, Nadat, and Atget, would make her international reputation.

Margarett climbed the five flights at rue Servandoni. "A stranger. Out of the blue," Abbott told me at ninety-three, chic in trousers, hair still elegantly short, scarf tied like an ascot at her neck. "I didn't know her well." The photographer, eight years younger than her subject, saw Margarett first on the threshold, illuminated in a spill of north light. She invited her to make herself at home while she set up. "I didn't have many props. The studio was simple. I used odd things." Margarett was immediately curious. They talked about what they had in common. Art? Paris? The old woman couldn't summon up their conversation, but she remembered Margarett's energy. "Paris was a magnet for a woman like that, looking for freedom."

Margarett had pulled back her hair rather severely and parted it on the side. She wore a suit with a pleated skirt, which reads gray in the black-and-white photograph, and under her jacket, to which was pinned an artificial flower, a thin sweater with narrow diagonal stripes. Abbott directed her to a mahogany chair with a curved back the same chair visible in other seated portraits she made that spring: of André Maurois, Leo Stein, James Joyce.

"I relied on the instincts of the moment," Abbott said, a gesture in which the person "would reveal something about herself." Margarett crossed her legs, leaned forward, set her right elbow on her knee, chin on her fist, and looked straight at the lens. "A portrait was a collaboration?" I asked. "An exchange," the old woman answered. What Margarett gave was a gaze that followed one everywhere in a room. Nothing remained of the girl Arnold Genthe caught in a youth-ful smolder of romantic challenge, or of the young mother shot by a student photographer at Prides, smiling, baby on her hip.

Margarett looks strong but uneasy; female but stripped of effemi-nizing clutter; handsome but not beautiful, not genderless exactly. You could imagine this woman lived and worked in Paris, that she was one of Abbott's famous female subjects: Sylvia Beach in a shiny black raincoat, caught in an almost violent expression; Jane Heap, hair cut like a man's, tuxedo and black tie, full lips darkly rouge; Janet Flanner, cross-legged on the floor, top hat decorated with one black, one white mask. But Margarett was not a resident of Paris who sought like-minded friends in a café at the end of the day or labored in the solitary light of a Left Bank studio. In spite of the sophisticated angularity of the photograph, the unassailed, even enraged, determination in her expression, the look in her eyes is lonely and frankly sad.

Margarett stands at an easel. A woman sits facing her, and Margarett is painting, not the woman's anger, but the longing and sadness beneath it. Abruptly, she picks up a wooden chair, slams it down on the floor. "Her face must disturb like a sudden, dangerous sound," I imagine her saying to no one in particular, then see her for a moment looking at herself in a mirror. The intensity in her eyes is not sadness and fear but what remains of work pursued that day, ideas argued through the night with artists who are her friends. Margarett paints and then she erupts into her loud, deep laugh and, with abandon, sitting in her chair, rocks back and forth in a rapture of having got it right.

"It was a time of hope," Berenice Abbott said, "that was the thing."

The Shadow Knows

BEVERLY LOWRY

By now, the shooting is old news, and Rush Springs, Oklahoma, has had its five minutes of notoriety. The story has been all over national magazines and newspapers and featured on prime-time television news—how, on a hot blistering day last July, Lonnie Dutton's two elder children, Herman, fifteen, and Druie, twelve, took a .243 deer rifle into the living-room of the trailer house where they lived, set the barrel of the gun against their sleeping daddy's head, just below his right ear, and blew him away, right there on the couch, a can of beer on the table beside him. How they killed him together, Herman steadying the gun while Druie pulled the trigger. How they had decided to do it—"kill Daddy"—that afternoon, when their sister, Alesha, who is ten, came out of the house crying and told them that their daddy had molested her. How the two boys were working in the field next to the trailer house that day—105 degrees and they'd been sent to chop and hoe—and decided that while they'd been putting up with their daddy's cruel mistreatment for years, this was different.

By mid-afternoon, all hush-hush to keep it secret from Alesha and their baby brother, Jake, eight, Herman and Druie Dutton had figured out what they had to do: their daddy had always told them that, if they ever discovered anyone fooling with their sister, they should pick up the .243 and shoot the son of a bitch in either the head, just below the ear, or the heart. Their daddy then poked the side of his head, to show where the bullet should go, then slapped the left side of his chest, to show them the heart, and then poked both boys in the side of the head repeatedly and hard, and then slapped their chests. He wanted to be sure they understood. Herman and Druie were good children; they did what they could to keep their daddy calm, including stealing, calling their mother names, biting her and throwing darts at her. And so they waited until they were sure that their daddy was good and asleep, so that he wouldn't draw out the nine-millimeter from underneath his overalls bib and shoot them first. Then they went inside the trailer house and killed him with the .243, which had been stolen from somebody in Lawton, Oklahoma, some eight years earlier.

In October, three months after the shooting, the Oklahoma sun still beats down like emergency floodlights. People in Grady County are used to it. The ones I've met are friendly, plain and very white, with flat, twangy accents. The women grow their hair long and leave it; the men drive pick-ups. The economy is down the tubes, politics what you would expect. On the turnpike between Oklahoma City and Chickasha, I pass a billboard saying SOCIALISM IS WRONG.

In Grady County, a woman on her own gets company fast. While driving, I watch as car after car pulls alongside, slows down, revs up; the drivers look over, I go on. It's a world in which bars are windowless and dark, their parking lots filled with pick-ups and the occasional Ranchero. My first night in Rush Springs, I stepped outside my motel to go for a short run. It was early evening, the sun was low, but there was plenty of light. A pick-up came by, slowed down; there were three men inside, raising cans to their lips. A couple of minutes later, a woman and a young girl in a brand-new, extended-cab pick-up stopped, and the woman asked where I lived and if I had seen the three men who were parked at the top of the road, waiting for me. She offered to take me back to the motel.

Eighteen miles south of Chickasha, at a yellow blinking caution light, I turn right off US 81, away from downtown Rush Springs. The telephone book gives "N of city" and "SW of city" as addresses. The house I am heading towards, the home of Luther Dutton, the dead man's father, is on a road with no name, "W of city."

When I spoke to Luther Dutton on the phone, he said he had no problem talking to me or anybody else. He wanted the story told right, and for that to happen, "There's only one way." Just so long as it wasn't for a book. He didn't go for the book stuff. "We're the only ones who know," he assured me. And he told me how to get to his house.

Southwest Oklahoma is farming country, watermelons and peanuts mostly—Rush Springs calls itself Watermelon Capital of the World. There are cattle, some sheep, some goats. The rolling countryside lies between mountains to the east and dry plains not that far to the west; and it is lush, green and wet, with heavy-headed oak and pecan trees and thick, webby undergrowth.

Scrub oaks line the road to the Dutton house. Mustang grapevines grow over the tops of the stunted trees like a shroud. Beyond them, all you can see is more scrub, denser brush. Just before the Dutton mailbox, there is a beat-up locked gate with a rusted sign hanging on it saying PRIVATE PROPERTY. Over the gate, five huge, dark, withering catfish heads swing in the breeze.

Luther Dutton's new mailbox is shaped like a barn. It is festooned with blue bows. There are bows on the fence and across the top of the gate.

The red clay road leading to the house slants down a little in a tunnel of overhanging trees, then curves to the right. The landscape opens up and there is a big house with a wide front porch set on a cleared, very pretty rise in the land. There is a refrigerator on the porch and a couple of nonfunctioning cars out front, but it isn't trashy. The trees are big, and the grass a deep green. Lonnie Dutton and his children lived on this same piece of land, back in the scrub oaks and underbrush, with nothing but a rutted cowpath for a way in or out. Nobody lives in the trailerhouse now.

It is six o'clock on a Friday evening. The season's first crop of peanuts has come in. The governor of Oklahoma is under investigation for illegal campaign funding. At seven o'clock that night, the unbeaten Rush Springs Redskins will take on the Hinton Comets in a Homecoming football game.

When I ring the doorbell, Luther Dutton answers. He is wearing jeans and a saggy white T-shirt. He has a kind of potato face, lumpy and uneven, a droopy lower lip and a bulbous nose. His hair is grey and thinning, uncombed. He is in his sixties, but he looks a good ten years older.

He invites me in, and we go through to a large room, kitchen, dining-room and living-room all in one. The room is clean and plain with fake wood paneling. There are little pictures on the wall including a child's "I-Love-You-Daddy" drawing which Luther says one of the kids made for Lonnie. A flyer is tacked on the refrigerator, announcing the town meeting in support of Herman and Druie held three months earlier, at which blue bows were sold to help pay legal expenses. The house is easy to keep and serviceable, with built-ins and new appliances.

We sit at a round table. Luther spits tobacco into a styrofoam cup, staring off in the general direction of the opposite wall and meeting my eyes only when it suits him.

He introduces me to his wife, Nancy. In rural areas, middle-aged women tend to fall into one of two categories: the chunk and the rail. The chunk puts on weight and acquires a bosom, hips, dimples, a double chin, a rolling gait; she has a girlish look and loves her food. The rail shrinks, her skin clings to her bones, her behind flattens, her neck turns into a column of folds. The rail usually chain-smokes, preferring cigarettes to food. A rail still in the ball game may cover up the damage with ice-blue eyeshadow and frosted pink lipstick; her hair will be dyed: black, yellow or red.

Nancy Dutton is a rail and has not been in the ball game for years. She could be eighty; it turns out she's sixty-one. In her thirties, she was institutionalized for mental and emotional problems and had shock treatments for more than a year; her daughter, Linda Munn, says that's why Nancy has a hard time remembering and sometimes seems so . . . flat. She sits on a barstool next to the breakfast bar, smoking steadily, and lets Luther do most of the talking.

Lonnie Dutton lived on his father's property for nine years. Records list him as an unemployed roofer, but no one can remember him ever doing a day's work for wages. He lived on the dole, getting food stamps and money from government programs and making his kids steal. When social services people came out for a home study, Lonnie pretended to live in Luther's house, and Luther and Nancy covered for him. The electricity in his trailer was illegally tapped from his father's line. His water supply came from his father's well. He would neither allow his parents to enter his trailerhouse, nor leave his own children with them when he went out. Wherever Lonnie Dutton went, his children went too. When he went to bars, they stayed in the truck until he was ready to go, no matter the temperature or the hour. If Lonnie came out drunk at two or three in the morning, fifteen-year-old Herman drove home.

Lonnie graduated from high school in Sterling, Oklahoma, one of only three boys in a class of thirty, and so he was elected Class Favorite, Most Handsome and Best Dancer, the other two boys being pretty squirrelly-looking. He had two elder sisters, Linda, now forty-three, and Dina, who is forty-one. Lonnie died four days short of his fortieth birthday. Nancy says his kids were planning a surprise party for him, and that Druie had asked her to make a cake with candles.

"He was a hard-working boy," Luther says of his son. "All his life he worked hard. He had a deformed heart you know . . . He raised registered hogs."

Luther makes statements like this, statements that clearly—to him—have some kind of resonance. And then he will pause, waiting for a response, I can't tell to what. After a beat, he goes on.

"Won nearly every prize in the county."

And he describes his son, the hard-working all-American farm boy, and Nancy tells me about Lonnie's deformed heart with the oversized valve and his high blood pressure.

As for school, "He didn't do no good. But he was a damned fine carpenter."

Luther Dutton backtracks, rethinks his story, checks himself. Nancy Dutton adds details, corrects small errors and contributes to Luther's main thrust, which is to let the world know that nobody understands what it has been like for him all these years, nobody. He is cagey, deft, sly, and thinks he can put one over on anybody. Luther and Nancy rarely use their son's name, but when they say "he," I always know who they mean.

Yes, Luther will admit, he did thrash his son with a belt from time to time, but that's what people did in those days, striped their sons' backsides. He was trying to straighten him out, that was all; of course it didn't do any good.

I go over some of the stories I have heard: how Lonnie made his wife, Marie, stand against the wall, then told his kids to throw darts at her; how he poured jalapeno pepper juice in her eyes; how he chased Herman with a two-by-four and kicked him between the legs with a steel-toed boot; how he used to shoot at the chicken coop while Herman and Druie were inside; and how he played William Tell with Druie by making him stand against a wall, then shooting bullets in a circle around his head. I ask him, have any of these stories been exaggerated?

Luther thinks a long time. When he shakes his head and says simply no, there is no knowing what his attitude is. When cornered, he has a mantra which goes: "I loved my son. I love my grandkids. My grandkids killed my son. And I have mixed emotions about that." At first, I thought by mixed emotions he meant he was confused, then later on I decided he meant exactly what he said.

Luther has been interviewed a lot. He often asks and answers his own questions.

"Were those children abused? I'd have to say, yes. Those children were belittled, berated, beat on, abused, called everything in the book. But you know, I never heard those boys use a cuss word."

Nancy shakes her head.

"They killed their daddy, yes. But they never used foul language."

And he waits a beat or two and then restates his theme: "Nobody knows what it was like, being a prisoner in your own home for years, nobody. But he was my son and I loved him. When you love somebody, you love them. Don't make no difference what they do."

Luther pulls up his shirtsleeve. "He cut me. Here." Traces a scar on his bicep. "Here." Touches his arm close to the wrist. "He shot me once—just birdshot, but I would have gone after him with my gun if my wife hadn't stopped me."

Luther says Lonnie never should have got married, and that on his wedding night he said he'd rather go coon hunting. "He hated women. He used to say, there's only one good woman in the world and that's her"—nods in Nancy's direction—"and all the rest are whores and liars." Thinking about why Lonnie believed this, Luther goes to the sink, paces, starts to say something, then stops, mentions family secrets, things he can't talk about. "But I'll tell you this," he finally says. "He was jilted and that's all I'll say. It was when he was a senior. He was always a man to hold a grudge, and that did it." As for his sisters, he probably hated them most of all. "But then," Luther says darkly, "he knew the things they did."

And so, at twenty-two, Lonnie married Rosemarie Standford, even though he didn't want to—"It was her wanted to," Nancy declares—and Luther says he would be the first to take the stand and say that, yes, Lonnie abused her and beat her up so bad you couldn't tell who she was. But as for the question of whether he molested Alesha, Luther Dutton says that's hard for him to know. "I'll tell you this, Lonnie hated a pervert. He had no use for homos. He hated a queer. And I ask myself, would he molest his own child? I have a hard time with that, you see. I have mixed emotions about that. But to answer your question, I'd have to say I don't think he ever did. Or not that I ever knew of."

At one point, Luther leaves the room and comes back in carrying a three-foot length of hard rubber tubing and a pistol in a holster. He puts them on the table.

"Now, ma'am," he says, " I don't meant to disrespect you, but you know what that is." He nods at the tube. "It's a tube from a pump to air up your tires." He pauses. "That's what he used to beat them with." He takes the pistol out of the holster. "Ma'am. I don't mean to disrespect you." The gun is an automatic. He takes the clip out. "This was his gun. He was left-handed. A left-handed man." He puts the nine-millimeter back in the holster. "He wore it here." He lays his hand across his heart. "In the bib of his overalls. Always."

Marie left Lonnie in 1989 and went to Texas to live with her mother. She took her children with her. A few months later, Lonnie went down there and made it up with Marie, saying he would change, they'd all move and make a life in Texas. Then things happened. Lonnie beat Marie up, Marie's mother called the police and Lonnie was thrown in jail. When he got out two weeks later, he went back home to Oklahoma. Soon afterwards, Herman and Druie asked to go back to live with their dad. This was before he started beating up on them, and anyway they didn't really trust their mother, especially after Lonnie had drilled certain facts into their heads and made them call her pig and whore dog. Lonnie filed a custody suit, which he won. Most people believe Luther helped his son pay for a good lawyer. Marie didn't have one.

Oklahoma has a law stating that, if a parent is absent from a child for twelve consecutive months and provides no support, then the parent's rights can be terminated without notice. As Marie Dutton has not seen her children in at least three years, she is no longer legally considered their parent. And one day recently, when the boys were in court, they were given the chance to see Marie. They refused. Druie eventually gave in and talked to her, but Herman stood firm.

Luther Dutton says he called the social services on "this very phone— so many times," and he gets out old telephone bills showing the calls to a Chickasha number. As for the police, Luther says, "The police are thirty-five miles away. You know what happens. Time they get here . . . And it's complicated. I mean, if you file charges, you have to stop and think, what's going to happen to the kids? We'd get into it over those kids. I'd see Herman with his head swollen up, Druie with a black eye, and we'd get into it. He'd tell me to mind my own damned business, those kids were his and he'd do what he damned pleased, and nobody better try to come between him and his kids. So . . ."

He shows me Lonnie's photograph album. There are diamond-shaped cuts in many of the snapshots, where Lonnie gouged out the face and body of Marie. One picture is of Lonnie on his wedding night, standing by a dog-pen, holding his arm over the coon hounds' heads to get them to jump up. He is trim, of medium build, a fairly good-looking young man. His smile is rascally, but not mean. In later photos, he is big and burly and will not look at the camera. In most of them, he is wearing a shapeless hat with a big brim, and you can see the gun holster sticking out of his overalls bib. I hold the pictures up in Nancy's direction. I would not have known, I say, that these were of the same person. She nods.

In one picture, it is Christmas, and Lonnie's four children and Nancy are lined up inside Luther and Nancy's house. Nancy is in the middle, looking pathetic in a droopy dress. The four children all hold rifles on their shoulders, like soldiers. Herman stands at one end, chin tucked in like a Marine, shoulders severely squared.

"See there," Luther points at the right side of Herman's head. "You can see how swollen up it is. And look at his mouth."

Herman's head looks soft and melonish on one side, and his mouth is twisted and off-centre. Druie has a black eye.

"That's the gun they shot him with." Luther taps the photo. "Right there." He points to the gun Herman has on his shoulder. "That's the .243."

Linda Munn, Lonnie's elder sister, has not lived in Rush Springs for ten years. But she has come back to Oklahoma to testify to her brother's brutality; there are pictures of her in the middle of the main street of Rush Springs, holding up a sign saying BRING OUR ANGELS HOME.

When I spoke to her later, her first words were, "You didn't believe everything Daddy said, did you? That's what scares me. That people will go out there and take everything he says at face value."

Linda Munn says her daddy beat up on her as far back as she can remember, once so badly she had blood streaks from the back of her neck to her ankles, and on Lonnie too—one time in the barn, so brutally that everybody went and hid so they couldn't hear. She also says that Lonnie didn't have a deformed heart or high blood pressure. "That's bull poop. He was lazy. If those little boys are going to have to tell the truth about what went on, then we should too. That place he says Lonnie cut him? My brother didn't cut Daddy there. He did that himself, welding. I told him I knew that, but he just said, 'Well, *they* don't.'"

When Linda Munn was fourteen, she got pregnant, got married and came home to her parent's house to live with her new husband. Those were bad years. Nancy was in hospital getting shock treatments, and Luther was beating up on all the kids.

Linda says that no girl was ever going to be good enough for Lonnie in her mother's eyes. "If she didn't use the recipes my mom used or clean house the way my mom did, she was ridiculed. Marie never had a chance."

Linda Munn says that she is prepared to believe just about anything that's said about her brother, and wonders about his sexual problems. She says he wouldn't let Marie change Alesha's diapers if anybody else was in the room, in case some man saw the baby's genitals and started getting ideas. When his daughter was a toddler, he used to introduce her as "my nigger" and "my little slut." Once, when Alesha was about four, she fell off the porch and cracked her head. Linda's son Wayne picked her up and held her on his lap to see if she was badly hurt, and Lonnie came running up, waving his pistol, and told Wayne to take that child off his lap; he knew what Wayne was thinking—Linda says, because Lonnie was having those thoughts himself. And there is the story about Lonnie beating up Marie to make her have sex with another man, then when she wouldn't, pouring alcohol down her throat until she did, then beating her up worse afterwards because she did it, and everybody blaming Marie because she didn't after all *have* to do it. Linda says she remembers her brother bragging that there was one thing he could say about Marie: she took an ass whipping better than any man he knew.

There are other houses on the road with no name, "W of city." Karen Caveny and her family live in a trailerhouse on the front part of their land, where they are building a home and share a fence line with the Dutton place. The living-room of the trailer is warm and comfortable, the walls covered with family portraits. Karen Caveny is a pleasant-faced woman in her mid-forties, smart and plain-spoken as a stop sign. She has a lot to say about what she heard out there. From 1984, when Lonnie moved his trailer on to his father's land and settled down with his pregnant wife and their three kids, she and her family never felt safe.

"Lonnie liked to shoot. My kids have dodged his bullets; we have bullet holes in the side of our house. When Lonnie and Marie first moved in, they had six white dogs. Those dogs were chasing livestock, and I sent my daughter Jodi to tell Herman to tell his daddy he had to do something about them. Next day, Herman told Jodi, "Daddy says you don't have to worry about those dogs any more. He stepped out on the front porch and shot them all."

Karen Caveny caught Lonnie Dutton peering in her windows at least twice, and one time he stalked a neighbor who complained about goats in her yard, following her car in his pick-up and parking alongside it while she went to church.

"What you have to understand about Lonnie is, he liked intimidating people. And when you're doing the kinds of things he was doing and enjoying them, then I'd have to say that was evil."

"Marie?" Karen Caveny's eyes fill. "Just after they moved in, we were in the house, the television was on, the washing machine was going, it was night, and on top of all that noise I heard screams. I thought it was one of the animals, but when I went outside, I knew it was a person. It went on for forty-five minutes. She was screaming his name out loud, begging him to stop."

Karen Caveny eventually went back inside and turned up the television so she couldn't hear any more. At a quarter to six the next morning, there was a knock at the door and there stood Marie, holding Druie by the hand with Alesha on her hip. She was pregnant with Jake. "That child was so big she was waddling. Her face was out to here, her eyes were black, and there wasn't a part of the whites of her eyes that was white; they were completely red. The blood vessels had all burst, I guess. Her mouth was busted and one ear was torn. She had black-and-blue marks all over her. She needed a ride into town, and so we took them and put her and the children on a bus to Texas. Next thing I knew she was back. She came to us lots of times. Nancy would call me and I'd lie: Oh, I haven't seen Marie, haven't seen her in a long time. Marie would hide the children, lay them down under some bushes and wait for the right car to come along and she'd get up and put them in the car and get a ride where she needed to go."

Karen Caveny says that she called the social services "between thirty and fifty times" but that "nobody came." She made the reports anonymously because for a long time she and her family were Lonnie Dutton's only neighbors. "He would know it was me turning him in. I had children of my own to think of. If he was doing the things he was doing to his own children, what would he do to mine?"

Lonnie liked to set off fires on other people's land, and one time a dozen or so people who lived in the area got together and called the sheriff. Nobody came out until eventually someone from another county told a friend, who was a special investigator from yet another county, about what was going on, and that person roused some members of the Grady County Sheriff's Department. And when they arrived, Karen Caveny told them the whole story, about the screams and about Lonnie being a peeping Tom. "They told us there was nothing they could do unless we caught him red-handed and held on to him until somebody came. Now can't you just see me saying, 'Lonnie, will you wait right there while I call the sheriff?' " And while this was not said outright, the message Karen Caveny got from the Sheriff's Department was: be your own vigilante; do what you have to do.

People who live outside the city limits don't always live there from necessity or because they are farmers. They live there because they get a kick out of having their own way, by God; and living where they don't see, by God, anybody else; and having, by God, beaten the system. The Cavenys never thought of moving because of, " Oh, the pioneer spirit. You don't let people run you off your property. You just don't."

On 12 July, some time between four and five in the afternoon, Karen Caveny heard there had been a shooting on the Dutton place, and she was not surprised. But she thought Lonnie had shot his dad. Why? "Because Lonnie was just that crazy and his dad was just that scared." When she heard what had really happened, she says it was the last thing she would have imagined. "I had a mental picture of those two little boys—you know, they're small; they look more like ten and twelve than twelve and fifteen—and I could see them holding that gun and praying to God that Lonnie wouldn't wake up before they pulled the trigger and I felt terrible for them. I wish they hadn't had to go through that. Nobody deserves to live the way they lived. They didn't just haul off and shoot their dad. He was a demon. He was living hell."

There are constant and hurtful questions in Grady County these days: who saw the bruises or heard the screams; who called the social services or the child-abuse toll-free number to make reports; who was responsible for the fact that, while there were a lot of people who thought that Lonnie Dutton was a man in need of a good killing, his kids were the only ones up to doing it?

Employees of the Department of Human Services can't talk about individual cases. The Sheriff's Department will only say that, if a child won't talk, there's nothing they can do. A math teacher at Herman's school once took the boy aside and asked him about the bruises and abrasions on his face. Herman made up some tale about the limb of a tree hitting him and, even when the teacher said he didn't believe him, held fast to his story. And people in Rush Springs want to make it clear, they didn't know what was going on, they didn't even know Lonnie Dutton, he never came into town.

Everybody thinks something had to go wrong for those children to have fallen through the cracks of the system, but nobody knows exactly what. And I find myself wondering if *anything* could have been done to stop Lonnie Dutton's bullying, short of his children rising up and shooting him. The Dutton family was isolated and secretive. Nobody much knew where the trailer was, and Lonnie had installed motion detectors in his yard, connected to lights. He slept on the couch, surrounded by guns. If the lights came on in the night, he started shooting. It didn't matter what was out there. He didn't wait, he didn't aim. He just shot.

As I leave "W of city," the sky is blood-red along the horizon. I keep thinking about Herman. Herman was the caretaker child, the one in charge; it was up to him to keep things on an even keel, take the hits for his brothers and sister, lie when anyone asked about his bruises, run round at lunch-time to make sure the other kids were OK. Herman never quit trying to be the good child and please his dad. When Lonnie took them all shoplifting, Herman knew he would beat up on whoever didn't steal enough and so he cut back on his take. Last year, after Herman had failed to do a chore exactly right, Lonnie went after him with a two-by-four and knocked him out cold in the back yard; there is a declivity in Herman's skull now, big enough to lay your finger in.

Herman is the smallest boy in his class—I have seen his school group picture. He is in the front row, sparky-looking, perfectly proportioned, wiry. He is standing at an angle to the camera, one hand loosely curled on his thigh. His blond hair is in big waves, dramatically dipped to one side, and he is wearing a bright western shirt, a black belt, tight jeans and cowboy boots. He may be tiny, but his body is taking an adult shape, and he has a great sense of style.

That July afternoon, Herman told Druie he would be the one to shoot their daddy, but when they got in there, he couldn't do it. At fifteen, Herman was old enough to know the consequences, legal and otherwise. So the younger, more concrete-thinking Druie took the gun, but he couldn't do it either, although he said that if Herman could steady the rifle, he thought he could pull the trigger. Lonnie wore a droopy moustache, sometimes a forked beard and had had his head shaved to give him a meaner look. I imagine the two boys standing beside him, passing the rifle between them, keeping a careful eye on the bald head, the moustache, the chin, the bulked-up body of their two-hundred plus pound dad in his overalls, the nine-millimeter automatic in a holster beneath the bib.

And so Herman aimed the .243 and put his finger on the trigger again, and just as he was about to lower the barrel once more, Druie pushed the trigger back. The bullet made a neat three-quarter-inch entry hole, then exploded inside Lonnie Dutton's skull. It did not exit. There was a lot of blood. Lonnie died instantly.

Herman and Druie ran out the front door. Alesha and Jake were playing in the back yard, Herman had made sure of that because he didn't mean for them to see; but Alesha heard the noise and ran in the back door, saw her daddy lying dead on the couch and started screaming.

Herman herded his brothers and sister together, and all four children ran down the rutted cow path to their daddy's pick-up, bawling. They were heading down to the main road, going God knows where, when their cousin, Linda Munn's son Wayne, who until a week before had been a Rush Springs policeman, drove in. Herman told him, "I think Daddy's dead." Wayne was not surprised; people had been expecting a shooting out there for years; they just didn't know who would end up dead. But he thought it would be Luther or one of the kids, not Lonnie.

The first police officer on the scene was Guy Huggins, the deputy Sheriff. He said that the trailerhouse was swept up and fairly clean, and that there were no illegal drugs on the premises. Later on, he went to pick up Herman and Druie at a relative's house, and all four kids were still bawling. Herman said that he was the one who shot his dad; then, when Huggins got the boys to the Sheriff's annex in Chickasha, where they were questioned separately, Druie said that Herman held the gun but that he pulled the trigger. Both boys knew what they had done and said they loved their daddy. When was the funeral? Could they go?

It is dark now. In Rush Springs, the Homecoming game is in progress. The scoreboard lights say ten minutes left in the second quarter, the Redskins leading by two. I park on the highway. The stadium lights up the pitch-black night. Everybody's there: men with their feet up on a fence rail, smoking; women selling tickets, talking to their daughters. Let loose in the warm night air, kids run around like wild things.

At half-time, I drive into the parking lot and buy a ticket. The band—mostly white children in red and black uniforms—has marched out and plays "Ebb Tide." Convertibles circle the field, as Homecoming maids perched atop the back seats smile and wave. They have a lot of hair, fizzed up, fanned out, shiny with goo. Their cars stop at the fifty-yard line, where each maid is escorted through a flower-decked arbour. The queen and king are crowned, flashbulbs pop.

The Dutton compound is only five miles off, but it's a long way from there to here. As the band and the Homecoming court leave the field, and the Redskins roll back on, I think about the boys, what might have been happening to them, right now, this minute, if they hadn't killed their father.

All four Dutton children have been made wards of the court, a ruling that Marie Dutton is still fighting. Alesha and Jake have been put into the temporary care of a relative. Herman and Druie were sent to the Oklahoma Juvenile Diagnostic and Evaluation Center, which recommended that a court trial be avoided. If Herman and Druie stay out of trouble until April 1996, their records will be clear.

Nobody knows when the four children will be together again. The court has ruled that any member of the Dutton family seeking custody must first agree to therapy.

Back on US 81, heading north, I wonder what secrets are buried with Lonnie Dutton and what Luther Dutton was making up. I wonder how all four kids will turn out. I think about Herman. Herman has his own room now, his own things. I wonder what his nights are like, what he thinks about, what kind of plans he is making.

Later that night I wake up screaming. A rat is at me, biting and biting me, and I cannot move.

All Things Censored:
The Poem NPR Doesn't
Want You to Hear

MARTÍN ESPADA

I was an NPR poet. In particular, I was an *All Things Considered* poet. *All Things Considered* would occasionally broadcast my poems in conjunction with news stories. One producer even commissioned a New Year's poem from me. "Imagine the Angels of Bread" aired on January 2, 1994, in the same broadcast as the news of the Zapatista uprising in Chiapas. But now I have been censored by *All Things Considered* and National Public Radio because I wrote a poem for them about Mumia Abu-Jamal.

As many readers may know, Mumia Abu-Jamal is an eloquent African-American journalist on death row, convicted in the 1981 slaying of police officer Daniel Faulkner in Philadelphia—under extremely dubious circumstances. Officer Faulkner was beating Mumia's brother with a flashlight when Mumia came upon the scene. In the ensuing confrontation, both Faulkner and Mumia were shot. Though Mumia had a .38 caliber pistol in his taxi that night, and the gun was found at the scene, the initial judgment of the medical examiner concerning the fatal bullet was that it came from a .44 caliber weapon. Several witnesses reported seeing an unidentified gunman flee, leaving both Faulkner and Mumia severely wounded in the street.

What happened in court was a tragic pantomime. The trial featured a prosecutor who assailed Mumia for his radical politics, including his teenaged membership in the Black Panthers. Witnesses were coached in their testimony or intimidated into silence by police. The trial was presided over by a judge notorious for handing out death sentences to black defendants, or manipulating juries to do the same, as in this case. A strong critic of the Philadelphia police—particularly with respect to their brutal treatment of the African-American collective called MOVE—Mumia was condemned by the very system he questioned.

In August 1995, Mumia came within ten days of being executed by lethal injection. He is seeking a new trial. Robert Meeropol, the younger son of Julius and Ethel Rosenberg, says: "Mumia is the first political prisoner in the U.S. to face execution since my parents."

Enter NPR. In 1994, National Public Radio agreed to broadcast a series of Mumia's radio commentaries from death row. The Prison Radio Project produced the recordings that April. Suddenly, NPR canceled the commentaries under pressure from the right, particularly the Fraternal Order of Police and Senator Robert Dole. Mumia and the Prison Radio Project sued NPR on First Amendment grounds.

In April 1997, I was contacted by the staff at *All Things Considered*, their first communication since my New Year's poem. Diantha Parker and Sara Sarasohn commissioned me to write a poem for National Poetry Month. The general idea was that the poem should be like a news story, with a journalistic perspective. They suggested that I write a poem in response to a news story in a city I visited during the month. Ms. Parker called to obtain my itinerary so that NPR could give me an assignment relevant to a particular city. Fatefully, they could think of no such assignment. But the idea had found a home in the folds of my brain.

Since April is National Poetry Month, I traveled everywhere. I went from Joplin, Missouri, to Kansas City, to Rochester, to Chicago, to Camden, New Jersey. And then to Philadelphia. I read an article in the April 16 *Philadelphia Weekly* about Mumia Abu-Jamal. The article described a motion by one of Mumia's lawyers, Leonard Weinglass, to introduce testimony by an unnamed prostitute with new information about the case. This became the catalyst for the poem.

I also visited the tomb of Walt Whitman in nearby Camden, and was moved. Whitman wrote this in "Song of Myself": "The runaway slave came to my house and stopt outside, / I heard his motions crackling the twigs of the wood pile, / Through the swung half-door of the kitchen I saw him limpsy and weak, / And went where he sat on a log and led him in and assured him, / And brought water and fill'd a tub for his sweated body and bruis'd feet." In my poem Whitman's tomb became a place of refuge for the "fugitive slave," first for a nameless prostitute, then Mumia. By poem's end, this place and poet came to represent our sacred compassion, our ceremonies of conscience, our will to resist, our refusal to forget.

I faxed the poem to NPR on April 21. On April 24, *All Things Considered* staff informed me that they would not air the poem. They were explicit: They would not air the poem because of its subject matter—Mumia-Abu Jamal—and its political sympathies.

"NPR is refusing to air this poem because of its political content?" I asked. "Yes," said Diantha Parker.

She cited the "history" of NPR and Mumia, a reference to their refusal to air his commentaries. She further explained that the poem was "not the way NPR wants to return to this subject." Such is the elegant bureaucratic language of censorship. Parker would later admit, in an interview with Dennis Bernstein of KPFA-FM, that she "loved" the poem, and that "the poem should have run, perhaps in a different context." This comment also debunks the idea that NPR was merely exercising its editorial discretion. The quality of the poem was never questioned. The criteria for the assignment had been met. "He did everything we asked him to do," said Parker to Bernstein.

A few days later, I met Marilyn Jamal, Mumia's former wife. I presented her with the poem and watched her struggle against tears. Then she said: "I promised myself that I wouldn't cry anymore." I concluded that NPR's censorship should come to light.

The people at *All Things Considered* expressed indignation that I was aware of their "history" with Mumia, and still wrote the poem anyway. Sara Sarasohn, the same producer who solicited my New Year's poem, told me: "We never expected you would write *this*!" Said Parker to Dennis Bernstein: "He should have known better."

How could I not write this poem once it came to me? How could I censor my imagination, making myself complicit in NPR's muzzling of Mumia?

I had given NPR the proverbial benefit of the doubt. I had hoped that a sense of fairness—a respect for opposing viewpoints—would compel *All Things Considered* to broadcast the poem, a broadcast that would address the concerns of listeners who felt that NPR "sold out" Mumia. Instead, I encountered a reaction based on cowardice and self-pity.

Confronted with the fate of a man on death row, the staff of *All Things Considered* could only think of their own discomfort, their own problems caused by the controversy, their own political and professional security. Worse, they insisted on implicitly comparing their suffering to the suffering of Mumia Abu-Jamal. Diantha Parker cited "safety concerns" for NPR staff in explaining the refusal to air a poem about a man facing execution. When contacted by Demetria Martínez, a columnist for the *National Catholic Reporter,* concerning this story, executive producer Ellen Weiss complained that the NPR-Mumia controversy "will follow me to my tombstone." *Her tombstone.* Compare this to the tombstone of a man who may soon die by lethal injection.

Surely, Weiss deserves the Liberal Media Sensitivity to Language Award.

Weiss, who at the time of this interview had not read the poem, also informed Martínez that NPR had a policy of not airing any commentaries or "op-ed" pieces about Mumia Abu-Jamal while his lawsuit against NPR was pending. Note how a poem became a "commentary," not a work of art, when that definition justified censorship. Strangely, the two people who made the decision not to air the poem, and informed me of that decision—Parker and Sarasohn—never mentioned such a policy in a telephone conversation of almost twenty minutes. Yet, some weeks later, Sarasohn told Dennis Bernstein: "It's a legal thing." Parker and Sarasohn also confessed to Bernstein that they did not consult their supervisors or NPR attorneys before deciding to suppress the poem.

The legal justification for this act of censorship amused me; apparently, the people at NPR forgot that I am also a lawyer. As fellow attorney Bill Newman, head of the western Massachusetts ACLU, pointed out, "The reason for silence in the face of pending litigation does not apply. As a poet, an independent person, you are not a corporate spokesman. You cannot bind the corporation. The reason corporations like NPR say 'no comment' is because they don't want the statements to be used against them in court. That rationale does not apply to a poet reading a poem. It makes no sense."

Furthermore, the subject of the lawsuit and the subject of the poem were totally different. The censored poem was not about Mumia's censored commentaries, nor about his First Amendment rights. Mumia's lawsuit against NPR did not concern his criminal case or his possible execution. Newman raised a question: "If Mumia were to dismiss his lawsuit, would they air this poem?" (In fact, a federal district court judge dismissed the suit in September 1997. That decision has been appealed.) Dennis Bernstein asked both Sarasohn and Parker if the poem might be aired following Mumia's execution, as an elegy. Both times, his question was greeted by silence.

NPR's policy, even if ex post facto, served as a punitive means to perpetuate Mumia's silence by silencing those who would speak for him. "First they censor him. Then, because he exercises his First Amendment right to remedy the violation, NPR compounds that affront to his freedom of expression by refusing to allow others to comment on his behalf," said Newman.

Subsequent to the original publication of this article in the July 1997 issue of *The Progressive* magazine, NPR stopped using the legal argument publicly to justify its actions. Producers Parker and Sarasohn were no longer available for comment. Instead, Kathy Scott, Director of Communications for NPR, told *The Hartford Courant* that, "We are a news organization and we don't take advocacy positions." Now the problem, apparently, was that "Espada was attempting to use NPR as an advocate for Mumia Abu-Jamal," as Scott expressed it in a statement to WCVB-TV in Boston. At one point, Scott said of Mumia: "My gosh, the man's life is at stake, and to influence that decision one way or another just would not be responsible on our part."

Like a top left spinning too long, NPR's spin had become wobbly. Newspapers, radio and television stations take positions, called "editorials," sometimes with the disclaimer that the opinions expressed in the editorial do not necessarily reflect those of management, a concept seemingly alien to the producers of *All Things Considered*.

In fact, NPR takes "advocacy positions" all the time. They are called "commentaries." Moreover, *All Things Considered* had aired my poems in the past—all poems of advocacy. The ultimate contradiction, however, was this: In July 1997, after discussions with NPR in Washington, WFCR-FM, the NPR affiliate in Amherst, Massachusetts, elected to air the poem in the context of a news story about the controversy. The poem was not used against NPR in court, nor was NPR's status as a news organization demolished by the presence on the air of an advocate for Mumia Abu-Jamal.

I once asked my friend David Velazquez, who worked as a farrier, about shoeing horses. He replied: "Imagine a creature that weighs fifteen hundred pounds and is motivated by fear." That's NPR, at least in terms of Mumia. Of course, the liberal media is notorious for timidity. To again quote my wise friend: "A liberal is someone who leaves the room when a fight breaks out."

Editorial decisions are made for political reasons on a daily basis. Rarely, however, is the curtain lifted to reveal the corroded machinery. Moreover, as a left-wing poet, I expect to be censored by mainstream media. But when so-called "alternative" media also censor the left, the impact is devastating. Ask Mumia Abu-Jamal.

This censorship also manifests itself on the streets. In November 1997, I gave a benefit reading, with a group of poets, for the Western Pennsylvania Committee to Free Mumia Abu-Jamal. A member of the organization, a graduate student from Germany named Gabriele Gottlieb, was posting flyers for the event when she was attacked and seriously beaten by a man denouncing Mumia as a "cop killer." Members of the Committee speculated that the attacker may have been an off-duty police officer. In less charitable moments, I imagine that he was essentially expressing the same urges as the people at *All Things Considered*, albeit more brutally.

Readers can call or write *All Things Considered* to urge that the poem be aired. They can urge, again, that Mumia's commentaries be aired, or at least released from the vaults of NPR so that others might have access to them. They can inform NPR that their financial contributions to National Public Radio will instead be diverted to the legal defense of Mumia Abu-Jamal. That address is: Committee to Save Mumia Abu-Jamal, 163 Amsterdam Ave. #115, New York, NY 10023. Checks should be made payable to the Bill of Rights Foundation ("for MAJ").

Meanwhile, I assume that *All Things Considered* has put my name on its blacklist. I wonder what poems I must write to be allowed on *All Things Considered* again. Maybe some cowboy poetry. What follows is the poem NPR does not want you to hear. I have made a few minor revisions, since, in the midst of this madness, with a poet's compulsive nature, I was trying to create a better poem.

Another Nameless Prostitute Says the Man Is Innocent
—for Mumia Abu-Jamal
Philadelphia, PA/Camden, NJ, April 1997

The board-blinded windows knew what happened;
the pavement sleepers of Philadelphia, groaning
in their ghost-infested sleep, knew what happened;
every Black man blessed
with the gashed eyebrow of nightsticks
knew what happened;
even Walt Whitman knew what happened,
poet a century dead, keeping vigil
from the tomb on the other side of the bridge.

More than fifteen years ago,
the cataract stare of the cruiser's headlights,
the impossible angle of the bullet,
the tributaries and lakes of blood,
Officer Faulkner dead, suspect Mumia shot in the chest,
the witnesses who saw a gunman
running away, his heart and feet thudding.

The nameless prostitutes know,
hunched at the curb, their bare legs chilled.
Their faces squinted to see that night,
rouged with fading bruises. Now the faces fade.

275

Perhaps an eyewitness putrifies eyes open in a bed of soil,
or floats in the warm gulf stream of her addiction,
or hides from the fanged whispers of the police
in the tomb of Walt Whitman,
where the granite door is open
and fugitive slaves may rest.

Mumia: the Panther beret, the thinking dreadlocks,
dissident words that swarmed the microphone like a hive,
sharing meals with people named Africa,
calling out their names even after the police bombardment
that charred their black bodies.
So the governor has signed the death warrant.
The executioner's needle would flush the poison
down into Mumia's writing hand
so the fingers curl like a burned spider;
his calm questioning mouth would grow numb,
and everywhere radios sputter to silence, in his memory.

The veiled prostitutes are gone,
gone to the segregated balcony of whores.
But the newspaper reports that another nameless prostitute
says the man is innocent, that she will testify at the next hearing.
Beyond the courthouse, a multitude of witnesses chants, prays,
shouts for his prison to collapse, a shack in a hurricane.

Mumia, if the last nameless prostitute
becomes an unraveling turban of steam,
if the judges' robes become clouds of ink
swirling like octopus deception,
if the shroud becomes your Amish quilt,
if your dreadlocks are snipped during autopsy,
then drift above the ruined RCA factory
that once birthed radios
to the tomb of Walt Whitman,
where the granite door is open
and fugitive slaves may rest.

Prisoner AM-8335:
A Postscript

MARTÍN ESPADA

Poetry, that curious and remarkable art, has taken me to some curious and remarkable places: from a Quaker meeting house to a boxing gym, from a stone mansion on the sea to a tortilla factory. And now death row.

Most of us who debate the issue of the death penalty, for or against, never imagine that this avenging angel might swoop down on someone we know and care about personally. I no longer have that luxury. Death row for me wears one particular human face.

In April 1997, I became entangled in a censorship controversy with National Public Radio when NPR's *All Things Considered* refused to broadcast a poem commissioned from me after two producers learned that the subject of the poem was Mumia Abu-Jamal. I never considered the consequences of confronting and alienating National Public Radio. By comparison, Mumia Abu-Jamal had a great deal more to lose. Moreover, a writer who thinks too much about consequences becomes ethically paralyzed, even stops writing, or at least writing anything worth reading.

As I wrestled with NPR, I became involved in the movement to win the radical African-American journalist a new trial and overturn his unjust conviction for the killing of a Philadelphia police officer. One year after the battle with NPR began, on May 2, 1998, I found myself sitting on death row, a few feet away from Mumia Abu-Jamal, at SCI-Greene in Waynesburg, Pennsylvania. This is the tale: how I arrived there, what we said to each other, and the creation of another poem unlikely to be aired on *All Things Considered*. (Parenthetically, the worst thing anyone can say to a poet is: "Don't say that." The poet will probably say it again.)

I would have considerable trouble visiting Mumia in my true capacity as a writer. Under the so-called "Mumia Rule," journalists and their equipment are barred from the Pennsylvania state prison system.

I could not bring in a camera, a tape recorder, a pad or a pencil. Mumia has not been photographed for some time, though he finds inventive ways to project his voice over the walls; a radio commentary broadcast on KPFA-FM, for example, was recorded on a telephone answering machine.

One of Mumia's frequent visitors is Marcus Rediker, a professor of history at the University of Pittsburgh and a member of the Western Pennsylvania Committee to Free Mumia Abu-Jamal. Marcus recalled that I am still licensed to practice law in the state of Massachusetts, though I have not actually practiced since 1993. He proposed the idea of having me visit Mumia as a lawyer, since Mumia is entitled to unlimited legal visits. Of course, I am not part of Mumia's legal team, but this distinction was lost on prison authorities. The Board of Bar Overseers in Boston faxed the prison a letter proving that I was an attorney, and the warden approved my visit for the following day.

SCI-Greene is a super-maximum security facility. The technocrats who designed the prison interior decided on pastel walls to complement the hairtrigger metal detectors. Though SCI-Greene may serve as an example of the latest incarceration technology, there is still razor wire festooning the outer walls, and a history of brutality within. For the briefest moment, Marcus Rediker and I crossed the threshold of this underworld to find Mumia.

Prisoner AM-8335 was waiting for us behind a Plexiglas window. His hands were cuffed—as they are whenever he comes out of his cell—and he wore a striped prison jumpsuit, in the fashion of the old Mississippi chain gangs. He seemed both in good health and in good spirits. We visited for more than two and a half hours, with the red "Legal Visit" sign strung across the door.

He spoke energetically of literature, history, and politics (former Panther Eldridge Cleaver had recently died). He would have fit in comfortably with a table of writers or activists at a coffeehouse. *One of us*. Only he was here, awaiting execution by lethal injection.

I realized then that my poem about Mumia, "Another Nameless Prostitute Says the Man Is Innocent," visualized the man's execution— even the moment of death, when "the fingers curl like a burned spider"—and that I had never considered the emotional impact of the poem on that man. I explained my perception that among many people, even among activists in the movement to free him, there is a sense of unreality about the case, the vague notion that the authorities of Pennsylvania would never dare to kill Mumia with the attention of the world upon them. I wanted to jolt readers into the realization that the execution might actually happen, to create an atmosphere of urgency, to move away from Mumia the icon and toward Mumia the human being in mortal danger, to make everyone on death row more tangibly human. But how did the poem's images of death make him feel?

His response was generous. "What you imagine in the poem is nothing I haven't imagined a thousand times myself," he said. "I found your approach refreshing."

I have known a number of former political prisoners—I was close to the poet Clemente Soto Vélez, locked up for his espousal of Puerto Rican independence—but I had never met a political prisoner who was still incarcerated. There has been some debate in left-liberal circles about whether Mumia is indeed a political prisoner. I refer the doubters back to the sentencing phase of Mumia's trial in 1982. The prosecutor chose that critical moment to introduce Mumia's membership as a teenager in the Black Panther Party, and cited remarks attributed to Mumia in a newspaper article in which the young Abu-Jamal quoted Mao's famous dictum: "Political power grows from the barrel of a gun." The prosecutor then used Mumia's political affiliations and beliefs to characterize him as an "executioner," influencing a jury that returned a sentence of death. To this day, Mumia's outspoken radicalism inflames his enemies, as the calls to kill him grow more shrill, ranging from a full page ad in *The New York Times* demanding his execution to a "Fry Mumia" rally on my own campus at the University of Massachusetts-Amherst.

In the two years prior to my encounter with Mumia, a wave of repression engulfed SCI-Greene, resulting in more than two hundred lawsuits filed by inmates and a series of articles in the *Pittsburgh Post-Gazette*. In one incident, according to the *Post-Gazette*, a guard arguing with a Cuban inmate named Antonio Noguerol knocked out the inmate's gold tooth with his nightstick, then scrawled the letters "KKK" in the prisoner's blood on the floor. As a professional journalist and jailhouse lawyer, Mumia counseled other inmates working to tell their story through the media and the courts.

The prison authorities found an insidious way to retaliate against Mumia and others like him. The state bureaucracy enacted a regulation requiring that inmates keep all personal possessions in a single box, twelve by twelve by fourteen inches. The practical effect was to deprive inmates of books and documents collected for years. One morning four guards entered Mumia's cell and looted seventeen cartons of books and papers, an entire library obliterated. He could afford to mail a few books home, but he could not keep any of it in the cell he occupied twenty-three hours a day. To Mumia, the political character of this action was clear; one guard even found a book with the word "Revolutionary" in the title and blurted out: "This is what we're supposed to get." Mumia and other inmates organized two hunger strikes. They won a concession: two boxes instead of one.

Mumia Abu-Jamal is not only a man unjustly imprisoned on death row. He is a writer, with three books and numerous articles to his credit. He is also a student, enrolled in a graduate program. Imagine a writer or student losing every book, every dog-eared, underlined, stained, sweet book. Then imagine being unable to walk through the doorway to begin the job of replacing them.

I realized that I was sitting in the company of a man who actually could answer that hypothetical question: If you were going to a desert island and could take only one book with you, which book would it be? So I asked: "What did you put in the box?"

"I put *Beloved* in the box," Mumia said.

He gazed over my shoulder, and continued: "I would rather be beaten than this assault on the life of the mind. . . . Giving up a book is like giving up a child, like parting with your own flesh. How do you choose between *Beloved* and *The Wretched of the Earth?*"

What happened next stunned us all into silence. Mumia's eyes filmed over. First one tear, then a second meandered down his face. The same man in a calm baritone had contemplated his own execution, the death of his body, only moments before; now the thought of his lost books, the lingering death of his mind, brought a grief that was impossible to control. As I studied his face I saw in the Plexiglas a reflection of the guards walking outside the room, and a phrase struck me: "Small blue men patrolling your forehead." It was the first line of what would become a poem.

Finally he spoke again, apologized for "blubbering," and was assured that there was no shame in it. When Marcus and I left, the guards steered us to a huge steel door that inexplicably refused to open for several minutes. Waiting, we glanced back at Mumia, who waved and tapped on the window. On the way out we bumped into Leonard Weinglass, Mumia's actual lawyer, who was informed by the guards upon his arrival that Mumia was already visiting with his attorney. Weinglass was gracious enough not to declare me an imposter, and waited patiently until I emerged to discover the identity of Mumia's new legal representative.

Mumia still waits for a new trial. His case is on appeal before Judge William Yohn, Jr., of the federal district court for the Eastern District of Pennsylvania. As the struggle for Mumia's life reaches its apex, he will be dehumanized, even demonized by the media, the state of

Pennsylvania, the Fraternal Order of Police. Hopefully, a few people will remember the Mumia Abu-Jamal I met on May 2, 1998.

I could not sleep that night. Whenever I closed my eyes, I saw Mumia's face painted on the caves of my eyelids. The next morning, on the plane home, I wrote another poem about Mumia Abu-Jamal so that I might sleep again. The poem attempts to grasp my visit with Mumia, to articulate his experience and mine in metaphor, but ultimately the poem deals with the love of books, and the greatest library I ever saw, which I never saw at all.

Prisoner AM-8335 and His Library of Lions
—for Mumia Abu-Jamal

When the guards handcuffed inmates in the shower
and shoved them skidding naked to concrete,
or the blueshirts billyclubbed a prisoner
to wrench the gold from his jaw,
to swirl KKK in his spat blood,
the numbered men pressed their fingertips
against the smooth cool pages of your voice,
that voice of many books,
and together you whispered in the yard
about lawsuits, about the newspapers.

From the battlements
the warden trumpeted a proclamation:
in every cell one box per inmate,
twelve by twelve by fourteen,
for all personal possessions. You say
four blueshirts crowded your death row cell
to wrestle seventeen cartons away,
wrinkled paperbacks in pillars
toppling, history or law collected and studied
like the bones of a fossilized predator,
a library beyond Carnegie's whitest visions of marble.
One guard would fondle a book emblazoned
with the word Revolutionary, *muttering:*
this is what we're supposed to get.

Today, after the hunger strike,
you sit windowed in the visiting room,
prisoner AM-8335: dreadlocks blooming
like an undiscovered plant of the rain forest,
hands coupled in the steel cuffs,

brown skin against the striped prison jumpsuit,
tapestry of the chain gang.

I would rather be beaten, you say,
than this assault on the life of the mind.
You keep Toni Morrison's book in your box
with the toothpaste.
You stare through the glass at the towering apparition
of your library, as if climbing marble steps.

And you say:
Giving up a book is like giving up a child,
like parting with your own flesh.
How do you choose between Beloved
and The Wretched of the Earth.

Your eyes pool.
A single tear is the scarification of your cheekbone,
a warrior's ceremonial gash on death row.
Across the glass a reflection of the guards walking,
small blue men patrolling your forehead.

In the parking lot, I turn again toward the prison,
walls ribboned with jagged silver loops of wire,
and see a great library
with statues of lions at the gate.

Sarajevo I

CHRISTOPHER MERRILL

30 May 1993

The shelling begins long before daybreak. I pull my sleeping bag up to my chin, dreaming of a thunderstorm. But when a shell screams past our house on Koševo Hill, landing less than a hundred meters away, I go downstairs to the living room, where three relief workers have rolled out their sleeping bags. A fourth, Pat Reed, is pacing in the hall. She says it is better to have a floor between us and the Serbs. So I lie in the dark, listening to a weird mixture of sounds: artillery and birdsong. First a series of blasts, then silence, then the birds resume singing.

"A good day to donate blood," John McCormick mutters.

It was a BBC report about a group of Bosnians trudging through the mountains, fleeing the Serbs, that convinced John to give up environmental lobbying and come to Sarajevo. One detail from that report haunts him: a woman recovering from childbirth left her newborn in the snow. But his original plan of working for a children's relief organization came to nothing. And his latest idea—to restore the sewage treatment plant—is unfeasible: the plant is in Serbian hands. If John has yet to figure out how to stave off outbreaks of dysentery, cholera, and hepatitis, he has nevertheless picked up some useful information. On my first day here he spread out a map to show me the most dangerous places in the city. With each explosion now his breathing grows heavier.

"They're slaughtering *kids* up there," he sighs.

Machine guns start firing in the hills surrounding the city, where Serbian shells are softening Bosnian front line positions. The shooting sounds like a hailstorm on a tin roof.

"Fucking Četniks," Vinnie Gamberale grumbles. A soft-spoken Australian with a military background, he has no respect for the armies fighting in Bosnia. "They're a drunken lot," he likes to say. "They have no discipline." This morning even Vinnie cannot sleep through all the noise.

"Did you hear the whistle from that shell?" says Vic Tanner, whose most recent assignment was to Somalia. "I hate that."

"When I look out at the ruins," says Pat Reed, "all I can think is, What a senseless war."

"This is the end of Sarajevo," says John.

"This is the end of something," says Vic.

Vinnie climbs out of his sleeping bag.

"Careful," says Pat. "I'm an old woman. My heart can take the shelling but not the sight of Vinnie in the nude."

At daybreak, when there is a pause in the shelling, I walk out into the haze and sit with John McCormick and Muha, a technician now commanding a squadron of troops on Sarajevo's western front. Muha is off this week, since there are not enough guns to go around. During his leave he studies English. John is teaching him grammar. This morning they are working on prepositions.

"*The book is under the table*," John says to Muha. "Which is the preposition in that phrase?"

There is a detonation nearby. I flinch.

"No problem," says Muha. "That's outgoing."

Since my last journey to the Balkans, the Clinton administration has adopted a feckless policy on Bosnia. The new president has reservations about the Vance-Owen peace plan—and no alternative. One week he fears that "the terrible principle of 'ethnic cleansing' will be validated, that one ethnic group can butcher another if they're strong enough," the next week he urges the Bosnians to negotiate within the framework of Vance-Owen. His campaign promise to lift the arms embargo on the Bosnians and use NATO air strikes on Serbian positions, which during his first weeks in office divided Europeans and gave the Bosnians false hope, is one of many he will break. Tyrants everywhere take note of Clinton's indecisiveness. Warren Zimmerman, our last ambassador to Yugoslavia, is not alone in believing the president has squandered American authority.

"I don't believe we can call ourselves the leader of the free world or the greatest superpower anymore," he said not long ago. "It rings hollow now because we haven't shown the fortitude that goes with that."

The moral dimension of American policy is also missing, as Elie Wiesel publicly reminded Clinton at the April opening of the Holocaust Museum in Washington. "I have been to the former Yugoslavia," cried the Nobel peace laureate, "and, Mr. President, I cannot not tell you something: we must do something to stop the bloodshed in that country." The president has a moral imperative to end the genocide in Bosnia, Wiesel went on to tell State Department officials. The president has a higher moral obligation, they replied: to maintain the liberal coalition he assembled to win the 1992 election. Bosnia is not worth sacrificing his presidency over.

Nor is Clinton alone in acting feebly. Though NATO planes patrol the skies over Bosnia to enforce the no-fly zone recently mandated by the UN Security Council, Operation Deny Flight, at a cost of $2 million a day in fuel alone, is just an exercise in overflying. Three weeks ago, the UN declared Sarajevo and the besieged cities of Bihác, Goražde, Srebrenica, Tuzla, and Žepa "safe areas," not "safe havens," the stronger designation, because UNPROFOR, the UN peacekeeping force, is not prepared to defend them. Bosnian Serb General Ratko Mladić, who herded tens of thousands of Bosnians into the eastern enclaves of Goražde, Srebrenica, and Žepa then shelled them with impunity, happily agreed to the UN's terms: among other things they required the Bosnians in the "safe areas" to disarm. Mladić knows he can overrun them whenever he likes.

Indeed the peacekeeping mandate will remain weak as long as the United States refuses to send troops to Bosnia, a Bush administration decision continued by Clinton. This only worsens relations with our NATO allies, particularly Britain and France, the countries with the most troops on the ground. Like the arms embargo, UNPROFOR is a fig leaf for the West's inability to act decisively, reinforcing the status quo in Bosina, i.e., the Serbian military advantage. Miloscvić's reaction is telling: "I appreciate very much that the United States will not be the world's policeman, to put everything in order in its own view." And the disarray in the international community has prompted Bosnian Croats, supported by Zagreb, to turn against the Bosnian government, overrunning Muslim villages in central Bosnia and besieging the Muslim side of Mostar, the capital of Herzegovina. The plan to divide Bosnia between Serbia and Croatia, hatched by Miloscvić and Tudman, is nearing completion.

Meanwhile, despite American ambivalence about the peace plan, Vance and Owen convened a conference in Athens earlier this month to bring the warring parties together. Milosevic, playing peacemaker now that greater Serbia is within his grasp, persuaded Radovan Karadzić to sign on to the plan. The Bosnian Serb leader did so knowing that his assembly in Pale would reject it.

"This is a happy day," Lord Owen announced at the conclusion of the conference, "and let's hope that this does mark the moment of an irreversible peace process for Bosnia-Herzegovina."

He could not have been more wrong.

Bosnia suffered another blow this month when Secretary of State Warren Christopher, traveling to several European capitals, failed to convince anyone to endorse Clinton's plan to lift and strike. Christopher's lackluster performance surprised European diplomats accustomed to receiving their marching orders from Washington, and infuriated the Bosnians. The Serbs hold 70 percent of Bosnia, and with no prospect of military support from the West the Bosnians launched an offensive three days ago to break the siege of the capital, now in its fourteenth month, where there is still no water or electricity. A Serbian counteroffensive is what awakened us on this first anniversary of the Security Council decision to impose sanctions on Serbia and Montenegro.

Just beyond the small apple orchard in our front yard is an elementary school—yesterday I heard the thwack-thwack of two Bosnian soldiers stroking a tennis ball on the playground. Across the valley, 400 meters away, houses climb the side of a hill; a Serbian shell struck one house last evening, killing eleven. At the foot of the hill, the gutted railroad station; at the top, the mangled radio and TV tower the JNA use for target practice, says Muha. From the backyard we can see the Olympic hockey stadium destroyed by the Serbs and the soccer field that has become a cemetery. The park below us was thickly wooded until last fall, when Sarajevans began cutting down the trees to heat their houses and apartments. New grave markers fill some of the empty space. Above the park is Koševo Hospital, where in the last year more than 20,000 wounded have been treated, the unpaid surgeons operating around the clock, often by flashlight. The hospital floors are streaked with blood—no water can be spared to clean them—and the refrigerated space in the morgue is too small to handle all the dead.

"This winter there were so many wounded they just dumped the amputated parts out with the trash," says John. "When the dogs got into the trash heaps they turned wild."

Muha shrugs. He is a wiry young man in blue jeans, with a patch of black hair growing on his Adam's apple. Shells fly overhead in both directions. "Stereo," he says with toothless grin. "The shooting at night is beautiful." He pulls out a knife and waves it at the hills. "Fire," he commands.

A shell lands by the hospital, striking a building (which houses an army logistical center) at the College of Medicine. Smoke rises into the air. "That's life," Muha says in a steady voice. But a moment later he is crying, "Why? Why no America? Why no Europe?" Another college building is hit. "What are you doing, Četniks?" Muha demands. "Sunday is no good for this."

He points at Mount Trebević, the steep face that forms a natural boundary on the southern edge of the city. "Četniks," he says. He points to the southwest, at Mount Igman. "Četniks," he says again. This he solemnly repeats, turning in a circle under the grape leaves, for each hill and mountain around Sarajevo. "Četniks everywhere."

A NATO jet roars overhead.
"Taking pictures," Muha sighs, "like a tourist."
At the pop of an outgoing round I flinch again.
"It's good," says Muha. "It's good."

Sarajevo was known as the Golden Valley before it fell to the Turks in 1429. From its founding in 1263 the frontier town was said to be blessed with wealth. The surrounding mountains yielded no gold, but merchants from Dubrovnik made fortunes mining iron ore. Under Ottoman rule Sarajevo became one of the empire's major cities, rivaled only by Thessaloníke and Edirne. It was far enough from Constantinople to insure some autonomy, and since it was a crossroads—the Bosna River, from which the country takes its name, has its source just outside the city and runs north into the Sava—trade flourished here. Even Sarajevo's name marks the way a variety of people, settling or passing through, gave the city its cosmopolitan air: *serai*, which descends from Turkish and Persian sources for *inn*, shares a root with the English word *caravansary*.

There is a legend that Turkish forces conquered the town by a ruse, setting thousands of fires in a nearby mountain village to frighten the soldiers in the garrison. The Sultan swept into the Golden Valley from the north, and at the sight of the Bosnians he cried, "*Kos! Kos!*"— "Run! Run!" So the part of the city where I am staying is called Koševo. And the village in which the fires were set the Turks named Pale: to light. A circle closed, then, half a millennium later, when Pale, now a ski resort, became the capital of the self-styled Republika Srpska, from which the siege of Sarajevo is being directed, a systematic violation of human rights, according to international legal scholars. In fact, the Security Council has just established an International War Crimes Tribunal at The Hague to investigate atrocities, including the indiscriminate shelling of cities. The Serbian gunners targeting Sarajevo this morning do not seem to be afraid of being charged for their crimes.

* * *

I am in the bathroom when a shell strikes the building next door. I rush out into the hall, pulling my pants up, mindful of Erasmus, the Slovenian knight killed, by cannon fire, in a squatting position.

On our way to the basement Pat says, "Whenever I go to the bathroom I wonder if this will be the time they get me."

Next to the garage is a small room with a mattress pushed up against the picture window. An open fire is burning from a gas line dangling in the wood stove, heating water for coffee; on the table are freesias and oleander blossoms in a vase. An old woman who has just come in from the street is holding her hand over her heart; her daughter, rubbing her shoulder, keeps looking at her leg, as if to see if it is still there. Another shell lands nearby.

"If that's how they are going to retaliate for every little bit of land we get," says Mirna, a young woman with cropped blond hair and bad skin, "let them just take the city."

Mirna is curled up on a cot, clutching her arms and pouting. She and her husband, Muha, moved into the basement when the International Rescue Committee (IRC) rented the house. A pharmacist by training, Mirna helps her father cook for the relief workers; her mother does the cleaning. She takes a kind of perverse pleasure in the knowledge that her father built the munitions factories supplying some of the shells landing all around us.

"Last night we drank a bottle of whiskey," Mirna says. "And when Muha tried to wake me up this morning I couldn't move, not until I heard that old woman screaming."

Muha smiles at her. She looks away. At the sound of a third explosion, this one less than seventy-five meters from the house, Mirna throws up her hands.

"Every night last summer three shells would hit somewhere in the neighborhood. I lost my mind," she says. "Once I tried to run outside, but my aunt held me back. She asked my father for some water so she could give me a pill. But his hands shook so much he spilled it all over her."

"The good thing is, it will probably be quiet for a while," says Pat. "They usually fire in threes. Don't ask me why. Of course I could be proved wrong at any moment, and that would be that."

The old woman and her daughter bow to us and leave.

"This is the kind of day the Četniks fire two thousand grenades, and we fire twenty," says Mirna. "That's how we spent last summer—each family in its cellar, with the music turned up as loud as it would go to drown out the shelling."

Muha switches on the radio. Sting is singing "Message in a Bottle," after which Vatican Radio broadcasts a Mass.

"It's a big day," says Muha. "I may have to go back to the front tonight."

"We have a friend on an anti-tank bridge," says Mirna. "He can see a Četnik get into his tank, fire a grenade, then climb back out and lie in the sun."

"The old part of town is suffering the most today," says Muha. "It's just the old people there."

"The ninety-year-old man next door has lived though five wars," says Mirna. "This is the worst, he says, because wars used to be fought between armies, and now it's soldiers against civilians. The Četniks will kill a thousand today if we fight back just to show us how futile it is to do anything."

Then the pop of an outgoing mortar.

"I have a feeling we'll be here for a while," says Pat.

"No tennis today," says Slaven, "only grenades."

He is standing in the doorway to the basement. Bosnia's former top-ranked junior tennis player works as a guard for IRC. Before the war, when injuries cut short his playing career, he made good money as a teaching professional in Germany. Now he is a heavy smoker who writes folk songs in his free time. Slaven hopes to work as a musician after the war.

"It will be difficult," he admits. "In Bosnia there may be only twenty thousand people to buy my records. In Yugoslavia there were ten times as many. So I may have to keep teaching tennis: fifty-five minutes on the court and five minutes to smoke!"

His wife and son are living in Belgrade; his marriage ended before the war, and not because she is Serbian. "Too much money, too much girls," he explains, showing me a photograph of the woman who "ruined" his marriage. "My wife's very angry at me."

He looks at my tape recorder.

"I have one of them," he says. "I put it under the bed when I make love to girls."

"Really," I say.

He tunes the radio to hear the news. "One of our commanders has lost his mind," he says after a minute. "They ordered him to stop firing his mortar, but he won't listen. Unfortunately, he's very close to us." He lights a cigarette. "It's bad," he says. "The news is very bad. The Četniks have retaken three positions and Sting is having troubles with his voice."

* * *

Everyone wants to hear about Damir's adventure.

"The other night I was walking home late," IRC's engineer begins. "I came to an intersection, and four cars converged on me, just like in the movies. They looked at my blue card [the identification card distributed to humanitarians and journalists by the UN High Commissioner for Refugees or UNHCR]. 'Why are you working for them?' they said. 'You should be defending your country.' They put me in a car with eight others and drove us up into the hills. In the morning I was digging trenches a hundred meters from the Četniks."

The commanding officer of Damir's work detail has a reputation for never excusing anyone from digging trenches. But by that evening IRC pressure on the government won the engineer his freedom; after all, he is restoring gas and water to the city.

"They took me to see the commander," says Damir. "I thought he would blackmail me or make me smuggle something for him. But he just wanted to know who caused him to spend all day on the telephone, and then he let me go."

Damir's story is exceptional in only one respect: his quick release. The warlords in the army often kidnap men and boys and force them to dig trenches at the front or work on the tunnel under the runway at the airport. Once the tunnel is finished, linking Dobrinja and Butmir, two government-controlled suburbs, arms and supplies can be smuggled into the city.

John McCormick repeats something he said earlier. "They're slaughtering kids up there."

Just before noon a shell lands in the top floor apartment of the next building over, severing the leg of an old woman who lost her husband to a sniper's bullet last month.

Ćiki appears in the doorway, clutching a five-pound piece of shrapnel from the shell, which left a hole in the façade of his in-laws' house. Ćiki is a Serbian architect married to a Muslim; at the start of the war they moved in with her parents, and when she fled the country, he went on living with his in-laws, though they despise him. No one trusts Ćiki, who manages the IRC warehouse: rumor has it he is calling in coordinates for strikes in this neighborhood. He chalks the date on the piece of shrapnel. Muha props it on the table next to the flowers.

"It looks like the devil's tooth," says John McCormick.

Now there are twelve of us in the basement—humanitarians and engineers and soldiers; a housewife, an architect, a tennis coach: Australian and American, British and French, Bosnians of all stripes— Serb, Croat, and Muslim. Ours is an unlikely caravan in a makeshift caravansary. And we have different ways of coping with the terror. John breathes heavily, Pat paces, I record in my notebook every conversation. Vinnie calmly explains military strategy.

"The way the momentum is going now the Bosnians will lose," he is saying. "Arms are getting in, but the Serbs and Croats are getting all of them. I try not to be pessimistic about it."

Mirna goes into the bedroom. "How dark it is," she exclaims—and then there is another explosion.

Pat opens a book called *The Destruction of Yugoslavia* but immediately closes it. "What should you read during an artillery attack?" she says. Not for the last time do I recall the story of the Serbian writer calling his Slovenian friends during the Ten-Day War to ask if they have read his new novel. I clutch my copy of St.-John Perse's *Collected Poems*. Vic has an anthology of erotica in his backpack. His is the better choice, everyone agrees; the ancient link between love and war, Venus and Mars, is proving stronger for the time being than poetry or *The Destruction of Yugoslavia*, which, in any case, we are experiencing firsthand. In fact, we are too scared to read at all. But Mirna has the best answer to Pat's question: "Marx and Lenin," she calls out from the bedroom. "They burn forever."

You cannot talk to John McCormick for long without hearing about John Jordan, the carpenter who came to Sarajevo to fight fires. Last fall, when Jordan learned that Serbian snipers were targeting firemen, he left his home in Rhode Island, vowing to stop them. He knows war as well as fire: the Vietnam veteran is a volunteer firefighter. What he lacks in diplomacy he makes up in passion.

"He's going on raw anger," John McCormick says during a pause in the shelling, "but the UN thinks he's playing with a full deck. In the States, on a handshake, he got three hundred firefighters suits, and now the fire brigade is fitted out with protective gear. That doesn't mean much when it comes to snipers and grenades. They've lost at least a dozen men and thirty wounded."

The shooting begins again. More shells land around us. It is some minutes before the lobbyist can resume his story.

"John Jordan believes this is the first time in history that firemen have been military targets. It's another development in warfare, like targeting schoolchildren or systematic rape. And he wants the UN to provide protection for his men. If they come under attack, UNPROFOR should return fire, then catch the sniper and take him before the world court."

Suddenly water is running from every faucet in the house. The Bosnians jump to their feet and, with shells falling nearby, rush to the garage to collect the dozen plastic fuel containers Vinnie scrounged up for just such an occasion. Soon we are all lined up like a fire brigade, filling and passing containers back out to the garage. A shell has struck a water line in the neighborhood, and there is no time to waste, since there is no telling how long the water might run. We fill the toilets and tubs on every floor. Mirna begins to wash dishes and clothes.

"It's a miracle," she says. "A real miracle."

The longer the shelling goes on, the closer we grow. Vic stayed out after curfew last night, playing a computer game in his office. With no telephone service in the city and his walkie talkie inexplicably switched off, he could not be contacted. John and Pat were worried about him. But when he strolled in after ten, their questions only upset him. He stormed off to bed. Now he apologizes. Meanwhile, Slaven is offering Ćiki cigarettes, and Vinnie, who regarded me with suspicion from the moment I moved in, seems to have decided that I am not all bad.

Vinnie hates journalists, especially freelancers. At dinner one night he attacked them at such length it was difficult for me not to take his words personally. "They arrive with fifty dollars in their pockets and expect us to show them around," he complained, perhaps forgetting that he too had come here without money or backing, relying on his wits—and a false ID—to set up IRC's operation. Only after prodding from Pat did Vinnie reveal another source of his anger: returning to Sarajevo from Split last week, he had lost his place on a UNHCR flight to a journalist from Alaska.

"Stefan Patterson?" said Pat.

"What about him?" Vinnie muttered.

"He's no journalist."

Pat and I had met Stefan (if that was his name) one night in the bar at the Hotel Split. He had been drinking, and when we said we could not help him—he was looking for Martin Bell, the famous BBC correspondent—he got a wild look in his eyes.

"Are you journalists?" he said.

"Why do you ask?" said Pat.

"They just fucking shut my operation down," he said.

"They" were UNPROFOR, and his operation was helping Sarajevans to escape from the city. Stefan claimed to have smuggled out hundreds of Bosnians, Croats, Macedonians, Muslims, and Jews. For the last eight months he had also snuck medicines and 6,000 pieces of mail a week into the capital. He had come to Bosnia with $40,000. He had $4,000 left.

"I've never asked for one fucking nickel from anyone," Stefan declared. "Plenty of mercenaries do what I do. But I'm a stand-up guy. And I'm going to pay the price on this."

His specialty was falsifying documents: press credentials, blue cards, medical evacuation orders; his mistake had been to try to pass off three children as journalists. He had managed to board them and five other Bosnians on a plane in Sarajevo (only peacekeepers, diplomats, humanitarians, and journalists were allowed to travel on UN flights), but by the time they landed in Split UNPROFOR had caught on to his ruse. They took away his own doctored blue card and threatened to arrest him. It was not clear why the Bosnians were allowed to stay in Croatia.

"Here's the bottom line," he said. "Strong people have to stand up for the weak. Who are you? I always knew who I was. This is my time. And I'm only talking now because I got caught."

It was no surprise to learn he had studied creative writing in college. An inventive storyteller, Stefan claimed to have earned his money working on the Exxon Valdez cleanup. With dummied-up ship captain's orders, he was made skipper of a boat responsible for clearing dead animals from the beaches in Prince William Sound. If Hemingway provided the myth for his adventure, Oscar Schindler offered him a model. "I would have been the man in World War Two," he insisted.

"But the first thing to know about refugees is they want to leave, then they want to go back," said Pat, pointing at the old Bosnian men scattered around the hotel lobby. "Look at their life. You smuggled out 236 people? That many go back every week."

Stefan was not listening. "There's a need for people like me who can walk between both worlds," he declared. "There's nothing more noble than trying to save people." He drained his beer. "The Bosnians realize their hope is false. They thought Bush might save them at Christmas. In the winter they held on because Clinton said we'll stand up to the Serbs. Now he tells the Bosnians, 'Fuck you. You're on your own.' And they're tattered. When their soldiers go to the front lines at two in the morning they look like they're walking out of Siberia. They know they'll lose, they're fighting with sticks and stones. Every night they put on a big show with a little gunfire. They have a couple of places around town to launch mortars, but they're defeated.

"The Serbs are brilliant! Like Goebbels. Now they're presenting themselves as peacemakers, and we buy it. But soon, very soon, the Sarajevans will try to break out, and they'll be slaughtered. You should listen to the wind. You can hear them. Do you know what I'm talking about?"

"Who are you working with?" said Pat.

"The Jewish Center," he replied.

"Is that all?" she said.

"I don't remember." He smiled. "But there's a saying, 'When the Jews leave, a city dies.' It hasn't happened yet, but it will. Just listen to the wind. Listen to outgoing. Listen to the incoming."

I needed a flak jacket to get on the UNHCR flight to Sarajevo. (In Split they rent for $100 a day.) Stefan was willing to trade his if we agreed to bring a duffel bag of mail into the capital. A fair exchange, said Pat. And my reservations about the veracity of his story vanished in the morning, when I met him at a bus stop under a palm tree. The sky was overcast, and a brisk wind swept in from the sea, where a freighter rode at anchor. The Bosnians Stefan had smuggled out were huddling together. "We are very grateful to the American," said a woman holding an infant. What ever made him think he could pass off a baby as a journalist? I wondered. But I said nothing. I needed his flak jacket.

The board members do not look happy. The three older men flew in this morning to determine if IRC should suspend operation. From the moment that John Fawcett, IRC's Sarajevo director, brought them into the basement they have sat stiffly on the cot, unwilling to remove their flak jackets and helmets. John and Vinnie, having failed to get a radio message through to tell them to delay their trip from Zagreb, adopt a new strategy: to convince them that it is not too dangerous to work here. When a shell strikes just outside the house Vinnie calmly explains that it landed 350 meters away.

"That's no problem," he says with a straight face. "The Serbs are trying to get a mortar in a house across the valley." He waves in the direction of the house the Serbs blew up last night. "I hope you won't take that to mean we should pull out of here. Safety's our first concern."

He asks Ćiki to describe, in his nervous, halting fashion, a new program: IRC is distributing vegetable seeds around the city. Soon gardens will be growing on balconies.

A NATO jet rumbles overhead.

"Our useless military," John McCormick sneers. "The Powell Doctrine is, We do deserts, we don't do mountains, jungles, or people who fight back."

"It's good to have someone careful at the Pentagon," a board member counters.

"The pundits are always making the analogy to Munich," says John Fawcett, "but for the wrong reason." He is leaning against the door, a thin man with a drooping mustache, and I assume he will defend the board member, because I do not yet know how courageous he is. As it happens, he is one of those humanitarians who will stay in Sarajevo until the bitter end. An unmistakable air of tragedy clings to him (a daughter's death, a broken marriage), which may explain the nonchalance with which he sets the board member straight. "In 1938 the British and the French needed time to rearm," he tells him. "We don't have that problem now. We could stop this."

"What do you know about Banja Luka?" said Stefan Patterson. "Do you know about the fertilizer factory? The pig farm? At night the Serbs pulverize the people they've killed and turn them into fertilizer. Once they took thirty people from the hospital, shot them, and fed them to pigs. What about Sanski Most? Last year the Serbs executed thirty-five hundred on the bridge in Sanski Most and pushed them into the river. Gypsies were brought in as a burial detail. But a few people escaped, and they came here to the mosque. I've verified their stories. You see, the Serbs are learning, just as the Germans did. It's very easy to fight an enemy that no longer exists. And guess what, boys and girls? I'm here to tell you the Germans have a new disguise, but the world isn't listening."

When John Fawcett drives off with the IRC board members, the conversation turns to flak jackets, prize items for the Bosnian warlords.

"My sister wants me to wear one that covers my private parts," Pat says with a laugh. "I tell her I'm not interested in having children."

"I don't know if it's better to be mugged by a Bosnian for wearing one or to walk through the streets without one," says Vic.

"I won't wear mine again," Vinnie declares, "until the Bosnians change their attitudes towards relief workers. They think we're just stuffing the chickens before the slaughter."

John shakes his head. "It's amazing to see a UN armored vehicle going fifty miles an hour down Sniper's Alley, and pedestrians in summer jackets scattering to get away from it. You can imagine what kind of attitude that creates. And of course the driver's wearing a flak jacket."

"I hate the way our jackets keep disappearing from the house," says Vic.

"As long as we have enough for the end," Pat says. "The Serbs are sending reinforcements here from Banja Luka. If they take the airport, it's all over."

"Which means what?" I say.

"We evacuate overland," she explains. "The UN estimates we'll lose 50 percent."

"That's peacekeepers and relief workers," Vinnie adds. "Not journalists."

John repeats a popular saying: "Easy to get into Sarajevo, impossible to leave."

Pat looks at me. "Whatever you do, don't get separated from your passport and blue card. You'll need them to get out."

Slaven tunes his guitar and begins to sing folk songs in Bosnian, English, and German. His nose is stuffed, his voice is raspy, his music is unbearably sad. But while he plays we feel—all of us there in the basement—a kind of peacefulness, until another shell lands just outside the house.

"They haven't had enough bloodshed yet," John says angrily.

Mirna takes Muha's hand. Ćiki lights a cigarette. Slaven sings a little louder.

Late in the afternoon, during a lull in the shelling, I go upstairs and out onto the balcony. Dust hangs in the sunlit air; an acrid smell rises from the ground. Ćiki's father-in-law is sweeping the street with a hand broom; his mother-in-law dusts the window next to the new hole in their façade. Someone is hammering in the distance. A house across the valley, which took a direct hit an hour ago, is burning. A year ago, during a similar assault on the city, an independent Belgrade television station broadcast an intercepted radio transmission of Mladić giving shelling instructions to his unit commanders. "Fire on Velušići," he said, mispronouncing the name of the neighborhood across the valley. "There aren't many Serbs living there." His strategic goal was more precise: "Shell them until they're on the edge of madness," he ordered. Needless to say, I am on that edge.

I lean on the railing, watching the smoke rise toward the radio tower. I am recalling a scene from Czeslaw Milosz's *Native Realm*. Nazi-occupied Warsaw. August 1944. Milosz and his future wife are on their way to visit a friend when all at once machine guns start firing. Pinned down in a potato field, one hundred yards—"a whole journey"—from the safety of their friend's house, Milosz never lets go of the book in his hand, T.S. Eliot's *Collected Poems*, because he needs it.

A bullet whizzes over my head. Through the doorway I dive, and while I lie on the floor, breathing heavily, the Bosnian officer in our neighborhood fires his mortar. I hurry down to the basement, needing the poems of St.-John Perse, which I left under a cot, in the same way that I need to put another layer of concrete between me and the soldiers firing at us from the hills.

"Do you want to hear another story?" Stefan Patterson said. "Ahmići. Vitez. The massacre. I was there, and I know who did it. I've been drunk with the son of a bitch. HDZ? Do you know about the HDZ? It goes right up to that prick Franjo Tuđman. I know who did it, I walked into the houses, I stepped over the bodies. There was a woman, a mother. One of her children was shot, and the blood from her body was splattered against the wall, and they pushed the mother down on all fours, with her head pulled back like a dog, and they fucked her up the ass, and then they poured benzene all over her, and they torched her. Her burned body stayed in the same position, like she was still getting fucked. And upstairs there was a boy, about twelve years old. Do you know what a roast pig looks like? It doesn't have any features. He was lying face up, completely burned. His little penis was sticking up in the air. Half his leg was burned off, six inches from his body. That's how hot the fire was. He had a bullet hole in his left side, and fresh blood was on the ground four days after he was shot. You know he lingered. You know he suffered. I will never be the same."

Dusk. Ćiki returns to his in-laws, a new guard replaces Slaven, and Muha leaves the house without saying where he is going. In the hills above Sarajevo the dead and wounded are carted away, trenches are dug, soldiers keep watch; in the city friends and families gather to remember the dead, journalists file their stories, and UN observers write up their reports. I am in bad shape, having wrenched my back diving away from the sniper's bullet; and when Mirna begins to cook dinner I find I am neither hungry nor thirsty. In fact, I have not eaten in two days, not since taking a sip of water from a bottle Mirna's father then warned me not to drink from. The fever I am running I attribute to nerves. The shelling persists into the night: there are tracers everywhere.

Pat says to me: "You know, you don't have to be here."

"I know," I say.

John and Pat put mattresses in the cluttered cubbyhole next to the garage. John fashions a bunk out of cardboard boxes, and Pat rolls out her sleeping bag. From the shelves I take three suitcases, stack them one on top of another, and lie down on the floor, with my legs resting on the suitcases to take the pressure off my back. Mirna climbs up on John's bunk, where he is lighting a candle. Pat switches on her short-wave radio to hear the BBC World Report.

"The good news is, we have earth on one side and two floors above us," says Pat. "The bad news, there are three barrels of fuel outside the door!"

BBC is reporting 24 dead and 170 wounded in Sarajevo. More than 1,000 shells struck the city today—an average day, by Bosnian standards. Upstairs, the new guard is rifling through my duffel bag; in the morning I will be $100 poorer. John lights another candle. The radio plays on.

Emergence

CAROLYN FORCHÉ

Infancy is what is eternal, and the rest, all the rest is brevity, extreme brevity.

       —*Antonio Porchia*

Inspiration is not the granting of a secret or of words to someone already existing: it is the granting of existence to someone who does not yet exist.

       —*Maurice Blanchot*

I was five months pregnant with my first and only child when we arrived in Johannesburg for what was to have been two years. It was summer in the southern hemisphere, the sky poached by sun and fog, and my first impression was such that in letters home we would describe this place as a "California with slavery." We had come to document Apartheid in photographs and text. Officially, my husband would work at the *Time* bureau, and I would accompany him as wife and expectant mother.

For a brief time, I was able to work with the Soweto parents of detained children, who wanted information about international human rights organizations. Without necessary police permits which were impossible to obtain, we were nevertheless able to enter townships and homelands, led by churchworkers who knew how to avoid police roadblocks, and as my womb swelled, I also grew invisible, no longer attracting police who would not wish to involve themselves with so pregnant a white woman. My husband concealed his cameras, passing me the exposed film to keep under my maternity dress. The images produced from this film would not often appear in the press, however, as the media tacitly respected much of South Africa's ban on "visual documentation of unrest." Those who defied this ban found their employees deported, or unable to renew their visas, as would eventually happen to us. These were the last years of Apartheid, as destiny would disclose, and South Africa was living under what was then called a "state of emergency."

Emergence, I wrote, *emergence: to rise, to come into the light, to rise up out of a liquid in which the subject has been submerged.*

My notebooks filled, as they had in other parts of the world: vignettes, aperçus, bits of utterance. There was world and paper, and each could cross the surface of the other, marking it lightly but indelibly. Writing was my way of knowing what was for me otherwise unknowable, and like Ryszard Kapuściński whom I admired, I preferred to work "in the forest of things, on foot, in the world," which I hoped to participate in, rather than experience.

There was never a question of my giving birth in Apartheid South Africa. The plan had been to drive overland to Zimbabwe when the time came. I'm not sure why I hadn't anticipated the arduousness of such a journey, nor recognized the risks incurred by a thirty-five-year-old "elderly *prima gravida*," electing to receive her prenatal care from obstetricians on three continents, but I had not yet experienced the sea-change of motherhood, holding rather to an image of life continuing much as it was, but with a sleeping baby tied to my back.

Suppressed perhaps were the labors of my childhood as the eldest daughter of seven, tri-folding clouds of diapers, running bed linens through the mangle, stirring Catholic school uniform shirts in pots of starch. Lost were the babies' cries, the slow-thickening puddings and white sauce, mounds of socks to be matched, and toddlers watched never closely enough. Left behind me, Saturday mornings scrubbing foyer and bath tiles with Fels Naptha, taking pails of oil soap to the rows of wooden dining chairs. I made lunch for the "little ones" when I was six, and by seven baked my first loaf of bread. So standing evenings at the open window over foaming dishes I began subliminally to narrate a bearable selfhood. During endless hours of menial work, I spoke to God, who surrounded me, then to voices in books, and finally to fields and sky, where a presence was. Writing, I thought, formed itself elsewhere and passed through me, coming out of my hands. It was mysterious and foreign, but the experience of its making could not be compared to anything else. In the act of writing, there was heightened being, which could be remembered as ecstatic. There was, first, what could be said, and later, the way of saying, which was superior to the said.

My mother and I shared the arduous work of caring for the six children she bore in the ten years after my birth. She would bring the newborns home, wrapped in delicate "receiving" blankets, and I would steal into the darkness of my parents' room to gaze at a new one asleep in the straw basinette, pale-haired and fragile, having made an arduous journey from God's world. My mother was almost a child herself when she began, or so it seems to me now. For reasons that can never be disclosed, she was perhaps ill-prepared for her brood: she had *wanted* many children, but had pictured us all as sleeping infants, wingless, perfect and from heaven. She made *Novenas* to the Mother of God, sang to us, wept, took to her bed, and told us we would understand when we were grown. At night, while I read and wrote by flashlight under my blankets, I heard the clacking of her Royal manual typewriter, and eventually discovered the silvery Christmas box of her poems and stories, some clipped from newspapers, hidden in her mysterious closet among evening clothes no longer worn.

"Join the convent," she would advise me above the din during some shared task or another. So it was not as if I hadn't known.

We left South Africa precipitously on March 17, 1986, a month to the day before my son was born because, among other reasons, we had broken unjust laws, and I was afraid to risk giving birth in jail. Specifically, we were accused of violating the restrictive "Group Areas Act" by having black houseguests, and it was suspected that we were also disseminating "images of unrest" to the outside world. Our arrest, fervently desired by our "Rhodesian" landlady, was considered by our lawyers unlikely but possible.

We left behind the tag-sale furniture we'd assembled into a serviceable household, including the straw cradle with its bridal mosquito net. In my hurry I left some of my notebooks, but these contained indecipherable drafts of poems and so would pose a problem for no one. I don't know if those lines will return to me in a patient hour, but the cradle appeared often for a time in my dreams.

I remember not feeling certain we were safe until the wheels were tucked into the belly of the plane. My son leapt and fluttered through the night. I wrote notes toward poems as we re-fueled in Madagascar, notes which had become, I thought, a substitute for what I had once considered "finished poems." We were en route to Paris, and as this was the last day of my pregnancy when I would be accepted as a passenger on a commercial carrier, my son would be born there. A French photographer, Gilles Peress, had offered us his place, as he would be returning to document "The Troubles" in Northern Ireland, and would not return to Paris again for some time.

So it was that we lived for a year at 11 rue Schoelcher, in an atelier identical to Simone de Beauvoir's, who lived beside us at 11 bis. until her death that April. The two-storey windows opened on a luminous fresco of clouds, and from the little *loggia*, it was possible to gaze out over the graves in the cemetery of Montparnasse. In the armoire, there were books, and little paper soldiers fighting the Franco-Prussian war. At the farm-table, I translated the poet Robert Desnos, many afternoons alone with the windows open, conjugating the *future perfect*, ivy shivering on the cemetery walls, waiting for the infant to come, a Desnos line revealing itself, and I thought: *how is it possible that I am living here*, as if a childhood dream had found an empty theatre in which to mount a small production of its hopes?

By proclivity and circumstance, I had in recent years often been in countries shattered by suffering and war. Why? I might have asked, or well might have, anticipating the birth of a child. Men and women came into my life, offering to teach me things I could not otherwise learn, and I said *yes* out of curiosity, ignorance, a need to please, and a desire to obey God, *for* whom language had first come, in the form of spontaneous prayer-songs spoken when I thought no one listening.

During my childhood, the stars were more thickly clustered, and they whispered. I was not "by myself" often, but when I was, sometimes felt that my "self" opened and left, remaining near*by* as the phrase would have us imagine. If I were in the house at those times, the furniture swelled toward me or diminished as if moving away, accompanied by a crescendo of air against glass, my own breath, some mysterious hum of world. This was a state my sister also experienced and it terrified us both. I would later understand that objects remain where they are, and space dilates between them as time passes. If I were outside, however, in the woods or fields behind the house, this was not so disturbing, perhaps because one does not expect fixity in nature. God was there.

Despite the efforts of the Sisters of St. Dominic, Order of Preachers, to promote the idea of a carceral earth and a juridical cosmos, I imagined rather that the earth was a school, and that humans and other life forms were *already* burning, as light issued visibly from them, and the world, if saved at all, would be saved entire. If this were so, there was work to be done, and I hoped to comport myself well enough that God would give instructions in a form I could understand. Such was my spiritual pridefulness that I appended a request that this instruction not be given by an apparition, which would surely frighten me to death. After many years in the labyrinth of such expectations, it quite circuitously became clear to me that my instructions were to say *yes*.

Until now, until Paris, this *yes* had entailed what I *thought* had been an acceptance of mortality, a willingness to forego self-protection as circumstances required, and a faith in the luminous web of souls dedicated to what may have been simplistically conceived as a teleological endeavor. However, I was now an expectant mother, and what I imagined I was doing was about to change, utterly and for my ever, not in increments but as a whole, not by extension but in essence. This would also happen to my "work," a place-holding term for the labor of nurturing the self-propagation of language.

One writes inescapably out of one's obsessions—linguistic, philosophical, formal, cosmological. During my formative years as a poet (and in my educational *milieu*), "form" was regarded as a container rather than a force, examined for its features and flaws rather than the consequences of its use. The poem was, as Charles Simic once put it, "an antique pinball machine with metaphors instead of balls." It was to be read as expressive of the sensibility of the poet, whose "voice" it conjured and as an unparaphrasable utterance of complex figural interplay and patterned sound. The reader installed herself in this poem, reading analytically or "closely," so as to discern the intricacies of its making, rather as a watch maker approaches the work with spring-pin tool and dust-brush. Thus machined, the poem was regarded as a species of discourse, to be valued for itself and for its utility as communicator of feeling and thought.

My first two published poetry books were written during my teens and twenties, in the mode of the first-person, free-verse lyric, a writing which seemed to me very much to corroborate *le monde vecu*, the lived world. I thought of words as the crystalline precipitate of conscious attention: particular, precise, and resonant with as much "poetic" euphony as I could "hear." At first, mother's college English textbook provided models, and I wrote mostly rhymed quatrains in unvaried iambic pentameter. Later, the nuns assigned the writing of "paragraphs," and after a demonstration which persuaded them that I had not been plagiarizing from an unknown source, permitted me to dispense with the topic-sentence/body/conclusion format, whereupon I wrote elaborate descriptions of natural phenomena. In early adolescence, I was startled to read lined free verse for the first time, which I did not understand but tried to imitate with disappointing results. There were some years of this. When my first book, *Gathering the Tribes*, was chosen for the Yale Prize, I received a letter from its judge, Stanley Kunitz, asking about my poetics, and as I was unaware of *having* a poetics, I wrote of my upbringing, and in response to questions regarding influences, named my mother and grandmother.

In my twenties, God's presence receded, and even the radiant and shivering poplars of my childhood achieved apparent visual stability. The world changed and changed again. I had been translating Salvadoran poet Claribel Alegria, because I was her daughter's friend, and because she was an older woman poet whose work had not yet appeared in English. So it was that when her nephew, Leonel Gomez Vides, appeared at my door for an unexpected three-day visit, I invited him in, whereupon he invited me to spend my Guggenheim year in El Salvador, then still at "peace," a euphemism for the silence of misery endured. I became what was later called a "human rights worker," and this work partially informed my second book, *The Country Between Us*, written feverishly but without the remotest sense of its "political" character or utility. Critical reception in the U.S. was unexpectedly intense and mixed, but my focus was then on the collective work of building a network opposed to military intervention in Central America. Toward that end, I traveled through the United States for three years; later, human rights work would bring me to Northern Ireland, Israel, the West Bank, Lebanon, and South Africa. During the time, I didn't focus on poetics as such, but not for lack of interest.

The safe harbor of France was where my intellectual and poetical life resumed. We lived in that small, sparsely furnished atelier in a manner more conducive to work than I had ever previously known. Wind carried the scent of narcissus from the graves to our open casements. Mornings the knife-sharpener cried up from the street, and like the other women, I raced out to have the kitchen knives honed. Our supply of milk and cheese was kept for a time on the sill, to the amusement of our *quartier*, until we bought a small refrigerator. Daily I wheeled my basket to rue Daguerre market, where I bought unfamiliar species of fish, seasonal fruits and vegetables, aged cheese, young wines, and such things as I have never managed to replace: hard Normandy cider, fresh lavender from Grasse. My command of French was still provisional, however, and I once mistakenly tried to buy two and a half kilos of parsley, to the amusement of *le commercant*.

Aside from domestic pursuits, I spent my days writing and reading [in those days Martin Buber, Emmanuel Levinas, Jean-Francois Lyotard, Phillipe Lacoue-Labarthe, Paul Celan, Francis Ponge and Edmond Jabes], while translating Desnos, because I thought this effort would revive and improve my French. On the day before my delivery I completed the work, discovering on the final page some lines I had inscribed in a notebook during my first trip to Paris in 1977, and thus finding a poet for whom I had searched in the intervening years:

> *J'ai reve tellement fort de toi*
> *J'ai tellement marche, tellement parle*

Telement aime ton ombre
Qu'il ne me reste plus rien de toi,
Il me reste d'entre l'ombre parmi les ombres
D'etre cent fois plus ombre que l'ombre
D'etre l'ombre qui viendra et reviendra
　　　Dans ta vie ensoleillee

[I have dreamed so strongly of you
I have walked so much, talked so much
So much I have loved your shadow
That there now remains for me nothing more of you,
It remains with me to be a shadow among shadows
To be a hundred times darker than the darkness
To be the shadow that will come and come again
　　　Into your sun-blessed life.]

The discovery seemed magical and auspicious, and the next morning my labor began, so lightly that I did not at first realize what it was, and regretted my life-long fear. After twenty-six hours, my son was delivered by caesarean, something I had not anticipated, but that my husband and the doctor had known was likely for weeks. I chose to be awake. I remember surgical lights, instructions in French, the intelligence of the eyes above the masks, a pressure, a sense of being pulled apart without pain, and then a weakening, more oxygen, a rapid exchange among the physicians, then my son held above me, silent and white then suddenly rosy and crying. For a moment, they let me hold him, and when he heard my voice the crying stopped. "He knows who this is," my husband said. I told him that I was his mother, and that everything would be all right. A day later I was given an emergency transfusion of two liters of whole blood. For some reason still unknown to the hematologists, I had stopped making red cells after the birth. There were tense hours, waiting for my body to begin its necessary work again. My son was beside me in an incubator, quiet, alert. I was utterly there, and when I came back I was still there, in a small hospital in Paris with the windows open.

We called him Sean-Christophe, this little one, this Other, who now called me to responsibility, and whom I could neither evade, comprehend nor possess as a *knowledge*. "The child lives," Martin Buber wrote, "between sleep and sleep . . . in the lightning and counter-lightning of encounter." With him I experienced a radiant interdependence of sensation and thought; he was of me but he was not "mine." He was as yet "unknown" to me, even though the egg that had contributed life to him had been with me since my own birth.

On paper in the following months, the "I" of my previous writing receded, having become an emptiness, replaced by a polyphonic and schoenbergian symphony of cacophonous utterance. Absent this *I*, whose selfhood the poems formerly served, words became material and translucent, no longer transparently communicative of the sensibility I no longer possessed. This movement did not entail a repudiation, but was marked by a radical sense of unfamiliarity. Each page began *mis en question*: white, open, each word in all its plenitude marked the site of a wound. Anxious at first, I returned to my notebooks filled with "notes toward poems," and discovered nascent versions of the same phenomenon. These were not notes but the work itself, begun during my pregnancy, and without my conscious collaboration.

This was a work happening *with* me which was not *about* me, having to do with attention rather than intention, a work which would eventually disclose itself as self-altering rather than self-expressive. Rather than writing discrete (individual) poems from beginning to end, and passing them through a sieve of revisionary practice, I found myself attending to the work's assemblage, aware that I was creating a reading-space to be explored rather than received, but in the manner of one caught in a web of consequence. The historical density of the language seemed to limit its play of signification, as the cry of suffering remains a cry. This poetry did not have the function of recording or representing, but rather of attending to the making of its utterance.

The poems I had previously written now seemed the graveyard of possibilities. Tedium had taught me to narrate a self-in-the-world to relieve tedium. *Writing*, older than glass, younger than music, was no longer for me merely the guardian of the past, but a way into the open and the future. Dining the milk-hours of earliest morning, my son nursed beside the two-storey windows filled with cloud islands of a forming world. He seemed to see something I did not see. The ancients thought that light traveled from the eye to the world and this seemed so with him. He was at the gates of language, where only the invisible is obvious. Or so it seems to me now.

Ah, Wilderness!
Humans, Hawks, and
Environmental Correctness on
the Muddy Rio Grande

DINTY W. MOORE

Y ou *can* steer, can't you?"
　　The question comes from Annie, a wiry, energetic woman of about fifty, with graying hair, dark eyes, a craggy face that belies countless hours under the sun. She wears Teva water shoes, neoprene bike shorts, black rowing gloves. I am here to relax, but clearly she is all business.

"Well, *can* you?"

Thirteen of us—three guides and ten paying customers—stand on the Texas side of the Rio Grande, just east of Big Bend National Park, about to launch eight canoes. The canoes sit low in the water, laden with tents, poles, food, paddles, pots, pans, stoves, water jugs, and a cumbrous portable toilet we will come to call "The Groaner."

In their wisdom, the guides have paired Annie and me together, but having sized me up in my old tennis sneakers, cheap T-shirt, and denim shorts, she seems not so sure. Steering a canoe is a dicey prospect under any circumstance, given the vagaries of water and wind; but in whitewater, steering can be life or death. Annie has reason to be cautious.

"You do have a draw stroke, right?" She is sensing my hesitation. "You *do* know how to read water?"

The simple answer is "yes," but the Rio Grande is capricious; a swirling mess of brown river, fast-moving and sided by high canyon and undercut rock. I *do* know a bit about steering a canoe, though not enough that Annie's aggressive questioning doesn't immediately make me forget it all.

The pairing remains, because the guides don't want to hear dissent. Worse yet, from Annie's perspective, I am awarded the stern, where the course is set and corrections made. The canoe's rear seat falls to me not because of gender or expertise, but because I outweigh Annie dramatically.

She reluctantly takes the bow, and one by one, the guides push the eight canoes into the swift current. When it is our turn, Annie commences paddling, paddling with immense effort, paddling at a rate easily three-times more vigorous than the bow paddler in any of the other five tandem boats. She paddles as if her very life depends on it, as if I have already announced loudly my plans to steer the canoe into the first dangerous hole I can find.

The evening before, thirteen of us meet in a motel in Odessa, Texas, home of the world's largest jackrabbit statue. We spend the following morning squeezed into a long blue Nantahala Outdoor Center van, riding across the endless flatness of the Permian Basin, all oil fields and dried out ranches. We drop down through Fort Stockton, Marathon, past the Tinaja Mountains, before we find the unmarked road to our river put-in, at Heath Canyon Ranch.

Aside from Annie, the guests on this trip include a pair of retired Vermont schoolteachers; a Bermuda physician named Thomas and his birdwatching British wife, Lu; Fiona, a young pharmaceutical saleswoman; two other doctors, both traveling solo; Bill, a retired engineer; and me. Both of the American doctors are named Dave, and so earn the quick nicknames Tall Doctor Dave and Bearded Doctor Dave.

To amuse ourselves during our lengthy van ride to the put-in, we speculate on what the trip might bring. Tall Doctor Dave can do better than speculate, however; he is a Sierra Club member, and the environmentalist group's magazine features an article on the stretch of river we will soon be travelling. He has brought the article, "Texas on My Mind (and Mexico on My Right)," and reads us snippets. Author Rebecca Solnit describes our destination as "a slow-moving opaque soup with the occasional clot of foam floating atop it."

In the van, we wince.

In another section, Solnit warns that we will be bobbing through "just about every type of pollution imaginable, including radioactive sediments, industrial toxins, mine wastes, agricultural runoff, erosion caused by mining and logging, and improperly treated sewage."

We wince again, more noticeably this time. Tall Doctor Dave confesses that he almost cancelled the trip and sacrificed his deposit when the magazine arrived in his mailbox, but he really needed a week away from the operating room.

Finally, Solnit writes that the Rio Grande "annually dries up altogether at four points and runs perilously low elsewhere," and details how, because of upstream agricultural diversion, there was barely even enough water for her raft trip to pass through the lower canyons, our destination. She eventually managed to drag her raft out, but leaves the distinct impression that the next party to boat through might get stuck for all time.

The guides mumble something about Sierra Club negativity, but for the most part the van ride ends in silence.

Saturday afternoon, on the river, paddling like a demon just to keep up with Annie, I see no clots of foam, just lots of cool, quick mud-colored water. The sky is glassy blue, the air sweet smelling, the cliffs gorgeous, and the *Sierra* article is forgotten.

Our first campsite, Borland Canyon, is only five miles off, and with Annie's windmill strokes, we are there in no time. We camp on the Texas side, and at sundown are treated to a light show somewhere south in the Chihuahuan Desert. I have never seen lightning quite like this before; sharp blazing bolts running flat along the horizon, as if the sky itself has been turned on its side.

We finish our evening meal and bed down, then brace for the arrival of the torrential rains that follow the lightning. The storm lasts only ten minutes, but for the duration my tent feels as if it might lift up into the sky.

Morning, though, comes with sunshine, chirping birds, the sound of our lead guide, Fritz, shouting "Cawww-feeeee," in a Southern drawl more like a yodel than a yell. Fritz, a woman despite her nickname, will spend the week keeping us alerted to meals, changes in plans, imminent dangers, and bathroom arrangements. The latter will become quite complicated.

We stumble out of our various tents and take good-natured inventory of our aches and pains, and our survival. The brief encounter with nature's fury seems to pick up everyone's spirits.

Except Tall Doctor Dave, who emerges sopping wet. His gear is already a running joke—he came on the trip equipped with more rigging than an astronaut, it seems, most of it fluorescent orange or yellow, all of it dramatic on his 6'4" frame. Though we are paddling in extreme heat, he wears enough layered Capilene and spandex that he would not look so out of place at a toxic chemical spill. He is a walking advertisement for REI, the catalog outfitter.

Despite his high-tech gear, though, it turns out that he somehow left Chicago without his fly—the taut, waterproof fabric square that stretches over a tent to deflect water away from the edges. As a result, the poor man slept much of the night in a puddle.

As most of us eat breakfast and remark on the beauty of the day, he morosely shoves his drenched equipment and saturated sleeping bag into his gear sack.

"If we can get into camp early," Fritz promises, "and if the sun is still out, and if we can find some trees, that stuff should dry out just fine."

It seems like a lot of ifs, but our first full day on the river is filled with such beauty and interest, that even the lanky physician soon forgets to worry.

The immediate riverbank is overwhelmed with bamboo, but the hills on either side host a variety of desert flora—prickly pear cactus, barrel cactus, mesquite, acacia, and ocotillo. The river is a migratory route for birds, since there is very little water elsewhere in this desert region, so we see abundant great blue heron, cliff swallows, black phoebes, Swainson's hawks. Lu, the birdwatcher, calls out the names for us.

The cliffs, and surrounding bluffs, grow more dramatic with each mile we cover. "Drink," Fritz shouts at regular intervals. "Keep drinking." Confined as we are between canyon walls, under a desert sun, we are baked goods—the real danger to our health and well being, given the gentleness of the rapids so far, is dehydration.

Annie, like the tall doctor, comes well-equipped. She wears a nylon water bag on her back, and drinks constantly from a hose that runs to her mouth. I, on the other hand, come poorly equipped, and am constantly filling, refilling, and dropping my empty Gatorade bottle into the mud on the bottom of the canoe, which always sends us off course, and sends Annie into a short panic.

In this fashion, we put seventeen miles behind us, then camp for our second night on a small, muddy ledge. The canyon walls cut us off from all but the faintest sunlight well before the sun actually sets, and since it is October, we light an early fire. Over a dinner of red beans and rice, we joke about Tall Doctor Dave's wet gear, about which paddling duo is slowest, which the most inept, and which duo bickers most constantly—the two Doctor Daves, it turns out, not Annie and me.

Tall Doctor Dave gives me his copy of the Sierra *article, and that night, in my tent, I underline passages, wondering whether Rebecca Solnit could possibly have been on the same river we now travel.*

Solnit bemoans "longhorn cattle grinding the riverbank into dust" and occasionally washing up dead, "further compromising the river." She mentions possible "killer bees," though she sees none, and "acrid, gritty dust that would blow into every crack in a tent and across every open dish, and onto our exposed skin." Her raft washes aground every few paragraphs, something she blames on all the farmers upstream and their wanton irrigation. At Hot Springs Rapid, our destination for the next evening, she even manages to encounter armed men that she assumes are with the Mexican army.

Solnit, it appears, feels threatened every step of the way; I have never seen such beauty in my life. The few longhorn cattle I see along the riverbank are handsome and welcome. To her, they are uninvited despoilers of the earth. The water on which we paddle is an opaque brown, from the mud, but I am nonetheless grateful for the water, for the heat, for the light dust, for all that I've seen on this first day.

I worried in the van when Tall Doctor Dave started reading the article, worried that the trip brochure promising wild and scenic wilderness was some scam. Now I'm worried about Solnit and her readers, and am more than willing to side with the guides and their terse dismissal of "Sierra negativism." I'm not sure what Solnit was looking for on her trip, but I doubt she and I came looking for the same thing.

This apparent contradiction in those most committed to environmentalism has been noted before—the very experience of nature, the deep calm and solid centeredness that comes from being in the desert, on the shore, in the forest, is often not available to them, because they are perpetually anxious. As stewards of our planetary survival, they sacrifice any opportunity they ever had of enjoying the nature they want to protect.

At one point, Solnit worries in print about the Sierra Blanca nuclear-waste dump. The proposed facility is not even open at the time she is writing (nor is it now), and if it were to open, it would be several hundred miles upstream, and sixteen miles from the river. But, Solnit notes, the proximity of a possible earthquake fault line "would add to the radioactive threats to the Rio Grande."

If they build it, and if some waste escapes, and if there is an earthquake . . . well, it could happen. But I'm thinking, no wonder Solnit's raft kept running aground—she came on her trip carrying a heavy load.

We enter the full force of the canyon on Monday, our third day on the river, and the view becomes truly breathtaking—one-thousand-foot sheer walls, castle-like bluffs, undercut canopies riddled with cliff swallow nests.

Equally striking is the absence of civilization. One other party—a couple in a canoe accompanied by a kayaker—pass by early that morning, but otherwise we seem to be the only humans on the river. Nor is there anyone visible on the adjoining land. The canyon walls make the riverbank, what there is of it, nearly inaccessible for about a seventy-mile stretch; that limits foot-travel, and it limits the canoe and raft traffic as well. Once into the lower canyons, you are in for the duration. It takes a commitment.

During the next few days, we will pass two, maybe three abandoned fishing camps, but see no one, just cows and birds. This remoteness from phones, e-mails, faxes, television, and other people, has a wonderfully calming effect. Even the guides eventually relax. We are, Fritz assures us, a "very low maintenance" group of guests.

Tall Doctor Dave encounters a new problem with his size-13 water sandals, but solves it by wrapping the sandals onto his feet with duct tape—fluorescent yellow duct tape. Fiona can barely stifle her giggles.

We stop around mid-day at a site the guides promise us is filled with fossils. "You can look at them, but you'll have to leave them where they are," Fritz instructs. A few trip members quote the ecologist's motto, "Leave nothing but your footprints, take nothing but your memories." Gary, one of the guides and a veteran of this canyon, lets us know that he has in fact seen the fossil field dwindle in the ten years or so that he has been making the trip. "They used to be everywhere," he says. "Now you really have to look."

And so we do, baking under the desert sun, turning over countless small sand-colored rocks. We find a few trilobite impressions, one or two fossilized clams, and a living scorpion or two.

We take nothing.

Or if anyone does, no one's telling.

Gradually, we enter deeper into the high canyon, and the river narrows, squeezing more water through an ever-tighter funnel of rock. As a result, the rapids become more potent, more dangerous.

And, as luck would have it, I am the first of the trip to be catapulted out of a boat. A miscalculation of mere inches and I shoot head over heels into Palmas Canyon rapid, a roiling mess of whitewater and rock. My boat, Annie at the bow, carries through the rapid without me. After feeling a blunt impact on my leg, I wash through as well, into a wide, shallow field of riffles and stone.

The guides are quick to throw ropes and shout lifesaving directives that I can't hear over the roar of the water, but none of this turns out to be necessary. Because the temporary widening has created a shallow area, I simply stand up and walk out. I earn a purple bruise the size of a bocce ball on my right thigh, but am otherwise unhurt.

My baptism becomes the source of much merriment, and we stop for lunch right where I fell, to mark the occasion. The unpacking of our lunch stores results, however, in a swarm of large, hovering, brown insects known as tarantula hawks.

They are wasps, actually, but very large wasps—roughly the size of small hummingbirds—and are given the striking name because their sting can paralyze a tarantula. The tarantula hawk will drag its immobilized victim away, then deposit its eggs in the body of the living spider. Later, the wasp larva will hatch, and eat their way out.

Gruesome stuff, but they don't sting us. What they desperately want, instead, are our slices of ham. The next twenty minutes consist of swatting and griping, until I distract the group by accidentally discovering a different sort of insect, a rainbow grasshopper. This one is shaped like the grasshopper most of us know, but instead of a dull green or brown, it is covered in bright orange and blue mosaic tiles. It does not seem real; the colors are far too spectacular. But it is. The eyes move cautiously back and forth.

I bring the grasshopper into the group on the twig to which it has attached itself, and everyone crowds around. Solnit never mentioned this.

All of us on the trip have varying levels of experience—with rivers, and with wilderness. The guides, of course, have seen plenty, and many of the paying guests have taken two, even three trips a year for many years running. Often, during our meal breaks, they trade information on destinations and guide companies, thinking ahead to their next excursion.

For me, though, this is a first. I have never experienced so much wilderness in my life, never been so removed from civilization, never been so aware of my own smallness. I would often visit Niagara Falls as a kid, and though there is no denying the majesty of those particular rapids, they somehow weren't as impressive as this canyon. The difference, I decide, must be this: At Niagara Falls, we stand back and observe; here, on this trip, we have become part of the canyon, dependent on the flow of the river, subject to rock and weather, benefiting from the beauty at the same time that we are at risk from the remoteness and harsh geography. We have Igloo coolers, canned ham, bagged rice, and bottled water, so we aren't completely linked to the canyon's ecosystem, but for these seven days, we are beyond doubt at the canyon's mercy. The canyon is mighty.

I know what Solnit would say! The canyon may look pristine, majestic, and intact, but all the while small pollutants we can't see are destroying the delicate natural balance. Just because something looks magnificent, doesn't mean it isn't being destroyed. Look at that footprint, over there! It's not just a footprint, it's erosion.

I appreciate her concern, but even a good thing can be carried too far.

Solnit acknowledges at one point in her article, in fact, that her trip companions, most of them Canadians, seem to be having quite the good time. "But then they were on vacation and determined to enjoy themselves," she writes.

What she doesn't seem to realize is that she seems just as determined not to enjoy herself.

I find one passage from Solnit's article almost laughable.

"After passing a herd of goats, I told my raft-mates the story of Esequiel Hernandez, the teenage goatherd who was shot in the back by U.S. Marines in Redford, Texas, not far from where we floated," she writes.

My God, I think—my last thought before I fall asleep—she must have been a hell of a fellow paddler on her raft trip. A real barrel of fun.

Wednesday, our fifth day together, the air turns cold, misty, gray, and the paddling grows harder, thanks to a persistent upstream wind. The trip members grow silent; even the guides recede into their thoughts, right down to the vigilant Fritz, who for the first few days would ask "is there anything you need" every twenty minutes.

The weather is surely a factor in our mood, but I think the "canyon effect" becomes part of it as well. None of us feels quite so significant as we did in our civilized lives. Our verbal cleverness doesn't seem quite so important to share. Who we are, what we own, our job titles— all of these are fairly irrelevant. Our perspective on nature has shifted, but more significantly, so has our perspective on ourselves. What we now see, I think, is closer to the truth of the matter.

Only Thomas and Lu remain a team for the full seven days. The rest of us play musical canoes every day or so, switching paddling partners, trying out new seats, new chemistry. Annie paddles now with Gary, one of the guides, and they quickly push out to the lead. Bearded Doctor Dave and I team up, and I'm finally switched to the bow, which affords a nicer view.

This day of dreary weather also brings a series of impassable rapids, or impassable at least in full boats with mid-level paddlers. To get by, we "line" the boats, which means we stretch out along the rocky bank, brace ourselves against boulders to resist the rushing current, and pull the canoes along one by one, passing them from hand to hand, sometimes hoisting them over rocks too narrow for them to pass through. This is the most dangerous work of the trip. We must take care that the canoes don't come up the line too fast, pinning someone against the rocks, breaking a limb, or worse, forcing one of us underwater where the danger of becoming trapped by the current is great.

After a bit more paddling, we knock off early at a spot called Burro Bluff, one of the highest points within a hundred-mile range. Gunshot thunder is coming from somewhere. Deep as we are in the belly of the canyon, it is hard to tell from exactly where. After our tents are staked and gear stored away, we hike up to the Bluff, past creosote, prickly pear, all manner of thorny plant life. It is a steep hike—better suited for burros, hence the name, than people—but we are promised a stunning vista.

It takes a good forty-five minutes to pull ourselves up the crisscrossing trail, and the view down into the canyon is, indeed, amazing. On a clear day, Fritz tells us, we could see deep into Mexico as well, but the heavy overcast cuts off our view.

We are on the Bluff for no more than two minutes before Fritz realizes the thunder is not so distant, that the storm is close, and bearing right down upon us. "Get your asses down the hill," she shouts, not needing to explain. We are standing on the highest point anywhere near, human lightning rods.

The run back down is a comic stumble, the small rocks catching under foot like ball-bearings, the cacti snagging and scratching, the wonderful view forgotten. The canyon rules all.

I do love the planet, though if Solnit were reading this essay as closely as I've read hers, I suspect she would not think so. I am firmly against acid runoff, nuclear spillage, diverted rivers, and a host of other ecological evils. I believe that men, and women, would do better to cooperate with the Earth's ecosystem rather than run it into the ground. I think myself a reasonable man. But Solnit might lump me in with the irrigators, the lumber harvesters, the cattlemen, and all the others guilty of insensitive exploitation.

After all, I'm only human.

Which is precisely my problem with what she, and many of the eco-extremists—those who seem to get the most notice and thus have the biggest voice in the environmentalist movement—have to say. It too often sounds as if the human species is the only thing separating a contaminated planet from Eden. If the "cancer" we call human beings were to be cut away, they seem to imply, then all problems would somehow be solved. Whatever we do, however we interact with the environment is unnatural; whatever every other species does is as natural as rain. On this trip, we are hauling out not just our garbage and food waste, but our human waste as well, in that big tin box called the Groaner. Yet cows and goats and pigs and birds have been defecating along this river forever. They didn't seem to ruin anything. Tarantula hawks lay their eggs inside of live spiders, so that their offspring can hatch and eat their way out, but that's natural. We, on the other hand, have to apologize for paddling up to the shoreline with our little tents, because we are flattening some grass, and maybe leaving a footprint or two.

What seems most pointless to me is the either/or nature of the argument. The Bible tells us that mankind has "dominion over the fish of the sea, and over the fowl of the air, and over the cattle, and over all the earth," and some interpret this to mean we can do as we please, when we please, without thought or moral center. The ecological extremists, on the other hand, seem to see us as the only species not entitled to interact with the Earth at all.

I don't see much of a future in either position.

Annie has made it clear to us that she shares some of Solnit's views, but with an added gender twist. "Back before the sky gods came, before history," she tells us during one of our snack breaks, "the earth was a matriarchy. There was no question where the power was—women were the one's who gave birth, so they had all the authority. Men had no idea if they even played a part in the birth process, so they had no sense of their own importance.

"But then women put men in charge of metallurgy, and everything changed," she explains. "That's why we're destroying the planet. The patriarchy is only concerned with maximum production. Men have no interest in nurturing, in preserving anything. All the patriarchy wants to do is produce more, more, more."

I am more than a little chagrined, then, when it is Annie who later catches me in an act of environmental misconduct.

So far we have camped on slabs of rock, on mud, on sand, once even on grass, but our Thursday evening campsite is a field of small stones. My ten-year-old daughter, Maria, collects stones, and when I wake up Friday, I can't resist the urge to gather a few of the more uniquely colored or patterned ones to bring her as my return gift. I am aware that this violates the strict "take nothing but your memories" rule, but my love for my daughter overtakes my conscience.

Annie, though, comes upon me as I collect a plastic baggie of pebbles. We are in a rock sea, billions of rocks washed down from the cliffs and unearthed by the river over thousands, maybe millions of years, but Annie catches on quickly to what I am doing, narrows her eyes.

Futilely, I try to convince her of my position. "A few rocks aren't going to make a difference," I say, pointing to the small stones all around.

That doesn't seem to impress her, so I lamely play a gender card, "They're for my daughter."

"You shouldn't take a thing," Annie answers with a chill. "Nothing."

This is the official position of the trip guides as well, but Fritz and her crew have no interest in policing our gear. Thomas and Lu, in fact, have for the last day or so been lifting rocks the size of footballs into their canoe. They are building a fireplace back home, and explain to me that they like to use rocks from each of their many adventure travel trips as architectural accents. Fritz says, "You really shouldn't do that" at one point, but otherwise lets the infraction slide. I don't know if Annie has said anything to them or not.

Later, Bearded Doctor Dave shares his own views of nature.

"Oh, these environmentalists are worrying for no reason," he says cheerfully. "We aren't going to destroy the planet. Nature always takes care of herself. When we get too many people around here, when things get too bad, nature will intervene."

"How?" I ask.

"Plague," he answers dispassionately. "It is only a matter of time before the planet is hit with its next widescale de-population. There are viruses out there we don't know about yet. Nature cleans its own house."

He is a physician, so we listen closely.

Moments later, Lu, reflecting on the imminent end of our trip, says, "My, we have been out of touch for so long. There are people out there wondering if we are still alive."

"We should be wondering if *they* are still alive," Bearded Doctor Dave answers quickly. "It's more dangerous in their world with all the car accidents, shootings, muggings, bombings, than it is out here. Why do you even assume at this point that your loved ones back home are still alive?"

We paddle the rest of the day with little said between us.

It has come down to this:

Rebecca Solnit is convinced that we are marring the planet willfully and with malice. Bearded Doctor Dave, it turns out, shares her views in his own odd way, but is instead focused on the ecosystem's coming revenge, the quiet shy planet striking back with a fury. Annie agrees with Solnit, and in addition, is pretty sure I'm one of the worst offenders. Thomas and Lu are collecting stones for their fireplace, and taking it all in stride. We are, all of us on the trip, dirty, tired, cold, scratched and bruised, and as best as I can tell, the river is doing just fine. No one has seen a single clot of toxic foam.

We have met nature, debated our place in it, and found little common ground.

As for me, I don't object to using a big tin box for a toilet, and I even take my turn carrying the heavy receptacle on and off the canoe each day; and I don't mind carrying away all of our trash, right down to straining out the few grains of rice that fall into our dishwater when we do the pots and pans; I even follow the rule to bag up my apple cores, though I still contend the wildlife would have been more grateful had we left them. I don't mind any of it, really, but I object to the implication that we somehow don't belong, that our every step is unnatural and unwelcome.

As careful as we are, the fact remains that at each of our seven campsites we have squashed some bugs, flattened some plants, inadvertently knocked the needles off a few cacti, and eroded a bit of soil off the muddy banks as we scrambled up with our considerable gear. Do I have to feel horrible about this?

A friend of mine, an Appalachian hiker, has explained to me that anti-environmentalists are guilty of exaggerating the environmentalist position, that the entire environmental movement is being tarred with an eco-extremist brush to make the environmentalists' views easier to dismiss.

This is an old tactic, and I'm sure he is right. I don't mean to contribute to this distortion, but I have Solnit's article in front of me; I'm not making it up. And Annie really said those things. And I gave those rocks to my daughter, and still feel vaguely uneasy about whether I did the right or wrong thing.

My behavior has not been blameless, maybe, but it hasn't been so bad. Yes, I believe in the beauty and importance of the environment, and I believe in protecting it. But I'd also like to be a part of it. Call it selfish if you will, but I'd be quicker to support the preservation of an ecosystem that includes me as a regular member.

I didn't visit the river in a bulldozer, after all.

I came by canoe.

Maps

JULIE CHECKOWAY

The town in which I was born was a tiny place, not much more than two miles wide and two miles deep, and the world in which I lived as a child—the immediate world that spun its tight circles around me—just as small and boundaried. That was the far northeastern coast of Massachusetts, just above Cape Ann, back in the nineteen sixties and seventies, when, before that part of the state became a Boston suburb, and easy hour-long commute down Route 495, it was still a stretch of isolated, sandy-soiled Puritan towns, dotting like punctuation the thirty miles of coast up to the New Hampshire line.

In the early nineteenth century, before the industrial revolution, my birthplace had been a prosperous port. The clinking of coins had echoed in the chandeliered lobbies of busy banks around town. Once, my town had rivaled Boston in a bid to become the capital of the state. Then the wide mouth of the river had silted up, shallowing the harbor, ending water trade. No longer were tall ships launched toward Asia in search of spices, indigo, and tea. Commerce shifted elsewhere then—to Lowell, to Lawrence, to Fall River—and those places, not my town, played out their especial American destinies, growing dim with factories and smoke.

By the time I arrived upon the scene, in the year Jack Kennedy died, my town was industry-less and dying, full of its own dailiness, full of plumbers and clam diggers, dentists and podiatrists. Spunky cheerleaders birthed babies out of wedlock and metamorphosed into the cranky clerks who stood in orthopedic shoes behind the counters of needlework and notions shops. Bright-toothed valedictorian boys became electricians—blue-uniformed, bill-capped, pot-bellied men who attended to the town's domestic circuitries.

In my received world, plans were cut short; schemes and dreams ran out of steam. My father was an automobile mechanic who longed to be a big band singer like Rudy Vallee or Mel Torme. My mother died of leukemia when she was forty-one. Hers was a sudden and unexpected illness. In the winter, she began to bruise and bleed. By summer she was gone. Afterward, for a week, the house rocked beneath us; from the living room and up the stairs wafted the moan of keening mourners. On every mirror lay a bedsheet, preventing us from looking on our own reflections. After that, my father refused to speak my mother's name or to display a single photograph of her. He carried her bureau, full of things, down to the basement, where her sweaters grew moldy and moth-eaten. Dressing for work in the mornings, my father often whistled the winsome tune "The Impossible Dream."

The landscapes of youth do much to shape whom we become. When I was growing up, on the bookshelves of our living room were not the full texts but the *Reader's Digest Condensed* versions of the classics—abridged Melville, Twain, and Dickens bound in faux leather spines—and three editions of the thirty-volume *World Book Encyclopedia* that my parents had begun but never finished collecting by redeeming Green Stamps at the Finast supermarket. We had *Aardvark* through *Aztec*, *Babel* through *Byzantium*, *Cadmium* through *Cathay*, beyond that no more.

When I was a girl, to the west of me was all of America; there were days, I swear, when I could feel the weight of the whole country at my back. To the east, just beyond the mouth of the Merrimack, lay the ocean—slate blue and cold and seemingly endless, an invitation and a dare. In my girl-hood, I used to walk my town from end to end in a couple of hours. I marched alone from the old iron bridge that spanned the river, past grand Federalist houses with their ornate lintels and gables and railed widow's walks, past smaller shingled homes no wider than the hoodspans of two Buicks, arriving at last at the dark stands of green trees and dairy farms of the neighboring town, believing I had gathered on my way—by virtue of breathing—everything there was to know: the smell of hay and sea salt, the stink of mackerel, gossip about local disasters of finance and of love, the perfume of roses growing fat and wild on splintered trellises, the screech of seagulls atop tall telephone poles, the screech of the wheels of the mortician's hearse.

Youth makes an imprint, indelible and certain, upon the table of memory. This imprint is the map by which we navigate our lives. Some of us remain where we are born. Others of us leave the sure horizons of our living rooms and tree-lined neighborhoods, our well-lit childhood streets and grassy playing fields and shallow wading ponds. We seek out broader vistas. We seek the planet.

We carry with us maps from long ago.

* * *

Human beings are born with a kind blindness to first loss. Then loss first enters all of us—early or late; it enters like a knife, reminding us forever after of *can be* and *cannot*, of *is*, and *was*, and *is no more*. My mother's unexpected death did that. It disturbed the known and certain order of my early world.

Psychologists say that the memory is inexact, that we recall screen memories, by which they mean that the mind is a filter on which the truth collects, by which they mean that the story of one's life is an aggregate of shards.

What I *do* know is when my mother died the month was July, the date the Fourth—that noisy patriotic American holiday it would be difficult for a five-year-old to misremember, a day marked by Jimmy Fund parades and white *sisk sisk* of sparklers set off at dusk and afterward the thunderous drone of fireworks, the blazing flames of bonfires. The air that day was thick and the day itself preternaturally still, as if it were waiting for something as grand as the earth's platectonic shift or as minute as the creaking of the rafters in our house or the slow settling of our foundation.

At midday, my father began to call his children into his room: "Your mother is gone," he told each of us—my three older sisters, my older brother, my younger brother, and me. "She's gone to a better place," he said. And with those words, there was the shutting of some door. A door shut on us—my family—on whom we had been before. Perhaps I could say, and be telling the truth by saying it, that the shutting of that door left us in a room in which we would become selves we had not planned to be. A door shut on my father and brothers and sisters, and a door shut on me, and as it did, I began to become the girl who would become the woman who would one day write *these words*, and *this* word. *And this.*

After my mother disappeared, my father no longer wished to look at us, his children. My older brother fled to college. My younger brother left one day with all of his belongings packed in two garbage bags; my father helped him pack. My father told my three sisters—with their almond-shaped eyes and round cheeks like my mother—that he wished never to see them again. Good-bye, he said. And they went away. Then he remarried, choosing a woman with three daughters who looked nothing like his own three older daughters or his dead wife, or like me.

I, alone, stayed on. I looked at my three stepsisters and saw nothing I resembled. And in our house we never spoke of my mother or my sisters again.

After that, only half of me moved forward in the world while the other half stayed stubbornly back, heels dug into the ground, as if one half of me knew something important, something I ought to be remembering. But what was it? I was awake and asleep, cognizant and somnolent. Never again, I vowed, would I fail to note the leafy elms that lined my street; never again would I fail to note the wondrous gusts of wind that whisked within our house's eaves. Secretly and always I vowed to look for my mother everywhere, around corners, in the thin evaporating air, to believe quietly that she must be waiting for me somewhere. Then vowing this, I grew tired, limp as a rag doll and wholly without will.

"Dig to China," my grandmother used to say to me when I was a child. "Dig to China," my mother's mother used to say of an autumn afternoon, sending me off to dig with a teaspoon in the cold and loamy, dark New England soil of my backyard after my mother had died. These were the days when my father still allowed my grandmother to visit our house. Soon he would tell her that she, too, must go. All of them gone. All the women whom I resembled gone.

"Dig to China," my grandmother would call insistently from the kitchen window or an open door, wiping her hands on her apron, peering at me with worried eyes, and dig I would, all afternoon, perspiring in my cap and scarf and parka, my hands numb in my mittens, fingers dull with redundant motion, dull and alive with wanting to reach the world's other side, through soil dry as ash.

Years later, when I went to China searching for the shadow world of Chinese women, I would remember my grandmother standing in the doorway, her brow furrowed with worry.

What on earth will become of that girl? she must have been thinking. *Where on earth will she go?*

This much I know: girls who have mothers inherit from them their womanhood, however complicated that womanhood is, however in need of unraveling. But girls whose mothers disappear can spend their whole lives digging and digging, searching the broad earth for images of themselves in near and distant mirrors.

I was twenty-four when I went to China. It was 1987, a year and a half before the bloodshed of Tiananmen Square, and I was a graduate of the Iowa Writers' Workshop, a fiction writer, a writer of truths thinly veiled. At Iowa I had learned more about writers than writing. There, great writers had thrived for decades, but I shriveled up, more like a seedling gone all bad. There was too much talk about publishing at Iowa, too little straight talk about craft. *Street smarts, thick skin, knowing to whom in New York to send your Christmas cards*, a classmate there once advised me. *That*, she said, swirling the ice in her enormous glass of gin, *is what a writer really needs*. A professor of mine once announced that a big-name editor from a big-name literary magazine was flying into town. *You ought to go to the cocktail party and meet the guy*, the professor told the young men and women around his seminar table. *You never know*, he added dryly. *You might have to go to bed with him someday.*

At Iowa, each time I typed a word on my old Smith-Corona I could not help but imagine a roomful of picky critics breathing down my neck. Instead of writing, I fell in love with Will Harrison, fifteen years my senior, a brilliant graduate student who was supposed to be writing his dissertation on the influence of Asian poetry on American poets. We were a matched set, he and I, both blighted by writer's block. We set up house together in a brown bungalow on a cul-de-sac called G Street. We planted a garden. I learned to cook. It seemed to me that Will drank too much—wine with dinner every night, just enough to conk him out. After a while, whole months passed without our making love. At night I fell asleep in front of the blue light of the TV. I watched the Weather Channel, with its warm and cold fronts skimming across America, its jet stream rising and falling, dependent on the season.

In winter, the winds whipped up and chilled me. In summer, the deep blue skies blackened up like clockwork each afternoon, and I searched the horizon almost hopefully for the fickle fingers of tornadoes that lurked at the very backs of storms. At twilight I walked across the bridge that spanned the modest expanse of the Iowa River and I wondered when my apprenticeship as a writer in the real and wider world would begin.

Instead of taking workshop courses, I found myself drawn to the study of anthropology. I met Margery Wolf, an anthropologist who had done definitive fieldwork on women in China and who had written a book on the subject called *Revolution Postponed*. Margery inspired something dormant in me to come alive. She spoke about the lot of Chinese women, the misogyny they had to face for centuries, and more importantly the secret networks which they had established amongst themselves. Rural women met down by the river where they washed their clothes, Margery said. In secret, the women discussed their husbands, fathers, sons.

In the evenings, according to Martin Yang, an anthropologist whom Margery cited, men would go off to the threshing grounds. At home, women would rush through their chores and head out not to threshing grounds but to the open spaces in the lanes between their homes. Later, they would rush back home, Margery said, so that the men could neither spy on their women's gathering nor learn what it was they had to say.

"The shadow government," Margery Wolf called the secret meetings of Chinese women. And the place where the women met I thought of as *the shadow world,* where women saw each other's true faces, where they told their secrets and were unafraid.

When I finished at the Iowa Writers' Workshop, I was rudderless as a skiff at sea. I needed a teaching job but had not published yet. Some of my classmates had taken positions at American College Testing, just on the outskirts of town, where, under bluish fluorescent lights, they spent their days writing reading-comprehension questions for standardized examinations. Others had taken on adjunct teaching positions that offered heavy workloads, no benefits, and measly pay. Will had little chance for a teaching assistantship at the university. He had taken too long on his dissertation, and his chances for support from the department were slim, diminishing. I bit my nails and worried hard.

"China," I said one night.

He looked up at me from his desk, his eyebrows curled like face-down question marks.

"Let's go," I said.

I pointed to the piles of empty legal pads upon his desk and mine. "It will be good for us," I said, waving in front of him a classified ad that I had found in the back of a catalogue. The ad read: *Teachers Wanted in the People's Republic.*

He nodded. *Yes.*

I arranged for us to serve as visiting professors for a year at a teachers' university in an industrial city four hours south of Beijing.

Soon it was summer in Iowa. In the Midwest heat, we packed up our books, shipped them early on a freighter, so they would arrive when we did, in the autumn. I tacked a map of China to our bedroom wall. I traced the lines of rivers and mountain ranges with my fingers. I plotted out a course.

Friends asked me *why China?* and I told them that digging to that country was something I had dreamed of when I as a child.

From Margery Wolf I had learned that China has a long history of casting its women in shadow. Ancient Chinese folk wisdom has it, for example, that all women possess a power called *nu hua* or female peril, by which they are able to drive men loony, kill off whole seasons of rice and cabbage, topple sturdy governments. Standard Chinese histories chronicle the tales of wily emperors' wives who, it was said, single-handedly felled whole dynasties. Confucius himself proclaimed that the very harmony of the universe, the bowl of heaven and the curve of the earth, depended upon the submission of dark feminine *yin* to the force of light—masculine *yang.*

Secretly lock the postern gate. Restrict her to courtyard and garden. Then misfortune and intrigue will pass you by, went the traditional advice given to Chinese bridegrooms. Foot-binding, a practice introduced in the tenth century, ensured that women could not venture far enough from home to cause much *ma fan*, trouble. *Why must the foot be bound?* went a Yuan dynasty rhyme. (*To prevent barbarous running around.*) According to the ancient Precepts for Women, a Chinese woman must cultivate "The Four Virtues": compliance, reticence, cleanliness, and domesticity. For centuries, women in China lived in a reticent, clean, domestic world, silenced and unseen. The ancient ideograph for "woman," meant, literally, a person shut behind a door.

When Mao Zedong came to power in 1949, he proclaimed his desire to eradicate feudalism from China and he made the liberation of women one of the cornerstones of his political agenda. Mao's 1950 Marriage Law forbade arranged and mercenary marriages; it outlawed child marriages, abolished polygamy and concubinage, and granted women the right to initiate divorce. Mao encouraged women's literacy. He welcomed women into the workforce as valued comrades. But the full liberation of half of China's population was a distant and future goal, Mao cautioned. Feudalism had deep and tangled roots. Women's emancipation was to be a methodical, intricate process taking place in stages over time. "To liberate women," Mao cautioned the Chinese people, "is not to build washing machines."

In 1987, more than a decade after Mao Zedong's death, great change was afoot once again in the People's Republic of China. The hysterical political rhetoric of the Cultural Revolution had been supplanted by the free-market frenzy encouraged by a reform-minded Deng Xiaoping. In the countryside, Mao's communes were dissolving, and farmers were free to reap the harvest of their own initiatives. In cities, workers in record numbers rejected their "iron rice bowls," or state factory jobs, and, with the blessing of Beijing, sought their fortunes in the sphere of private enterprise.

In Deng Xiaoping's so-called "market economy with socialist characteristics," China's 200 million women seemed to be more liberated than ever before. Women cast off their baggy unisex Mao suits and donned tailored skirts and high heels. They put down Mao's Little Red Book of political proscriptions and picked up fashion magazines advising them on everything from the correct application of eye makeup to means of bust enhancement. Rural women flocked to urban centers and to China's special economic zones, hoping, as nearly everyone in China did at the time, to get rich quickly and gloriously.

But Deng's economic reform brought about a backlash against

women. In a profit-hungry PRC, Chinese women were nearly universally considered, as they had been in the days of Confucius, "goods on which one loses money." In state-run factories, women were channeled into inferior jobs. They brought home substantially less money than their male counterparts for comparable work. In privately run factories, executives, in an effort to get an edge against their competition, did away with maternity leave and on-site day care. Women were forced to retire several years earlier than men. Across China, female infanticide and spousal abuse was on the rise. Women's literacy was on the decline; according to official government figures, in the late 1980s, 70 percent of China's women could neither read nor write. For the equivalent of two thousand U.S. dollars, Chinese women were being kidnapped and sold into slave marriages.

As the date of my departure for the PRC neared, I held a yard sale, sold my furniture. I let my backyard garden go wild, the rhubarb shunting up unchecked, the fuzzy leaves as broad as palm fronds, the tomatoes dropping heavily off their vines, the Boston lettuce bolting until it spouted milky juice.

Will studied Chinese at an institute in Indiana.

I took language lessons in Iowa City from a graduate student who hailed from Shanghai. Three nights a week and throughout the days I studied flash cards, listened to tapes. I repeated words and phrases and tried to sing the four clear tones of Mandarin, aware that only when I arrived on Chinese soil would I begin to truly learn this language of notes and signs.

While waiting to leave, I took up weaving. I bought a four-harness treadle loom, which arrived by parcel post from a mail-order company in New Hampshire. I ran my hands along the broad and oaken beams of the loom. I pressed the pedals, listening for the sensuous rush of the waxed ropes in the sanded pulleys. I wove with ragged wools and silks; I worked in vivid reds and blues and greens. Sometimes—on a whim—I wove a length of ribbon in.

"Every story is two stories," the writer Grace Paley once told me. "Every story is two stories," she said, meaning: *the story of the story and the story of the storyteller.* Two strands.

Looking back, I see how the writer of a memoir is a kind of weaver. And I remember how, before I left for China, a bolt of cloth grew in my hands, strand by strand by patient strand, each pass of the bobbin a small advancement in the pattern, the finished cloth not unlike a story one might tell—the combination of the warp and weft of different threads.

Murder

BARRY LOPEZ

In June of 1964 I left a friend's home in Santa Fe at dawn, drove north through Abiquiu, where Georgia O'Keeffe was then living, passed slowly through a lovely valley high in the San Juans that holds the town of Chama, and turned west for Durango. I crossed the Utah border west of Dove Creek, and ate lunch in the Mormon stillness of Monticello.

I was twenty, headed for Wyoming to work the summer on a friend's ranch, wrangling horses. And I was innocently in love, as perhaps you can only be at that age. The young woman lived in Salt Lake City. Anticipating each encounter—with her, beginning that night in Salt Lake, and the months afterward working with horses in Jackson Hole—made the sense of covering miles quickly in good weather an exquisite pleasure.

The highway north from Monticello runs ribbon-smooth through bleak, wild country. When I left the café I fell back into a rhythm with it. The performance of the car, the torque curves through all four gears and so the right moment to shift, was well known to me. Flying down U.S. 191 and double-clutching out of the turns eased the irritation that had grown in me in Monticello, under the stares of café patrons. "No, sir, we don't serve any coffee," the waitress had said. And, "No, sir, we don't have any ashtrays. We don't smoke here."

I rifled over the road course, holding a steady seventy through the turns and rises. The only traffic was a pickup or a car, sometimes a tractor-trailer rig, every six or eight minutes. I had a Ruger Single-Six .22 magnum pistol under the seat. In a leather case in the trunk was a rifle. In those days in that country a young man traveled with guns as a matter of course, with no criminal intent.

The two-lane highway passed clean beneath the hiss of new tires. Wind coming through the windows vibrated softly in the interior of the car. I remember the sight of the chrome tachometer, fitted to the steering column, gleaming in the sunshine, the spotless black nap of the floor carpets. I can recall the feel of the rolled seat covers under my thighs. In the seat opposite me sat my dog, a mongrel coyote I'd caught in the woods of southern Michigan as a pup. We'd driven the country for days at a time together, trips to New York City, to Helena, to Louisiana, the wind roaring at the windows, the tires whispering and thudding over the rain-slicked concrete roads, the V-8 engine with its four-barrel carburetor, guttering through straight exhaust pipes.

A small, nondescript hill rises just south of Moab. The road climbs its gentle southern slope for several hundred yards and then falls off so abruptly a driver headed north confronts for a moment a blind spot. I hit the hill at probably eighty, imagining details of the evening ahead with Jan in Salt Lake. I saw a police car making a K-turn in the road a hundred yards in front of me as I came over the rise. The steering wheel seemed to stiffen, to resist in that moment, but that is likely a false memory. I never touched the horn, there was no time, no point. I focused on missing him, as he continued to back up slowly across the midstripe. I hurtled past on the left, going off the road in a spray of sand and dirt and whacking sagebrush with the rear fender as I tried to pull the car back on the road. It being the police, I thought it best just to keep going. His barn-size stupidity was a flat trade-off, I figured, with my speeding. I got the skidding car back up on the road and drove on to Moab at a touch under the legal sixty, with the police cruiser right behind me.

I slowed to the designated thirty-five at the city limit and a few blocks into town turned in to an A&W Root Beer stand. The police car went by. I tried to detect from the corner of my eye without turning my head whether he was turning his and staring at me through his sunglasses. He was. I continued to study the hand-scripted legend on the menu board in front of me. When the waitress came over I ordered a hamburger and what many people then called a black cow, a root beer float.

The air beneath the awning where I was parked was still and cool. I could feel the sweat drying on the back of my thighs. I got out and took the dog without a leash to a patch of dry grass and weeds in the harsh light at the edge of the parking lot. I noticed two young women there while I waited, sitting in a black 1960 Thunderbird backed up against a fence.

I ate my lunch slowly, scanning my Utah map and scrutinizing its detailed diagram of the streets of Salt Lake. I had the radio on. From time to time I glanced over at the two women in the Thunderbird.

They had a child with them, a boy just a few years old. The women and I made eye contact once or twice. I smiled.

It occurred to me the cop would have had a tough time trying to force a ticket on me for speeding.

The sound of a door closing made me look up. One of the women in the Thunderbird, the one on the passenger side, had gotten out and was walking over. She looked seventeen or eighteen. She was very pregnant. My dog sat still in her seat as the woman approached the window. She leaned down and looked in, but didn't say anything. I reached for the dog and at my touch she turned and stepped nimbly into the backseat. Without a word the woman opened the door and got in.

"Hi," I said, conscious of being very casual.

"You live around here?" she asked.

"No. I'm coming from Indiana, from school there."

"Where're you going?"

"Wyoming."

She stared ahead in silence. I remember seeing the sweat beaded up on her small hands, her stout fingers, the maternity blouse billowing in a pink-and-white pattern over her lap.

"What do you think you might do for a woman?"

"What's that?"

"For a woman that might be in trouble, might have lots of trouble."

In the cool air under the metal awning, out of the glaring desert light, her language seemed dreary, detached.

"What kind of trouble is that?"

"Family trouble."

"You need money?"

"Would you kill my husband?"

The ebb of my nonchalance in this conversation was now complete. I sensed a border I did not know.

"I've got a gun over there in that car. He's in a garage outside of town, working on his car. All you have to do is walk in there, walk right up to him, and shoot him. He won't know you. There's no one else there. No one could hear."

I stared at her, her pallid cheeks, her full breasts.

"I'm not a liar. He's there. And I want to kill him."

She turned halfway to me, for the first time, no longer speaking to the windshield. Her milky blue eyes were both desperate and distant.

"He's working on his car. He doesn't care." She inclined her head. "That woman over there? Her sister's gonna have his kid too. I'd kill him myself, but I can't. I'd screw up. He'd beat me up so bad, I'd lose the baby."

I was afraid to say anything, make any movement. Her voice edged on hysteria, on laughter.

After a few moments of my silence her hand went to the door handle. "If you want to do it, no one would know. You could throw the gun away. I wouldn't say anything. I don't even know your name."

When the stillness hung on she said, "Well, forget it. Just forget it. Forget I even got in here." She got out, closed the door firmly, and walked away, reaching across to her right temple with her left hand in a prolonged, deliberate movement to sweep her blonde hair off her face, a movement that carried her across the sunlit lot to the Thunderbird. She sat there sullen and tight-lipped. When the boy came to her from the backseat she shoved him away, as if he were a younger brother she had to baby-sit.

I paid for my lunch and left. The peculiar tone of muscle in my young body, the quickness of my hand reflexes that made driving seem so natural, so complete a skill, was gone. I drove slowly north through town. The same officer sat austerely in the same car, parked just past the bridge over the Colorado River at the edge of town. I drove under the speed limit for more than an hour. I passed one or two buildings that could have been garages but there was no sign of life.

I crossed the Green River and turned north for Price on U.S. 6. After a bit I pulled over and let the dog out. She bounded with exuberance through the sage and, a time or two, stood poised, looking back at me. I leaned against the car, smoking a cigarette. I couldn't remember if I'd loaded the pistol the night before when I was putting things in my car in Santa Fe. I thought of being with Jan that night, and suddenly impatient, whistled for the dog with exasperation.

Going Back to Bisbee

RICHARD SHELTON

It is July 20, 1989, early afternoon, monsoon season in the Sonoran Desert, and I am going back to Bisbee. As I drive east out of Tucson, the temperature is 106 degrees and the humidity must be in the forties. Huge white thunderheads are building up in the south, drawing moisture from the Gulf of Mexico, but they don't look very promising yet. Too white and too far apart. Between them the sky is cerulean under a fierce sun. The heat doesn't seem to have anything to do with the sun. It comes up from the ground and just hangs there, almost solid. Perhaps the clouds mean a storm later in the afternoon, or perhaps they will just drift north like idle promises. No blue-black horizon yet. No thunder. But the breeze is from the southeast, what there is of it, and a monsoon can move in quickly at this time of year, especially late in the afternoon.

The desert could certainly use a storm right now to cool things off and lower the humidity. I am reminded of what somebody said about a fundamentalist fire-and-brimstone preacher. "It's not the heat so much as the humility." I've been on the road only a few minutes and already my backside is melting into the car seat. The sane part of me says, "Stop! Roll up the windows and turn on the air conditioner!" The insane, masochistic part of me answers, "No! You will be leaving the desert floor soon, climbing out of this furnace and into the rangeland where it will be cooler. Don't be a pantywaist." I engage in these dialogues with myself about the air conditioner quite often. They have as much to do with the history of the van I am driving as they do with my own warped point of view.

The van bug bit me a few years ago when Rosalie Sorrels, the folk singer from Idaho, came to visit us, driving her elderly van, which she had named Mabel Dodge. Rosalie and Mabel Dodge had been batting around the country doing concerts. In fact, Rosalie had been batting around the country so much that she was known as "The Travelin'

Lady" from the title of one of her best known songs. The romantic notion of a home on wheels attracted me at once. Why couldn't I get a van and bat around the country doing whatever it is I do, and I wasn't exactly sure what that was, but the idea felt good. So my wife and I started looking for a used van. I didn't want any furniture or fancy trappings, just room to stretch out in. With a sleeping bag and an ice chest I would be fine.

And soon, on one of her trips to West Texas to visit her family, my wife found the almost-perfect van. She called me from Ft. Worth.

"Happy birthday. I bought you a van."

"Great! Wonderful! What color is it?"

"It's the color of your eyes." My wife can be a little romantic herself sometimes, especially when she has just driven a hard bargain.

"Good lord! I don't want a red, white, and blue van."

"No, it's blue all over, inside and out."

It was a 1978 Dodge with one previous owner and a considerable number of miles on its odometer. It had front seats and a bench across the back and was otherwise devoid of furniture. But it was gloriously, decadently carpeted—floor, walls, and ceiling—with a deep shag, light blue carpet. Sleeping in it, I was soon to find out, was like sleeping in a blue womb. Otherwise its personality was masculine. I named it Blue Boy.

Other than a Rickenbacker owned by my grandparents, which was an elegant antique when I was a child, Blue Boy is the only automobile for which I have ever felt genuine affection, and we have had many adventures together from Canada to the tip of Baja California and from the Atlantic to the Pacific. Blue Boy is badly faded now, like my eyes, from years of Arizona Sun, and he has a gash near the rear where my wife backed him into a paloverde outside of our garage. (When asked how it happened, she said, "God moved a tree," and she sticks to that story.) He is a little loose in the joints and has many rattles as the results of some of the worst roads on the North American Continent but he continues to purr along like the perfect traveling machine he is.

But Blue Boy had one peculiarlity which was linked to the fact that he had lived all his previous life in West Texas, although I didn't make that connection until years later. His motor ran cool enough, even with the air conditioner on, until the outside temperature rose above one hundred degrees. Then he began to overheat when the air conditioner was on. From the depths of my ignorance of automobile mechanics, I assumed that Blue Boy's engine was not powerful enough to take on the added burden of the air conditioner at such high temperatures, and I simply got used to driving without the air conditioner most of the time, and always when the outside temperature was very high. I took a certain macho pride in being able to "tough it out," as my father used to say, and had a tendency to sneer at the occupants of other vehicles as they rolled down the highway all sealed up in their air-conditioned capsules.

This went on for several years until last summer when we took a trip from Tucson to the West Coast, during which my wife wept, complained, and threatened to faint nearly all the way to Los Angeles. She flew home and announced that she was never going anywhere in Blue Boy again in the summer. My wife is resolute. When she makes up her mind, she makes up her mind; and when she issues an ultimatum, there is no getting around it.

The situation called for drastic action. So I decided to take Blue Boy to a mechanic to see if anything could be done about his peculiarity. The upshot was that my diagnosis had been wrong. Blue Boy's engine was quite powerful enough—how could I have doubted? But his radiator was all clogged up, and his circulatory system couldn't cool the engine properly. His radiator was clogged because his previous owner had put West Texas water in it, and West Texas water is loaded with minerals and alkali and God knows what, causing deposits to build up to the point that the radiator was functioning at less than half its normal capacity. I gave Blue Boy a new radiator and his peculiarity disappeared. Now he can go up the steepest hill in the Southwest in August and never overheat.

But I am a creature of habit and stubborn in my own way. I have driven for so many years in the desert without an air conditioner that I still rarely use it unless I have passengers—one passenger in particular. I have the notion that in order to see the landscape properly one must experience the temperature as well. I agree with one of my dogs who keeps telling me, "What good is it to travel if you don't slow down enough to smell the country?" But right now, as my van pulls away from the sunset and my bottom slowly melts into the driver's seat, I would like to see and smell and feel a good slap-dash Southern Arizona monsoon storm. I think Blue Boy would enjoy it too.

I love the Sonoran monsoons when they finally arrive. They are usually brief, violent, and incredibly dramatic, with enough thunder, lightning, and hard-driven rain to make life exciting, even precarious. After the clouds build up into great white cathedrals, as they are trying to do now but without much success, the desert turns suddenly dark and still. The light is dim, green, and eerie. Everything seems to be holding its breath, waiting. The air becomes languid, palpable with humidity. Low thunder begins to roll around in the distance, almost comforting after the unnatural silence. Then somebody up there starts flipping light switches. Enormous panels of sheet lightning go on behind the clouds, hold for a few seconds, then go off. The effect is totally theatrical, as if some wizard lighting technician were playing bravura pieces on the control board offstage, never quite repeating the same brilliant display twice.

Then all notions of theatricality are destroyed and things get serious. The entertainment is over but the show has just begun. And if you are in it, that is, if you are out in it and cannot get out of it, you will never forget it. Suddenly there is a wrenching, shrieking explosion as a lightning bolt connects with the ground nearby. It sizzles, pops, and sputters. The air smells strange, pungent with ozone. Another bolt strikes, and another. The desert has become an exploding mine field. Thunder breaks directly overhead, so loud and close you can almost see it, as if a huge chasm had opened in the clouds. The vibration makes you duck and nearly knocks you off your feet. Reverberations rattle away in the distance. More bolts of lightning strike—to the left, to the right, straight ahead. The temperature is plummeting. It can drop more than thirty degrees in a few minutes. In the flashes of lightning you see paloverde and ocotillo lashing in the wind, which seems to come from all directions at once. Cottontails huddle at the base of a greasewood, ears down, noses twitching, black eyes huge and shining with terror. A young javelina, the peccary or wild boar of the Sonoran Desert, panics, breaks from shelter, and runs wildly down the arroyo, snorting at every step. The sharp crack of thunder, the spluttering pop of lightning, and the screaming of the wind are reaching unbearable levels. The world has gone mad.

Almost imperceptibly under all this, then growing louder, another sound like the tattoo of a million tiny drums rises to a crescendo. Rain. But "rain" is not the right word. Rain is what comes to the Sonoran Desert in the spring, if we are lucky. It is gentle and civilized. But this is neither gentle nor civilized—it is brutal. Huge drops in tight formation strike the earth with such velocity that they often bounce four feet in the air. Thunder and lightning continue, but now the dominant element of the storm is water, which seems to be almost solid, not so much falling in drops as poured from some vast container and driven by the fury of the wind. Water is everywhere. There seems to be no air left to breathe. And it is cold, the cold plunge after the steam bath. It comes down much faster than the earth can absorb it and runs in sheets over the desert pavement, the thin layer of small stones and gravel which holds the earth in place and without which the desert soil would quickly be carried away.

Within a half hour after the first real clap of thunder, the storm is usually over, leaving the desert bedraggled but the air soft and aromatic with the smell of wet greasewood. The danger, however, is not over so quickly. Flash floods can race down arroyos and across roads with a bore like that of the sea rushing into a narrow inlet at high tide. The floods reach their peak after the storm is over and often inundate low-lying areas far downstream. Midwesterners quote the old saw: "If you don't like the weather, just wait a minute." But we could change that to a more sinister desert version: "If the lightning doesn't get you, wait for the flood."

Both lightning and flood do get some of us every year. Prominent signs—DO NOT ENTER WHEN FLOODED—are posted where arroyos cross roads, but some people choose to ignore them, and often they drown. The water crossing a road might look shallow, but the current can be extremely strong. Many years ago a friend who was on his way to our house for dinner in his VW Bug entered a seemingly shallow arroyo after a brief summer storm. He discovered that his vehicle had a watertight bottom. It carried him on a fast half-mile boat trip down a twisting, roaring arroyo before it bumped, like the basket carrying Moses, into a safe harbor. By that time the Bug was a wreck and so was our friend. One of the first things I remember seeing when I arrived in Tucson in the late fifties was a pickup truck stranded in about eight feet of water in a downtown railroad underpass. Three people were on its roof, screaming for help. Before they could be rescued, one of them was swept into the current and drowned.

According to Southwestern tradition and folklore, the *chubascos*, or monsoon storms, are supposed to begin two days after Summer Solstice, on June 24, or San Juan's Day. But they are usually late and some years seem to have great difficulty getting it all together, teasing for weeks and then finally materializing in late July, as they have this year. But how fitting that they should be associated with San Juan's Day, which isn't the day of St. John the Apostle, but of Señor Juan, John the Baptist himself, who said, "I baptize you with water." And he didn't mean he was going to sprinkle a little on. He went into the desert and lived on locusts and honey, but we associate him with rivers and with wrath, a fierce and dramatic wrath. I never witness a chubasco without thinking of him, of his cleansing fury and his promise for the future. And when I see a bona fide member of the "generation of vipers" beginning to crawl with all haste toward higher ground as a storm approaches, I chuckle to myself and say, "A wise move, Mr. Pharisee. A very wise move. Señor Juan wants to baptize you good."

Since few desert creatures like to swim, although a remarkable number of them can if they have to, most of them head for high ground before a summer storm. We live in the Tucson Mountains. Our house sits on the saddle of a low hill with an arroyo on either side. It did not occur to us when we built the house many years ago that the hill on which we built undoubtedly served as a place of refuge when the arroyos became torrential rivers. And so, without knowing it, we built a shelter for more than ourselves. It seems as though desert creatures must have a universal communication network. When a storm is approaching, I think they must drop all predatory inclinations. I can imagine the spiders telling the toads who tell the lizards who tell the snakes who tell the rats who tell the squirrels who tell the rabbits, "*Arriba! Arriba! Vamos a la casa.*"

And they come. Walking, running, hopping, and crawling, they come. Spiders of all denominations, shiny or shaggy, large or small. Iridescent beetles. Toads the size of salad plates. The little banner-tailed kangaroo rat and the big rock squirrel, whose front end is gray while his rear end is brown. And many kinds of snakes, mostly harmless, but some dragging their little noisemakers behind them. Some stay only until the storm is over, but others move in for more extended periods. In their attempts to stay in the house or in the courtyard just outside the kitchen door, some are incredibly, pathetically persistent. None more so than the tarantula.

I have a considerable affection for tarantulas. They are the victims not only of our aversion to spiders, but of a very bad press which portrays them as quite different creatures than they are. The mythic, and I'm afraid still predominant, view of tarantulas seems to have originated in Southern Italy, in the seaport of Taranto, whose citizens, between the fifteenth and the seventeenth centuries, were visited with repeated epidemics of a strange disease that created frenzy. This came to be known as tarantism and was thought to result from the bite of a tarantula. From this comes the name of a somewhat frenzied folk dance, the tarantella. Evidently the spider was named after the town, the disease was named after the spider, and the dance was named after the disease. But at the bottom of all this, the spider was innocent. I don't think we know what really caused tarantism. Perhaps it was just a particularly potent wine in the stomachs of some volatile Italians with a natural tendency for body language. At any rate, the tarantula took the rap and has henceforth been thought to be a sinister, even deadly, creature.

But the tarantula is not significantly dangerous to humans. It almost never bites, even when tormented; and if it does, its bite is no more potent than the sting of a bee. It is true that the sexual practices of the female tarantula will not hold up to the close scrutiny of a moralist, but as far as I'm concerned, sexual practices are inexplicable throughout the entire phyllogenetic scale, and let those without sin get out their stones. Tarantulas are somewhat large and hairy, to be sure, but less so than many of the creatures we choose as pets. In fact, tarantulas make excellent pets if they are given the full run of the house in order to find sufficient food.

So I have a considerable fondness for tarantulas, but my wife does not share this feeling. While she allows some varieties of large spiders to remain in the house and even refers to them as my "friends," she draws the line at tarantulas. I have explained to her that tarantulas are quiet, well-behaved house guests who pay for their lodging by eating flies and small insects. I have told her that they eat ticks, which are troublesome to our dogs, although I am not absolutely sure this is true. I have even hinted that a few tarantulas around the house would have a tendency to cut down on the number of other long-staying guests, including relatives. When she said she was afraid of stepping on a tarantula while she was barefooted, I told her that the possibility was very remote because they usually climb up the walls. This did not seem to comfort her very much. My wife is resolute. No tarantulas!

Consequently, when a tarantula lumbers in, lifting one leg at a time and lowering it with great care and deliberation, I am expected to put it out. But tarantulas are also resolute, and persistent. I have put the same tarantula out as many as five times in one evening, each time placing it farther from the house. And each time it would laboriously turn itself around and head back for the open door from which it had just been ejected, like a stray dog who has adopted a new home and will not be discouraged. On its third or fourth entry, it will even begin to take on some of the mannerisms of a stray dog unsure of welcome— tentative, cringing a little, trying to be inconspicuous. But a tarantula crossing the kitchen floor with its slow, stately, inexorable walk has difficulty being inconspicuous, and my wife notices it every time. Several times I have managed to keep one hidden for a day or two, but eventually it grows bold and strikes out across the floor or up a wall, and as soon as my wife sees it, expulsion is inevitable.

Tarantulas probably come in the house to avoid summer storms, but they are also attracted to light. I once thought that this was because light attracts some of the small insects on which they feed, but perhaps they are attracted to light for its own sake or for some reason we do not understand. Edmund C. Jaeger in his book *Desert Wildlife* tells about camping in the Sonoran Desert with two companions and being visited by a "number of tarantulas, which seemed to be attracted by the firelight. They rapidly approached the fire, then suddenly about-faced when they felt the heat. Time and again they returned, only to repeat the withdrawal." Jaeger also mentions their astonishing longevity, which has been documented. Some female tarantulas live for twenty-five years.

There is another persistent creature who makes its appearance in large numbers at our house during the monsoon season, either coming inside or congregating in the small courtyard just outside the kitchen door, where I have seen as many as nine of them at a time. I call it Bufo, short for *Bufo alvarious*, the Colorado River toad. But I can manage very little affection for Bufo, partly because it is ugly by just about any standard one wants to apply, and partly because it is dangerous to our dogs, of which we always have several, usually several more than we should have. On the scale of natural beauty, I would have to place Bufo somewhere near the bottom as compared to other desert creatures. It presents an aesthetic problem I cannot overcome. Bufo is large, often seven inches long and almost as wide, olive-gray to nearly black-brown, with an amazing assortment of lumps, bumps, and wart-like protuberances all over its head and body. I am sure it would have these on its neck if it had a neck, but it doesn't seem to have one. Some of these lumps and bumps are glands. Others seem to be—and I hesitate to use the words—purely decorative. But Bufo's skin is not the real aesthetic problem for me. The problem is the casual relationship between Bufo's skin and everything it contains. The toad moves with a queasy, sloshing, rolling, jiggling motion, like a rubber bag only partly filled with some viscous fluid. When Bufo hops, and it can hurl this entire, loosely organized arrangement through the air with great force and cover more than three feet in a single hop, it lands with a loud, sickening plop, and everything sloshes around for a while before settling into repose. None of this seems to bother Bufo, who wears an expression of absolute equanimity, if not stolidity; but it is a real aesthetic problem for me.

Another thing which probably affects my judgment is that Bufo's skin is covered with a slimy substance whose chemical makeup closely relates it to cobra venom. This helps protect the toad from predators, such as coyotes, but it also has a devastating effect on any domestic dog foolish enough to lick or bite Bufo. The dog immediately has a seizure, which in some cases can be fatal, and goes down head-first, splay-legged, gasping for breath. Evidently the toxin paralyzes the dog's respiratory system. The remedy is to wash the dog's mouth out with water, being careful not to drown the dog by letting water run down its throat.

We once had a Doberman who could never resist grabbing a Colorado River toad whenever she encountered one. She was unable to make a connection between the toad and the terrible things that happened to her immediately afterward. But our present three dogs, Big, Bigger, and Clydesdale, have sense enough to leave Bufo alone, in spite of the fact that only two of them were desert-raised. The third is probably just too lazy to be bothered, or else, like me, he has an aesthetic reservation about Bufo.

When I left the dogs about a half hour ago, they had all gone into an extended pout. They are pessimists. When they see me putting clothes into the van in preparation for a trip, they assume it is going to be a long one and do their dying-swan routine, which includes tragic looks from piteously drooping, glistening eyes. When this fails to impede my preparations, they go into a pout. They turn away and stare, fixedly, at the wall, uttering long, dejected sighs. One of them can sigh in such a way that it sounds exactly like a wrenching sob. The others encourage her to longer and deeper sobs. "Let him have it, Sadie. Break his heart."

Nevertheless, I and my stony heart got into Blue Boy and drove away. I am going back to Bisbee, and it feels good in spite of the heat and humidity. No storm yet, and I haven't turned on the air conditioner. I am only a few miles from the intersection of Highway 83, which will take me south and up into the grasslands where it will be cooler. I am driving over a fairly level alluvial plain, the desert floor, which stretches up from the Santa Cruz River. The river is dry now, as usual, but waiting to be transformed into a real hell raiser if the storm materializes.

The basin I am driving through is almost completely surrounded by mountains. Behind me and on the other side of the river is the jagged, toothy outline of the Tucson Mountains, in the foothills of which is the house where three dogs are probably still pouting. The Tucsons are older than most of the large mountain ranges in the vicinity, and not as high, worn down to a kind of runic grandeur. Their foothills, which were almost untouched desert twenty-five years ago, have become the suburbs of sprawling Tucson's west side. In spite of this, their higher peaks, protected from development by a county slope ordinance as well as Saguaro National Monument West and Tuscon Mountain Park, are full of mystery and the play of shadows.

Because of their starkness and their science-fiction shapes, I think of the Tucsons as "the mountains of the moon." When a winter storm comes over them from the west, they are dramatic in the way the Alps are dramatic, but on a much smaller scale of course. Clouds and mist swirl and billow around their peaks, and their deeply eroded canyons become places of mystery. Once every few years they are even covered with snow, a brief but glorious transformation that usually lasts until about noon the following day. And in spite of their stark contours, their surfaces are pelagic, almost shaggy when seen in the slanting light of late afternoon, covered with a heavy growth of desert plants that includes thick stands of saguaros, a sizable part of the last significant saguaro forest left in the world.

I have wandered through the Tucson Mountains at all times of the day and night, have climbed many of their peaks and followed their arroyos for miles, and yet they remain a mystery to me. Some presence is there, some numen which I am aware of but cannot describe nor come to grips with. It is powerful, wonderful, and I fear it is dying. I have tried to write about the Tucsons and that presence many times, and have always failed. Years ago, when I did not know them as well as I do now, I wrote,

> you could get here from anywhere
> but once you are here
> there are many places you can never go

That is from a failed poem called "The Upper *Bajadas*," a technical term identifying a kind of landscape that includes the foothills and talus slopes of the Tucson Mountains. I am fascinated with the term because it seems to be contradictory—upper lowlands, although *bajada* actually means "slope"—and includes words from both English and Spanish, suggesting two elements of the complex mix of cultures now living in this area. And somehow, for some reason I do not entirely understand, I have continued to live in the upper *bajadas* for more than a quarter of a century, which is no time at all in terms of the life of the mountains, but it is the entire lifespan of a very lucky tarantula, and it is a long time for me.

Range after range of mountains as far as I can see and much farther. To my left, making up the entire northern horizon, is an enormous mass, dark blue now in the shadow of the thunderheads. It is actually three ranges of mountains extending from almost due north of Tucson to a point far to the southeast, the Catalinas, Tanque Verdes, and

Rincons. The Catalinas are the most spectacular in terms of height and bulk. They are young, vital, awesome mountains. Their steep, treeless sides suggest nothing of what is above and beyond. It is hard to believe, as I drive across the oven of the desert floor, that up there about forty miles away is a large sub-alpine forest of pines and firs and a ski resort where the high temperature today is in the upper sixties.

Directly south of me are the Santa Ritas, which are much larger and more formidable than they appear to be from here. They too have a heavy growth of timber on their upper elevations and were the source of much mineral wealth in Spanish Colonial times, causing Tubac, on the Santa Cruz River just west of the Santa Ritas, to become the earliest center of colonial culture in this area. In 1752 the first nonnative woman to set foot on what is now Arizona soil arrived in Tubac. Nobody seems to know who she was, but she was undoubtedly Spanish, probably *creole*—of pure Spanish descent but born in New Spain, now Mexico. I doubt that any contemporary women envy her her small niche in history. Her life, by our standards, must have been hell.

Range after range of mountains. To the east the Whetstones, and south of them the Huachucas. Farther east the Dragoons and the magnificent Chiricahuas where a couple of months ago I and one of the dogs climbed Silver Peak to an elevation of 7,975 feet. Fortunately it was the smallest of the large dogs—the largest weighs more than I do—because he collapsed near the top of the mountain and I had to carry him most of the way down. When we got to Cave Creek, I dumped him in, for which he has never forgiven me, but it cooled him down and probably saved his life. As my less-than-courageous dog found out just before he tried to crawl under my sleeping bag while I was in it, the Chiricahuas have a considerable population of black bears, wildcats, and javelinas. The mountains are also attracting a large population of campers and tourists, nearly all of whom seem to be frantically searching for the same reclusive and very beautiful bird, the coppery-tailed trogon. Someone should start a rumor that the coppery-tailed trogon is a myth invented by the Bureau of Tourism, that there is no coppery-tailed trogon. It might save an entire mountain range from destruction at the hands and feet of hordes of binocular-carrying faddists.

This is pure basin and range country—mountain ranges of all sizes which once had deep and extensive valleys between them. But through the process of erosion, the valleys have filled in and leveled off to become vast basins that we refer to in a general way as the desert floor. A glance at the map shows Interstate 10, on which I am driving, twisting across Southern Arizona like a huge snake crawling from the New Mexico border to Phoenix. A closer look at the map shows why it takes such an indirect route. Range upon range of mountains, between which it must twist, trying to stay on low and fairly level ground. These ranges extend generally north and south or northwest and southeast, so that a road from east to west is doomed to encounter them broadside and must constantly maneuver around and between them. The section of freeway on which I am driving is heading straight southeast on its way to Lordsburg, New Mexico, considerably to the north.

I am moving down the length of a broad, relatively flat corridor bordered on both sides by extensive mountain ranges. From here it is difficult to tell where one range ends and another begins. Distances in the desert are tricky, where visibility is often more than sixty miles and mountain ranges thirty miles apart appear to be flat, tissue-paper collages with one range pasted directly on the range behind it. Human depth perception cannot deal with such distances accurately, especially in the brilliant light and usually dry air. Perhaps that is why many travelers along this road hardly notice the mountains at all. They will say it is "just flat desert. Nothing much to see." The mountains look less solid and real than the thunderheads above them and appear to be painted on the sky in colors ranging from the most delicate pastels to the darkest purple. At the moment, the lower slopes of the Santa Ritas are a soft yellow-green, fuzzy with vegetation.

This stretch of the desert floor is also much greener than usual, shockingly green in contrast with what it looked like a few weeks ago before the rains came. This area must have had several good soakers recently. The predominant growth here is greasewood, a sea of greasewood with an occasional stand of jumping cholla or ocotillo and once in a great while a stunted mesquite. Most of the year this stretch has a faded, desiccated look, suggesting either severe overgrazing or the presence of caliche close to the surface. Probably both in this case.

Even at its most verdant, greasewood is not a lush plant, but it is the most commonly found plant in the Sonoran Desert and often seems to be able to grow where almost nothing else will. It is delicate and lacy, with bare, silvery-gray stems and bright metallic-green leaves. Along here it averages about three-and-a-half feet tall but can grow to be a very tall plant if it gets more water. When I first moved into the desert, I watered the greasewood near the house from time to time. Within two years I had a fifteen-foot-high jungle. At the moment, the foliage of the greasewood has distinct glints and undertones of yellow, indicating that many of the plants are in bloom, but the tiny yellow blossoms, each with five petals twisted like the blades of a fan, are too inconspicuous to be seen clearly from a distance.

The saguaro has come to be the plant which is most often used to symbolize the Sonoran Desert, and as much as I admire these giants, each with its individual style and personality, they are not nearly as widespread and typical of this desert as is the humble greasewood. Nor is the saguaro, except for its size, any more surprising. The unassuming greasewood is a truly amazing plant. It is an evergreen which often displays buds, blossoms, and fruit on the same plant at the same time. The fruit is a small, furry, silver-white globe that can quietly stick to fur or fabric and hitchhike for miles. As a greasewood matures, it sends up concentric circles of new shoots from the same root. Eventually the central and original part of the plant dies and disintegrates while the peripheral "clones" continue to grow. Some of these individual plant colonies, shaped like doughnuts with the original portion in the center long since dead, are more than sixty-five feet across. The botanist Frank Vasek recently radiocarbon-dated one of these colonies in the desert of Southern California at 9,400 years old, making it the oldest living plant known to man, and bumping the bristlecone pine from that prestigious position.

And in another way, greasewood is the signature plant of the Sonoran Desert. Its leaves are resinous, slightly sticky to the touch, although not unpleasantly so. This substance, called lac, gives the Sonoran Desert its distinctive smell, especially after a rain. Each desert in the United States has a distinctive smell, and that smell is usually caused by a specific plant. I always associate the Great Basin Desert with the bracing odor of sage. And everybody who has known the Sonoran Desert associates it with the smell of greasewood after a rain, a slightly medicinal but exhilarating smell.

Those who have lived in the Sonoran Desert for any period of time never forget that smell, and no matter how far away they go, many of them can never get over it. I meet them when I am doing poetry readings in many different parts of the country, when I am reading poems about the desert. They approach me after the readings and softly speak the magic words like a litany: "desert," "greasewood," "saguaro," "rain." Sometimes they have tears in their eyes as they tell me where they once lived in the desert and how they can never get it out of their minds. Each time I realize that I am in the presence of a kindred spirit and that we who love the desert speak a language whose significance others cannot entirely understand. And each time I am thankful that I, too, am not an exile, that the circumstances of life have not forced me to leave the desert.

Most botanists would probably raise at least one eyebrow at my use of the name greasewood to identify the plant which is technically known as *Larrea tridenta*, claiming that it should be called creosote bush to distinguish it from two other desert plants—one found in the Mojave and one in the Great Basin—called greasewood. But I stick to my guns and call it greasewood, as most of us who live in the Tucson area do. We prefer this name probably because of our proximity to the native Tohono O'odham people (previously called Papago), who refer to the plant as greasewood rather than creosote bush and rely on its medicinal properties for a wide range of ailments. In fact, in O'odham folklore, greasewood was the first thing that grew, and from its resin, or lac, Earth Maker formed the mountains. When the lac dried, the mountains stiffened and remained in place. There's probably a principle in that which could be used as a symbol of the basic difference between the Anglo and the Native American points of view. I would have a tendency to think that the plant was created from the mountains, but the O'odham believe the mountains were created from the plant.

The whole greasewood vs. creosote controversy reminds me of the subject of popular taxonomy and the way things get their names. This is the science of what-you-call-it, and I think of it as an absolute science because it often seems to make absolutely no sense. In the case of the greasewood and creosote problem, what you call it depends not only on where you are, but on who you are. People interested in or baffled by this science often ask me such questions as: "Does the jumping cactus really jump?" I have several answers to this question depending on what mood I'm in. Sometimes I say, "Only when your back is turned." At other times I answer with another question. "Does the weeping willow really weep?" And although they seem contradictory, there is a sense in which both these answers suggest the truth. That's the way it is with the science of what-you-call-it.

The popular, as opposed to the scientific, names for plants and animals are often based on figurative language, the language of impression and comparison, the language of poetry. These names are descriptive, concrete, highly compressed, and usually require some kind of imaginative leap. I am not a linguist, but it seems to me that the more "primitive" a language is by our standards, the more it relies on such names.

At the moment, looking south and back a little to the west, I can see clouds hanging in delicate long streamers like veils. The streamers do not reach the ground, and the clouds are moving steadily northwestward. It is a common phenomenon in the desert—rain which is falling in a localized area but evaporating before it reaches the ground. The name which comes into my mind is *walking rain*, an expression translated from the language of a Native American culture. It is descriptive, concrete, accurate in a metaphorical sense, and so highly compressed as to require a slight leap of the imagination. It is also beautiful. Somewhere rain is falling but never comes to rest on the earth, while at the same time it is moving. *Walking rain.*

The name jumping cholla, the official, nonscientific name found in all the respectable books, was arrived at in the same way and is based upon close observation of the plant's structure and resultant behavior. The jumping cholla is one of the great beauties of desert vegetation and it is a true devil. Its trunk is a tube of intricately woven wooden mesh, very strong and very light, often found transformed into ugly lamps in curio shops. Above the cholla's trunk it produces soft, fleshy green segments, each connected to the one before it by means of a delicate joint, and each covered with barbed spines. When you brush against the plant, even ever so lightly, the spines pierce flesh and the barbs hold them in place. As you pull back or move away, the joint neatly disconnects and the entire fleshy segment remains embedded in its victim—in this case, you. Only the slightest contact is required. These large green spiny monsters seem to jump on you and hang on.

But this is only the beginning. The subtle lengths to which this plant will go in order to do you bodily harm are truly insidious and diabolical. If you should step on one of the fleshy segments which has already fallen on the ground, and they often cover the ground around a plant in great profusion, you will squash it, exposing its slimy, slick inner pulp. Its spines will often attach the segment lightly to the sole of your shoe. As you take the next step and your foot comes up behind you, the upward thrust of your foot will cause the spines to dislodge, and the lubrication of the slimy inner pulp will aid the segment in sliding easily over the sole of your shoe. The entire segment will fly up behind you, or jump up behind you, and impale you in the back of the lower leg, penetrating even heavy trousers.

When this happens, if you don't have a comb with you, you can be in considerable trouble. If you try to dislodge the segment with your hand, you will find that your hand is immediately attached to the back of your leg by means of the cholla segment, leaving you bent over in an awkward position while you slowly fry in the sun. The thing to do, while you still have at least one hand free to do it with, is to slide a comb between your flesh and the cholla segment and lift it away with one quick, hideously painful jerk. And it's a good idea to do this as quickly as possible because the cholla still has one more card to play in its diabolical game. Poison. It is the only cactus whose spines are coated with a slightly toxic substance which can cause severe festering and has been known to cripple horses when the spines are not removed soon enough.

And yet the jumping cholla is a beautiful thing, especially when seen as I am seeing them now, from a safe distance. Even more so when seen in the moonlight. They are about the height of a person, and moonlight turns the long pale spines which cover their tops to platinum blond. They look like many statuesque 1930s starlets standing out there waiting to be discovered. But drive on, drive on! To touch that glamorous creature even once is to know pain and learn the cruelty of a truly ruthless beauty.

About twenty miles out of Tucson I swing south off the freeway and onto Highway 83, which will take me up into the rangeland. I haven't turned on the air conditioner, and suddenly the heat seems unbearable, probably because of my reduced speed and because I know it will be a little cooler soon. The storm clouds seem to be stalled just above the southern horizon. "*Ven, Chubosco!*" I chant. "*Ven, ven, Chubasco!*" There is no immediate response.

I always talk to things more than I do to people. I talk to stones, plants, animals, and even the weather, but I have a superstitious belief that when I address the natural things of this region, I must use Spanish. Their experience with Spanish goes back to the sixteenth century, while they have heard English for only about 150 years. I have a feeling that it takes the natural things of the world a long time to get used to a new language. And since I don't know any Pima or Apache, I try to use Spanish. But my Spanish is dreadful. I not only speak it very poorly, I hear it even worse. If I can ask the right question, I can't understand the answer. And to be asked a question in Spanish which requires more than a *si* or *no* is a nightmare from which I cringe. It's much easier to speak Spanish to things which cannot or do not reply. Also, the plants and animals are less critical. They do not correct my mistakes. And I'm sure the stones and mountains have heard much garbled and ungrammatical Spanish since one spring day in 1540 when the twenty-nine-year-old Francisco Vázquez de Coronado and his ill-fated band struggled down the valley of the San Pedro River past the point at which I will be crossing it in less than an hour.

I still blush when I remember one of my classic blunders in Spanish. Although it was only one of many, it stands out in my mind. I had just arrived in Cuernavaca after a three-day train and bus ride from Nogales. I was exhausted and sick. The taxi driver deposited me and my luggage in front of the house where I had rented a room from a

Mexican family. My landlady-to-be, a truly gracious person, came out to the sidewalk to meet me and escort me in. Looking at my haggard face, she asked in Spanish, "Are you tired?" The word is *cansado*. But I confused it with *casado* (married), and in my impeccable Spanish replied, "Yes, I have been tired for fifteen years and I have a twelve-year-old son." Her eyes opened wider for a moment, but she merely nodded, patted me on the shoulder with compassion, and led me into the house to rest after my long ordeal.

Historically, however, it seems fitting for me to speak in Spanish to the things which make up this landscape, no matter how bad my Spanish is, since the landscape was part of New Spain until 1821, when Mexico gained its independence, and then part of Mexico until 1854 as a result of the Gadsden Treaty, although the United States did not take possession of it until 1856. This 27,305 square miles of what is now Southern Arizona, plus 2,365 square miles of what is now New Mexico, cost the United States ten million dollars. It was not, as is generally believed, purchased from the Mexican people or from any duly constituted Mexican government. It was privately and secretly sold by the one-legged dictator, Antonio López de Santa Anna, who had already played a leading role in Mexico's loss of another chunk of real estate now known as Texas.

Santa Anna became dictator of Mexico four different times before that infant country was forty years old. In his day, he was thought of by many of his fellow citizens as Mexico's savior. Most contemporary historians, looking back, see him as its nemesis, one of the darkest of the dark angels who ministered to that bleeding young republic. He must have been a fairly good general, at least he could raise an army when almost nobody else could, but he was treacherous, unscrupulous, vain, and childlike. He billed himself the "Napoleon of the West," and needed much money to maintain his army and his style. As a dictator, he had chosen the title "His Most Serene Highness," which was indicative of his style. He lived in gilded, rococo luxury, and loved parties and huge celebrations, especially when they were in his honor. And his sale of a large part of what was left of Mexico in order to make ends meet was not the most shameful transaction he engaged in. He also sold the natives of Yucatan as slaves to Cuban plantation owners at twenty-five pesos each.

When we look back on Santa Anna and the Gadsden Purchase, the recent outrage of the United States government, upon discovering—lo and behold—that the Dictator of Panama was selling drugs, seems strident and exaggerated. For Latin American dictators, such things have often been a matter of style. And for us, it seems to be a matter of whether or not we want what they happen to be selling at the moment. When it was the land through which I am now driving, we did.

The United States government wanted a southern railroad route to the fabled land of California. California had just fallen, like a ripe avocado, into the hands of the United States in 1848, the same year large chunks of gold were found lying around in its rivers and streams. So we bought the strip of desert land from His Most Serene Highness, or "Old Santy Anny" as the Texans call him, who had found himself temporarily short of cash and was eager to sell.

But when President Pierce paid Santa Anna his ten million dollars—seven immediately and the balance upon completion of the border survey—a big page in history's book flipped over for this land which is now part of Southern Arizona. And although that page has subsequently become a palimpsest of notations, forgotten dates, and appointments with destiny, it is the page we still live on if we live in Arizona south of the Gila. Whatever our backgrounds, our foregrounds are shaped by the rip-roaring, boom-or-bust American Era, which arrived with the Gadsden Purchase and is still going strong all around us. What Faulkner said about the Deep South is true here as well: "The past is not dead; it is not even past."

The American Era arrived in Tucson, a one-story adobe town of about six hundred people, in the spring of 1856 when a detachment of United States Dragoons marched into town while the Mexican troops marched out. Even that quiet transition included a foretaste of what was to come. The newcomers just couldn't wait. Some of the Gringo residents, one of whom was later to become a judge in the Territory of Arizona, tied several mesquite poles together and hoisted an American flag over Miles' store, with loud cheers, while the Mexican troops were filing past on their way out of town. It was an insult. An ugly incident ensued. Fortunately, nobody started shooting. In that respect the incident was unusual.

The civilian Mexican population was quiet and polite. Some packed up and moved south across the newly established border. Many of the older residents stayed. They had already lived under two governments, although on the ragged frontier of both, and they would wait and see if this one would be different. Certainly neither of the others had done much for them in their frontier isolation, danger, and poverty. Nobody had consulted them about whether or not they wanted to become part of the American Era. And nobody had asked the mountains or desert basins or plants or animals about it. But not since the mid-tertiary age, vaguely twenty million years earlier, had the landscape known such sudden and dramatic changes as it was about to undergo. And nobody had asked the native Pimas or Tohono O'odham or Apaches if they wanted to enter the new era, which would bring their cultures to the brink of annihilation and sometimes beyond. The Americans, the restless changers and movers, had come. In less than 150 years we have changed everything in the region except the weather, and during this, the hottest summer on record in Southern Arizona, we are beginning to wonder if we haven't changed that too.

As I drive through the heat toward the low hills which skirt the Santa Rita Mountains, much of what I see reminds me of how thoroughly we have changed this landscape. Layer upon layer of our discarded history lies everywhere around me, more obvious than the aluminum cans and broken glass along the road. I am a product of the American Era, of that dream of the endless frontier, of that push toward new lands to use up for my purposes, of that greed. And I am going back to Bisbee, where I will look down into a gigantic crater, an inverted mountain of empty space which was, seventy-five years ago, a real mountain. I will not be shocked. Along the way, I will see no antelope where once they were everywhere, and I will not be shocked. I will drive through valleys where grass once grew shoulder-high and where now only the ubiquitous greasewood is able to find a foothold in what is left of the soil, and I will not be shocked. I am a product of the American Era. It is my heritage.

And I am going back to Bisbee, not really knowing why. Perhaps it is because two years of my life were left there, put behind me, and now I have reached an age at which I cannot afford to forget even two years out of those allotted me. Perhaps I am looking for the spirit of a mountain I never knew, a mountain which became a crater on whose edge I lived for two years, happily, while the landscape and even the earth around me was being destroyed. Or perhaps it is just nostalgia. I was happy there, while the destruction went on twenty-four hours a day, and now I want to go back.

We are starting to climb. Blue Boy feels it, and I feel a wave of something like euphoria. Sunflowers and brilliant white prickle poppies flaunt themselves beside the road. The storm is beginning to build more rapidly now, and I want to feel cold water on my face. Maybe I am suddenly happy just because I am going somewhere, anywhere. I have put down roots in the last thirty years, but I am still the child of those who kept moving, always westward. Did they ever look back? The record of the birthplaces of my mother, father, aunts, and uncles reads like a trail map from the Mississippi River to Oregon. Once, when I asked my mother where one of her younger brothers was born, she said, "In a wagon. I think it was somewhere in Arkansas." I am the child of those who were born along the road, and it was a long, long road.

Blue Boy was raised in West Texas, so he likes flat country best. He's no mountain goat when it comes to climbing hills, but he's had plenty of experience since he came to Arizona. He's slow but steady. He puts his head down and takes the incline at his own speed. At first all the jackrabbits—the Datsuns and Hondas—pass him. Then, as the hill gets steeper, they begin to falter, but he keeps on at the same dogged pace. If it's a long hill, by the time we are near the summit he is steadily passing most of them. And when we start downhill, I can't hold him in. Even in low gear he tends to run away, careening around curves, tires squealing. I don't always enjoy the downhill part as much as he does. His center of gravity is a little too high for me to feel secure, although I appreciate the view from up here. Sometimes, when he leans at an extreme angle around a downhill curve, I have the sickening sensation that all four of his wheels are not entirely in contact with the road. Going downhill he reminds me of a horse, a big rawboned sorrel I had when I was a kid. As soon as we turned toward home, he would break into a wild gallop no matter how hard I tried to slow him down, and all I could do was grab the saddle horn and remember to duck low as we sailed through the barn door, which was just low enough to knock me off. It wasn't an act of aggression. At that moment he had his mind on something else.

Just now Blue Boy is starting a steady, winding climb. Not too steep, but enough to make him lean into it. We aren't into real rangeland yet, but these low hills, rising toward the Santa Ritas, are cattle country. The sea of greasewood is giving way to more varied, widely spaced vegetation. Ocotillo, yucca, and prickly pear are most obvious, each plant standing out smartly with plenty of space around it, guarding its territory. The ground is rocky and eroded, with here and there a pastel tint of green—new grass just coming up after the recent rains and not yet discovered by the cattle. It won't last long. There isn't a building in sight, and sight is a long way, but I can see a cattle pond near a dirt road, and I know there are a few ranch houses scattered miles apart off to the left, tucked away in the clefts of the low-lying Empire Mountains.

I should enjoy this stretch of the road, especially now when it is greener than usual. The view is expansive, and the shapes of the hills are intrinsically pleasing, like curves of the female body in repose. The growth is varied and dramatic. Soft greens, soft browns, soft grays, with here and there a burst of sunflowers or a prickle poppy waving brilliant white handkerchiefs. But all of a sudden this stretch of the road begins to get on my nerves. Bad memories. These low, rolling hills depress me, and the past isn't past enough as I drive through them.

There must be millions of people who live in the East who would look at this landscape and consider it paradise, who would give anything they have to live on one of these sprawling cattle ranches. The easygoing pace, the magnificent vistas, the hard, honest work close to nature. Haven't most of us dreamed of it at one time or another? Isn't this one of the dreams that drove our grandparents and great-grandparents across the plains and over the mountains, suffering and dying as they came west, always west. Unlimited sun and space. Land, and the opportunity to work on it, to be one's own boss. Air not breathed by anyone else. Some of the lucky ones, the tough ones, or the unscrupulous ones secured that dream and created a way of life that was to become the dominant idyllic symbol of American culture, translated through literature and film to all the world. And in spite of the fact that we know the translation was generally romantic and inaccurate, it is also somehow comforting to know that somebody, sometime, somewhere really did live on those cattle ranches in a manner even remotely similar to the one portrayed in books and films. With the addition of a few more gadgets and technology, somebody still does. Right over there on the other side of that low hill.

I don't know exactly how many acres of this particular kind of country it takes to support one cow, but I know the ranches have to be very big in order to support a sizable herd. When I hear ranchers talking about hundreds of thousands of acres in a single spread, my mind goes blank. I cannot envision it. Years ago when I spent some happy weekends riding horseback on one of the larger ranches in Southern Arizona, I could never really fathom how big it was. I knew I could ride north thirty miles from the ranch house and I would still be on the ranch, but I could never come to grips with all that land actually being part of a single piece of property.

And with the exception of the enormous land grants made by the Spanish kings and later the Mexican government, many of which were ultimately disallowed and split up by the United States government, it is difficult to figure out exactly how these huge ranches got that way. The Homestead Act of 1862 said that the maximum number of acres of public land allowed to a homesteader was 160, or 320 for a man and wife. Even if a homesteader had a wife and ten grown children, not an unusual size for a family in 1862, they could jointly obtain only 1,920 acres, small potatoes as compared with many of the cattle ranches in Arizona, then or now. And although some exceptions were made, the magic figure of 160 acres was never changed until President Franklin Roosevelt withdrew what was left of the public domain from homestead entry in 1934.

The Homestead Act of 1862 was a foolish, catch-all piece of legislation. It was part of the Jeffersonian plan to insure a nation made up of small, independent farmers; but in the West it didn't. East of the hundredth meridian, where there was rich soil and abundant rainfall, 160 acres was plenty of land to support a family, often more than one family could work. But in the West, especially in the Southwest, with little rainfall, no irrigation, and alkaline soil, 160 acres wasn't nearly enough land for one family to survive on. And the major loophole in the Homestead Act was that it did not regulate transference of deeds and consequently could not prevent land speculation.

Yankee ingenuity in its most flagrant forms circumvented the Homestead Act and its corollaries—the Desert Land Act and the Timber and Stone Act. Homesteaders often built bird houses on their land so they could swear that the land had been improved. Or they dumped a barrel of water on it and paid a witness to swear that the land had been irrigated. Some claimed many 160-acre parcels under different names and using false identification papers. Historians have estimated that about 95 percent of the final proofs of land improvement under the Desert Land Act were fraudulent. But such fraudulent acquisition of public land represented a relatively small portion of the total land available. Enterprising land speculators acquired whole empires by obtaining, for a song, deeds to homesteaders' land, Spanish and Mexican land grants, and railroad land, often for European investors.

Many of the Mexicans who had settled in what is now Southern Arizona before the Gadsden Purchase, who did not speak or read English and did not understand Anglo ways of doing business, lost their land to Anglo homesteaders or speculators. Some were simply driven off their land at the point of a gun and fled south into Mexico, leaving no legal record of ownership. And the Southwest was won, for some homesteaders at least. The dream became a reality. But dreams which require such desperate methods to achieve often have a tendency to turn into nightmares somewhere down the road. One of them did, recently and right down that dirt road which cuts off from the highway and over the hill to a comfortable ranch house on a ranch which is not very large by local standards.

I know a young man who was raised in that ranch house. His name is Chad. He is well built and handsome, with a thick mane of dark, curly hair. Chad married the daughter of one of our neighbors in the

Tucson Mountains. I attended their wedding. They settled on Chad's father's ranch and had a baby. It was all part of the Southwestern American dream—a beautiful young couple and their beautiful child on a ranch in a magnificent landscape. But Chad's father had had a long-standing land dispute with a neighboring rancher. I don't know how much land was disputed or why, but one day Chad's father took his gun to his neighbor's ranch and killed the rancher. Then he killed himself with the same gun. Then I lost track of Chad for a few years, although he continued to live on the ranch and work it. But he wasn't living there the last time I saw him. He was in the state prison. When the Southwestern version of the American dream starts to turn back on itself, there is no end of troubles.

Safford is a small farming community on the Gila River in the southeastern part of the state. It must have been sometime in 1981 that I went to the state prison there to visit a creative writing class. I didn't know Chad was there and didn't recognize him at first. Somehow, you don't expect to run into part of the American dream in a state prison. In 1980 Chad had been tried for unlawful imprisonment, kidnapping, and aggravated assault. Because he had a very good lawyer and the case was tried in Tucson, Chad was found guilty only of aggravated assault, but that crime carried a mandatory five-year sentence because it involved the use of a deadly weapon which was, of course, a gun.

During the trial, Chad admitted that he had detained a twenty-year-old Mexican man at gunpoint, padlocked a chain around his neck, chained him to a toilet, and left him for a day and a night without food or water. The Mexican's name was Manuel, and he was an illegal alien whom Chad had employed to work on the ranch for seven dollars week. Chad believed that Manuel had stolen three thousand dollars worth of tools from the ranch, although Manuel had denied it. Somebody else later admitted to having taken the tools from Chad to settle an outstanding debt. At the trial, Chad said he had chosen to place the chain around Manuel's neck because "it looked like the most comfortable place." He also said, "I liked Manuel. I liked him for a long time. He was a friend of mine."

Rural farm workers and cattle hands in Mexico are called *campesinos*, which translates, literally, peasants. Thousands of campesinos come across the border in search of work each year, and they are often employed by Southern Arizona ranchers. I have seen groups of them many times, tramping resolutely down some dirt road, carrying little but a plastic jug of water, the one thing essential to survival in this country. Often I have given them rides, being careful not to ask them questions that would give me unwanted information about their status, since it is against the law to transport an illegal alien. But they usually speak little English, and my Spanish is so wretched that it isn't difficult to avoid finding out what I don't want to know. Blue Boy is commodious, and if people are willing to sit on the floor and scrunch up a little, he can carry a good many. I have sometimes wondered, idly, what I would do if I were caught near the border transporting a van load of illegal aliens, but it doesn't bear dwelling on.

The employment of illegal campesinos on ranches in Southern Arizona is traditional and has been a common practice as long as there have been American ranches in Southern Arizona. Recently the federal government has taken fairly drastic steps to try to stop this practice, but my feeling is that the government is trying to bail out the ocean with a tea cup. The attitudes of many Arizona ranchers toward these ragged campesinos is strangely ambivalent. They want to employ them, since the campesinos are experienced and will work for little pay, but at the same time the ranchers accuse the campesinos of slaughtering their cattle and stealing from their ranches.

In Chad's case, the fact that he assumed his tools had been stolen by an illegal alien, rather than by one of his Anglo acquaintances, is significant and fairly typical. And the particular nature of his treatment of Manuel is also significant. Some of the ranchers don't seem to feel that the aliens are quite human. They seem to think of them as varmints, almost like coyotes, which most ranchers routinely exterminate. For every case like Chad's that was reported by "an anonymous tip" to the United States Border Patrol, there are undoubtedly many which are not reported. And legal records would suggest that until quite recently even reported cases were not usually prosecuted.

Chad's case did not receive very much publicity. I had not heard about it before I encountered him in the prison. But one similar case received so much publicity that it monopolized the front pages of Arizona newspapers, off and on for years. Seldom has the dirty laundry of the Southwestern American dream been so thoroughly exposed for all to see. Legally, it was a complex proceeding, and much of its complexity arose from the attitudes of the people of Southern Arizona, quite a few of whom, before it was over, sat on one or the other of its three juries.

The original defendants were George Hanigan, a wealthy, politically active rancher, and his two sons, Tom and Pat. All three were accused of detaining, robbing, and torturing three campesinos on the Hanigan ranch. The ranch extends on both sides of Highway 80 between Bisbee and Douglas, but closer to Douglas, where the highway parallels the Mexican border about two miles away. Before the first trial, however, the father died. The two young sons—Tom was under twenty and Pat was in his very early twenties—stood trial three times, and each time with a different result.

The first was an Arizona Superior Court trial in Bisbee in 1977, at the conclusion of which both defendants were acquitted. The federal government then stepped in, basing its case on an interstate commerce act which it claimed had been violated when the three victims were detained and not allowed to pursue employment. The first federal trial took place in Tucson in 1980 and resulted in a hung jury. The second federal trial, necessitated by the hung jury of the preceding one, was held in Phoenix in 1981. Obviously, each subsequent trial was being moved farther and farther away from the cattle ranch area in the southeastern corner of the state in order to obtain an unbiased jury. Bisbee is less than 25 miles away from the Hanigan ranch, Tucson is about 120 miles away, and Phoenix is about 240 miles away. It is noteworthy, I think, that Phoenix is north of the Gila River and well beyond the land included in the Gadsden Purchase. It is surrounded by farming and industrial areas and has a distinctly different style and outlook from the predominantly ranching-mining communities farther south. In the federal trial held in Phoenix, Tom was acquitted, but Pat was found guilty and sentenced to four years in prison.

The next year, while Pat was serving his sentence in a Pennsylvania federal prison, Tom was tried in Tucson for possession of five hundred pounds of marijuana, which had been found in the Hanigan barn. He was acquitted. Apparently Tom's trial for possession had no connection with the preceding legal actions, but it does suggest another thread in the tangled social fabric of life on the great ranches along the Mexican border.

Perhaps I shouldn't be depressed when I see those low hills on my left that remind me of Chad and the last time we met. Perhaps I should see in all this some progress being made toward respect for the human body and the human spirit. Chad's arrest came after the Hanigan case had received so much publicity. Without that publicity, the "anonymous tip" which resulted in Chad's arrest might never have been made. Without that publicity, whoever called the Border Patrol might not have had the courage to do so. Perhaps there is a force at work in recent years here in Southern Arizona that will make ranchers think twice before they torture or kill an illegal alien. Chad's lawyer admitted as much when he said his client felt that the trial came as a result of "Hispanic pressures." But in his closing statement to the jury, Chad's lawyer also said, "If the so-called victim was not a Mexican alien and this had not happened in the Southwest, this trial never would have happened." That means, I guess, that if you live in Lansing, Michigan, and you take your employee hostage at gunpoint, put a chain around his neck, chain him to a toilet and leave him there for twenty-four hours you will not be prosecuted. I don't know. I've never been to Lansing, Michigan. I'm sure the people there have problems of their own, but I doubt that they have this one.

Nobody knows how many unmarked graves are hidden in all those thousands of miles of the Southwestern American dream along the border. And nobody knows how many cases of murder, torture, or rape have gone unreported or unprosecuted in this beautiful country through which I am driving. The bones of dead bodies are soon scattered by coyotes in this country, and nothing is left to record what happened. So I am depressed on this stretch of the road through lovely, undulating hills somewhere between grassland and desert. I keep thinking about the sparrows and wondering if God's eye is really on them. Maybe it's like the Messenger says about the sparrows in Mac-Leish's play *J.B.*: " 'Hardly ever see one dead.' And a girl asks, 'What happens to them?' The Messenger replies, 'They get over it . . . over being there.' "

And I guess that's how I'll get over it, too, by getting over the next hill, and the next and the next.

Flying in the Middle of Art

ANNIE DILLARD

Dave Rahm lived in Bellingham, Washington, north of Seattle. Bellingham, a harbor town, lies between the San Juan Islands in Haro Strait and the alpine North Cascade Mountains. I lived there between stints on the island. Dave Rahm was a stunt pilot, the air's own genius.

In 1975, with a newcomer's willingness to try anything once, I attended the Bellingham Air Show. The Bellingham airport was a wide clearing in a forest of tall Douglas firs; its runways suited small planes. It was June. People wearing blue or tan zipped jackets stood loosely on the concrete walkways and runways outside the coffee shop. At that latitude in June, you stayed outside because you could, even most of the night, if you could think up something to do. The sky did not darken until ten o'clock or so, and it never got very dark. Your life parted and opened in the sunlight. You tossed your dark winter routines, thought up mad projects, and improvised everything from hour to hour. Being a stunt pilot seemed the most reasonable thing in the world; you could wave your arms in the air all day and all night, and sleep next winter.

I saw from the ground a dozen stunt pilots; the air show scheduled them one after the other, for an hour of aerobatics. Each pilot took up his or her plane and performed a batch of tricks. They were precise and impressive. They flew upside down, and straightened out; they did barrel rolls, and straightened out; they drilled through dives and spins, and landed gently on a far runway.

For the end of the day, separated from all other performances of every sort, the air show director had scheduled a program titled "Dave Rahm." The leaflet said that Rahm was a geologist who taught at Western Washington University. He had flown for King Hussein in Jordan. A tall man in the crowd told me Hussein had seen Rahm fly on a visit the king made to the United States; he had invited him to Jordan to perform at ceremonies. Hussein was a pilot, too. "Hussein thought he was the greatest thing in the world."

Idly, paying scant attention, I saw a medium-sized, rugged man dressed in brown leather, all begoggled, climb in a black biplane's open cockpit. The plane was a Bücker Jungman, built in the thirties. I saw a tall, dark-haired woman seize a propeller tip at the plane's nose and yank it down till the engine caught. He was off; he climbed high over the airport in his biplane, very high until he was barely visible as a mote, and then seemed to fall down the air, diving headlong, and streaming beauty in spirals behind him.

The black plane dropped spinning, and flattened out spinning the other way; it began to carve the air into forms that built wildly and musically on each other and never ended. Reluctantly, I started paying attention. Rahm drew high above the world an inexhaustibly glorious line; it piled over our heads in loops and arabesques. It was like a Saul Steinberg fantasy; the plan was the pen. Like Steinberg's contracting and billowing pen line, the line Rahm spun moved to form new, punning shapes from the edges of the old. Like a Klee line, it smattered the sky with landscapes and systems.

The air show announcer hushed. He had been squawking all day, and now he quit. The crowd stilled. Even the children watched dumbstruck as the slow, black biplane buzzed its way around the air. Rahm made beauty with his whole body; it was pure pattern, and you could watch it happen. The plane moved every way a line can move, and it controlled three dimensions, so the line carved massive and subtle slits in the air like sculptures. The plane looped the loop, seeming to arch its back like a gymnast; it stalled, dropped, and spun out of it climbing; it spiraled and knifed west on one side's wings and back east on another; it turned cartwheels, which must be physically impossible; it played with its own line like a cat with yarn. How did the pilot know where in the air he was? If he got lost, the ground would swat him.

Rahm did everything his plane could do: tailspins, four-point rolls, flat spins, figure 8's, snap rolls, and hammerheads. He did pirouettes on the plane's tail. The other pilots could do these stunts, too, skillfully, one at a time. But Rahm used the plane inexhaustibly, like a brush marking thin air.

His was pure energy and naked spirit. I have thought about it for years. Rahm's line unrolled in time. Like music, it split the bulging rim of the future along its seam. It pried out the present. We watchers waited for the split-second curve of beauty in the present to reveal itself. The human pilot, Dave Rahm, worked in the cockpit right at the plane's nose; his very body tore into the future for us and reeled it down upon us like a curling peel.

Like any fine artist, he controlled the tension of the audience's longing. You desired, unwittingly, a certain kind of roll or climb, or a return to a certain portion of the air, and he fulfilled your hope slantingly, like a poet, or evaded it until you thought you would burst, and then fulfilled it surprisingly, so you gasped and cried out.

The oddest, most exhilarating and exhausting thing was this: he never quit. The music had no periods, no rests or endings; the poetry's beautiful sentence never ended; the line had no finish; the sculptured forms piled overhead, one into another without surcease. Who could breathe, in a world where rhythm itself had no periods?

It had taken me several minutes to understand what an extraordinary thing I was seeing. Rahm kept all that embellished space in mind at once. For another twenty minutes I watched the beauty unroll, and grow more fantastic and unlikely before my eyes. Now Rahm brought the plane down slidingly, and just in time, for I thought I would snap from the effort to compass and remember the line's long intelligence; I could not add another curve. He brought the plane down on a far runway. After a pause, I saw him step out, an ordinary man, and make his way back to the terminal.

The show was over. It was late. Just as I turned from the runway, something caught my eye and made me laugh. It was a swallow, a blue-green swallow, having its own air show, apparently inspired by Rahm. The swallow climbed high over the runway, held its wings oddly, tipped them, and rolled down the air in loops. The inspired swallow. I always want to paint, too, after I see the Rembrandts. The blue-green swallow tumbled precisely, and caught itself and flew up again as if excited, and looped down again, the way swallows do, but tensely, holding its body carefully still. It was a stunt swallow.

I went home and thought about Rahm's performance that night, and the next day, and the next.

I had thought I knew my way around beauty a little bit. I knew I had devoted a good part of my life to it, memorizing poetry and focusing my attention on complexity of rhythm in particular, on force, movement, repetition, and surprise, in both poetry and prose. Now I had stood among dandelions between two asphalt runways in Bellingham, Washington, and begun learning about beauty. Even the Boston Museum of Fine Arts was never more inspiriting than this small north-western airport on this time-killing Sunday afternoon in June. Nothing on earth is more gladdening than knowing we must roll up our sleeves and move back the boundaries of the humanly possible once more.

Later I flew with Dave Rahm; he took me up. A generous geographer, Dick Smith, at Western Washington University, arranged it, and came along. Rahm and Dick Smith were colleagues at the university. In geology, Rahm had published two books and many articles. Rahm was handsome in a dull sort of way, blunt-featured, wide-jawed, wind-burned, keen-eyed, and taciturn. As anyone would expect. He was forty. He wanted to show me the Cascade Mountains; these enormous peaks, only fifty miles from the coast, rise over nine thousand feet; they are heavily glaciated. Whatcom County has more glaciers than the lower forty-eight states combined; the Cascades make the Rocky Mountains look like hills. Mount Baker is volcanic, like most Cascade peaks. That year, Mount Baker was acting up. Even from my house at the shore I could see, early in the morning on clear days, volcanic vapor rise near its peak. Often the vapor made a cloud which swelled all morning and hid the snows. Every day the newspapers reported on Baker's activity: would it blow? (A few years later, Mount St. Helens did blow.)

Rahm was not flying his trick biplane that day, but a faster, enclosed plane, a single-engine Cessna. We flew from a bumpy grass airstrip near my house, out over the coast and inland. There was coastal plain down there, but we could not see it for clouds. We were over the clouds at five hundred feet and inside them too, heading for an abrupt line of peaks we could not see. I gave up on everything, the way you do in airplanes; it was out of my hands. Every once in a while Rahm saw a peephole in the clouds and buzzed over for a look. "That's Larsen's pea farm," he said, or "That's Nooksack Road," and he changed our course with a heave.

When we got to the mountains, he slid us along Mount Baker's flanks sideways.

Our plane swiped at the mountain with a roar. I glimpsed a windshield view of dirty snow traveling fast. Our shaking, swooping belly seemed to graze the snow. The wings shuddered; we peeled away and the mountain fell back and the engines whined. We felt flung, because we were in fact flung; parts of our faces and internal organs trailed pressingly behind on the curves. We came back for another pass at the mountain, and another. We dove at the snow headlong like suicides; we jerked up, down, or away at the last second, so late we left our hearts, stomachs, and lungs behind. If I forced myself to hold my heavy head up against the g's, and to raise my eyelids, heavy as barbells, and to notice what I saw, I could see the wrinkled green crevasses cracking the glaciers' snow.

Pitching snow filled all the windows, and shapes of dark rock. I had no notion which way was up. Everything was black or gray or white except the fatal crevasses; everything made noise and shook. I felt my face smashed sideways and saw rushing abstractions of snow in the windshield. Patches of cloud obscured the snow fleetingly. We straightened out, turned, and dashed at the mountainside for another pass, which we made, apparently, on our ear, an inch or two away from the slope. Icefalls and cornices jumbled and fell away. If a commercial plane's black box, such as the FAA painstakingly recovers from crash sites, could store videotapes as well as pilots' last words, some videotapes would look like this: a mountainside coming up at the windows from all directions, ice and snow and rock filling the screen up close and screaming by.

Rahm was just being polite. His geographer colleague wanted to see the fissure on Mount Baker from which steam escaped. Everybody in Bellingham wanted to see that sooty fissure, as did every geologist in the country; no one on earth could fly so close to it as Rahm. He knew the mountain by familiar love and feel, like a face; he knew what the plane could do and what he dared to do.

When Mount Baker inexplicably let us go, he jammed us into cloud again and soon tilted. "The Sisters!" someone shouted, and I saw the windshield fill with red rock. This mountain looked infernal, a drear and sheer plane of lifeless rock. It was red and sharp; its gritty blades cut through the clouds at random. The mountain was quiet. It was in shade. Careening, we made sideways passes at these brittle peaks too steep for snow. Their rock was full of iron, somebody shouted at me then or later; the iron had rusted, so they were red. Later when I was back on the ground, I recalled that, from a distance, the two jagged peaks called the Twin Sisters looked translucent against the sky; they were sharp, tapered, and fragile as arrowheads.

I talked to Rahm. He was flying us out to the islands now. The islands were fifty or sixty miles away. Like many other people, I had picked Bellingham, Washington, by looking at an atlas. It was clear from the atlas that you could row in the salt water and see snow-covered mountains; you could scale a glaciated mountainside with an ice ax in August, skirting green crevasses two hundred feet deep, and look out on the islands in the sea. Now, in the air, the clouds had risen over us; dark forms lay on the glinting water. There was almost no color to the day, just blackened green and some yellow. I knew the islands were forested in dark Douglas firs the size of skyscrapers. Bald eagles scavenged on the beaches; robins the size of herring gulls sang in the clearings. We made our way out to the islands through the layer of air between the curving planet and its held, thick clouds.

"When I started trying to figure out what I was going to do with my life, I decided to become an expert on mountains. It wasn't much to be, it wasn't everything, but it was something. I was going to know everything about mountains from every point of view. So I started out in geography." Geography proved too pedestrian for Rahm, too concerned with "how many bushels of wheat an acre." So he ended up in geology. Smith had told me that geology departments through-out the country used Rahm's photographic slides—close-ups of geo-logic features from the air.

"I used to climb mountains. But you know, you can get a better feel for a mountain's power flying around it, flying all around it, than you can from climbing it tied to its side like a flea."

He talked about his flying performances. He thought of the air as a line, he said. "This end of the line, that end of the line—like a rope." He improvised. "I get a rhythm going and stick with it." While he was performing in a show, he paid attention, he said, to the lighting. He didn't play against the sun. That was all he said about what he did.

In aerobatic maneuvers, pilots pull about seven positive g's on some stunts and six negative g's on others. Some gyrations push; others pull. Pilots alternate the pressures carefully, so they do not gray out or black out.

Later I learned that some stunt pilots tune up by wearing gravity boots. These are boots made to hook over a doorway; wearing them, you hang in the doorway upside-down. It must startle a pilot's chil-dren, to run into their father or mother in the course of their home wanderings—the parent hanging wide-eyed upside-down in the door-way like a bat.

We were landing; here was the airstrip on Stuart Island—that island to which Ferrar Burn was dragged by the tide. We put down, climbed out of the plane, and walked. We wandered a dirt track through fields to a lee shore where yellow sandstone ledges slid into the sea. The salt chuck, people there called salt water. The sun came out. I caught a snake in the salt chuck; the snake, eighteen inches long, was swimming in the green shallows.

I had a survivor's elation. Rahm had found Mount Baker in the clouds before Mount Baker found the plane. He had wiped it with the fast plane like a cloth and we had lived. When we took off from Stuart

Island and gained altitude, I asked if we could turn over—could we do a barrel roll? The plane was making a lot of noise, and Dick Smith did not hear any of this, I learned later. "Why not?" Rahm said, and added surprisingly, "It won't hurt the plane." Without ado he leaned on the wheel and the wing went down and we went somersaulting over it. We upended with a roar. We stuck to the plane's sides like flung paint. All the blood in my body bulged on my face; it piled between my skull and skin. Vaguely I could see the chrome sea twirling over Rahm's head like a baton, and the dark islands sliding down the skies like rain.

The g's slammed me into my seat like thugs and pinned me while my heart pounded and the plane turned over slowly and compacted each organ in turn. My eyeballs were newly spherical and full of heartbeats. I seemed to hear a crescendo; the wing rolled shuddering down the last ninety degrees and settled on the flat. There were the islands, admirably below us, and the clouds, admirably above. When I could breathe, I asked if we could do it again, and we did. He rolled the other way. The brilliant line of the sea slid up the side window bearing its heavy islands. Through the shriek of my blood and the plane's shakes I glimpsed the line of the sea over the windshield, thin as a spear. How in performance did Rahm keep track while his brain blurred and blood roared in his ears without ceasing? Every performance was a tour de force and a show of will, a *machtspruch*. I had seen the other stunt pilots straighten out after a trick or two; their blood could drop back and the planet simmer down. An Olympic gymnast, at peak form, strings out a line of spins ten stunts long across a mat, and is hard put to keep his footing at the end. Rahm endured much greater pressure on his faster spins using the plane's power, and he could spin in three dimensions and keep twirling till he ran out of sky room or luck.

When we straightened out, and had flown straightforwardly for ten minutes toward home, Dick Smith, clearing his throat, brought himself to speak. "What was that we did out there?"

"The barrel rolls?" Rahm said. "They were barrel rolls." He said nothing else. I looked at the back of his head; I could see the serious line of his cheek and jaw. He was in shirtsleeves, tanned, strong-wristed. I could not imaging loving him under any circumstance; he was alien to me, unfazed. He looked like G.I. Joe. He flew with that matter-of-fact, bored gesture pilots use. They click overhead switches and turn dials as if only their magnificent strength makes such dullness endurable. The half circle of wheel in their big hands looks like a toy

363

they plan to crush in a minute; the wiggly stick the wheel mounts seems barely attached.

A crop-duster pilot in Wyoming told me the life expectancy of a crop-duster pilot is five years. They fly too low. They hit buildings and power lines. They have no space to fly out of trouble, and no space to recover from a stall. We were in Cody, Wyoming, out on the North Fork of the Shoshone River. The crop duster had wakened me that morning flying over the ranch house and clearing my bedroom roof by half an inch. I saw the bolts on the wheel assembly a few feet from my face. He was spraying with pesticide the plain old grass. Over breakfast I asked him how long he had been dusting crops. "Four years," he said, and the figure stalled in the air between us for a moment. "You know you're going to die at it someday," he added. "We all know it. We accept that; it's part of it." I think now that, since the crop duster was in his twenties, he accepted only that he had to say such stuff; privately he counted on skewing the curve.

I suppose Rahm knew the fact, too. I do not know how he felt about it. "It's worth it," said the early French aviator Mermoz. He was Antoine de Saint-Exupéry's friend. "It's worth the final smashup."

Rahm smashed up in front of King Hussein, in Jordan, during a performance. The plane spun down and never came out of it; it nose-dived into the ground and exploded. He bought the farm. I was living then with my husband out on that remote island in the San Juans, cut off from everything. Battery radios picked up the Canadian Broadcasting Company out of Toronto, half a continent away; island people would, in theory, learn if the United States blew up, but not much else. There were no newspapers. One friend got the Sunday *Times* and no one mentioned that it was last week's.

One day, Paul Glenn's brother flew out from Bellingham to visit; he had a seaplane. He landed in the water in front of the cabin and tied up to our mooring. He came in for coffee, and he gave out news of this and that, and—Say, did we know that stunt pilot Dave Rahm had cracked up? In Jordan, during a performance: he never came out of a dive. He just dove right down into the ground, and his wife was there watching. "I saw it on CBS News last night." And then—with a sudden sharp look at my filling eyes—"What, did you know him?" But no, I did not know him. He took me up once. Several years ago. I admired his flying. I had thought that danger was the safest thing in the world, if you went about it right.

Later I found a newspaper. Rahm was living in Jordan that year; King Hussein invited him to train the aerobatics team, the Royal Jordanian Falcons. He was also visiting professor of geology at the University of Jordan. In Amman that day he had been flying a Pitt Special, a plane he knew well. Katy Rahm, his wife of six months, was sitting beside Hussein in the viewing stands, with her daughter. Rahm died performing a Lomcevak combined with a tail slide and hammerhead. In a Lomcevak, the pilot brings the plane up on a slant and pirouettes. I had seen Rahm do this: the falling plane twirled slowly like a leaf. Like a ballerina, the plane seemed to hold its head back stiff in concentration at the music's slow, painful beauty. It was one of Rahm's favorite routines. Next the pilot flies straight up, stalls the plane, and slides down the air on his tail. He brings the nose down—the hammerhead—kicks the engine, and finishes with a low loop.

It is a dangerous maneuver at any altitude, and Rahm was doing it low. He hit the ground on the loop; the tail slide had left him no height. When Rahm went down, King Hussein dashed to the burning plane to pull him out, but he was already dead.

A few months after the air show, and a month after I had flown with Rahm, I was working at my desk near Bellingham, where I lived, when I heard a sound so odd it finally penetrated my concentration. It was the buzz of an airplane, but it rose and fell musically, and it never quit; the plane never flew out of earshot. I walked out on the porch and looked up: it was Rahm in the black and gold biplane, looping all over the air. I had been wondering about his performance flight: could it really have been so beautiful? It was, for here it was again. The little plane twisted all over the air like a vine. I trailed a line like a very long mathematical proof you could follow only so far, and then it lost you in its complexity. I saw Rahm flying high over the Douglas firs, and out over the water, and back over farms. The air was fluid, and Rahm was an eel.

It was as if Mozart could move his body through his notes, and you could walk out on the porch, look up, and see him in periwig and breeches, flying around in the sky. You could hear the music as he dove through it; it streamed after him like a contrail.

I lost myself; standing on the firm porch, I lost my direction and reeled. My neck and spine rose and turned, so I followed the plane's line kinesthetically. In his open-cockpit, black plane, Rahm demonstrated curved space. He slid down ramps of air, he vaulted and wheeled. He piled loops in heaps and praised height. He unrolled the scroll of the air, extended it, and bent it into Möbius strips; he furled line in a thousand new ways, as if he were inventing a script and writing it in one infinitely recurring utterance until I thought the bounds of beauty must break.

From inside, the looping plane had sounded tinny, like a kazoo. Outside, the buzz rose and fell to the Doppler effect as the plane looped near or away. Rahm cleaved the sky like a prow and tossed out time left and right in his wake. He performed for forty minutes; then he headed the plane, as small as a wasp, back to the airport inland. Later I learned Rahm often practiced acrobatic flights over this shore. His idea was that if he lost control and was going to go down, he could ditch in the salt chuck, where no one else would get hurt.

If I had not turned two barrel rolls in an airplane, I might have fancied Rahm felt good up there, and playful. Maybe Jackson Pollock felt a sort of playfulness, in addition to the artist's usual deliberate and intelligent care. In my limited experience, painting, unlike writing, pleases the senses while you do it, and more while you do it than after it is done. Drawing lines with an airplane, unfortunately, tortures the senses. Jet bomber pilots black out. I knew Rahm felt as if his brain were bursting his eardrums, felt that if he let his jaws close as tight as centrifugal force pressed them, he would bite through his lungs.

"All virtue is a form of acting," Yeats said. Rahm deliberately turned himself into a figure. Sitting invisible at the controls of a distant airplane, he became the agent and the instrument of art and invention. He did not tell me how he felt, when we spoke of his performance flying; he told me instead that he paid attention to how his plane and its line looked to the audience against the lighted sky. If he had noticed how he felt, he could not have done the work. Robed in his airplane, he was as featureless as a priest. He was lost in his figural aspect like an actor or a king. Of his flying, he had said only, "I get a rhythm and stick with it." In its reticence, this statement reminded me of Veronese's "Given a large canvas, I enhanced it as I saw fit." But Veronese was ironic, and Rahm was not; he was literal as an astronaut; the machine gave him tongue.

When Rahm flew, he sat down in the middle of art, and strapped himself in. He spun it all around him. He could not see it himself. If he never saw it on film, he never saw it at all—as if Beethoven could not hear his final symphonies not because he was deaf, but because he was inside the paper on which he wrote. Rahm must have felt it happen, that fusion of vision and metal, motion and idea. I think of this man as a figure, a college professor with a Ph.D. upside down in the loud band of beauty. What are we here for? *Propter chorum*, the monks say: for the sake of the choir.

"Purity does not lie in separation from but in deeper penetration into the universe," Teilhard de Chardin wrote. It is hard to imagine a deeper penetration into the universe than Rahm's last dive in his plane, or than his inexpressible wordless selfless line's inscribing the air and dissolving. Any other art may be permanent. I cannot recall one Rahm sequence. He improvised. If Christo wraps a building or dyes a harbor, we join his poignant and fierce awareness that the work will be gone in days. Rahm's plane shed a ribbon in space, a ribbon whose end unraveled in memory while its beginning unfurled as surprise. He may have acknowledged that what he did could be called art, but it would have been, I think, only in the common misusage, which holds art to be the last extreme of skill. Rahm rode the point of the line to the possible; he discovered it and wound it down to show. He made his dazzling probe on the run. "The world is filled, and filled with the Absolute," Teilhard de Chardin wrote. "To see this is to be made free."

CONTRIBUTORS

JULIE CHECKOWAY is the author of a book of literary nonfiction, *Little Sister: Searching for the Shadow World of Chinese Women* (Viking, 1996), and the editor of *Creating Fiction,* a collection of essays on writing, which was named by Amazon.com as one of the ten best books on writing published in 1999. Her work on the mail-order bride business in America has appeared in a variety of magazines and newspapers, including *The New York Times.* She is the Director of the Creative Writing Program at the University of Georgia.

ALAN CHEUSE is a novelist, story writer, and journalist—the author, among other books, of *The Grandmothers' Club* and *The Light Possessed,* and the memoir *Fall Out of Heaven.* He serves as book commentator for NPR's evening news-magazine *All Things Considered* and his work appears regularly in a number of national publications. His recent essay collection, *Listening to the Page, Adventures in Reading and Writing,* was published by Columbia University Press.

STANLEY L. COLBERT has been a magazine and book editor, a literary agent in New York, Beverly Hills, and Canada, group vice-president of HarperCollins Publishers, and president and CEO of HarperCollins Canada. He has also been a published writer and produced screenwriter, a film and television producer, and a television network executive. He is currently a distinguished visiting professor in the Creative Writing Department at the University of North Carolina at Wilmington, which recently awarded him an honorary Doctor of Fine Arts degree in recognition of his life's work.

ANNIE DILLARD is the author of numerous books of nonfiction, including *For the Time Being, An American Childhood, Living By Fiction, The Writing Life, Teaching a Stone to Talk, Holy the Firm, Encounters with Chinese Writers, Tickets for a Prayer Wheel,* and *Pilgrim at Tinker Creek,* which won the Pulitzer prize for nonfiction in 1974.

MARTÍN ESPADA'S fifth book of poetry, *Imagine the Angels of Bread,* won an American Book Award and was a finalist for the National Book Critics Circle Award. Another volume of poems, *Rebellion is the Circle of a Lover's Hands,* won both the Paterson Poetry Prize and the PEN/Revson Fellowship. His latest collection of poetry, *A Mayan Astronomer in Hell's Kitchen,* has recently been published by W.W. Norton. He is the author of a book of essays, *Zapata's Disciple,* which won the

Independent Publisher Book Award for creative nonfiction. He is a professor in the Department of English at the University of Massachusetts.

PHILIP FURIA is the author of *The Poets of Tin Pan Alley: A History of America's Great Lyricists* (Oxford, 1990), *Ira Gershwin: The Art of the Lyricist* (Oxford, 1996), *Irving Berlin: A Life in Song* (Schirmer Books/Simon & Schuster, 1998), and *Pound's "Cantos" Declassified* (Penn State Press, 1984). He has also written about American popular song and American poetry in *The American Scholar, In Theater*, and other journals and magazines. A native of Pittsburgh, he studied at Oberlin College (B.A., 1965), the University of Chicago (M.A., 1966), and the Iowa Writers Workshop (M.F.A., 1970). He received his Ph.D. in English in 1970 from the University of Iowa and taught for twenty-five years at the University of Minnesota, where he was also Chair of the Department of English and Associate Dean for Faculty of the College of Liberal Arts. He is currently a professor in the Department of Creative Writing at the University of North Carolina at Wilmington.

LEE GUTKIND, founder and editor of the popular journal *Creative Nonfiction*, has performed as a clown for Ringling Brothers, scrubbed with heart and liver transplant surgeons, wandered the country on a motorcycle, and experienced psychotherapy with a distressed family— all as research for eight books and numerous profiles and essays. His books include the award-winning *Many Sleepless Nights*, an inside chronicle of the world of organ transplantation, and *An Unspoken Art*, a Book-of-the-Month Club selection recently published in the Republic of China. The University of Southern Illinois Press has reissued Gutkind's book about major-league umpires, *The Best Seat in Baseball, but You Have to Stand!* Also a novelist and filmmaker, Gutkind is editor of the Creative Nonfiction Reader (a series of anthologies, from Tarcher/Putnam) and Emerging Writers in Creative Nonfiction book series from Duquesne University Press, and director of the Mid-Atlantic Creative Nonfiction Writers' Conference at Goucher College in Baltimore. Former director of the writing program at the University of Pittsburgh and currently Professor of English, he has been mentoring editors and reporters at National Public Radio in Washington, DC.

ROBIN HEMLEY is the author of five works of nonfiction and fiction and has won a number of awards for his prose, including the Independent Press Book Award, Story Magazine's Humor Award, two Pushcart Prizes, The Nelson Algren Award from the Chicago Tribune, and others. He teaches creative writing at Western Washington University and in the low-residency M.F.A. Program at Vermont College.

NICHOLAS S. HENTOFF is Senior Counsel and Director of Legal Education for the Foundation for Individual Rights in Education (FIRE). He graduated from Cornell University in 1984, with honors in philosophy, and from the University of Arizona Law School in 1988, where he served as an Executive Editor of the Arizona Law Review. Following law school, he clerked for the Honorable Charles L. Hardy, United States District Judge for the District of Arizona. In Arizona, Hentoff maintained a private practice specializing in criminal defense, civil rights, and civil liberties litigation and appeals. Prior to joining FIRE, he was a Senior Associate Counsel with the Center for Individual Rights in Washington, DC. Hentoff has written on issues of civil rights, civil liberties, and criminal justice for *The Washington Post*, *The New York Times*, *The Wall Street Journal*, and *The Nation*, among other publications.

PHILLIP LOPATE is the author of three personal essay collections (*Bachelorhood, Against Joie de Vivre, Portrait of My Body*), a book of movie criticism (*Totally Tender Criticism*), and one about education (*Being With Children*). He has edited *The Art of the Personal Essay* and *Writing New York*. He is a professor at Hofstra University.

BARRY LOPEZ is the author of four works of nonfiction, including *Arctic Dreams* and *Of Wolves and Men*; seven works of fiction, including *Field Notes* and *Winter Count*; and a novella-length fable, *Crow and Weasel*. His work is regularly published in *Harper's,* the *Paris Review, The Georgia Review,* and other national journals. He has received numerous literary awards, including the National Book Award, and lives in western Oregon.

BEVERLY LOWRY was born in Memphis, Tennessee and grew up in Greenville, Mississippi. The author of six novels—including *Come Back, Lolly Ray, Daddy's Girl,* and *The Track of Real Desires*—she now writes primarily nonfiction, including essays, feature journalism, book reviews, profiles and two books: *Crossed Over, A Murder a Memoir,* and *Her Dream of Dreams, the Rise and Triumph of Madam C.J. Walker* (January, 2002.) She directs the Creative Nonfiction track of the MFA program at George Mason University.

CHRISTOPHER MERRILL is the author of four collections of poems, including *Watch Fire,* for which he received the Peter I.B. Lavan Younger Poets Award from the Academy of American Poets; three works of nonfiction, *The Grass of Another Country: A Journey Through the World of Soccer, The Old Bridge: The Third Balkan War and the Age of the*

Refugee, and *Only the Nails Remain: Scenes from the Balkan Wars;* and many edited volumes and works of translation. He directs the International Writing Program at The University of Iowa.

BRENDA MILLER is Assistant Professor of English at Western Washington University. She received two Pushcart Prizes for her work in creative nonfiction, and her essays have appeared in such periodicals as *The Georgia Review, The Sun, Utne Reader, Prairie Schooner, The Seneca Review, The Journal, Fourth Genre, Northern Lights,* and *Yoga Journal.* Her work is included in the books *Storming Heaven's Gate: An Anthology of Spiritual Writings by Women,* (Penguin, 1997), and *In Brief: Short Takes on the Personal* (Norton, 1999). She is the editor of *The Bellingham Review.*

E. ETHELBERT MILLER lives in Washington D.C. He is the author of several collections of poems. Miller was awarded the 1995 O.B. Hardison Jr. Poetry Prize. In 1996, he received an honorary doctorate of literature from Emory & Henry College. He is the co-chair of the Humanities Council of Washington D.C.

DINTY W. MOORE is the author of two books of nonfiction, *The Emperor's Virtual Clothes: The Naked Truth About Internet Culture* and *The Accidental Buddhist: Mindfulness, Enlightenment, and Sitting Still American Style;* as well as a collection of short fiction, *Toothpick Men.* He has written essays for *The New York Times Sunday Magazine,* the Philadelphia *Inquirer,* and *The Philadelphia City Paper,* and is a 1992 National Endowment for the Arts Fellow in Fiction Writing. He teaches at Penn State Altoona.

HONOR MOORE'S most recent book is *The White Blackbird: A Life of the Painter Margarett Sargent by Her Granddaughter,* a New York Times Notable Book in 1996. Her new book of poems, *Darling,* will be published by Grove Atlantic in September 2001; *Memoir,* a previous collection, appeared in 1989 and remains in print. *Mourning Pictures,* her verse play based on her mother's death, was produced on Broadway in 1974 and published in *The New Women's Theatre: Ten Plays by Contemporary American Women.* Moore has received awards in poetry from the National Endowment for the Arts (1981) and the Connecticut Commission on the Arts (1992) and in playwriting from the New York State Council on the Arts (1975). Her work has appeared in *The New Yorker, The New York Times, The Nation, The New Republic, The Paris Review, Seneca Review, Conjunctions,* and many other magazines, journals, and anthologies. In 1997 she was Visiting Distinguished Writer in Creative Nonfiction at the University of Iowa. She has lectured in nonfiction at Bennington Writer's Workshops M.F.A. program, and was in 2000 the visiting poet at Wesleyan University. She is currently on the faculty of the M.F.A. writing program at New School University.

JUDITH ORTIZ COFER is the author of *Woman in Front of the Sun: on Becoming a Writer,* a collection of essays; of a novel, *The Line of the Sun;* of *Silent Dancing,* a collection of essays and poetry; of two books of poetry, *Terms of Survival* and *Reaching for the Mainland;* and of *The Latin Deli: Prose and Poetry.* Her work has appeared in *The Georgia Review, Prairie Schooner, Kenyon Review, Southern Review, Glamour,* and other journals. Her work has been included in numerous textbooks and anthologies including: *Best American Essays 1991, The Norton Book of Women's Lives, The Norton Introduction to Literature, The Norton Introduction to Poetry, The Heath Anthology of American Literature, The Pushcart Prize,* and the *O. Henry Prize Stories.* She is the Franklin Professor of English and Creative Writing at the University of Georgia.

MICHAEL PEARSON is the director of the creative writing program at Old Dominion University. He has published essays and stories in *The New York Times, The Baltimore Sun, The Atlanta Journal-Constitution, The Boston Globe, The Journal of American Culture, The Southern Literary Journal,* and *Creative Nonfiction,* among others. He is the author of four books, including *Imagined Places: Journeys Into Literary America,* a New York Times Notable Book of 1991, and *Dreaming of Columbus: A Boyhood in the Bronx* (1999), of which William Morris, former editor of *Harper's,* observed, "Michael Pearson is one of our finest memoirists. *Dreaming of Columbus* should give him the reputation among American writers he so richly deserves."

BOB REISS'S newest book about the victims, science and politics of global warming, *The Coming Storm,* will be published by Hyperion Publishers in August, 2001. Two of his recent novels were bought by Paramount Pictures. His *Outside* magazine articles about the Amazon were finalists in the National Magazine Awards.

RICHARD SHELTON is the author of nine books of poetry, five of which were published by University of Pittsburgh Press. His first major book, *The Tattooed Desert,* won the *United States Award* of the International Poetry Forum, and his memoir, *Going Back to Bisbee,* won the Western States Award in Creative Nonfiction. He teaches in the

Creative Writing Program at the University of Arizona, and was a co-founder of that program in the 1960's. He is the recent recipient of a $100,000 grant from the Lannan Foundation.

HARVEY A. SILVERGLATE graduated from Princeton University (cum laude) and Harvard Law School. He is a partner in the Boston law firm of Silverglate & Good and specializes in criminal defense and civil liberties law. He has lectured and taught at the Cambridge Rindge & Latin School, University of Massachusetts College III, and Harvard Law School. He is a long-time member of the American Civil Liberties Union and has held various offices in its Massachusetts state affiliate. Silverglate is the civil liberties columnist for *The Boston Phoenix* and *The National Law Journal* and writes a periodic column for *Inc. Magazine*. His op-ed pieces have appeared in *The Wall Street Journal, The Boston Globe, The Philadelphia Inquirer, The Village Voice, Media Studies Journal,* and elsewhere. His articles and book reviews have been published in *The Harvard Law Review, The Harvard Civil Rights-Civil Liberties Law Review,* the now-defunct *Civil Liberties Review,* and a number of other professional journals. *The Shadow University* (co-authored with Alan Charles Kors) is his first full-length published book.

LAUREN SLATER, a 1999 National Magazine Award nominee, holds a master's degree in psychology from Harvard University and a doctorate from Boston University. Her books include *Prozac Diary, Welcome to My Country,* and *Lying.* Her work was chosen for *Best American Essays/Most Notable Essays* of 1994, 1996, 1997, 1998, and 1999. She is the winner of the 1993 New Letters Literary Award in creative nonfiction and the 1994 Missouri Review Award. She lives with her family in Massachusetts.

LAURA WEXLER is the author of a forthcoming nonfiction book to be published by Scribner's about the 1946 Moore's Ford lynching. She has published essays and articles in *DoubleTake, The Oxford American,* and the *Utne Reader,* as well as other newspapers and magazines.

TERRY TEMPEST WILLIAMS is the author of *Refuge: An Unnatural History of Family and Place, An Unspoken Hunger, Desert Quartet,* and most recently, *Leap.* She is the recipient of a John Simon Guggenheim Fellowship and a Lannan Literary Award for creative nonfiction. She lives in Castle Valley, Utah. *Red: A Desert Reader,* a collection of her wilderness essays, will be published by Pantheon Books in 2001.

INDEX